T0336044

Current Issues and Trends in E-Government Research

Donald F. Norris
University of Maryland, Baltimore County, USA

Cybertech Publishing

Hershey • London • Melbourne • Singapore

Acquisitions Editor:	Kristin Klinger
Development Editor:	Kristin Roth
Senior Managing Editor:	Jennifer Neidig
Managing Editor:	Sara Reed
Assistant Managing Editor:	Sharon Berger
Copy Editor:	Nicole Dean
Typesetter:	Amanda Appicello
Cover Design:	Lisa Tosheff
Printed at:	Integrated Book Technology

Published in the United States of America by
    CyberTech Publishing (an imprint of Idea Group Inc.)
    701 E. Chocolate Avenue
    Hershey PA 17033
    Tel: 717-533-8845
    Fax: 717-533-8661
    E-mail: cust@idea-group.com
    Web site: http://www.cybertech-pub.com

and in the United Kingdom by
    CyberTech Publishing (an imprint of Idea Group Inc.)
    3 Henrietta Street
    Covent Garden
    London WC2E 8LU
    Tel: 44 20 7240 0856
    Fax: 44 20 7379 0609
    Web site: http://www.eurospanonline.com

Library of Congress Cataloging-in-Publication Data

Current issues and trends in e-government research / Donald Norris, editor.
    p. cm.
  Summary: "This book provides a complete synopsis of the latest technologies in information policy, security, privacy, and access, as well as the best practices in e-government applications and measurement, as well as the most current issues in hardware and software technology, adoption, diffusion, planning, management and philosophy"--Provided by publisher.
  Includes bibliographical references and index.
  ISBN 1-59904-283-5 (hardcover) -- ISBN 1-59904-284-3 (softcover) -- ISBN 1-59904-285-1 (ebook)
  1. Internet in public administration. 2. Information technology--Research. 3. Electronic government information. 4. Public administration--Technological innovations. I. Norris, Donald F.
  JF1525.A8C87 2007
  352.3'802854678--dc22
                          2006031362

British Cataloguing in Publication Data
A Cataloguing in Publication record for this book is available from the British Library.

Current Issues and Trends in E-Government Research

Table of Contents

Preface

Electronic government (or e-government) has come a long way since its modest beginnings a mere 10 or so years ago. Governments throughout the world and at all levels—national, sub-national (state or provincial governments), and local—have adopted some form or forms of e-government. As shown in the latest United Nations benchmarking report (U.N., 2005), the more developed nations, nations with stronger economies, and nations with democratic political structures tend to lead in e-government adoption.

Yet, the findings of that report as well as of other studies (e.g., Coursey & Norris, 2006) suggest that e-government has a long way to go to reach the predictions of its principal normative models (Baum & DiMaio, 2000; Layne & Lee, 2001; Hiller & Belanger, 2001; Ronaghan, 2001; Wescott, 2001). These models predict that e-government adoption will move from the informational to the interactive, transactional, integrative, and transformational. The available evidence, however, shows that for the most part e-government is and remains mainly informational with relatively little real integration and relatively few interactive and transactional functions or services available on governmental Web sites.

Finally, although numerous claims are made in the literature for the transformative capability of e-government, no studies have been undertaken to ascertain if such transformation is occurring as a result of e-government. Perhaps since e-government is only 10 years old, it is too soon to inquire about its transformative impact. It may also be that the transformation hypothesis itself is flawed (e.g., Danziger & Anderson, 2002; Kraemer & King, 2006; Coursey & Norris, 2006).

Current Issues and Trends in E-Government Research endeavors to bring to both scholars and practitioners the latest and best in research into the phenomenon of e-government. This volume presents a wide range of research studies about a variety of aspects of e-government.

Assessing Digital Government at the Local Level Worldwide: An Analysis of Municipal Web Sites throughout the World, by James Melitiski, Marist College, and Marc

Holzer, Rutgers University – Campus at Newark (USA), examines and evaluates the performance of the Web sites of 84 cities around the world. The authors used a five-stage framework employing 92 measures to analyze these Web sites. Their study found that Seoul, Hong Kong, Singapore, New York, and Shanghai were the top five large cities in terms of the provision of on-line information and services.

The Impact of the Internet on Political Activism: Evidence from Europe, by Pippa Norris,[1] Harvard University (USA) and the United Nations Development Program, addressed some of the political consequences of the rise of knowledge societies. Norris uses survey data and key measures of political activism from the 19-nation European Social Survey, 2002, in particular, to examine the capacity of the Internet for strengthening democratic participation and civic engagement. Her chapter summarizes current debate about the impact of the Internet on the public sphere. Norris argues that the main influence of this development, as it is theorized in a market model, will be determined by the "supply" and "demand" for electronic information and communications about government and politics. She predicts that the primary impact of knowledge societies in democratic societies will be upon facilitating cause-oriented and civic forms of political activism which will strengthen social movements and interest groups, versus impacts on conventional channels of political.

E-Government in Canada: Transition or Transformation? by Jeffrey Roy, Dalhousie University (Canada), examines e-government in Canada. Roy provides a definition (albeit somewhat normative) for this elusive topic, discusses certain conceptual dimensions of e-government, particularly those around service and security and transparency and trust, and assesses Canada's public sector response to e-government. With respect to the latter, he notes the top-down (federal government) nature of e-government in Canada as well as barriers to the full implementation of e-government. Finally, Roy observes the political nature of e-government by noting that a change in party control of the federal government has the potential to change the emphasis if not the nature of e-government in Canada.

In *Motives, Strategic Approach, Objectives and Focal Areas in E-Gov-Induced Change,* Hans J. (Jochen) Scholl, University of Washington (USA), discusses an exploratory study of eight propositions derived from the private-sector literature that focus on business process change induced by e-government. Scholl employed a purposive sample to survey top managers in New York State government and in the governments of the city of Seattle, Washington (USA) and King County, Washington (USA) who had had responsibility for at least one e-gov project. His principal finding was that e-government does, indeed, induce major business process changes in governmental organizations as predicted by the private sector literature.

E-Government-Induced Business Process Change (BPC): An Empirical Study of Current Practices presents Scholl's follow-on and companion piece to the previous chapter. Here, using the same methodology and research propositions as in the previous chapter, Scholl asks whether e-government related BPC practices are different from or similar to BPC practices in the private sector. Among other things, he found considerable similarities between BPC practices in the public and private sectors. However, one important difference stood out—the importance of stakeholder involvement in successful e-government projects. He attributed this to the differences in governance in the two sectors. Scholl argues that because of this difference, BPC projects are more complex and take longer in the public sector, but also are more likely to succeed.

Computer Security in Electronic Government: A State-Local Education Information System, by Alison Radl , Iowa Department of Human Services (USA), and Yu-Che Chen, Iowa State University (USA), examines security issues associated with e-government projects. The authors employ the CIA (confidentiality, integrity, and availability) model to examine factors affecting security through a case study of an educational information system in Mid-Western American state involving a state department of education and 370 local school districts. Radl and Chen examined a number of factors potentially associated with security (e.g., district size, software selection, technology staffing, technology competence and support, and others). They found that technology support was an important factor in security but that other hypothesized factors did not achieve statistical significance.

Measuring and Explaining the Quality of Web Sites in the (Virtual) House of Representatives, by Kevin M. Esterling, University of California, Riverside, David M. J. Lazer, Harvard University, and Michael A. Neblo, Ohio State University (USA) examines how members of the U.S. House of Representatives use the Internet to provide information and services to and promote interaction. They used data from the 2002 Congressional Management Foundation (CMF) evaluation of Congressional Web sites. They also developed three measurement tools from the 37 variables examined in that study (overall quality, content quality, and usability). They then conducted multiple regression analyses using a variety of independent variables (e.g., tenure in office, margin of victory in last election, political party, Internet connectivity of district, median district income, and others) to predict Web site quality. The authors' principal findings were that shorter tenure in office, closer electoral margin, internet connectivity of constituents, and socioeconomic status of district were all correlated with high-quality Web sites.

The next four chapters address aspects of what has come to be known as e-democracy, or the use of electronic means to encourage citizen participation in governmental programs, activities, and decision-making. E-democracy is predicted by some of the normative models of e-government to be an "end-state" of e-government.

In *Electronic Democracy at the American Grassroots*, I examine local e-democracy in the U.S. using data from focus groups with officials from 37 leading edge municipal and county governments from across the U.S. My principal questions were: why American local governments adopted e-government and whether e-democracy was among the reasons for its adoption; whether e-government had produced or affected local e-democracy; and what plans, if any, these governments had with respect to e-democracy in coming years.

I found that American local government adopted e-government mainly to deliver governmental information and services and to provide citizen access to governmental officials. Local e-government did not operate in a manner that either produce or impact local e-democracy (at least, as I define the term). Finally, few American local governments have any plans whatsoever regarding e-democracy—it simply is not on their radar screens.

Next, in *A Brave New E-World? An Exploratory Analysis of Worldwide E-Government Readiness, Level of Democracy, Corruption and Globalization,* Zlatko J. Kovačić, The Open Polytechnic of New Zealand (NZ), employs a number of data sources to examine the relationship between e-government readiness, level of democracy, corruption, and globalization for 191 nations. He hypothesizes that more democratic nations, those with less corruption, those with higher international economic integration would be more positive toward increasing the level of e-government readiness. He also hypothesizes that nations that actively work to increase their levels of e-government readiness would have higher democratic ratings. He found, for the most part, moderate support for hypotheses. However, globalization did not appear to contribute to e-government readiness.

Scenarios for Future Use of E-Democracy Tools in Europe, by Herbert Kubicek, University of Bremen, and Hilmar Westholm, Institute for Information Management Bremen, (GmbH) (Germany), present possible scenarios for the future of e-democracy and the use of ICTs to facilitate e-democracy in Europe. Their chapter is based on work undertaken by scholars at RAND Europe, the Danish Technological Institute and the Institute of Technology Assessment of the Austrian Academy of Sciences.

Kubicek and Westholm present and describe three plausible future scenarios titled "A more prosperous and just Europe," "A turbulent world," and "Recession and reorientation," and examine the implications of these scenarios for the use of ICT tools for e-democracy. They note that different scenarios result in different mixes of the use of e-democracy tools and different outcomes. However, they also found that in none of the scenarios are ICTs "the key to solving the problem of political apathy."

In *The Quest for Advocates: Exploring the Missing Political Good Will for E-Democracy in Europe,* Harald Mahrer, Vienna Institute of Economics and Business Administration & METIS Institute for Economic and Political Research (Austria), reports on a case study of 220 parliamentarians from 25 EU countries regarding their views toward e-government and e-democracy. In particular, he was interested in learning whether parliamentarians were supportive of efforts toward e-democracy or whether they exhibited characteristics of what has come to be known as the "middleman paradox."

Mahrer found that while parliamentarians generally were quite supportive of e-administration and felt that current barriers to achieving more complete diffusion of it, they were not as sanguine about e-democracy. Here, he noted that the parliamentarians believed that there were numerous barriers to achieving e-democracy, that overcoming the barriers would difficult, and that, in any event, they were uncomfortable with the prospect of being replaced by forms of digital democracy. These findings clearly suggest the existence of the middleman paradox regarding e-democracy across Europe. Finally, Mahrer noted some differences between the orientations of Eastern (former Communist) and Western European parliamentarians toward e-democracy.

E-Gov Research 2003-2006: Improvements and Issues, by Åke Grönlund and Annika Andersson, Örebro University (Sweden), assesses the maturity of the field of e-government research through examination of papers presented at leading e-government conferences (HICCS 2003, European Conference on Electronic Government 2003, and EGOV 2003, 170 papers; and HICCS 2006 and EGOV 2005, 117 papers). After an exhaustive examination of the contents of these papers, Grönlund and Andersson report that the maturity of the field has, indeed, improved during this period. Papers presented in the later conferences exhibited greater consistency with research publication standards; were more closely linked to the literature; had fewer dubious claims; and were more empirical. However, they also noted continuing limitations in this literature, including an increase in purely descriptive works and only a slight increase in theory creation and testing.

E-Government Research: Capabilities, Interaction, Orientation, and Values, by Kim Viborg Andersen and Helle Zinner Henricksen of the Copenhagen Business School, Denmark, provides an in-depth analysis of recent literature about e-government, particularly to understand the conceptual domains and application areas being examined. Building on the framework developed by Danziger and Andersen (2002), the authors reviewed 110 articles in peer-reviewed journals, Andersen and Henricksen found that this research focuses mainly on e-government capabilities and interactions and less frequently value distributions and policy orientations. Their key finding is that this orientation suggests that e-government research follows in the path of previous IS research and that little research into e-government is being conducted from more of a public administration or governmental perspective.

Finally, in *E-Government Adoption in Canadian Municipal Governments: A Survey of Ontario Chief Administrative Officers,* Christopher G. Reddick, The University of Texas at San Antonio (USA), examines citizen-initiated contacts with government as the result of e-government. Reddick surveyed the chief administrative officers of Ontario municipalities with populations of 10,000 or greater. His survey achieved a response rate of 74%. Among other things, he found that municipal Web sites in Ontario, not unlike those in the U.S. are mainly informational, with few transactions. Additionally, he found that the chief administrative officers believed that e-government has increased citizen contact with government. However, he did not find that factors typically associated with citizen-initiated contact explained increased contact in Ontario municipalities. Municipalities with more on-line services and separate IT departments reported increased citizen initiated contact arguably more than other municipalities.

Electronic government has been around for only slightly over a decade. This means that research into e-government is also fairly new. Hopefully, the research reported here, which is on the leading edge of contemporary e-government research, will not only be informative to readers but will also stimulate further research into this exciting and important new governmental phenomenon.

Donald F. Norris
University of Maryland, Baltimore County
Editor-in-Chief
International Journal of Electronic Government Research

References

Baum, C. H., & Di Maio, A. (2000). *Gartner's four phases of e-government model*. Retrieved October 15, 2003, from http://www.gartner.com

Coursey, D., & Norris, D. F. (2006). Models of e-government: Are they correct? An Empirical Assessment. Under review by *Public Administration Review.*

Danziger, J. N., & Andersen, K. V. (2002). The impacts of information technology on public administration: An analysis of empirical research from the 'golden age' of transformation. *International Journal of Public Administration, 25*(5), 591-627.

Hiller, J. S., & Belanger, F. (2001). Privacy strategies for electronic government. In M. A. Abramson & G. E. Means (Eds.), *E-government 2001*. Boulder, CO: Rowman and Littlefield.

Kraemer, K. L., & King, J. L. (2006). Information technology and administrative reform: Will e-government be different? *International Journal of Electronic Government Research, 2*(1), 1-20.

Layne, K., & Lee, J. (2001). Developing fully functional e-government: A four stage model. *Government Information Quarterly, 18*(2), 122-136.

Ronaghan, S. A. (2001). *Benchmarking e-government: A global perspective*. New York: United Nations Division for Public Economics and Public Administration and American Society for Public Administration. Retrieved October 1, 2003, from http://www.unpan.org/e-government/ Benchmarking% 20E-gov%202001.pdf

United Nations, Division for Public Administration and Development Management, Department of Economic and Social Affairs. (2005). *UN global e-government readiness report, 2005: From e-government to e-inclusion*. New York: Author. Retrieved on April 10, 2006, at http://www.unpan.org/dpepa-egovernment%20readiness%20report.asp

Wescott, C. (2001). E-government in the Asia-Pacific Region. *Asian Journal of Political Science, 9*(2), 1-24.

Endnote

[1] While Pippa Norris and the editor of this volume share a surname, they are not related.

Chapter I

Assessing Digital Government at the Local Level Worldwide:
An Analysis of Municipal Web Sites throughout the World

James Melitski, Marist College, USA

Marc Holzer, Rutgers University – Campus at Newark, USA

Abstract

Throughout the world, government agencies are looking to use information technology as a tool for strategically enhancing their performance and creating public value. Our research examines 84 cities worldwide and evaluates their performance using a five-stage framework. The framework builds on existing e-government literature utilizing 92 different measures. The research was conducted between June and October of 2003. Our instrument was translated into the native language of each city and the assessment of each municipal Web site was conducted by a native speaker of the municipality's language. We review relevant e-government literature for evaluating Web sites in the U.S. and internationally, discuss our sample selection, methodology, theoretical framework, findings, and recommendations. Our results indicate that Seoul, Hong Kong, Singapore, New York, and Shanghai are the top five large cities providing digital government opportunities to citizens online. In addition, our research suggests a difference in the digital government capabilities between the 30 developed nations belonging to the Organization for Economic Co-operation and Development (OECD) and lesser-developed (non-OECD) nations.

Assessing Municipal Web Sites

As academics have debated the impact of flatter organizations on democratic accountability, organizations using information technology to provide information, process transactions, and communication have become flatter. Information technology advocates come in all shapes and sizes. Individuals seeking to automate transactions look to technology to increase organizational efficiency. Conversely, those seeking to increase the quality of services and increase democratic participation in government also see information technology as part of their solutions. Increasingly, information technology is seen as the answer to the question: "How can the public sector achieve efficiency and effectiveness, at the same time balancing those concerns with equity in service delivery?" (Holzer & Gabrielian, 1998) and "How can the public sector bring about a more honest dialogue between citizens and their governments?" (Nathan quoted in Holzer & Gabrielian, 1998, p. 79). Since public organizations should be efficient and effective, productive internally, and pursue such democratic values as equality, equity, and participation for a better society externally, both dimensions are important to service delivery.

Champions of information technology in the public sector suggest that information and communication technologies (ICTs) are conducive to both efficient and effective public organizations. In addition, they have argued that ICTs enable citizens to engage in policy deliberation. Following this logic, in recent years, e-government researchers have examined how public organizations are using the Internet. They often sought to answer two questions: (1) Why do public organizations adopt new initiatives, such as e-government programs? (2) Why are some initiatives more successful than others?

One way that researchers determine success is to assess performance of organizations that adopt e-government by developing criteria and conducting a content analysis of government Web sites. Unfortunately, most of this literature focuses on state and federal governments in the U.S. in terms of examining trends in digital government (the Center for Digital Government and Microsoft Corp., http://www.centerdigitalgov.com/; West, 2002, 2003). At the local level, a notable survey was conducted of local government managers in conjunction with the International City/Country Management Association and Public Technologies Inc. (Norris, Fletcher, & Holden, 2001; Holden, Norris, & Fletcher, 2003).

Little research has been conducted on analyzing the worldwide movement to digital government from a comparative perspective. Researchers at Brown University, led by Darrell West, have conducted a nationwide content analysis of state and federal government Web sites in the U.S. since 2000; they also completed a worldwide analysis of central government Web sites in 2001 and a summary of the results was published in the *Public Administration Review* (West, 2004). West's research finds an improvement of digital service delivery at federal, state, and local levels, as well as internationally.

Previous research, however, lacks a comprehensive framework for evaluating digital government. Such studies have paid attention to a few aspects of digital service delivery, comparing limited aspects of public organizations. They have not provided specific exemplars of practices and conditions necessary to successfully reproduce each best practice. Furthermore, their research evaluating Web site content consists of only 27 dichotomous variables (West, 2004). This research attempts to take a more comprehensive approach, by utilizing 92 measures, of which 45 are dichotomous and 47 are measures that use a four-point scale.

This research also utilizes a theoretical framework that is consistent with e-government and e-government literature. In 2002, Moon developed a framework for e-government analysis that consists of five stages: Information dissemination/catalogue; two-way communication; service and financial transactions; vertical and horizontal integration; and political (citizen) participation.

Based on Moon's research, one can imply performance improvement as a progression from "Stage 1. Information Dissemination" through "Stage 5. Citizen Participation." From a theoretical perspective, Ho (2002) describes performance improvement as a paradigm shift from a bureaucratic paradigm toward an e-government paradigm. According to Ho, "the new (e-government) paradigm transforms organizational principles in government. While the bureaucratic model emphasizes top-down management and hierarchical communication, the new model emphasizes teamwork, multidirectional networks, direct communication between parties, and a fast feedback loop" (Ho, 2002).

Ho argues that while the shift between paradigms is occurring at the city level, socioeconomic and organizational barriers are slowing the process to the point where city government Web sites are not reaching their fullest potential. Similarly, Norris and Moon (2005) demonstrate that local government Web sites are maturing and local governments are becoming more transactional and integrated. However, adoption of transactional initiatives remains slow. Other researchers argue that technology is used to reinforce the status-quo (Norris & Moon, 2005; Kraemer, 1991). For example, Melitski (2003) argues that e-government and the use of the Internet by public organizations is value neutral. While Melitski's IT and public administration paradigms are similar to Ho's bureaucratic and e-government paradigms, Melitski argues that the adoption of internet technologies does not automatically progress to open, accountable government (e.g., the public administration paradigm).

Instead, Melitski argues for the existence of two competing paradigms, similar to Burrell and Morgan (1979). Melitski further argues that organizational and cultural factors influence whether public managers will use the Internet and e-government to exert central control over their organization (IT paradigm), or decentralize and empower their organization (public administration paradigm). In other words, while other e-government theorists argue that adoption of e-government leads to the idealistic use of technology to empower citizens, we believe that competing paradigms within public organizations may hinder such a paradigm shift. Despite our value neutral view of technology, we do believe that the greatest potential for Internet use in public organizations lies in applications designed to facilitate open communication between agencies and create dialogue between citizens and their government. As a result, this research uses a five-stage continuum based on previous research, with citizen participation as the fifth stage.

Along with these theoretical movements, our society has been engaged in an ongoing transformation process from the industrial to the information society. Rapid change in ICTs has further expedited this trend. Moreover, technological change creates new challenges and opportunities for social and political organization (Kamarck & Nye, 2002; O'Looney, 2002). In order to facilitate efficiency and effectiveness in digital government, public organizations have begun to apply performance measurement to examine digital government initiatives.

Following the adoption of ICTs, public service delivery by the public, as well as the private sectors, could be restructured to meet the needs of their citizens or customers effectively and efficiently. Simply put, digital government refers to the directed influence of social processes through virtual means. Unlike traditional offline government, citizens have the choice of when and where to access government services via digital government.

Even though there has been a growing use of digital government, there are also certain problems, which prevent efficient and effective implementation. For instance, in terms of the digital divide, there has always been a gap between those people and communities that can make effective use of ICTs and those that cannot. Now, more than ever, unequal adoption of technology excludes many from reaping the fruits of the economy (Norris, 1999). In addition, there are recent calls for increased security, particularly of our public information infrastructure. Concern over the security of the information systems underlying government applications has led some researchers to the conclusion that e-government must be built on a secure infrastructure that respects the privacy of its users (Kaylor et al., 2001).

International Digital Government Efforts

Digital government development is now constant and conspicuous. It has received considerable attention through a steady stream of events at the national and international levels (Bertelsmann Foundation, http://www.begix.de/en/index.html; Global Forum 2003 at Mexico City; UN & ASPA, 2002; World Bank, http://www1. worldbank.org/publicsector/egov/egovstudies.htm; DigitalGovernance.org Initiative, http://65.110.68.184/artman/publish/index1.shtml). The Bertelsmann Foundation conducted research on "Balanced E-Government," to identify criteria of success for outstanding e-government performance in local and governmental administration. The project evaluated both e-administration—"transaction of user-oriented services offered by public institutions that are based on information and communication technologies"—and e-democracy—"digitally conveyed information (transparency) and the political influence (participation) exerted by citizens and business on the opinion-forming processes of public—state and non-state—institutions"—and how far the integration of both concepts has progressed (The Bertelsmann Foundation, 2001).

Digital government has become a high priority throughout the world. No country wants to be left behind in the movement to improve government through electronic delivery of information and services (Pardo, 2000). While most of the research on digital government has focused on advanced countries, the World Bank E-Government Web site focuses on digital government in developing countries (www1.worldbank. org/publicsector/egov). The World Bank provides cases studies as a source of ideas in the areas of better service delivery to citizens, improved services for business, transparency and anticorruption efforts, empowerment through information, and efficient government purchasing.

In addition to the World Bank, The DigitalGovernance.org initiative focused on digital governance in developing countries in terms of building accountable and democratic governance institutions using ICTs (Figures 1-5). They present five generic e-governance models: broadcasting model, critical flow model, comparative analysis models, e-advocacy model, and interactive service model, as well as many case studies in developing countries.

In 2001, an international report on national Web sites was published by the United Nations and the American Society for Public Administration in consultation with the National Center for Public Productivity at Rutgers University-Campus at Newark. The report, "Benchmarking E-government: A Global Perspective," used a framework similar to our research. According to the report, "National government Web sites were analyzed for the content and services available that the average citizen would most likely use. The presence or absence of specific features contributed to determining a country's level of progress. The stages (emerging Web presence, enhanced Web presence, interactive presence, transactional Web presence, and fully integrated Web presence) present a straightforward benchmark which objectively assesses a country's online sophistication" (United Nations; American Society of Public Administration, 2001).

Digital government has become a new part of the government structure. However, parochial perspectives limit opportunities to increase experimentation, innovation and organization learning pertinent to digital government. It is important to understand existing gaps in government theory and practice, including both traditional and digital perspectives, between Western and non-Western nations (Welch & Wong, 1998). Fortunately, the global study of digital government is advancing, and such efforts may contribute to its continued development.

In this context, our research evaluates the current practice of digital government in municipalities worldwide. This research focuses on the evaluation of current practice on the supply side (government), not the demand side (citizen). Our emphasis is on the evaluation of each city government Web site in terms of security, usability, and content, the type of online services currently being offered, and citizen response and participation.

Sample

This research examines cities throughout the world based on their population size, the total number of individuals using the Internet, and the percentage of individuals using the Internet. The cities were selected using International Telecommunication Union's (ITU) "Internet Indicators" (2002). The ITU data lists the online population for each of 196 countries[1], and our initial sample consisted of the largest municipalities within the 98 U.N. member countries with an online population greater than 100,000. For example, in the U.S. and South Korea, New York and Seoul were chosen, respectively. In addition, Hong Kong SAR and Macao SAR were added to the 98 cities selected, since they have been considered as independent countries for many years and have high percentages of Internet users.

The rationale for selecting the largest municipalities stems from the e-government literature, which suggests a positive relationship between population and e-government capacity at the local level (Moon, 2002; Moon & deLeon, 2001; Musso et al., 2000; Weare et al., 1999). Table 1 is a list of 100 cities selected.

For our purposes, the main city homepage was defined as the official Web site where information about city administration and online services are provided by the city. City Web sites typically included information about the city council, mayor, and executive branch of the city. Separate homepages for agencies, departments, or the city council, were examined only if the sites were linked to the menu on the main city homepage. If the Web site was not linked, it was excluded from evaluation.

Table 1. One hundred cities selected by continent (2004 population in 1,000s)**

Africa (12) Country	Pop.	Asia (30) Country	Pop.	Europe (34) Country	Pop.	North America (12) Country	Pop.	South America (10) Country	Pop.	Oceania (2) Country	Pop.
Algiers (Algeria)*	2004	Almaty (Kazakhstan)	1025.7	Amsterdam (Netherlands)	742.3	Ciudad de Mexico (Mexico)	8705.1	Asuncion (Paraguay)	539.2	(New Zealand)	374.3
Cairo (Egypt)	1790.7	Amman (Jordan)	1308.3	Athens (Greece)	762.1	Guatemala City (Guatemala)	999.4	Buenos Aires (Argentina)	11928.4	Sydney (Australia)	4305.5
Cape Town (South Africa)	8113.6	Baku (Azerbaijan)*	1240.8	Montenegro	1126.9	Havana (Cuba)*	2359.2	Caracas (Venezuela)	1719.6		
Casablanca (Morocco)*	2984.1	Bangkok (Thailand)	6709.2	Berlin (Germany)	3396.3	Kingston (Jamaica)*	594.5	Guayaquil (Ecuador)	2044.7		
Dakar (Senegal)*	3741.2	Beirut (Lebanon)	446.3	Bratislava (Slovak Republic)	428.8	New York (United States)	8134.8	La Paz (Bolivia)	850		
Dar-es-Salaam (Tanzania)*	2613.7	Bishkek (Kyrgyzstan)*	841.1	Brussels (Belgium)	983.9	Panama City (Panama)	445.8	Lima (Peru)	8380.3		
Harare (Zimbabwe)*	1976.4	Colombo (Sri Lanka)	669.7	Bucharest (Romania)	1897.1	Tobago	50.6	Montevideo (Uruguay)	1346.9		
Lagos (Nigeria)*	8682.2	Dhaka (Bangladesh)	9363.1	Budapest (Hungary)	1729.8	San Jose (Costa Rica)	346.8	(Colombia)	6981.5		
Lome (Togo)*	695.1	Dubai (United Arab Emirates)	940.6	Copenhagen (Denmark)	1100.7	San Salvador (El Salvador)	513.4	Santiago (Chile)	4434.9		
Nairobi (Kenya)	2504.4	Ho Chi Minh (Vietnam)	3452.1	Dublin (Ireland)	1027.9	Tegucigalpa (Honduras)	2240.5	Sao Paulo (Brazil)	10333.2		
Port Louis (Mauritius)*	143.6	(SAR)	6855***	Helsinki (Finland)	590.6		470.5				
Tunis (Tunisia)*	704.7	Istanbul (Turkey)	9631.7	Kyiv (Ukraine)	2598	Toronto (Canada)	4558.8				
		Jakarta (Indonesia)	8987.8	Lisboa (Portugal)	560.7						
		Jerusalem (Israel)	708.5	Ljubljana (Slovenia)	258.7						
		Karachi (Pakistan)	10889.1	London (United Kingdom)	7465.1						
		Kuala Lumpur (Malaysia)	1440.3	Luxembourg City (Luxembourg)	79.8						
		Kuwait City (Kuwait)*	152.1	Madrid (Spain)	3290.9						
		Macao SAR (Macao SAR)	445***	Minsk (Belarus)*	1682.9						
		Manama (Bahrain)	154.7	Moscow (Russia)	11246.6						
		Mumbai (India)	12622.5	Oslo (Norway)	799.2						
		Muscat (Oman)*	880.2	Paris (France)	2107.6						
		Nicosia (Cyprus)	200.7	Prague (Czech Republic)	1165.2						
		Quezon City (Philippines)	10330.1	Reykjavik (Iceland)	116.5						
		Riyadh (Saudi Arabia)	3822.6	Riga (Latvia)	687.7						
		Seoul (Korea)	9551.8	Rome (Italy)	2453.1						
		Shanghai (China)	13278.5	Herzegovina	602.5						
		Singapore (Singapore)	3499.5	Sofia (Bulgaria)	1084.7						
		Tashkent (Uzbekistan)	2299.4	Stockholm (Sweden)	1264.8						
		Tehran (Iran)	7317.2	Tallinn (Estonia)	372.1						
		Tokyo (Japan)	8273.9	Vienna (Austria)	1504.1						
				Vilnius (Lithuania)	544						
				Warsaw (Poland)	1676.6						
				Zagreb (Croatia)	682.3						
				Zurich (Switzerland)	351.7						

* Official city Web site unavailable

** Population data from the 2004 World Gazetteer (except for Hong Kong and Macao): www.world-gazetteer.com

*** Population data for Hong Kong and Macao from the 2004 World Sourcebook: http://www.odci.gov/cia/publications/factbook/

Sixteen of the initial 100 cities were excluded from our research for lack of an official city Web site: eight in Africa (67%), four in Asia (13.33%), one in Europe (2.94%), and three in North America (25%). As a result, this research evaluated only 84 cities of the 100 cities initially selected.

Our research examines local government services using an e-government model of increasingly sophisticated e-government services. As noted above, Moon (2002) developed a framework for categorizing e-government models based on the following components: information dissemination, two-way communication, services, integration, and political participation. Our methodology for evaluating e-government services includes such components; however, we have added the additional factors security and usability.

The additional e-government factors are grounded in recent calls for increased security, and the need to make digital government more citizen-friendly. Concern over the security of the information systems underlying government applications has led some researchers to the conclusion that e-government must be built on a secure infrastructure that respects the privacy of its users (Kaylor et al., 2001).

Methodology

Our instrument for evaluating city and municipal Web sites builds on previous research which identifies content, transactional services and citizen participation as critical components of e-government (Moon, 2001). Furthermore, in recent years many U.S. citizens have become more aware of the need for increased security and privacy of government. A recent poll conducted by Hart-Teeter in conjunction with the Council for Excellence in Government (2003) found that Americans are cautiously aware of possible risks associated with digital government. According to the Hart-Teeter poll, "This concern about privacy and security translates into a cautionary tone from Americans: a 54% majority think that government should proceed slowly in relying on the Internet for communication between citizens and government" (Hart-Teeter, 2003). We have added an additional area of emphasis for our analysis that examines Web site usability. Our final instrument consists of five components: (1) security and privacy; (2) usability; (3) content; (4) services; and (5) citizen participation. Table 2 summarizes the measures used in our research to assess a Web site's capabilities in each of those five categories.

Previous e-government research varies in the use of scales to evaluate government Web sites. For example, while West (2000, 2001, 2004) uses an index consisting of between 27 or so dichotomous (yes or no) measures, other assessments use a four-point scale (Kaylor et al., 2001) for assessing each measure. Our research instrument goes well beyond previous research, utilizing 92 measures, of which 45

Table 2. E-government measures

E-government Category	Number of Key Concepts	Raw Score	Weighted Score	Keywords
Security/Privacy	19	28	20	Privacy policies, authentication, encryption, data management, and use of cookies
Usability	20	32	20	User-friendly design, branding, length of homepage, targeted audience links or channels, and site search capabilities
Content	19	47	20	Access to current accurate information, public documents, reports, publications, and multimedia materials
Service	20	57	20	Transactional services involving purchase or register, interaction between citizens, businesses and government
Citizen Participation	14	39	20	Online civic engagement, internet based policy deliberation, and citizen based performance measurement
Total	92	203	100	

are dichotomous. For each of the five components in our theoretical framework, the study applies 14 to 20 measures, and each measure was coded on a four-point scale of increasing technological sophistication (0, 1, 2, 3; see Table 3). Furthermore, in developing an overall score for each municipality, we have equally weighted the five categories so as not to skew the research in favor of a particular category (regardless of the number of questions in each category). The remaining 47 measures were scored according to the scale in Table 2-3. The dichotomous measures in the "service" and "citizen participation" categories correspond with values on our four point scale of "0" or "3"; dichotomous measures in "security/ privacy" or "usability" correspond to ratings of "0" or "1" on our four point scale.

Table 3. E-government scale

Scale	Description
0	Information about a given topic does not exist on the Web site
1	Information about a given topic exists on the Web site (including links to other information and e-mail addresses)
2	Downloadable items are available on the Web site (forms, audio, video, and other one-way transactions, popup boxes)
3	Services, transactions, or interactions can take place completely online (credit card transactions, applications for permits, searchable databases, use of cookies, digital signatures, restricted access)

Our instrument places a higher value on some dichotomous measures, due to the relative value and technical complexity of the different e-government services being evaluated. For example, evaluators using our instrument in the "service" category were given the option of scoring Web sites as either a "0" or "3" when assessing whether a site allowed users to access private information online (e.g., educational records, medical records, point total of driving violations, lost property). "No access" equated to a rating of "0." Allowing residents or employees to access private information online was a higher order task that required more technical competence, and was clearly an online service, or "3," as defined in Table 3.

On the other hand, when assessing a site's privacy statement or policy, evaluators were given the choices of scoring the site as "0" or "1." The presence or absence of a security policy was clearly a content issue that emphasized placing information online, and corresponded with a value of "1" on the scale outlined in Table 2-3. The differential values assigned to dichotomous categories were useful in comparing the different components of municipal Web sites with one another.

To ensure reliability, each municipal Web site was assessed by two evaluators, in the site's native language, and in cases where significant variation (+ or – 10%) existed on the raw score between evaluators, Web sites were analyzed a third time. Furthermore, an example for each measure indicated how to score the variable. Evaluators were also given comprehensive written instructions for assessing Web sites.

Framework

This section details our theoretical framework and discusses specific measures used to evaluate Web sites. The discussion of security and privacy examines privacy policies and issues related to authentication. Discussion of the usability category involves traditional Web pages, forms, and search tools. The content category is addressed in terms of access to contact information, access to public documents and disability access, as well as access to multimedia and time sensitive information. The section on services examines interactive services, services that allow users to purchase or pay for services, and the ability of users to apply or register for municipal events or services online. Finally, the measures for citizen participation involve examining how local governments are engaging citizens and providing mechanisms for citizens to participate in government online.

The first part of our analysis examined the security and privacy of municipal Web sites in two key areas, privacy policies and authentication of users. In examining municipal privacy policies, we determined whether such a policy was available on every page that accepted data, and whether or not the word "privacy" was used in the link to such a statement. In addition, we looked for privacy policies on every page that required or accepted data. We were also interested in determining if privacy policies identified the agencies collecting the information, and whether the policy identified exactly what data was being collected on the site.

Our analysis checked to see if the intended use of the data was explicitly stated on the Web site. The analysis examined whether the privacy policy addressed the use or sale of data collected on the Web site by outside or third party organizations. Our research also determined if there was an option to decline the disclosure of personal information to third parties[2]. This included other municipal agencies, other state and local government offices, or businesses in the private sector. Furthermore, we examined privacy policies to determine if third party agencies or organizations were governed by the same privacy policies as the municipal Web site. We also determined whether users had the ability to review personal data records and contest inaccurate or incomplete information.

In examining factors affecting the security and privacy of local government Web sites, we addressed managerial measures that limit access of data and assure that it was not used for unauthorized purposes. The use of encryption in the transmission of data, as well as the storage of personal information on secure servers, was also examined. We also determined if Web sites used digital signatures to authenticate users. In assessing how or whether municipalities used their Web sites to authenticate users, we examined whether public or private information was accessible through a restricted area that required a password and/or registration.

A growing e-government trend at the local level is for municipalities to offer their Web site users access to public, and in some cases private, information online. Other research has discussed the government issues associated with sites that choose to charge citizens for access to public information (West, 2001). We add our own concern about the impact of the digital divide if public records are available only through the Internet or if municipalities insist on charging a fee for access to public records. Our analysis specifically addresses online access to public databases, by determining if public information such as property tax assessments or private information like court documents is available to users of municipal Web sites. In addition, there are concerns that public agencies will use their Web sites to monitor citizens or create profiles based on the information they access online. For example, many Web sites use "cookies" or "Web beacons"[3] to customize Web sites for users, but the technology can also be used to monitor Internet habits and profile visitors to Web sites. Our analysis examined municipal privacy policies to determine if they addressed the use of cookies or Web beacons.

This research also examined the usability of municipal Web sites. Simply stated, we wanted to know if sites were "user-friendly." To address usability concerns we adapted several best practices and measures from other public and private sector research (Giga, 2000)[4]. Our analysis of usability examined three types of Web sites: traditional Web pages, forms, and search tools. To evaluate traditional Web pages written using hypertext markup language (html), we examined issues such as branding and structure (e.g., consistent color, font, graphics, page length, etc.). For example, we looked to see if all pages used consistent color, formatting, "default colors" (e.g., blue links and purple visited links) and underlined text to indicate links. Other items examined included whether system hardware and software requirements were clearly stated on the Web site.

In addition, our research examined each municipality's homepage to determine if it was too long (two or more screen lengths) or if alternative versions of long documents, such as .pdf or .doc files, were available. The use of targeted audience links or "channels" to customize the Web site for specific groups such as citizens, businesses, or other public agencies was also examined. We looked for the consistent use of navigation bars and links to the homepage on every page. The availability of a "sitemap" or hyperlinked outline of the entire Web site was examined. Our assessment also examined whether duplicated link names connect to the same content.

We examined online forms to determine their usability in submitting data or conducting searches of municipal Web sites. We looked at issues such as whether field labels aligned appropriately with field, whether fields were accessible by keystrokes (e.g., tabs), or whether the cursor was automatically placed in the first field. We also examined whether required fields were noted explicitly, and whether the tab order of fields was logical. For example, after a user filled out their first name and pressed the "tab" key, did the cursor automatically go to the surname field? Alternatively, did the page skip to another field such as zip code, only to return to the surname later?

We also checked to see if form pages provided additional information about how to fix errors if they were submitted. For example, did users have to reenter information if errors were submitted, or did the site flag incomplete or erroneous forms before accepting them? Also, did the site give a confirmation page after a form was submitted, or did it return users to the homepage?

Our analysis also addressed the use of search tools on municipal Web sites. We examined sites to determine if help was available for searching a municipality's Web site, or if the scope of searches could be limited to specific areas of the site. Were users able to search only in "public works" or "the mayor's office," or did the search tool always search the entire site? We also looked for advanced search features such as exact phrase searching, the ability to match all/ any words, and Boolean searching capabilities (e.g., the ability to use AND/ OR/ NOT operators). Our analysis also addressed a site's ability to sort search results by relevance or other criteria.

Content is a critical component of any Web site. No matter how technologically advanced a Web site's features, if its content is not current, if it is difficult to navigate, or if the information provided is not correct, then it is not fulfilling its purpose. When examining Web site content, our research examined five key areas: access to contact information, public documents, disability access, multimedia materials, and time sensitive information. When addressing contact information, we looked for information about each agency represented on the Web site.

In addition, we also looked for the availability of office hours or a schedule of when agency offices are open. In assessing the availability of public documents, we looked for the availability of the municipal code or charter online. We also looked for content items, such as agency mission statements and minutes of public meetings. Other content items included access to budget information and publications. Our assessment also examined whether Web sites provided access to disabled users through either "bobby compliance" (disability access for the blind, http://www.cast.org/bobby) or disability access for deaf users via a TDD phone service. We also checked to see if sites offered content in more than one language.

Time sensitive information that was examined included the use of a municipal Web site for emergency management, and the use of a Web site as an alert mechanism (e.g., terrorism alert or severe weather alert). We also checked for time sensitive information such as the posting of job vacancies or a calendar of community events. In addressing the use of multimedia, we examined each site to determine if audio or video files of public events, speeches, or meetings were available.

A critical component of e-government is the provision of municipal services online. Our analysis examined two different types of services: (1) those that allow citizens to interact with the municipality, and (2) services that allow users to register for municipal events or services online. In many cases, municipalities have developed the capacity to accept payment for municipal services and taxes. The first type of service examined, which implies interactivity, can be as basic as forms that allow users to request information or file complaints. Local governments across the world use advanced interactive services to allow users to report crimes or violations, customize municipal homepages based on their needs (e.g., portal customization), and access private information online such as court records, education records, or medical records. Our analysis examined municipal Web sites to determine if such interactive services were available.

The second type of service examined in this research determined if municipalities have the capacity to allow citizens to register for municipal services online. For example, many jurisdictions now allow citizens to apply for permits and licenses online. Online permitting can be used for services that vary from building permits to dog licenses. In addition, some local governments are using the Internet for procurement, allowing potential contractors to access requests for proposals or even bid for municipal contracts online. In other cases, local governments are chronicling the procurement process by listing the total number of bidders for a contract online, and in some cases listing contact information for bidders.

This analysis also examined municipal Web sites to determine if they developed the capacity to allow users to purchase or pay for municipal services and fees online. Examples of transactional services from across the United States include the payment of public utility bills and parking tickets online. In many jurisdictions, cities and municipalities allow online users to file or pay local taxes, or pay fines such as traffic tickets. In some cases, cities around the world are allowing their users to register or purchase tickets to events in city halls or arenas online.

While, this research evaluates a city's capacity or ability to implement transactional services, it should be noted that the research does not account for the total number of transactions a city offers. As such, cities that offer three transactional services received the same score as cities with twenty. In addition, we recognize that not all transactions are equal, and technological sophistication among different transactional services varies. In other words, while we evaluate a city's capacity to implement basic transactional services, we do not determine whether the transactional service implemented is one of greater or lesser technological sophistication.

Finally, perhaps the most untapped area of e-government, or e-governance in this context, involves using the Internet to engage citizens in democratic processes. Citizen participation in government is a ripe area for e-government, in part because the Internet is a convenient mechanism for citizen-users to engage their government, and also because of the potential to decentralize decision-making. Despite that potential, very few public agencies offer online opportunities for civic engagement. We looked at several ways public agencies at the local level were involving citizens. For example, do municipal Web sites allow users to provide online comments or feedback to individual agencies or elected officials?

Our analysis examined whether local governments offer current information about municipal government online or through an online newsletter or e-mail listserv. We also examined the use of Internet based polls about specific local issues. In addition, our research examined whether communities allow users to participate and view the results of citizen satisfaction surveys online. For example, some municipalities used their Web sites to measure performance and published the results of performance measurement activities online.

Still other municipalities used online bulletin boards or other chat capabilities for gathering input on public issues. Most often, online bulletin boards offer citizens the opportunity to post ideas, comments, or opinions without specific discussion topics. In some cases, agencies attempt to structure online discussions around policy issues or specific agencies. Our research looked for municipal use of the Internet to foster civic engagement and citizen participation in government.

This study does have some limitations—unique cultural, customary, and institutional considerations—even though we have made concerted attempts to reduce such matters. We do offer this research as progress in solving the problems of developing reliable and valid evaluation criteria for digital government.

Findings and Recommendations

Table 4 lists the top 20 cities in digital government. The table lists city scores in each of the five categories of our framework. The maximum score for each category was 20 and the maximum total score was 100. Of the top five cities, four ranked first in at least one category from our framework. For example, Seoul excelled in service delivery and citizen participation, Hong Kong, ranked highest in privacy/security, as well as usability and New York's led all cities in providing content on its municipal Web site.

Tables 5 through 10 list the top 10 cities in the categories of privacy and security, usability, content, service delivery, and citizen participation.

Our research also suggests a difference in the digital government capabilities between the 30 developed nations belonging to the Organization for Economic Co-operation and Development (OECD) and lesser-developed (non-OECD) nations.

For example, Table 11 shows that although the average score for digital government in municipalities throughout the world is 28.49 out of 100, the average score in OECD countries is higher, 36.34, while the average score in non-OECD countries

Table 4. Top 20 cities in digital government

Ranking	City	Country	Score	Privacy	Usability	Content	Service	Participation
1	Seoul	Republic of Korea	73.48	11.07	17.50	13.83	15.44	15.64
2	Hong Kong SAR	Hong Kong SAR	66.57	15.36	19.38	13.19	14.04	4.62
3	Singapore	Singapore	62.97	11.79	14.06	14.04	13.33	9.74
4	New York	United States	61.35	11.07	15.63	14.68	12.28	7.69
5	Shanghai	China	58.00	9.64	17.19	11.28	12.46	7.44
6	Rome	Italy	54.72	6.79	14.69	9.57	13.16	10.51
7	Auckland	New Zealand	54.61	7.86	16.88	11.06	10.35	8.46
8	Jerusalem	Israel	50.34	5.71	18.75	10.85	5.79	9.23
9	Tokyo	Japan	46.52	10.00	15.00	10.00	6.14	5.38
10	Toronto	Canada	46.35	8.57	16.56	9.79	5.79	5.64
11	Helsinki	Finland	45.09	8.57	15.94	11.70	6.32	2.56
12	Macao SAR	Macao SAR	44.18	4.29	17.19	11.91	7.72	3.08
13	Stockholm	Sweden	44.07	0.00	13.75	14.68	10.00	5.64
14	Tallinn	Estonia	43.10	3.57	13.13	12.55	6.67	7.18
15	Copenhagen	Denmark	41.349	4.643	13.438	9.787	5.789	7.692
16	Paris	France	41.338	6.429	14.375	7.660	5.439	7.436
17	Dublin	Ireland	38.85	2.50	13.44	11.28	7.02	4.62
18	Dubai	United Arab Emirates	37.48	7.86	10.94	7.87	8.25	2.56
19	Sydney	Australia	37.41	6.79	12.19	9.15	5.44	3.85
20	Jakarta	Indonesia	37.28	0.00	16.56	9.79	6.32	4.62

Table 5. Top 10 cities in privacy/security

Rank	City	Country	Score
1	Hong Kong SAR	Hong Kong SAR	15.36
2	Singapore	Singapore	11.79
3	New York	United States	11.07
3	Seoul	Republic of Korea	11.07
5	Tokyo	Japan	10.00
6	Shanghai	China	9.64
7	Helsinki	Finland	8.57
7	Toronto	Canada	8.57
9	Auckland	New Zealand	7.86
9	Dubai	United Arab Emirates	7.86

Table 6. Top 10 cities in privacy/security

Rank	City	Country	Score
1	Hong Kong SAR	Hong Kong SAR	15.36
2	Singapore	Singapore	11.79
3	New York	United States	11.07
3	Seoul	Republic of Korea	11.07
5	Tokyo	Japan	10.00
6	Shanghai	China	9.64
7	Helsinki	Finland	8.57
7	Toronto	Canada	8.57
9	Auckland	New Zealand	7.86
9	Dubai	United Arab Emirates	7.86

Table 7. Top 10 cities in usability

Rank	City	Country	Score
1	Hong Kong SAR	Hong Kong SAR	19.38
2	Jerusalem	Israel	18.75
3	Seoul	Republic of Korea	17.50
4	Macao SAR	Macao SAR	17.19
4	Shanghai	China	17.19
6	Auckland	New Zealand	16.88
7	Jakarta	Indonesia	16.56
7	Toronto	Canada	16.56
9	Vienna	Austria	16.25
10	Helsinki	Finland	15.94

Table 8. Top 10 cities in content

Rank	City	Country	Score
1	New York	United States	14.68
1	Stockholm	Sweden	14.68
3	Singapore	Singapore	14.04
4	Seoul	Republic of Korea	13.83
5	Hong Kong	Hong Kong	13.19
6	Tallinn	Estonia	12.55
7	Macao	Macao	11.91
8	Helsinki	Finland	11.70
9	Dublin	Ireland	11.28
9	Shanghai	China	11.28

Table 9. Top 10 cities in service delivery

Rank	City	Country	Score
1	Seoul	Republic of Korea	15.44
2	Hong Kong SAR	Hong Kong SAR	14.04
3	Singapore	Singapore	13.33
4	Rome	Italy	13.16
5	Shanghai	China	12.46
6	New York	United States	12.28
7	Auckland	New Zealand	10.35
8	Stockholm	Sweden	10.00
9	Sao Paulo	Brazil	9.12
10	Sofia	Bulgaria	8.42

Table 10. Top 10 cities in citizen participation

Rank	City	Country	Score
1	Seoul	Republic of Korea	15.64
2	Rome	Italy	10.51
3	Singapore	Singapore	9.74
3	Tegucigalpa	Honduras	9.74
5	Jerusalem	Israel	9.23
6	Auckland	New Zealand	8.46
7	Copenhagen	Denmark	7.69
7	New York	United States	7.69
9	Paris	France	7.44
9	Shanghai	China	7.44

is lower, only 24.26. Whereas 19 of 28 cities in OECD countries are above the world average, only 16 of 52 cities in non-OECD countries are above that average. Interestingly, 32 of 52 cities in non-OECD countries are below the average score for that group of countries.

In addition, 67% of cities selected in Africa, 13% in Asia, 3% in Europe, and 25% in North America have not established official city Web sites. Every city selected in South America had its own official Web site. Whereas cities in Africa have not paid attention to developing their capabilities in digital government, most cities in other continents are interested in developing those capabilities.

Table 11. Comparison by OECD membership

	OECD countries	Non-OECD countries
Above 36.58	12	8
36.34	Average Score in OECD countries	
36.58 – 28.49	8	7
28.49	Average Score Throughout the World	
28.49 – 24.55	2	5
24.26	Average Score in Non-OECD Countries	
Below 24.55	6	32

There were also regional differences. For example, 67% of cities in Africa, 13% in Asia, 3% in Europe, and 25% in North America do not have official city Web sites. Interestingly, every city selected in South America has its own official Web site. Whereas cities in Africa have not paid attention to developing their capabilities in digital government, most cities in other continents are interested in developing those capabilities.

A one-way ANOVA (Table 12) suggests difference in the level of digital government at the municipal level between OECD and non-OECD countries at a significance level of 0.05. This is consistent with our concern over the disparity in e-government between governments in developed versus lesser-developed countries.

The apparent gap between developed and under-developed countries, suggests the need for international organizations such as the U.N. and cities in advanced countries to attempt to bridge the digital divide. We recommend developing a comprehensive policy for bridging that divide. A comprehensive policy should include capacity building for municipalities, including information infrastructure, content, and applications and access for individuals. Parallel to improving citizens' access to digital government, it is important to develop relevant content for citizens and innovative applications in digital government considered as best practices throughout the world.

The data we have developed underscore several concerns. First, given the low scores on privacy (mean 2.53, median 1.07) and participation (mean 3.26, median 2.18), cities worldwide need to work diligently to increase Web site security and to encourage citizen participation. There are many established criteria for improved

Table 12. ANOVA

OECD membership

	Sum of Squares	Df	Mean Square	F	Sig.
Between Groups	2654.411	1	2654.411	13.696	.000
Within Groups	15117.039	78	193.808		
Total	17771.450	79			

Table 13. Descriptive statistics for the 84 cities surveyed

	Privacy	Usability	Content	Service	Participation
Min	0	3.44	0.43	0	0
Max	15.36	19.38	14.68	15.44	15.64
Mean	2.53	11.45	6.43	4.82	3.26
Median	1.07	11.72	5.635	4.2105	2.18

NOTE: Maximum score for each category was 20

Web security, and an increasingly rich and accessible set of best practices studies on citizen participation.

Second, the apparent gap between developed and underdeveloped countries suggests the need for international organizations, such as the U.N. and the World Bank, as well as cities in the more advanced countries, to work assiduously to bridge the digital divide—within countries and between countries. The digital divide is a challenge that democratic and democratizing societies must address, and it refers to the divide between those with Web access and Web-related skills, and those without such capacities. Even though the online population worldwide is increasingly reflective of communities offline, the reality of a digital divide means that certain segments of the population are effectively excluded from online access and public policy deliberation.

Thus, the divide undermines the Internet as a mainstream and inclusive participatory medium, as it disproportionately impacts lower socio-economic individuals who have historically played an insignificant role within the public policy process. We recommend the development of comprehensive policies to bridge that divide. A comprehensive policy should include capacity building for government Web sites, including information infrastructure, content, and applications and access for individuals and their representative organizations. Parallel to improving citizens' access to digital government, it is important to develop relevant content, and to emulate innovative applications and best practices of digital government throughout the world.

References

Bertelsmann Foundation. (2001). *Balanced e-government*. Retrieved December 24, 2003, from http://www.begix.de/en/index.html

Burrell, M. G. (1979). *Sociological paradigms and organizational analysis*. London: Heinemann.

Giga Consulting. (2000). *Giga scorecard analysis of the New Jersey Department of Treasury*. [An unpublished report to the NJ Department of Treasury.] Additional information about the Giga Balanced Scorecard can be found at www.forrester.com

Hart-Teeter. (2003). *The new e-government equation: Ease, engagement, privacy and protection*. A report prepared for the Council for Excellence in Government.

Ho, A. (2002). Reinventing local governments and the e-government initiative. *Public Administration Review, 62*(4), 434-444.

Holden, S. H., Norris, D. F., & Fletcher, P. D. (2003). Electronic government at the local level: Progress to date and future issues. *Public Performance & Management Review, 26*(4), 325-344.

Holzer, M., & Vatche, G. (1998). Five great ideas in American public administration. In J. Rabin, W. Bartley Hildreth, & G. J. Miller (Eds.), *Handbook of public administration* (2nd ed.) (pp. 49-101). New York: Marcel Dekker.

Kaylor, C., et al. (2001). Gauging e-government: A report on implementing services among American cities. *Government Information Quarterly, 18*, 293-307.

Kraemer, K. (1991). Strategic computing and administrative reform. In C. Dunlop & R. Linking (Eds.), *Computerization and controversy: Value and social choices* (pp. 167-80). Boston: Academic Press.

Melitski, J. (2003). Capacity and e-government performance: An analysis based on early adopters of Internet technologies in New Jersey. *Public Performance and Management Review, 26*(4), 376-390.

Moon, M. J. (2002). The evolution of e-government among municipalities: Rhetoric or reality? *Public Administration Review, 62*(4), 424-433.

Moon, M. J., & deLeon, P. (2001). Municipal reinvention: Municipal values and diffusion among municipalities. *Journal of Public Administration Research and Theory, 11*(3), 327-352.

Musso, J., et al. (2000). Designing Web technologies for local governance reform: Good management or good democracy. *Political Communication, 17*(1), 1-19.

Norris, D. F., Fletcher, P. D., & Holden, S. (2001). *Is your local government plugged in? Highlights of the 2000 electronic government survey.* Washington, DC: International City/Country Management Association.

Norris, D. F., & Moon, M. J. (2005). Advancing e-government at the grassroots: Tortoise or hare. *Public Administration Review, 65*(1), 64-75.

Norris, P. (1999). Who surfs? New technology, old voters and virtual democarcy. In Kamarck & Nye (Eds.), *Democracy.com? Governance in a networked world* (pp. 71-94). Hollis, NH: Hollis Publishing.

Pardo, T. (2000). *Realizing the promise of digital government: It's more than building a Web site.* Albany, NY: Center for Technology in Government.

United Nations; American Society of Public Administration. (2001). *Benchmarking e-government: A global perspective.* Retrieved from http://www.aspanet. org/about/pdfs/BenchmarkingEgov.pdf

Weare, C., et al. (1999). Electronic democracy and the diffusion of municipal Web pages in California. *Administration and Society, 31*(1), 3-27.

West, D. M. (2000). *Assessing e-government: The Internet, democracy, and service delivery by state and federal governments.* Retrieved from http://www.inside-politics.org/egovtreport00.html

West, D. M. (2001). *WMRC global e-government survey, October, 2001.* Retrieved from http://www.insidepolitics.org/egovt01int.html

West, D. M. (2002). *Global e-government, 2002.* Retrieved from http://www.in-sidepolitics.org/egovt02int.pdf

West, D. M. (2003). *Global e-government, 2003.* Retrieved from http://www.in-sidepolitics.org/egovt03int.pdf

West, D. M. (2003). *Urban e-government, 2003.* Retrieved from http://www.inside-politics.org/egovt03city.pdf

West, D. (2004). E-government and the transformation of service delivery and citizen attitudes. *Public Administration Review, 64*(1), 15-13.

Welch, E., & Wong, W. (1998). Public administration in a global context: Bridging the gaps of theory and practice between Western and non-Western nations. *Public Administration Review, 58*(1), 40-50.

Endnotes

[1]   International Telecommunication Union. (2002). Internet indicators: Hosts, users and number of PCs. Retrieved June 12, 2003, from http://www.itu.int/ITU-D/ict/statistics/

[2]   The New York City privacy policy (www.nyc.gov/privacy) defines third parties as follows: "third parties are computers, computer networks, ISPs, or application service providers (ASPs) that are non-governmental in nature and have direct control of what information is automatically gathered, whether cookies are used, and how voluntarily provided information is used."

[3]   The New York City privacy policy (www.nyc.gov/privacy) gives the following definitions of cookies and Web bugs or beacons: "Persistent cookies are cookie files that remain upon a user's hard drive until affirmatively removed, or until expired as provided for by a pre-set expiration date. Temporary or 'session cookies' are cookie files that last or are valid only during an active communications connection, measured from beginning to end, between computer or applications (or some combination thereof) over a network. A Web bug (or beacon) is a clear, camouflaged or otherwise invisible graphics image format (GIF) file placed upon a Web page or in hyper text markup language (HTML) e-mail and used to monitor who is reading a Web page or the relevant email. Web bugs can also be used for other monitoring purposes such a profiling of the affected party."

[4]   Additional information about public sector Web site usability can be found online at the U.S. Department of Human Services site (www.usability.gov). Examples of private sector usability criteria and benchmarks include Moffitt (http://www.unt.edu/benchmarks/archives/2002/august02/access.htm) and Nielsen (http://www.useit.com/alertbox/990711.html).

Chapter II

The Impact of the Internet on Political Activism:

Evidence from Europe

Pippa Norris, Harvard University, USA &
United Nations Development Program

Abstract

The core issue for this study concerns less the social than the political consequences of the rise of knowledge societies; in particular, the capacity of the Internet for strengthening democratic participation and civic engagement linking citizens and government. To consider these issues, Part I summarizes debates about the impact of the Internet on the public sphere. The main influence of this development, as it is theorized in a market model, will be determined by the "supply" and "demand" for electronic information and communications about government and politics. Demand, in turn, is assumed to be heavily dependent upon the social characteristics of Internet users and their prior political orientations. Given this understanding, the study predicts that the primary impact of knowledge societies in democratic societies will be upon facilitating cause-oriented and civic forms of political activism, thereby strengthening social movements and interest groups, more than upon conventional channels of political participation exemplified by voting, parties, and election campaigning. Part II summarizes the sources of survey data and the key measures of political activism used in this study, drawing upon the 19-nation

European Social Survey, 2002. Part III examines the evidence for the relationship between use of the Internet and indicators of civic engagement. The conclusion in Part IV summarizes the results and considers the broader implications for governance and democracy.

Introduction

The rise of knowledge societies represents one of the most profound transformations that has occurred in recent decades. The diffusion of information and communication technologies (ICTs) promises to have major social consequences by expanding access to education and training, broadening channels of expression and social networks, as well as revolutionizing the nature of work and the economy. The primary impact of this development has been evident in affluent societies, but the Internet has also been widely regarded as an important instrument for social change in poorer nations around the globe (Franda, 2002; UN, 2002).

Part I: Theories of the Impact of Knowledge Societies on Democracy

There are multiple theories about how the growth of knowledge societies could potentially influence civic engagement in contemporary democracies. Four main perspectives can be identified in the literature.

The Internet as a Virtual Agora

The most positive view is held by cyber-optimists who emphasize the Panglossian possibilities of the Internet for the involvement of ordinary citizens in direct, deliberative, or "strong" democracy. Digital technologies are thought to hold promise as a mechanism facilitating alternative channels of civic engagement exemplified by political chat rooms, remote electronic voting in elections, referenda, plebiscites, and the mobilization of virtual communities, thereby revitalizing levels of mass participation in public affairs (Barber, 1998; Budge, 1996). This view was certainly popular as the Internet rapidly expanded in the United States during the mid-1990s and the radical potential of digital technologies for democracy continues to be expressed by enthusiasts today (Gilder, 2000; Rash, 1997; Rheingold, 1993; Schwartz, 1996).

Moreover, the general claim that the knowledge society will stimulate widespread citizen deliberation in affairs of state so that the Internet functions like a virtual Agora while attractive as a normative ideal, became less plausible once it was widely recognized by many observers that there are substantial disparities in who becomes involved in digital politics. Studies of politically-oriented discussion groups, bulletin boards, and online chat rooms have found that these largely fail as deliberative forums, instead serving as places to reinforce like-minded voices due to their "easy entrance, easy exit" characteristics (Davis, 1999; Davis & Owen, 1998; Wilhelm, 2001). The survey evidence from many countries indicates that those who take advantage of the opportunities for electronic civic engagement are often activists who were already most predisposed to participate via the traditional channels of political participation (Hill & Hughes, 1998; Selnow, 1998; Toulouse & Luke, 1998). The Internet is a medium of choice par excellence, so it seems improbable that political Web sites, chat rooms and online news will reach many citizens who are otherwise disengaged, apathetic, or uninterested, if they choose to spend their time and energies on multiple alternative sites devoted to everything from the stock market to games and music (Bonfadelli, 2002; Johnson & Kaye, 2003). In this regard, the Internet seems analogous to the segmented magazine market, where some subscribe to the *Atlantic Monthly* and the *Economist* and *Foreign Affairs*, but others pick *Golfing Weekly* or *Playboy*. Therefore, claims for the potential of the knowledge society to revitalize mass participation or strong democracies find little support from the available empirical studies.

The Knowledge Elite and Social Inequalities

As the Internet evolved during the last decade, a darker vision developed among cyber-pessimists who regard the knowledge society as a Pandora's Box reinforcing existing inequalities of power and wealth and generating deeper divisions between the information rich and poor. In this perspective, the global and social divides in Internet access mean that, far from encouraging mass participation, the knowledge society will disproportionately benefit the most affluent sectors in the developed world (Golding, 1996; Hayward, 1995; Murdock & Golding, 1989; Weber, Loumakis, & Bergman, 2003). For example, the first phase of the UN World Summit on the Information Society (WSIS) held in Geneva in December 2003 concluded that the Internet holds great prospect for development for billions of people around the globe, endorsing ambitious principles and action plans, and yet no agreement was reached about the transfer of financial and technological resources necessary to facilitate wider electronic access in poorer nations (ITU, 2003). Despite the great potential for technological innovations leading towards political change, observers suggest that in established democracies, traditional interest groups and governments have the capacity to reassert their control in the virtual political sphere, just as traditional multinational corporations have the ability to reestablish their predominance in the world of e-commerce (Hill & Hughes, 1998; McChesney, 1999; Selnow, 1998; Toulouse & Luke, 1998). In authoritarian regimes, as well, studies have found that access to publishing and disseminating information on the Internet, can be strictly restricted by governments, such as limitations imposed in Cuba, Saudi Arabia, and China (Boas, 2000; Drake, Kalathil, & Boas, 2000; Hill & Hughes, 1999; Kalathil & Boas, 2003).

Politics as Usual

The third perspective, which has become more commonly heard in recent years, is articulated by cyber-skeptics who argue that both of these visions are exaggerated. In this view, the potential of the knowledge society has failed so far to have a dramatic impact on the practical reality of "politics as usual," for good or ill, even in countries such as the United States at the forefront of digital technologies (Margolis & Resnick, 2000). This perspective stresses the embedded status quo and the difficulties of achieving radical change to political systems through technological mechanisms. For example, commentators suggest that during the 2000 American election campaign, George W. Bush and Al Gore used their Web pages essentially as glossy shop windows, fundraising tools, and campaign ads, rather than as interactive "bottom up" formats facilitating public comment and discussion (Foot & Schneider, 2002; Media Matrix, 2000). During the 2004 presidential election in the United States, the fundraising function also seems to have predominated in the campaign for Vermont Democratic Governor, Howard Dean, and the Kerry-Edwards Web site.

Elsewhere, content analysis of political party Web sites in countries as diverse as the United Kingdom, France, Mexico, and the Republic of Korea has found that the primary purpose of these Web sites has been the provision of standard information about party organizations and policies that were also widely available offline, providing more of the same rather than anything new, with still less interactive facilities.

Party presence on the Internet seems to represent largely an additional element to a party's repertoire of action along with more traditional communication forms rather than a transformation of the fundamental relationship between political parties and the public, as some earlier advocates of cyber-democracy hoped. (Gibson, Nixon, & Ward, 2003)

Studies of the content of government department Web sites in many countries at the forefront of the move towards e-governance (e.g., the United States, Canada, and India) and surveys of users of these Web sites have also found that these Web sites are often primarily used for the dissemination of information and the provision of routine administrative services. The Internet thereby serves as an aid to good governance by increasing government transparency, efficiency, and customer-oriented service delivery, but it does not function as a radical medium facilitating citizen consultation, policy discussion, or other democratic inputs into the policymaking process (Allen, Jullet, & Roy, 2001; Chadwick & May, 2003; Fountain, 2001; Haque, 2002; Stowers, 1999; Thomas & Streib, 2003). In the skeptical view, technology is a plastic medium that flows into and adapts to pre-existing social molds and political functions.

The Political Market Model

The last theoretical perspective—the one developed in this study—can be characterized as the political market model. In this account, the impact of the knowledge society depends upon the interaction between the "top-down supply" of political information and communications made available via the Internet, e-mail, and the World Wide Web from political institutions, notably government departments, parliaments, political parties, the news media, interest groups, and social movements, and upon "demand" in the use of information and communications about politics among the online public.

This model suggests that, in turn, demand depends upon the social characteristics of the online population, especially the preponderance of younger, well-educated citizens who are commonly among the heaviest users of the Internet, and their prior political interests and propensities. The theory suggests that, given these assumptions, use of the Internet in the public sphere is most likely to strengthen and reinforce cause-oriented and civic-oriented dimensions of political activism, which are more popular among the well-educated younger generation, while having far less impact upon traditional channels of participation through voting, parties, and election campaigns (Norris, 2001, 2002).

Therefore, rather than accepting that either everything will change as radical forms of direct democracy come to replace the traditional channels of representative governance (as optimists hope), that the digital divide will reinforce socio-economic disparities in politics (as pessimists predict), or alternatively that nothing will change as the digital world merely replicates "politics as usual" (as the skeptics suggest), the political market model suggests that it is more sensible to identify what particular types of democratic practices will probably be strengthened by the rise of the knowledge society, understanding that these developments remain a work in process.

Part II: Conceptual Framework, Evidence, and Data

What evidence would allow us to examine these propositions, particularly testing the impact of the Internet upon political activism? To understand these issues, we need to recognize that involvement in public affairs can take many different forms, each associated with differing costs and benefits. This study compares the impact of frequency of use of the Internet on four main dimensions of activism: voting, campaign-oriented, cause-oriented, and civic-oriented. These are summarized into

Table 1. Political activism in Europe, ESS-2002

Percentage that have...	Regular internet user (%)	Not regular user (%)	Activism Gap (%)	Sig
VOTING				
Reported voting in the last national election	28	26	+2	***
CAMPAIGN-ORIENTED				
Contacted politician	22	13	+9	***
Worn campaign badge	12	6	+6	***
Donated money to party	11	7	+4	***
Worked for party	6	4	+2	***
Been a party member	6	5	+1	***
CAUSE-ORIENTED				
Bought product for political reason	41	17	+24	***
Signed petition	35	16	+19	***
Boycotted product	25	11	+14	***
Demonstrated legally	10	5	+5	***
Protested illegally	2	1	+1	***
CIVIC-ORIENTED				
Been a member of a sports club	35	14	+21	***
Been a member of a trade union	33	17	+16	***
Been a member of a consumer group	25	11	+14	***
Been a member of a hobby group	20	10	+10	***
Been a member of an educational group	12	4	+8	***
Been a member of a professional group	14	6	+8	***
Been a member of an environmental group	9	4	+5	***
Been a member of a humanitarian group	9	4	+5	***
Been a member of a church group	15	11	+4	***
Been a member of a social club	11	10	+1	***
TOTAL 21-POINT ACTIVISM INDEX				
Mean index score	4.43	2.56	+1.87	***

Source: European Social Survey, 2002 (ESS-19). Pooled sample N. 31741 in 18 ESS nations, excluding Germany (where Internet use was not monitored).

Note: For the specific items used in the construction of the Index, see the Technical Appendix. "Regular Internet user" is defined as reported personal use of the Internet, e-mail, or World Wide Web at least weekly. The "activism gap" is measured as the percentage of regular Internet users minus the percentage of regular non-users who engage in this activity. A positive gap indicates that regular Internet users are more active than non-users. The total activism index counts participation in each form of activity as one and sums the 21-point scale. Significance tested by Chi-squares and by ANOVA. *** .001 ** .01 * .05 N/s Not significant.

a 21-point "Political Activism Index" combining all dimensions[1]. The basic items used to develop this Index are listed in Table 1 and reported fully in Appendix A.

Voting in regular elections is one of the most ubiquitous forms of citizen-oriented participation, requiring some initiative and awareness for an informed choice but making fairly minimal demands of time, knowledge, and effort. Through the ballot box, voting exerts diffuse pressure over parties and elected officials, and the outcomes of elections affect all citizens. Participating at the ballot box is central to citizenship in representative democracy, but due to its relatively low costs, the act is atypical of other more demanding forms of participation. The Internet can be expected to encourage voting participation mainly by lowering some of the information hurdles to making an informed choice, although the provision of remote electronic voting through a variety of new technologies can be expected to have a more radical impact on turnout (Tolbert & McNeal, 2003).

Campaign-oriented forms of participation concern acts focused primarily on how people can influence parliament and government in representative democracy, mainly through political parties in British politics. Verba, Nie, and Kim (1978) focus on this aspect when they define political participation as "...those legal activities by private citizens that are more or less directly aimed at influencing the selection of governmental personnel and/or the actions they take." Work for parties or candidates, including party membership and volunteer work, election leafleting, financial donations to parties or candidates, attending local party meetings, and get-out-the-vote drives, typifies this category. Parties serve multiple functions in representative democracies, notably simplifying and structuring electoral choices, organizing and mobilizing campaigns, aggregating disparate interests, channeling political debate, selecting candidates, structuring parliamentary divisions, acting as policy think tanks, and organizing government. Not only are parties one of the main conduits of political participation, they also serve to boost and strengthen electoral turnout. If mass party membership is under threat, as many indicators suggest, this could have serious implications for representative democracy (Mair & Biezen, 2001; Scarrow, 2001).

Campaigning and party work typically generate collective rather than individual benefits, but require greater initiative, time, and effort (and sometimes expenditure) than merely casting a ballot. The Internet can be expected to provide new opportunities for activism in parties and election campaigns (e.g., through downloading information, joining parties or donating funds, and participation in discussion groups hosted on party or candidate Web sites) (Gibson, Nixon, & Ward, 2003; Hague & Loader, 1999; Norris, 2001). Experience of campaign-oriented activism is gauged in this study by a five-battery item, including whether people are members of a party and whether they have donated money to a party, worked for a party, contacted a politician, or worn a campaign badge during the previous 12 months.

Cause-oriented activities are focused primarily upon influencing specific issues and policies. These acts are exemplified by consumer politics (e.g., buying or boycotting certain products for political or ethical reasons), taking part in demonstrations and protests, and organizing or signing petitions. The distinction is not watertight; for example, political parties can organize mass demonstrations, and social movements often adopt mixed action strategies that combine traditional repertoires such as lobbying representatives, with a variety of alternative modes such as online networking, street protests, and consumer boycotts. Nevertheless, compared with campaign-oriented actions, the distinctive aspect of cause-oriented repertoires is that they are most commonly used to pursue specific issues and policy concerns among diverse targets, both within and also well beyond the electoral arena.

These acts seek to influence representative democracies within the nation-state through the conventional channels of contacting elected officials, ministers, civil servants, and government departments, but their target is often broader and more diffuse, possibly in the non-profit or private sectors, whether directed at shaping public opinion and lifestyles, publicizing certain issues through the news media, mobilizing a networked coalition with other groups or non-profit agencies, influencing the practices of international bodies such as the World Trade Organization or the United Nations, or impacting public policy in other countries. Experience of cause-oriented activism is measured in this study by a five-battery item, including whether people have signed a petition, bought or boycotted products for a political reason, demonstrated legally, or protested illegally during the previous 12 months.

Lastly and by contrast, **civic-oriented** activities involve membership and working together in voluntary associations, as well as collaborating with community groups to solve a local problem. The core claim of Toquevillian theories of social capital is that typical face-to-face deliberative activities and horizontal collaboration within voluntary organizations far removed from the political sphere (exemplified by trade unions, social clubs, and philanthropic groups) promote interpersonal trust, social tolerance, and cooperative behavior. In turn, these norms are regarded as cementing the bonds of social life and creating the foundation for building local communities, civil society, and democratic governance. In a win-win situation, participation in associational life is thought to generate individual rewards, such as career opportunities and personal support networks, as well as facilitating community goods by fostering the capacity of people to work together on local problems. Putnam suggests that civic organizations such as unions, churches, and community groups play a vital role in the production of social capital where they succeed in bridging divisive social cleavages, integrating people from diverse backgrounds and values, promoting "habits of the heart" such as tolerance, cooperation, and reciprocity, thereby contributing towards a dense, rich, and vibrant social infrastructure (Pharr & Putnam, 2000; Putnam, 1993, 1996, 2000, 2002). This dimension involves direct action within local communities (e.g., raising funds for a local hospital or school) where the precise dividing line between the social and political breaks down.

Trade unions and churches, in particular, which have long been regarded as central pillars of civic society in Europe, have traditionally served the function of drawing citizens into public life. For a variety of reasons, including the way that voluntary associations can strengthen social networks, foster leadership skills, heighten political awareness, create party linkages, and facilitate campaign work, people affiliated with church-based or union organizations can be expected to participate more fully in public life (Cassel, 1999; Radcliff & Davis, 2000). Access to the knowledge society can be expected to expand social networks and information, facilitating membership in civic associations and social groups, although the evidence as to whether the Internet strengthens or weakens social capital remains under debate (Bimber, 1998; Horrigan, Rainie, & Fox, 2001). Experience of civic activism is measured here by a 10-point scale summarizing membership in a series of different types of voluntary organizations and associations, including traditional sectors such as trade unions, church groups, and social clubs, as well as "new" social movements exemplified by groups concerned about the environment and humanitarian issues.

The summary 21-point Political Activism Index, which provides an overview, is composed very simply by adding together experience of each of these different types of acts (each coded 0/1). It should be noted that in this conceptual framework, this study focuses upon political *activity*; we are concerned with *doing* politics rather than being attentive to public affairs or having psychological attitudes such as trust in parliament or political efficacy, which are thought to be conducive to civic engagement. The study, therefore, does not regard exposure or attention to mass communications, including following campaign events in newspapers or watching party political broadcasts during the election, as indicators of political activism per se. These factors may, indeed, plausibly contribute towards participation and thereby help explain this phenomenon as prior pre-conditions, but they are not, in themselves, channels that citizens can use for expressing political concerns or mobilizing group interests.

Survey Evidence and Data Sources

To establish the extent and significance of the role of the Internet on political activism, the primary source of evidence for this study is drawn from the 19-nation European Social Survey 2002 (ESS-19). This is a new, academically driven study designed to chart and explain the interaction between Europe's changing institutions and the attitudes, beliefs, and behavior patterns of its diverse populations[2]. The survey includes a wide range of items designed to monitor citizen involvement, including a battery of a dozen items that can be used to create a summary political activism scale, as well as multiple indicators of political interest, efficacy, trust, party allegiances, subjective well-being, family and friendship bonds, and a rich array of detailed socio-demographic data, including household composition, ethnicity, type of area, and occupational details. This survey provides recent evidence, and it also facilitates comparison among similar advanced industrialized European societies and democratic states. The size of the total pooled sample (with over 36,000 cases) also allows us to monitor differences among smaller European populations, such as ethnic minorities.

The survey currently includes four nations in Scandinavia (Norway, Sweden, Finland, and Denmark), six nations in Northern Europe (Britain, Germany, Luxembourg, Ireland, the Netherlands, and Switzerland), four from Mediterranean Europe (Greece, Spain, Italy, Portugal, and Israel), and four post-Communist societies in Central Europe (the Czech Republic, Hungary, Poland, and Slovenia). All these countries were classified by Freedom House in 2001-02 as fully "free" in their political rights and civil liberties, using the Gastil Index. Most can also be categorized as affluent post-industrial economies, with an average per capita GDP in 2002 ranging from $16,000 (in Greece) to $30,000 (in Norway), although all of the post-Communist states except Slovenia fall below this level.

Internet Use

In some of these societies, the knowledge society has been widely diffused, with two-thirds or more of the public using the Internet at least occasionally. By contrast, in other societies, few of the public accesses the Internet. The survey monitored Internet use by the question in Example 1.

Example 1

```
Now, using this card, how often do you use the Internet, the World
Wide Web, or e-mail -- whether at home or at work -- for your
personal¹ use?

No access at home or work        00 (41%)        }
Never use                        01 (17%)        }
Less than once a month           02 (3%)         } Regular use
Once a month                     03 (2%)         }
Several times a month            04 (4%)         }
--------------------------------------------------------------
Once a week                      05 (5%)         }
Several times a week             06 (11%)        }
Every day                        07 (16%)        }
(Don't know/No answer)
_____

¹ "Personal use'" is defined by the ESS-2002 as private or recreational use that does not have
to do with a person's work or occupation.
```

This is a limited measure that does not gauge what people do online or where they commonly seek information, nor does it distinguish among access to the Internet, email, or World Wide Web. These are only some forms of access to the knowledge society, and other electronic technologies may be equally important, such as text messaging; mobile or cell phones; or cable, satellite, and interactive television. In addition, people may also use the Internet at work, and the measure does not attempt to monitor the length of experience of using the Internet. Nevertheless, this item provides a standard measure of exposure to the Internet widely used in other studies, which gives a suitable benchmark for cross-national comparison.

The main cross-national contrasts that emerged on this item are illustrated in Figure 1, which compares a third of Europeans in the sample who report that they *regularly* use the Internet (defined here as personal use of the Internet at least weekly) in the ESS-19. The remaining two-thirds say they never used the Internet or used it far less regularly than weekly. As many other Eurobarometer surveys have regularly reported, sharp differences are evident in Internet access within Europe (Norris, 2001). In Scandinavia (notably Denmark, Sweden, and Norway), regular Internet use is widespread among the majority of the population. Many of the countries fall into the middle of the distribution where anywhere from one-fifth to one-half use

Figure 1. Proportion of regular Internet users in Europe, ESS-2002

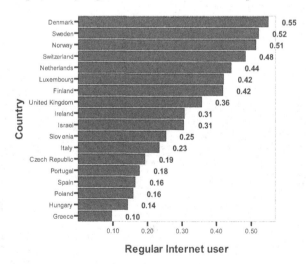

Regular Internet user

Source: European Social Survey, 2002, Pooled sample

Note: Regular Internet users is defined as those who personally use the Internet, e-mail or the World Wide Web at least once a week.

the Internet at least weekly. By contrast, in some countries in Mediterranean and post-Communist Europe, less than a fifth of the public made regular use of this technology, notably in Greece, Hungary, Poland, and Spain, which were all at the bottom of the distribution.

Part III: Analysis and Results

How do those Europeans who are and are not regular users of the Internet compare across the different types of political activism? We can first compare the overall patterns using the pooled ESS-19 sample without using any prior social or attitudinal controls, and then go on to consider the results of the multivariate analysis and differences among European nations. One important qualification to note is that in the analysis, we cannot establish the direction of causality in these models; with a single cross-sectional survey, it is impossible to disentangle satisfactorily whether use of the Internet facilitates and encourages political activism, or whether prior habits of political engagement lead towards continuing activism via electronic channels. To establish causality in any media effects, we really need either to analyze repeated panel surveys among the same respondents over successive years, or to examine experimental research designs, neither of which are available on a cross-national basis (Kent, Jennings, & Zeitner, 2003; Norris, 2000; Norris & Sanders, 2003). In the model, based on standard theories of political socialization, we assume that the cultural values and norms of behavior are acquired from formative experiences with family, school, and community in early youth. We theorize that these processes are likely to shape long-term and enduring political orientations and habitual norms of behavior, such as patterns of partisan identification, ideological values, and forms of activism. We assume that use of the Internet is a relatively recent and, therefore, short-term influence that will facilitate and reinforce the cognitive and attitudinal factors associated with habitual political activism (e.g., expanding people's awareness of election issues or party policies) but will not necessarily alter or transform broader patterns of civic engagement.

Given these assumptions, Table 1 shows a clear and consistent pattern: regular Internet users are significantly more politically active across all 21 indicators. The overall score on the mean Political Activism Index, which summarizes this pattern, was 4.43 for regular Internet users compared with 2.56 for others, a substantial and significant difference. Yet the size of the activism gap does vary among different types of engagement; it is relatively modest in reported voting turnout as well as across most of the campaign-oriented forms of activism, such as party membership, party volunteer work, and party donations. By contrast, the gap is substantial (in double digits) among many forms of cause-oriented activism, such as buying or boycotting products for political reasons and signing petitions, as well as in membership of certain types of civic organizations notably belonging to sports clubs, trade unions, consumer groups, and hobby groups.

To see whether this activism gap was an artifact of the way that regular Internet use was measured, Figure 2 illustrates the mean distribution of the political activism index across all categories of Internet use, ranging from no access at home or work to personal use of the Internet every day. The figure confirms that the overall scale of political activism rises sharply and steadily with each category of Internet use, more than doubling across the whole scale.

Moreover, if the patterns are analyzed by country, again similar results are evident in every society. As Figure 3 shows, political activism rises steadily with increasing Internet use in nearly all nations, and the only exceptions to this are Portugal and Poland where levels of technological diffusion remain very limited.

Despite this clear and important pattern, the theoretical framework in this study suggests that, given the characteristics of the online population, we should find systematic variations in engagement by the different types of political activism, and, indeed, this is confirmed by the data. Figure 4 illustrates the strong and significant linear relationship between use of the Internet and civic activism in a wide range of voluntary organizations and local associations (R=318***). The cause-oriented activism scale is also significantly associated with the frequency of using the Inter-

Figure 2. Internet use and political activism index

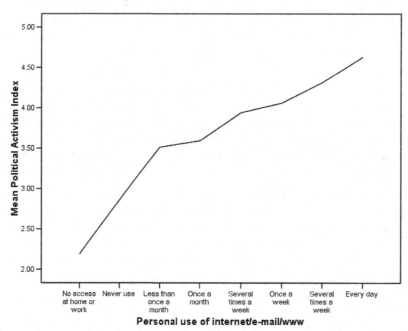

Source: European Social Survey, 2002 Pooled sample

Figure 3. Internet use and political activism index by nation

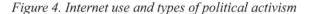

Source: European Social Survey, 2002

Figure 4. Internet use and types of political activism

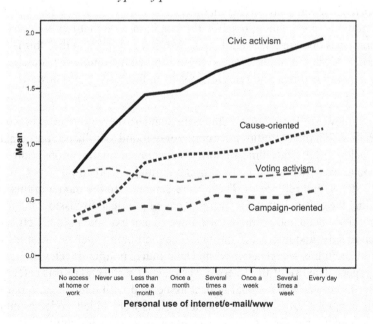

Source: European Social Survey, 2002 Pooled sample

net (R =.318***). Nevertheless, voting activism is relatively flat across levels of Internet use, and the correlation proves to be significant but negative in direction (R= -0.024**), while the campaign-oriented activism scale shows only a modest positive correlation (R=.136). The results suggest that any association between access to the Internet and political activism is heavily contingent upon the particular forms of participation that are under analysis.

Nevertheless, many factors may be influencing this process, including the prior social characteristics and cultural attitudes of Internet users. To examine these issues we need multivariate regression models. The main explanations of political activism can be categorized into the following four groups:

1.   *Structural* explanations emphasizing the resources that facilitate civic engagement; notably, time, education, and income, which are closely associated with demographic groups and social status;

2.   *Cultural* accounts focusing upon the motivational attitudes that draw people into public affairs, such as a sense of political efficacy, institutional confidence, and citizenship duty;

3.   *Agency* explanations prioritizing the role of mobilizing organizations such as churches and unions, as well as the role of the news media and informal social networks, which bring people into public affairs. The use of the Internet can best be conceptualized in this model as a mobilizing agency;

4   *Historical* accounts suggesting that there could be a regional effect generated by traditions in each area; notably, the length of time that representative democracy has operated in Scandinavia, Western Europe, and the "third-wave" democracies in the Mediterranean region and post-Communist societies that only experienced free and fair elections from the early 1990s onward.

Given this framework, Table 2 first includes the standard demographic and socioeconomic variables that many studies have commonly found to influence participation, including belonging to an ethnic minority, educational qualifications, household income, social class, work status, total hours normally worked per week, marital and family status, and religiosity. These were entered into the model in this order before adding the cultural attitudes of frequency of political discussion, the importance of politics, social and political trust, internal and external political efficacy, a sense of civic duty, and interest in politics. The mobilizing agency variables were then entered, including social networks and attention to politics on television, radio, and newspapers. The use of the Internet was entered at the end of this category to see whether there was any residual impact associated with this technology net of all other factors. Lastly, the major European regions were added, coded as dummy variables, where the Nordic region was the default category for comparison.

Table 2. Impact of Internet use on political activism, with controls

	B	Std. Error	Beta	Sig.
(Constant)	-1.39	0.28		0.00
SOCIAL STRUCTURE				
Gender	-0.17	0.05	-0.03	0.00
Age (years)	0.02	0.00	0.13	0.00
Belong to ethnic minority	0.03	0.13	0.00	0.81
Educational qualifications	0.22	0.02	0.11	0.00
Income	0.07	0.01	0.06	0.00
Work status	0.38	0.06	0.06	0.00
Total hours per week in main job + O/T	0.00	0.00	0.00	0.88
Married	0.19	0.05	0.03	0.00
Have children at home	0.13	0.05	0.02	0.01
Importance of religion	0.12	0.05	0.02	0.01
CULTURAL ATTITUDES				
Discuss politics/current affairs, how often	-0.14	0.01	-0.09	0.00
Important in life: politics	0.01	0.01	0.01	0.54
Social trust	0.02	0.00	0.04	0.00
Trust in national political institutions	-0.02	0.01	-0.03	0.01
Trust in international institutions	-0.03	0.01	-0.04	0.00
Internal political efficacy	0.27	0.01	0.18	0.00
External political efficacy	0.12	0.01	0.08	0.00
Civic duty scale	0.04	0.00	0.11	0.00
How interested in politics	-0.34	0.04	-0.09	0.00
MOBILIZING AGENCIES				
How often socially meet with friends, relatives or colleagues	0.17	0.02	0.08	0.00
TV watching, news/ politics/current affairs on average weekday	-0.12	0.02	-0.05	0.00
Radio listening, news/ politics/current affairs on average weekday	0.03	0.01	0.02	0.06
Newspaper reading, politics/current affairs on average weekday	0.09	0.03	0.03	0.00
Personal use of internet/e-mail/www	**0.10**	**0.01**	**0.10**	**0.00**
REGION				
Northern Europe	-0.30	0.06	-0.05	0.00
Mediterranean Europe	-1.35	0.08	-0.16	0.00
Post-Communist Europe	-1.73	0.09	-0.23	0.00
Adjusted R^2	.373			

Source: European Social Survey, 2002 (ESS-19). Pooled sample N. 31741 in 18 ESS nations, excluding Germany (where Internet use was not monitored).

Note: The models represent the result of ordinary least squares regression analysis where the total political activism index is the dependent variable. The index counts participation in each form of activity as one and sums the 21-point scale. The figures represent the unstandardized beta coefficient (B), the standard error (s.e.), the standardized beta coefficient (Beta), and the significance (sig). The default dummy regional variable was the Nordic region. All variables were checked to be free of problems of multi-collinearity by tolerance statistics. See Table 1 for the items in each scale.

The results in the pooled model confirm the significance of many of these factors upon the political activism scale. The only exceptions proved to belong to an ethnic minority, the amount of hours in the paid workforce, and the salience of politics, which all proved to be non-significantly related to participation, contrary to expectations. But after adding the complete battery of controls, use of the Internet continued to be significantly related to political activism, suggesting that this relationship is not

Table 3. Impact of Internet use on types of political activism, with controls

Type of activism	B	Std. Error	Beta	Sig.	Adjusted R²
Voting	.005	.001	.034	.002	.145
Cause-oriented	.036	.004	.095	.000	.213
Campaign-oriented	.006	.004	.018	.102	.161
Civic-oriented	.042	.006	.073	.000	.308

Source: European Social Survey, 2002. Pooled sample N. 31741 in 18 ESS nations, excluding Germany (where Internet use was not monitored).

Note: The models represent the result of ordinary least squares regression analysis on each form of activism as the dependent variables. For the full range of prior controls in the models (not reported here), see Table 2. The figures represent the unstandardized beta coefficient (B), the standard error (s.e.), the standardized beta coefficient (Beta), and the significance (sig).

simply explained away as a result of the prior social or attitudinal characteristics of those who are most prone to go online. The most important factors predicting activism (measured by the strength of the standardized regression coefficients) concern internal political efficacy (a feeling that the person could influence the political process), age, education, region, and civic duty. After these factors, use of the Internet proved the next strongest predictor of activism, which was more important than other indicators such as social and political trust or use of any of the news media. The overall model explained more than one-third of the variance in activism ($R^2 = .37$).

Similar regression models were then run with identical controls to predict the four types of political activism under comparison, using the pooled sample. Without showing all the coefficients, the summary of the results in Table 3 shows that use of the Internet was significantly associated with voting, cause- and civic-oriented forms of activism, but not with campaign-oriented forms of activism. This confirms that, rather than claims about the effect of the knowledge society on activism, we do need to distinguish among the types of participation that generate different effects. The reason for these differences most probably lies in the residual effect of the typical social background and the political values of Internet users, notably the propensity of well-educated younger generations to predominate online, as noted in many studies of the well-known "digital divide" (Norris, 2001).

Part IV: Conclusion and Discussion

The theory developed in this study considers the more pessimistic claims that the development of the Internet will serve to reinforce the voices of the powerful, the more skeptical arguments that it will merely reflect "politics as usual," and the more optimistic view that the knowledge society will transform governance as we know it and strengthen levels of mass political participation. The study hypothesizes that contemporary democracies are a market where the impact of the Internet depends in part upon the "supply" of political information and communications, primarily from political agencies, and also upon the "demand" for such information and communication from the mass public. In turn, the public's demand comes from the social and cultural profile of the online population reflecting long-standing patterns of civic engagement. As a result, use of the Internet is significantly related to overall patterns of political activism, even with multiple prior controls, but there are several distinct dimensions or channels of activism. The survey evidence analyzed in this study confirms that the rise of the knowledge society in Europe has indeed had the greatest positive consequences for politics by strengthening cause-oriented and civic-oriented activism, rather than by encouraging mass participation in campaigns and elections.

What are the broader implications of this pattern for democracy and for the future of electronic governance? We can speculate that the primary beneficiaries of this process will probably be political actors lacking traditional organizational resources that are useful in politics, such as those without a large-scale, fee-paying mass membership base, substantial financial assets, and paid full-time bureaucratic officials. This type of organization is exemplified by new social movements, transnational advocacy networks, alternative social movements, protest organizations, community activists and development workers, single-issue causes from all shades of the political spectrum, as well as minor parties. The knowledge society is not expected to drive these insurgent movements, but rather to facilitate their organization, mobilization, and expression (Keck & Sikkink, 1998). These organizations have the greatest incentives and the fewest constraints to using the knowledge society. If this perspective is correct, then the result of the rise of the Internet may be greater pressures on governments to respond to the demands of single-issue groups and more amorphous social networks. By contrast, established political parties and traditional interest groups can be expected to adapt far more slowly to the knowledge society, because they are capable of drawing upon alternative organizational and financial resources, including legal authority, full time paid officials, press officers, lobbyists, and grassroots fee-paying mass memberships. Yet these are the umbrella organizations, particularly parties, which are capable of aggregating diverse issues into broader programmatic platforms, encouraging compromise, deliberation, and bargaining among members and channeling demands on a more predictable basis into government. It remains to be seen how far these developments alter the channels of participation in representative democracy in Europe and elsewhere, but the consequences will probably provide government with greater opportunities to connect with citizens and to greater challenges in the inevitable pressures that arise from satisfying multiple fragmented zero-sum constituencies represented by single-issue politics.

References

Allen, B.A., Juillet, L., Paquet, G., & Roy, J. (2001). E-governance & government on-line in Canada: Partnerships, people & prospects. *Government Information Quarterly, 18*(2), 93-104.

Barber, B. R. (1998). Three scenarios for the future of technology and strong democracy. *Political Science Quarterly,* I(4), 573-589.

Bimber, B. (1998). The Internet and political transformation: Populism, community and accelerated pluralism. *Polity XXXI*, (1), 133-160.

Bimber, B. (2001). Information and political engagement in America: The search for effects of information technology at the individual level. *Political Research Quarterly, 54*(1), 53-67.

Boas, T. C. (2000). The dictator's dilemma? The Internet and U.S. policy toward Cuba. *The Washington Quarterly, 23*(3), 57-67.

Bonfadelli, H. (2002). The Internet and knowledge gaps: A theoretical and empirical investigation. *European Journal of Communication, 17*(1), 65-84.

Budge, I. (1996). *The new challenge of direct democracy*. Oxford: Polity Press.

Cassel, C.A. (1999). Voluntary associations, churches, and social participation theories of turnout. *Social Science Quarterly, 80*(3), 504-517.

Chadwick, A., & May, C. (2003). Interactions between states and citizens in the age of the Internet: "E-government" in the United States, Britain and the European Union. *Governance, 16*(2), 271-300.

David, R. (1999). *The Web of politics*. Oxford: Oxford University Press.

Davis, R., & Owen, D. (1998). *New media and American politics*. New York: Oxford University Press.

Drake, W.J., Kalathil, S., & Boas, T. C. (2000, October). Dictatorships in the digital age: Some considerations on the Internet in China and Cuba. *iMP: The Magazine on Information Impacts.* Retrieved from www.cisp.org/imp

Foot, K.A. & Schneider, S.M. (2002). Online action in campaign 2000: An exploratory analysis of the US political web sphere. *Journal of Broadcasting & Electronic Media, 46*(2), 222-244.

Fountain, J. E. (2001). *Building the virtual state: Information technology and institutional change*. Washington, DC: Brookings Institution Press.

Franda, M. (2002). *Launching into cyberspace: Internet development and politics in five world regions*. Boulder, CO: Lynne Rienner.

Gibson, R., Nixon, P., & Ward, S. (Eds.). (2003). *Political parties and the Internet: Net gain?* London: Routledge.

Gilder, G. (2000). *Telecom: How infinite bandwidth will revolutionize our world.* New York: Free Press.

Golding, P. (1996). World wide wedge: Division and contradiction in the global information infrastructure. *Monthly Review, 48*(3), 70-85.

Hague, B. N. & Loader, B. D. (Eds.). (1999). *Digital democracy: Discourse and decision making in the information age.* New York: Routledge.

Haque, M.S. (2002). E-governance in India: Its impacts on relations among citizens, politicians and public servants. *International Review of Administrative Sciences, 68*(2), 231-250.

Hayward, T. (1995). *Info-rich, info-poor: Access and exchange in the global information society.* K.G. Saur.

Hill, K. A. & Hughes, J. E. (1998). *Cyberpolitics: Citizen activism in the age of the Internet.* Lanham, MD: Rowan & Littlefield.

Hill, K. & Hughes, J. E. (1999). Is the Internet an instrument of global democratization? *Democratization, 3,*29-43.

Horrigan, J., Rainie, L., & Fox, S. (2001). Online communities: Networks that nurture long-distance relationships and local ties. *Pew Internet & American Life Project.* Retrieved from www.pew internet.org

ITU. (n.d.). Retrieved from http://www.itu.int/wsis/

Johnson, T.J., & Kaye, B.K. (2003). Around the World Wide Web in 80 ways: How motives for going online are linked to Internet activities among politically interested Internet users. *Social Science Computer Review, 21,*(3), 304-325.

Kalathil, S., & Boas, T. C. (2003). *Open networks closed regimes: The impact of the Internet on authoritarian rule.* Washington, DC: Carnegie Endowment for International Peace.

Keck, M. E., & Sikkink, K. (1998). *Activists beyond borders: Advocacy networks in international politics.* Ithaca, NY: Cornell University Press.

Kent, J. M., & Zeitner, V. (2003). Internet use and civic engagement: A longitudinal analysis. *Public Opinion Quarterly, 67*(3), 311-334.

Mair, P., & van Biezen, I. (2001). Party membership in twenty European democracies 1980-2000. *Party Politics, 7*(1), 7-22.

Margolis, M., & Resnick, D. (2000). *Politics as usual: The cyberspace "revolution."* Thousand Oaks, CA: Sage.

McChesney, R. W. (1999). *Rich media, poor democracy.* IL: University of Illinois Press.

Media Matrix (2000, October). *Campaign 2000: Party politics on the World Wide Web.* Retrieved from www.media metrix.com

Murdock, G., & Golding, P. (1989). Information poverty and political inequality: Citizenship in the age of privatised communications. *Journal of Communication, 39*, 180-195.

Norris, P. (2000). *A virtuous circle.* New York: Cambridge University Press.

Norris, P. (2001). *Digital divide.* New York: Cambridge University Press.

Norris, P. (2002). *Democratic Phoenix: Reinventing political activism.* New York: Cambridge University Press.

Norris, P. (2003). The bridging and bonding role of online communities. In P. N. Howard & S. Jones (Eds.), *Society online: The Internet in context.* Thousand Oaks, CA: Sage.

Norris, P., & Sanders, D. (2003). Medium or message? *Political Communications.*

Pharr, S., & Putnam, R. (Eds.). (2000). *Disaffected democracies: What's troubling the trilateral countries?* Princeton, NJ: Princeton University Press.

Putnam, R. D. (1993). *Making democracy work: Civic traditions in modern Italy.* Princeton, NJ: Princeton University Press.

Putnam, R. D. (1996). The strange disappearance of civic America. *The American Prospect, 24.*

Putnam, R. D. (2000). *Bowling alone: The collapse and revival of American community.* New York: Simon and Schuster.

Putnam, R. D. (Ed.). (2002). *Democracies in flux.* Oxford: Oxford University Press.

Radcliff, B., & Davis, P. (2000). Labor organization and electoral participation in industrial democracies. *American Journal of Political Science, 44*(1), 132-141.

Rash, Jr., W. (1997). *Politics on the Net: Wiring the political process.* New York: W.H. Freeman.

Rheingold, H. (1993). *The virtual community: Homesteading on the electronic frontier.* Reading, MA: Addison Wesley.

Scarrow, S. (2001). Parties without members? In R. J. Dalton & M. Wattenberg (Eds.), *Parties without partisans.* New York: Oxford University Press.

Schwartz, E. (1996). *Netactivism: How citizens use the Internet.* Sebastapol, CA: Songline Studios.

Selnow, G.W. (1998). *Electronic whistle-stops: The impact of the Internet on American politics.* Westport, CT: Praeger.

Shah, D.V., Kwak, N., & Holbert, R.L. (2001). "Connecting" and "disconnecting" with civic life: Patterns of Internet use and the production of social capital. *Political Communication, 18*(2), 141-162.

Stowers, G.N.L. (1999). Becoming cyberactive: State and local governments on the World Wide Web. *Government Information Quarterly, 16*(2), 111-127.

Thomas, J.C., & Streib, G. (2003). The new face of government: Citizen-initiated contacts in the era of e-government. *Journal of Public Administration Research and Theory, 13*(1), 83-101.

Tolbert, C.J., & McNeal, R.S. (2003). Unraveling the effects of the Internet on political participation? *Political Research Quarterly, 56*(2), 175-185.

Toulouse, C. & Luke, T. W. (Eds.). (1998). *The politics of cyberspace.* London: Routledge.

United Nations/American Society for Public Administration (2002). *Bench marking e-government: A global perspective.* New York: United Nations/DPEPA.

Verba, S., Nie, N., & Kim, J.-on (1978). *Participation and political equality: A seven-nation comparison.* New York: Cambridge University Press.

Weber, L.M., Loumakis, A., & Bergman, J. (2003). Who participates and why? An analysis of citizens on the Internet and the mass public. *Social Science Computer Review, 21*(1), 26-42.

Wilhelm, A. (n.d.). *Democracy in the digital age: Challenges to political life in cyberspace.* New York: Routledge.

Endnotes

[1]   Since the dimensions are theoretically defined and constructed, based on understanding the role of different forms of participation in representative democracy, the study did not use factor analysis to generate the classification or measurement.

[2]   For more details of the European Social Survey, including the questionnaire and methodology, see http://naticent02. uuhost.uk.uu.net/index.htm. Data for an initial nineteen countries, along with comprehensive documentation, is accessible at http://ess.nsd.uib.no. The survey is funded via the European Commission's 5th Framework Program, with supplementary funds from the European Science Foundation which also sponsored the development of the study over a number of years. I am most grateful to the European Commission and the ESF for their support for this project and to the work of the ESS Central Coordinating Team, led by Roger Jowell, for making this survey data available.

[3]   *"Personal use'"* is defined by the ESS-2002 as private or recreational use that does not have to do with a person's work or occupation.

This chapter was previously published in the International Journal of Electronic Government Research, 1(1), 20-39, January-March 2005.

Chapter III

E-Government in Canada:
Transition or Transformation?

Jeffrey Roy, Dalhousie University, Canada

Abstract

The objectives of this chapter are first, to examine the main conceptual dimensions of electronic government and second, to critically assess Canada's public sector. The following definition of e-government is a starting point: the continuous innovation in the delivery of services, citizen participation, and governance through the transformation of external and internal relationships by the use of information technology, especially the Internet. For some, e-governance is distinguishable from e-government in that the former comprises a more fundamental sharing and reorganizing of power across all stakeholders and the citizenry, whereas the latter is more focused on modernizing existing state processes to improve performance with respect to existing services and policies. In the short term, digital technologies continue to serve primarily as a platform for incremental changes to the service and security architectures. Yet, broader pressures and questions about transparency and trust continue to build. A key question is whether or not a new government is prepared to embrace a more holistic redesign of political institutions predicated on information openness and public engagement.

Introduction[1]

The objectives of this chapter are twofold: first, to examine the main conceptual dimensions of electronic government (e-government); and second, to critically assess both the current responses and future prospects of Canada's public sector. In order to be more precise on the scope of this chapter, the following definition of e-government is useful as a starting point: *the continuous innovation in the delivery of services, citizen participation, and governance through the transformation of external and internal relationships by the use of information technology, especially the Internet.*[2]

This definition helps to underscore the links between government and governance in such a context—and the fluid nature of roles and relationships both within the public sector and across various external stakeholders externally. The latter term, governance, may be defined in a general way as the manner and mechanisms by which resources are coordinated in a world where power and knowledge are increasingly distributed (Paquet, 1997). The rise of electronic governance (e-governance) then denotes processes of coordination made possible or even necessary by the advent of technology, and the spreading of online activities in particular (Allen, Juillet, Paquet, & Roy, 2001).

This broad starting point has been extended even further by other groups, such as the Organization for Cooperation and Economic Development (OECD) that refer to e-government as simply about achieving good government. This perspective underscores the widening canvass of e-government as digital technologies and online activities permeate most all aspects of the public sector. For some, e-governance is distinguishable from e-government in that the former comprises a more fundamental sharing and reorganizing of power across all stakeholders and the citizenry, whereas the latter is more focused on modernizing existing state processes to improve performance with respect to existing services and policies (Peristeras, Tsekos, & Tarabanis, 2002; Riley, 2003).

For others, and more in line with the definitions adopted above, e-government must be viewed as encompassing both administration and democracy (Bertelsmann, 2002). Despite rather fluid terminology, such viewpoints offer useful guidance, as the interdependence of such inward and outward considerations also matters due to the holistic context of a public sector encompassing both internal and external dimensions.

Service and Security

Remarkably new by any historical measure, the rapid emergence of e-government around the world and the specific nature of its current evolution can be viewed as stemming from two separate yet inter-related episodes over the past decade: on the one hand, the rise of the Internet and electronic commerce (e-commerce) during the 1990s; and on the other hand, the terrorist attacks of September 11, 2001. While their origins are quite distinct, they share many contemporary governance challenges.

With respect to the Internet and e-commerce, it is indeed remarkable that the world's online population has now surpassed half a billion people worldwide. Yet, despite progress in most regions of the world this population remains relatively concentrated in the developed world, within the most advanced economies of Asia, Europe, and North America (Geiselhart, 2004). This concentration stems, in part, from the catalytic role played by the private sector as competition and innovation spurred not only the digital infrastructure for online activity but the growing plethora of content products and user processes that lead to the Internet's permeation across organizations and institutions.

Indeed, within industry the Internet has served three main purposes in shaping market behaviour and organizational dynamics: a source of product and process innovation, an efficiency tool, and an alternative channel of client service. The widening scope of digital technologies and online activity means that few, if any, industries are exempt from some degree of transformation (Andal-Ancion, Cartwright, & Yip, 2003).

For governments, all of these Internet-induced changes are relevant. Indeed, much of e-government reflects private sector activity that has both encouraged and pressured public sector organizations to act in a similar manner. Much of the need for organizational innovation stems from similar drivers—efficiency and customer service—of e-commerce and new business models based on digital tools and virtual capacities. Fiscal constraints imposed by a quasi-competitive system of global investors and domestic politics, as well as a strategic desire to generate cost savings and reallocate spending to new and politically attractive priorities make the nexus between technology management and efficiency a central concern in government today (McIver & Elmagarmid, 2002; Pavlichev & Garson, 2004).

A key dimension of this concern is the organizational or enterprise architecture to coordinate resources, formulate policies, and deliver services. As with industry, the delivery of services online offers a potentially significant form of cost savings in comparison to other, existing service delivery channels (ibid.). Moreover, the willingness of governments to compare themselves to private sector organizations in terms of technology challenges and client (or citizen) expectations also matters: the public is encouraged to expect the same sorts of changes and service strategies across both sectors. In this perspective, multinational corporations and national governments (and large subnational ones) are viewed as similar entities in terms of their priorities and opportunities in seeking to deploy new governance capacities (Cairncross, 2002).

A more careful examination of government, however, reveals important differences across the private and public sectors. With respect to efficiency and customer service, two key and intertwined distinctions are relevant: first, government's abilities to realize efficiency savings are dramatically different than those of private corporations; and secondly, the roles and expectations of politicians and the public shape government in ways that are unique and unlike similar dynamics in industry. Efficiency, for example, is a much more politically contested principle in government. Stakeholders such as unions and political parties may oppose worker mobility and job cuts, moves generally applauded in the market sector. Equally important, whereas private corporations may aggressively cater to specific customer groups, defining them and providing incentives to shape their behaviour, governments remain wedded to broader public interest responsibilities involving all citizens.

These public interest considerations are tied to political accountabilities that, in turn, shape both the feasibility and the perceived appropriateness of e-government as a service-delivery strategy. The modest and uneven results of online service delivery by governments, even in those countries leading in Internet use, is indicative of both the complexities and diverse preferences characterizing a citizenry and their relations with their governments (Hart Teeter, 2003). Indeed, it is not clear whether citizens are demanding online services or governments are pushing them and the requisite mix of incentives and results to in move citizens online remain elusive (Roy, 2003). This elusiveness, in turn, is reflected in dispersed and uneven political leadership both in terms of the relative importance of online service delivery as a strategic objective and the level of resources and authority allocated to undertake necessary change.

These necessary changes are primarily about fostering more horizontal governance to cut across traditionally separate vertical entities, perhaps the single most crucial organizational challenge to realizing citizen-centric portals and service delivery mechanisms (Fountain, 2001; Allen, Paquet, Juillet, & Roy, 2005). Achieving this horizontal collaboration therefore requires political will and a set of organizational mechanisms to facilitate information sharing and joint action. There are both structural and cultural impediments to such mechanisms, reflecting traditional resource allocation processes and separate accountability systems based on vertical hierarchy and, in the case of Parliamentary models, Ministerial accountability (ibid.).

The danger is that in the absence of strong action to overcome these limitations, the rhetoric of portals as a basis for integrative services, one stop encounters and more seamless governance remains just rhetoric. Moreover, strengthened government-wide coordination, implying some degree of central authority runs counter to the thrust of new public management reform in the 1980s and early 1990s that emphasized organizational autonomy and flexibility. Striking a new balance is proving to be a formidable challenge is realizing e-government benefits (as the Canadian experience, subsequently examined, demonstrates).

The terrorist acts of September 11, 2001 have brought out similar governance dilemmas, albeit with an added sense of urgency. Governments have been quick to establish new anti-terrorism and homeland security measures that often create new pressures for horizontal coordination and government-wide action. Information management and inter-operability over a safe and secure digital architecture become precursors to improved security for citizens. Homeland security efforts are in keeping with the definition of e-government offered at this article's outset.

Since its inception, online service delivery has relied upon a secure infrastructure in order to underpin the technological feasibility of interacting and transacting via the Internet (Holden, 2004). Nonetheless, today cyber-security may also be viewed as one element in a broader public safety or homeland security agenda that denotes an important reshaping of e-government in terms of purpose and focus. A commonality of service delivery and homeland security is an emphasis on coordination across government and capacities to transcend organizational boundaries in order to focus on the needs of the citizen. A similar necessity for both agendas is a sophisticated and reliable digital architecture to underpin government wide capacities for action.

There are differences as well that are important in shaping how e-government is viewed both within and outside of the public sector. On the service delivery side, most governments had pursued a more collaborative model, facilitating horizontal coordination across separate units in an effort to achieve better results for the citizen as a consumer of public services (Allen et al., 2005). In comparison, the dramatic imposition of homeland or domestic security as a response to recent terrorist activities has accentuated a more centralized form of organizational response. The United States Department of Homeland Security is a case in point, internalizing coordination within a broader, more central command and control structure accountable directly to a senior cabinet appointee of the president. Yet, challenges of balancing hierarchies and networks, structure and flexibility, control and collaboration remain stark (Kamarck, 2004).

It may well be that a heightened political profile of security and terrorism corresponds to a public demand for action and clarity and as a result, stronger and more centralized forms of leadership. This point underscores how an evolution or dramatic shift in the mood of the public can shape the organization of government. The heightened security-minded focus on centralization and clarity is accelerating attention and investments made in cyberspace, technology and internal governance reform, changes that may well bolster the level of seriousness and internal competencies within government devoted to deploying and managing digital technologies (Dutta & McCrohan, 2002; Clifford, 2004).

How and to what ends such deployments occur are dependent on many variables, particularly the views of the citizenry and their elected representatives. Internet use is expected to rise and grow more prevalent, suggesting that more individuals will look to conduct their affairs with their governments online when feasible (Hart-Teeter, 2003). Uncertainty remains, however, as public attitudes are intertwined with both their informational and transactional encounters with government authorities (online and offline) and perceptions of the relative importance of priorities requiring attention and responses.

Privacy of information is a case in point. Certainly in North America prior to 2001 there was trepidation in the minds of citizens with respect to government collecting, sharing, and using personal information—even if better and faster service were the result (Joshi, Ghafoor, & Aref, 2002). More recently, despite real and legitimate debates on the nature of security-driven measures to gather similar forms of information in more direct and intrusive ways, governments are comforted, and perhaps even driven by a public now rebalancing security and privacy concerns. Still, despite this rebalancing and even with broad support for stronger homeland security measures, the American public remains highly suspicious of government handling of personal information (Hart-Teeter, 2004).

This contrast, openness versus secrecy, a major point of departure between deploying digital technologies as a means of serving citizens versus one centred on public safety, brings to light the central and related aspects of transparency and trust as two, interrelated and important dimensions of both e-government and e-governance.

Transparency and Trust

According to some observers of governance and the Internet, we live in the age of transparency (Tapscott & Ticoll, 2003). Although this particular invocation targets private corporations facing heightening investor and public scrutiny that ultimately renders traditional forms of secrecy and information containment and communications strategies counter-productive, the message and underlying forces driving it also hold much relevance for government. Transparency drives this need for greater openness and responsiveness, and secrecy would seem to be an increasingly risky prospect potentially resulting in questions, exposure and increased costs and complexities down the line (Mitchinson & Ratner 2004).

Indeed, government has arguably long been viewed as inherently more transparent than business—as any first year text on public administration argues with respect to the fishbowl of government life.[3] From one perspective, e-government has accelerated this emphasis on openness as not only have governments themselves moved to provide much more information online, but the Internet has underpinned expanded capacities for neutral observers and vested interests to find and share information, expose secrets and shortcomings, and mobilize public opinion accordingly.

The notion of trust in government and political processes is multi-faceted and complex. Parent, Vandebeek, and Gemino (2004) distinguish between specific and diffuse forms of political trust: "Specific support refers to satisfaction with government outputs and the overall performance of political authorities. Diffuse support refers to the public's attitude toward regime-level political objectives…diffuse support encapsulates the intrinsic" (p. 1). This differentiation underscores the potentially different ways in which citizens may judge precise forms of government action and democratic institutions more generally. There may therefore be related differences in how e-government is viewed as a set of customer relationship mechanisms (defined primarily by service delivery and responsiveness) versus how e-governance might come to be viewed (encompassing broader elements of legitimacy and accountability).

In their own discussion of how e-government might contribute to rising trust in the public sector, Tolbert and Mossberger (2003) offer a more encompassing approach bridging to some degree these two dimensions. The authors point to potential improvements in both administrative and democratic systems by making government more responsive, transparent and accountable, accessible, responsible, efficient and effective, and participatory. Their findings provide cautious testament to the notion that e-government's degree of online transparency is positively correlated to the level of trust accorded by citizens along some of these dimensions (Tolbert & Mossberger, 2003; Parent et al., 2004). Similarly, some experts see online information reporting as a key (and still under utilized) component of performance management and heightening both political and managerial accountability to the citizenry (Lee, 2004).

The relationship between trust and transparency is both complex and consequential, and it is bound to become more so as online access widens and usage expands. Greater transparency does not necessarily guarantee heightened trust, as openness imposed on governments that exposes error or fraud is likely to impact the attitudes of the citizenry differently than more proactive measures by political authorities to invite scrutiny and share information. Moreover, citizens may carry different views according to specific functions and roles carried out by certain segments of the public sector, meaning general assertions of government may be less relevant than support for specific initiatives and their handling.

The relationship between homeland security, transparency and e-government is illustrative. In the United States, despite an expanded realm of powers and secrecy, public opinion would seem to accord dramatically higher levels of confidence in those public organizations pursuing security-related matters (particularly front-line emergency services, but also intelligence agencies) than in the federal government generally (Hart-Teeter, 2004). At the same time the forces of transparency have not rescinded due to this security imperative and they continue to exert influence on the sorts of responses put forth by government.[4]

Government contracting is a case in point. Prior to the Internet, transparency was arguably minimal at worst or carefully managed at best. Procurement processes typically featured efforts to maintain a fair and open process by disseminating government needs, sharing information in an open but highly technical manner. This type of openness was limited to what was arguably a closed network of vendors and buyers. Breaches of fairness would occur, and would most often be dealt with quietly and discreetly in order to preserve the relative stability of the system for all participants.

With the Internet and increasingly ubiquitous digital technologies, complexity now defines the very fabric of government operations reliant on closer forms of collaboration and partnering between private sector specialists and government organizations. Adding to this complexity is a much greater focus on openness in procurement processes and a loss of the traditional common ground joining industry and government. This loss may not necessarily be negative as both sectors seek new arrangements to foster more collaborative governance in a much more open and transparent manner—with transparency extended to the widest possible range of stakeholders tied to the contractual or collaborative arrangement (Paquet, 1997). In navigating such volatility, an essential element in fostering effective collaboration between the public and private sectors is trust (Lane & Roy 2000; Lawther, 2002).

Yet this point applies more generally to the broad spectrum of relational governance challenges driving e-government. Trust is centrally positioned at the nexus between the primarily internally driven administrative reforms of e-government's architecture and the related, and more externally rooted pressures for e-governance reflected in widening debates on openness and engagement. Thus, the nature of trust is likely to be increasingly tied to not only online performance measures such as information and transactions provided by governments per se, but also to online process considerations more in line with a broader participatory and multi-stakeholder governance environment that challenges conventional notions of power, authority and accountability (Northrup & Thorson, 2003).

In such an environment, democratic legitimacy—the importance of maintaining and/or strengthening trust between public sector institutions and citizens, is a central concern for governments today—as movements such as "citizen engagement imply a more meaningful and ongoing role for the public in their democratic governance beyond merely electing representatives to act on their behalf. The Internet is a powerful venue for a more widely informed and highly educated citizenry disgruntled with largely representational systems of democratic governance (Palfrey, 2004; Geiselhart, 2004).

Accordingly, a reconsideration of the relative balance between representational and more participative forms of democracy is taking hold and it is intuitive to see why the Internet is a proxy not only for greater openness but also for more participation. The Internet's potential to facilitate a broader conversation across all stakeholders and the public at large is also an argument for inclusiveness that many optimists and proponents of e-democracy espouse. Conversely, the difficulties in structuring such a conversation, and indeed questions surrounding whether online exchanges can facilitate a meaningful forum for debate, learning and compromise are very real, and they represent critical design issues in terms of system of functioning democracy making use, or partial use of cyberspace (Norris, 2000; Oliver & Sanders, 2004).

There is, nonetheless, widening experimentation with democratic reform, many of which involve online capacities to varying degrees (MacIntosh, Malina, & Farrell, 2002). Much depends on the political culture and the relative balance of representation and participation historically permitted and nurtured, but a general observation is that the systemic introduction of more digital and participative forms of democracy would constitute a major revolution in the structure and functioning of the public sector apparatus (Fountain, 2004). While a wholesale redesign of democratic governance seems unlikely in the short term, ongoing mixes of acceptance, resistance and incremental change have resulted (Allen et al., 2001).

In all aspects of online activity, questions surrounding the level of trust and confidence of citizens in the digital technologies themselves are important (Bryant & Colledge, 2002). Much like online service delivery channels have been slow to evolve in many jurisdictions, it will not be any time soon when online mechanisms for voting, consultation and decision-making replace current practises. Moreover, as with homeland security, approaches and demands may vary with circumstance—as a strong public appetite for action and clear accountability may, at times, co-exist uneasily with demands for greater participation and power sharing. This latter tension must be highly contested—as it is a debate that goes to the heart of how democratic government and governance will co-evolve and adapt to the new circumstances of an online and inter-connected world.

In sum, this emerging set of opportunities and challenges in managing the complexities of transparency and trust across both high level discussions and initiatives surrounding democratic reform, and more precise governance and policy agendas—such as service delivery and homeland security strategies will shape e-government's scope as well as its impacts.

E-Government and E-Governance in Canada

Canada provides a useful basis for examining e-government. One of the world's most advanced countries by measures of economic wealth, quality of life, and Internet access and affordability, the public sector in Canada has been aggressively bolstering its usage of digital technologies in order to realize the promise of e-government.

The impetus for a key component of e-government federally evolved from a broader effort, *Connecting Canadians* that was crafted in the mid-1990s and led by the federal Department of Industry. In the Speech from the Throne on October 12, 1999 outlining its objectives and priorities, the Government of Canada stated: By 2004, our goal is to be known around the world as the government most connected to its citizens, with Canadians able to access all government information and services online at the time and place of their choosing:

The government on-line initiative (GOL) was launched to meet this commitment. The goal of GOL is to provide Canadians with electronic access to key federal programs and services. The initiative focuses on grouping or "clustering" online services around citizen's needs and priorities, rather than by government structures. The vision of GOL is seamless, citizen-centred service delivery. (Coe, 2004, p. 6)

The government showcases citizen satisfaction as progress.[5] Canada's reputation internationally has also been bolstered by international observers, such as Accenture Consulting that ranked Canada as a global leader—recognition largely predicated on the Government of Canada portal (www.gc.ca) that, in the spirit of integrated service delivery offers choices not according to government function and department—but rather by clusters of services formed on the basis of needs and interests of the citizen-user.[6]

Despite such acclaim, evidence suggests that the changes and investments made to date have been insufficient to overcoming the inertia of more traditional and vertical processes of Ministerial accountability and silo operations that comprise primarily separate and autonomous political fiefdoms:

GOL initiatives have accelerated the move toward a more horizontal, networked approach...However, with individual Minister accountability as sacrosanct, "silos continue to reign, within departments, across departments and across levels of

*government"...The Government of Canada will need to develop new governance
and accountability mechanisms that allow for collaboration.* (Coe, 2004, p. 18)

Coe's (2004) interviews with those responsible for the GOL projects, designed
as inter-departmental experiments to integrative services, are revealing. There is
no shared accountability to facilitate collaboration, as lead departments become
responsible for process and results; managers felt frustrated by tensions between
horizontal intent strategically and vertical constraints operationally (ibid.).

In a similar review of GOL, the auditor general underscores the absence of a coordinated architecture as a major weakness plaguing government's ability to realize benefits currently predicated more on vision than solid planning: "With only
high-level expected outcomes, there is no clearly defined end state for GOL. The
government will have difficulty measuring progress and performance toward 2005
objectives" (Auditor General of Canada, 2003, p. 10). Such findings are indicative
of the growing need for more rigorous collaborative mechanisms and performance
frameworks to both facilitate shared action and gauge progress, particularly in
service delivery agendas that transcend traditional reporting relationships (Public
Policy Forum, 2003; Stowers, 2004).

Similar challenges characterize security efforts. Over the past three years security has
become a high political priority with both financial investments and organizational
reorganizations to improve domestic capacity.[7] In findings remarkably similar to the
GOL experience, the Auditor General again concluded that horizontal coordination
has been inadequate: "Overall, these gaps and deficiencies point to a requirement to
strengthen the management framework of issues that cross agency boundaries, such
as information systems, watch lists, and personnel screening" (Auditor General of
Canada, 2004, p. 39).

The centrality of information sharing and inter-operability lie at the heart of both
GOL and security. Notably, despite the added and significant possibility of invok-
ing national security in the latter case, unlike the former, privacy concerns remain
a significant barrier to cross-agency action, although the Auditor General herself
remains suspicious that its relevance is not properly understood or defined: "We
noted that privacy concerns were often cited as the reasons why agencies could
not exchange information. However, officials were not able to show us any legal
opinions, specific references to legislation, or judgements as a basis for that position" (ibid., p.17).

Beyond these more systemic barriers, failures to foster coordinated action in a collaborative and informal manner, in the security realm, mirror many of the difficulties
exposed by Coe in her GOL assessment. In one example, the auditor general reports
on an effort to create an Integrated National Security Assessment Centre (INSAC) in

2003 to "use intelligence from nay sources to produce timely analyses and assessment of threats to Canada" and distribute this information accordingly. The findings of the auditor general illustrate the difficulties in achieving joint action:

The latter four organizations (Foreign Affairs, Citizenship and Immigration, Solicitor General and Privy Council Office) have not yet provided a representative. Foreign Affairs said that its resources should more properly address the threat to its personnel and assets abroad and that increasingly scarce resources from a "foreign ministry" should not be devoted to matters that are better left to domestic agencies. Immigration told us it supports the concept and attributes its absence to the lack of permanent funding available for that purpose. Solicitor General Canada said that although it has not assigned a specific representative, its officials are fully engaged in all functions and work initiated by the Centre. The Privy Council Office told us that it has no intelligence collection mandate but is actively involved on a daily basis in the processing of information produced by INSAC.

In a separate, closely related study, the Senate Standing Committee of National Security and Defence conducted a three-year review of security readiness and emergency preparedness and found similar concerns concerning government-wide capacities. The Senate report quotes a senior official's assessment of what is required for the newly formed Office of Critical Infrastructure Protection and Emergency Preparedness (OCIPEP) to fulfill its coordination role in responding to a major emergency: "The challenge, he said, is that this would require an unprecedented level of cooperation inside and outside of government" (Standing Senate Committee on National Security and Defence, 2004, p. 14).

An important lesson of governance would seem applicable to both GOL and security. In both cases, despite a similar need for horizontal action, capacities for doing are lacking. In the case of security, even with considerably more financial resources and political leadership devoted to the cause the difficulties encountered were very similar to barriers plaguing GOL's development. Moreover, there are important connections between GOL and security: a major component of the former is the secure channel, initially conceived as a core mechanism to conduct transactions with citizens but now also a central focus of cyber-security and a likely important element of government information management and sharing policies within the realm of security. For example, OCIPEP is the government's primary agent in improving cyber-security. Thus, their separate fortunes may also shape their collective and integrative prospects for success.

The responses of the recently reconstituted federal government (under a new prime minister in December 2003) address some of these dilemmas on the security side of the equation in a familiar manner—namely, centralization of political and bureaucratic authority within an enlarged entity and, it is hoped, a clear and decisive mandate to ordain the coordination necessary to the result of improved homeland security[8]. Thus, the earlier attempts to pursue a more collaborative and horizontal approach to security management have been significantly abandoned in favour of a more centralizing approach. Given the disappointing results of GOL to take hold and strengthen government-wide capacities, It is not unreasonable to expect that similar centralizing tendencies may result here as well—particularly as security becomes a common plank of both service delivery and homeland safety.

There are two major problems with such an evolution. First, the inward and centralized focus does not address the growing important of inter-governmental aspects to public sector governance and performance; and second, it is out of step with the increasingly participative nature of governance and management more in line with e-governance and changing expectations tied to openness and engagement within the public sector and across the citizenry.

On this first point the senate report provides an important examination of the extended implications and dangers of stymied federal coordination for the country as a whole. Simply put, the Senate Committee found major inter-governmental blockages that are particularly harmful to local governments and front-time delivery agents most in need of informational and tangible resources in order to respond to crises of various sorts (ibid.). The inquiry into the handling of the SARS epidemic, concentrated in Toronto, reported similar findings that, in turn, bolster the Senate's lament of what essentially amounts to an absence of inter-operability between levels of government, a major limitation to the effectiveness of governance capacities for the Canadian public sector as a whole.[9]

In terms of the second point, the failure of a more collaborative mindset to take hold within the federal government is in keeping with a broader characterization of parliamentary government in Canada and elsewhere as an intensely centralized governance model increasingly shaped by the dominance of the prime minister that breeds suspicion and reactive management internally while distancing the government from its citizens and stakeholders externally (Savoie, 1999).

As a response, discussions and proposals offered by the new government to reform and improve democratic governance are meant to counter this view. The over-riding emphasis has been placed on parliamentary—in an effort to re-engage elected officials in policy making and accountability through a variety of measures to lessen the dominance of the centre (prime minister's office) and widen the spheres of influence within Parliament. In short, the emphasis is on refurbishing the existing representational model in very precise manners in the hopes of reversing its steady decline in the eyes of the citizenry.[10]

Yet, alongside such debates a problem stems from contradictions generated by the federal government itself in terms of the messages conveyed to citizens. This contradiction stems from the emphasis on citizen engagement as a principle embraced by the government—particularly within the public service (i.e., the un-elected portions of the executive branch answerable to Ministers). Supported and reinforced by Ministers who routinely convey similar sentiments in public, citizen engagement promises a more direct voice to the public and to key stakeholders in shaping policy decisions and service delivery processes through new and innovative forms of consultation and participation.

Whereas notions of bringing citizens into government processes were radical propositions a few decades ago, it is rare to find a speech today by a senior government manager or Minister (particularly those engaged in e-government efforts) that does not articulate both a recognition of the desire of Canadians to play a greater role and a determination by government to accommodate this desire, both online and offline. Indeed, beyond rhetoric, the government has staked out cyberspace as one means of pursuing expanded public engagement, stating online that it "is committed to finding new and innovative ways to consult with and engage Canadians"[11].

The gap between reforming parliament and engaging Canadians is considerable, as there is little that is new and innovative about the formal committees and processes of the former. Moreover, digital technology—and the Internet specifically, are utterly absent in terms of both usage and debate from parliamentary chambers—the supposed focal point of open and public deliberation (Lenihan, 2002b). It is perhaps for this reason that while service and security initiatives can muster enough interest due to external events and environmental and demographic forces, they have failed to be complemented by broader and bolder governance reforms. Unlike their elected leaders, public servants have fewer qualms envisioning a different future—hypothetically by 2013:

Representative democracy in Canada has not been replaced, but it has become more participative. The powers of effective information and knowledge management are maximized to enable more open, transparent and better decision-making...Democracy is no longer just voting every four or five years, but a continuous, engaged, informed and collaborative dialogue involving all players. (E-Government Policy Network, 2004, p. 9)

Within the parliamentary model, however, whether and how officials should be engaged in this dialogue is a source of tension.[12] Moreover, as Canadians seek a more direct voice in the absence of clarity on how to do so, the impacts of transparency are felt in an increasingly bitter fashion within government due to a relentless series of scandals involving waste, mismanagement or alleged corruption.[13] This more reactive form of transparent reporting, or uncovering, provides testament to the view that while it is unlikely, or at least unclear that governments are failing more, their failures are without question being exposed more often and to greater affect. Trust and cynicism are then likely to become inversely related in an accelerating and negative cycle of decline.

Such difficulties support the notion that e-government, if unaccompanied by significant efforts at political and institutional reform, may do little more than reinforce the existing tendencies of a particular state system (Karakaya, 2003; Wilson & Welch 2004). In the case of the Canadian parliamentary model, the problem is compounded by the tension between these inward, reactionary tendencies of government on the one hand, and the intensifying outward pressures for greater openness and participation on the other.

Transformative Collaboration

If there is a commonality across the four e-government dimensions, it is the widening challenge of collaboration. Presently, collaboration is viewed more as a cost than a virtue—even by many managers and elected officials who routinely espouse the benefits of collaborative activity. Horizontal governance within the public sector must be collaborative to take hold: in the present system, running to counter to tradition, creating such mechanisms and a corresponding culture takes time and energies that can paradoxically be seen as vices on the quick action and strong decision-making required to respond to new realities. Similarly, a more participative and consultative form of politics often contradicts how we most regularly frame leadership—as decisive and unwavering.

While leadership is a key lens through which the conduct and interpretation of leadership must be understood, it is also a symptom of the larger organizational and managerial paradigm in good currency not only in government but in all sectors. Yet, it is government more than elsewhere that has continued to rely on the foundational pillars of Weberian bureaucracy that include hierarchy, clarity, and specialized (or stove pipe) organization. In this largely vertical world, the interface between formal structures and informal culture creates a reflexive preference for top-down management and process control.

The notion of control is fundamental here to understanding the reframing that must occur. All organizations and institutions require some form of control, but the widening interest in new governance systems is testament to the need to view control as less a means to shape every aspect of behaviour (i.e., process control) and more a basis for coordinated and shared actions orchestrated on the basis of outcomes and objectives. From the perspective of more horizontal but in reality networked governance solutions that are the essence of service transformation and effective security strategies, the fundamental challenge remains that of coordinating information flows, technical architectures and human behaviour across agency boundaries (Fountain, 2001, 2004).

A key argument derived from this investigation is that addressing this challenge requires much more meaningful reforms to the political apparatus surrounding the organizational mechanisms in transition. It is only if new technologies—and the attitudes derived from using these new technologies in categorically different processes, begin to permeate the institutions of democracy (and relationships between the executive and legislative branches as well as both with the citizenry at large) that a more meaningful change management program can be expected throughout the public service.

Here the implications for e-government becoming a new paradigm of governance (one more connected, networked, and collaborative) extend beyond the realm of the public sector. The difficulties of navigating transitional and transformative change are occurring at levels of society and across the private sector in particular. What is becoming increasingly clear is that the evolution of work and living in this digital era is thus far a mixed story of opportunity and empowerment for some, and precarious and high stress living for many others—including many of those described as the professional class of knowledge workers.

Not surprisingly, there are some early signs of a backlash against the "benefit" of being digitally connected to the workplace and to one another in a manner reminiscent of predictions that the most affluent and fortunate will be those able to consciously disconnect themselves from technology, thereby preserving private or individualized space. Indeed, in some limited instances private corporations are responding in-kind. Product developers at Google, for instance, receive a day a week of personal time to focus on pet project ideas, irrespective of how closely aligned such ideas are from current corporate strategy. Online platforms are then used to share the results of such creativity and spur new, collaborative initiatives that have become an important source of innovation for the technology company.

To some degree governments have much to learn from individual corporations that are reinventing both structure and culture through a nexus of technological and organizational innovation. Yet, at the same time governments must also preserve their distinctiveness in terms of democratic accountability and the public interest in not only specific service offerings but also serving as a model for working and living in a digital age. E-government must therefore be viewed as not only a new way of operating within the public sector but also a new way of organizing politically and acting in concert with other stakeholders and the public.

This new way entails a collaborative ethos that must ideally render e-government a more participatory model of co-governing between public servants, elected officials and the citizenry that, in turn, will shape the nature of government's relationships with other sectors–notably industry. In this respect, more collaborative relationships between industry and government are not about nurturing cozy ties in a technocratic organizational environment—with token transparency on a technical but highly limited scale. Such relationships must rely on, generate and preserve trust from the public, as well as key public servants and politicians.

A path of transformative collaboration (as opposed to transitional change) is therefore likely to require a stronger empowerment of decentralized sub-units within federal and provincial governments on the one hand, and municipal governments on the other. Collaboration across all of these levels will be required, but as argued throughout the preceding chapters it can only come about through less lopsided governance arrangements more conducive to both inter-governmental partnering and making use of the relevance and importance of proximity that remains as crucial for democratic performance as it does for innovation and competitiveness in Silicon Valley and the many communities attempting to replicate its market-based collaborate model.

In short, e-government's first decade in Canada has been about seeking growing but limited opportunities for public sector reforms denoted largely by the realms of service and security that are most visible and resource intensive at the national level. Pressures associated with heightened transparency and shifting and more complex determinants of trust are exposing the shortcomings of this trajectory, as traditional political and bureaucratic control overshadows the potential for new and more collaborative governance forms to take hold. If e-government is to usher in a positive transformation of both democratic engagement and public sector management, it will entail a truly federated strategy of localized experimentation coupled with a much greater willingness to make use of digital technologies as collaborative and discursive platforms than is presently the case. Such is the truly transformative challenge for e-government's second decade (Roy, 2006).

Conclusion

With the arrival of a conservative minority government to power in January 2005 (led by Prime Minister Stephen Harper) there is at the least the potential for a recasting of political priorities and actions and an alternative set of mechanisms to be designed to pursue them (the first change in political parties controlling government since 1993).

While initial indications are that the new government intends to continue with the expanded emphasis on service and security underway, there are important differences that may emerge in the managing of information and decision-making within this governance architecture. For example, the centrepiece of the campaign and the first legislative action in 2006 is the Federal Accountability Act—designed to increase transparency and oversight in most all aspects of government decision-making. Furthermore, the government has promised to proceed with a planned review of access to information laws and how they can be strengthened.

What will be important to watch is the extent to which this emphasis on openness and strengthened accountability extends into the realm of security or rather stops short. The findings of two judicial inquiries also represent an important variable. The first, the Gomery Commission, created in the aftermath of the so-called federal sponsorship scandal stemming from corrupt contracting practises between the Liberal Party and advertising companies in Quebec in the aftermath of the 1995 provincial referendum on sovereignty, concluded its efforts on February 1, 2006. A major factor in the demise of the previous government, the thrust of this commission has been to reinforce conservative directions for openness and accountability, both politically and within the public service. The result is likely to be at least a modest reduction in secrecy in many aspects of federal operations—particularly with regards to financial and program management. The extension of this reduction into the epicentre of government secrecy—security and public safety, remains to be seen.

Perhaps the most important influence on this latter question is the second judicial inquiry set to report later in 2006. The Arar Commission, established to investigate the deportation of a Syrian-born Canadian, Maher Arar, from the U.S. to Syria where he was held and tortured for more than one year, carries implications for information management and accountability both domestically and bilaterally (i.e., appropriate levels and mechanisms of cooperation with U.S. authorities). The commission itself has faced resistance from the previous government during its hearings regarding the public release of various information sources deemed overly sensitive, and it has been far less publicly visible and galvanizing than that of Gomery. Nonetheless, its findings are likely to strengthen the case for openness and oversight in the realm of security and the Conservatives will face important decisions in terms of their response. In the short term, then, digital technologies continue to serve primarily as a platform for incremental changes to the service and security architectures. Yet, broader pressures and questions about transparency and trust continue to build.

The key question for e-government's evolution in the coming years is whether or not a new government is prepared to embrace a more holistic redesign of political institutions, one predicated on greater information openness and public engagement through both traditional and online channels.

References

Allen, B., Juillet, L., Paquet, G., & Roy, J. (2001). E-government in Canada: People, partnerships and prospects. *Government Information Quarterly, 30*(1), 36-47.

Allen, B. A., Paquet, G., Juillet, L., & Roy, J. (2005). E-government as collaborative governance: Structural, accountability and cultural reform. In M. Khosrow-Pour (Ed.), *Practising e-government: A global perspective* (pp. 1-15). Hershey, PA: Idea Group Publishing.

Andal-Ancion, A., Cartwright, P., & Yip, G. S. (2003). The digital transformation of traditional business. *MIT Sloan Management Review*, Summer.

Auditor General of Canada. (2003). *Information technology: Government line*. Ottawa: Office of the Auditor General of Canada.

Auditor General of Canada. (2004). *National security in Canada: The 2001 anti-terrorism initiative*. Ottawa: Office of the Auditor General of Canada.

Bertelsmann Foundation. (2002). *E-government: Connecting efficient administration and responsive democracy*. Postfach: www.begix.de

Bryant, A., & Colledge, B. (2002). Trust in electronic commerce business relationships. *Journal of Electronic Commerce Research, 3*(2), 32-39.

Cairncross, F. (2002). *The company of the future*. Cambridge, MA: Harvard Business School Press.

Clifford, M. (2004). *Identifying and exploring security essentials*. Upper Saddle River, NJ: Pearson Prentice Hall.

Coe, A. (2004). *Innovation and accountability in 21ˢᵗ century government: Government on-line and network accountability*. Working paper, Kennedy School of Government, Harvard University.

Dutta, A., & McCrohan, K. (2002). Management's role in information security in a cyber economy. *California Management Review, 45*(1), 67-87.

E-Government Policy Network, Government of Canada. (2004). Transforming government and   governance for the 21ˢᵗ century: A conceptual framework. In L. Oliver & L. Sanders (Eds.), *E-government reconsidered: Renewal of governance for the knowledge age*. Regina: Canadian Plains Research Center.

Fife, R. (2004). Ottawa plans $500M security fix. *National Post,* 22/04, p.1.

Fountain, J. E. (2001). *Building the virtual state: Information technology and institutional change*. Washington, DC: Brookings Institution Press.

Fountain, J. E. (2004). Digital government and public health. *Public Health Research, Practise, and Policy, 1*(4), 1-5.

Geiselhart, K. (2004). Digital government and citizen participation internationally. In A. Pavlichev & G. D. Garson (Eds.), *Digital government: Principles and best practises*. Hershey, PA: Idea Group Publishing.

Hart-Teeter (2003). *The new e-government equation: Ease, engagement, privacy and protection*. Washington, DC: Council for Excellence in Government.

Hart-Teeter (2004). *From the home front to the front lines: America speaks out about homeland security*. Washington, DC: Council for Excellence in Government.

Holden, S. H. (2004). *Understanding electronic signatures: The key to e-government*. Washington, DC: IBM Center for the Business of Government.

Joshi, J. B. D., Ghafoor, A., & Aref, W. G. (2002). Security and privacy challenges of a digital government. In W. J. McIver & A. K. Elmagarmid (Eds.), *Advances in digital government: Technology, human factors and policy*. Boston: Kluwer Academic Publishers.

Kamarck, E. C. (2004). Applying 21st-century government to the challenge of homeland security. In J. M. Kamensky & T. Burlin (Eds.), *Collaboration: Using networks and partnerships*. IBM Center for the Business of Government: Rowman and Littlefield Publishers Inc.

Karakaya, R. (2003). *The use of the Internet for citizen participation: Enhancing democratic local governance?* Paper presented to Political Studies Association Annual Conference, University of Leicester.

Kotkin, J. (2000). *The new geography: How the digital revolution is reshaping the American landscape*. New York: Random House.

Lane, G., & Roy, J. (2000). Building partnerships for the digital world. *Lac Carling Government Review, 2*(1), 23-29.

Lawther, W. (2002). *Contracting for the 21st century: A partnership model*. Washington: PricewaterhouseCoopers Endowment for The Business of Government.

Lee, M. (2004). *E-reporting: Strengthening democratic accountability*. Washington, DC: IBM Center for the Business of Government.

Lenihan, D. (2002a). *E-government, federalism and democracy: The new governance*. Ottawa: Centre for Collaborative Government.

Lenihan, D. (2002b). *E-government: The message to politicians*. Ottawa: Centre for Collaborative Government.

MacIntosh, A., Malina, A., & Farrell, S. (2002). Digital democracy through electronic petitioning. In W. J. McIver & A. K. Elmagarmid (Eds.), *Advances in digital government: Technology, human factors and policy*. Boston: Kluwer Academic Publishers.

Marche, S., & McNiven, J. D. (2003). E-government and e-governance: The future isn't what it used to be. *Canadian Journal of Administrative Sciences, 20*(1), 74-86.

McIver, W. J., & Elmagarmid, A. K. (Eds.). (2002). *Advances in digital government: Technology, human factors and policy*. Boston: Kluwer Academic Publishers.

Miles, M., & Roy, J. (2001). Corporate governance as culture in industry and government. *Optimum, 31*(1). Retrieved from www.optimumonline.ca

Mitchinson, T., & Ratner, M. (2004). Promoting transparency through the electronic dissemination of   information. In L. Oliver & L. Sanders (Eds.), *E-government reconsidered: Renewal of governance for the knowledge age*. Regina: Canadian Plains Research Center.

Norris, P. (2000). Global governance and cosmopolitan citizens. In J. S. Nye & J. D. Donahue (Eds.), *Governance in a globalizing world*. Cambridge: Brookings Institution Press.

Northrup, T. A., & Thorson, S. J. (2003). The Web of governance and democratic accountability. In *Proceedings of the 36ᵗʰ Hawaii International Conference on System Sciences*.

Nugent, J. H., & Raisinghani, M. S. (2002). The information technology and telecommunications security imperative: Important issues and drivers. *Journal of Electronic Commerce Research, 3*(1), 1-14.

Oliver, L., & Sanders, L. (Eds.). (2004). *E-government reconsidered: Renewal of governance for the knowledge age*. Regina: Canadian Plains Research Center.

Palfrey, J. G. (2004). *Submission to the Workshop on Internet Governance* (International Telecommunications Union). Harvard Law School: Berkman Center for Internet and Society.

Paquet, G. (1997). States, communities and markets: The distributed governance scenario. In T. J. Courchene (Ed.), *The nation-state in a global information era: Policy challenges the Bell Canada Papers in economics and public policy* (Vol. 5, pp. 25-46). Kingston: John Deutsch Institute for the Study of Economic Policy.

Parent, M., Vandebeek, C. A., & Gemino, A. C. (2004). Building citizen trust through e-government. *Proceedings of 37ᵗʰ Hawaii International Conference on System Sciences*.

Pavlichev, A., & Garson, G. D. (Eds.). (2004). *Digital government: Principles and best practises*. Hershey, PA: Idea Group Publishing.

Peristeras, V., Tsekos, T., & Tarabanis, K. (2002). *E-government or e-governance: Building a domain model for the governance system.* University of Macedonia: United Nations Thessalokiki.

Public Policy Forum. (2003). *Clusters and gateways survey: Preliminary results.* Ottawa.

Riley, T. B. (2003). *E-government vs. e-governance: Examining the differences in a changing public sector climate.* Ottawa: Commonwealth Centre for E-Governance.

Roy, J. (2003). The relational dynamics of e-governance: A case study of the city of Ottawa. *Public Performance and Management Review, 25*(Summer), 1-13.

Roy, J. (2005). Services, security, transparency and trust: Government online or governance renewal in Canada? *International Journal of E-Government Research, 1*(1), 48-58.

Roy, J. (2006). *E-government in Canada: Transformation for the digital age.* Ottawa: University of Ottawa Press.

Savoie, D. (1999). *Governing from the Centre: The concentration of power in Canadian politics.* Toronto: University of Toronto Press.

Standing Senate Committee on National Security and Defence (2004). *National Emergencies: Canada's Fragile Front Lines.* Ottawa: Parliament of Canada.

Stowers, G. N. L. (2004). *Measuring the performance of e-government.* Washington: IBM Center for The Business of Government.

Tapscott, D., & Ticoll, D. (2003). *The naked corporation: How the age of transparency will   revolutionize nusiness.* Toronto: Viking Canada.

Tolbert, C., & Mossberger, K. (2003). *The effects of e-government on trust and confidence in government* [working paper]. OH: Kent State University.

Wilson, W., & Welch, E. (2004). Does e-government promote accountability? A comparative analysis of Web site openness and government accountability. *Governance: An International Journal of Policy, Administration and Institutions, 17*(2), 275-297.

Endnotes

[1]   A previous version of this chapter, drawing on many of the early sections, first appeared in 2005 in the *International Journal of Electronic Government Research* (Roy, 2005).

[2]   The government of Mexico has recently adopted this definition although its precise origins are unknown.

3   The fishbowl of public administration and management typically refers to the wider range of stakeholders monitoring government activity in some direct or indirect manner that exceeds the normal levels of oversight and scrutiny in the private sector—although in today's context of heightened corporate governance debates the parameters of this contrast are perhaps more fluid than in the past (Miles & Roy, 2001).

4   Decisions made by governments today that likely would not have been monitored and questioned publicly in the past are now regularly openly and politically. For instance, a recent study on the attitudes of Americans on this topic shows majority support for the Patriot Act but a strong desire to see its performance and suitability publicly debated (Hart-Teeter, 2004).

5   Coe presents some examples of evidence from government of Canada surveys. Canada leads all other Western industrialized nations in the take-up of on-line government services. Further, 77% of Canadians agree that the Internet has made it easier to find information about government programs and services. Finally, electronic service delivery has raised overall client satisfaction levels with federal services. There has been about a seven percent increase in overall satisfaction with federal services since 1998. Canadians satisfaction with on-line government services is 68%, whereas their satisfaction with services available by phone is only 56%.

6   There are three main sub-selections from the main portal: Canadians, non-Canadians and businesses, the logic being that the sorts of information and services required by online visitors generally falls into one of these three camps. Accordingly, with just a few clicks users are more likely able to find the information they seek.

7   Specifically, in the 2001 federal budget the government allocated $7.7 billion in new funds over five years on a range of initiatives and reforms centred on public security and safety and anti-terrorism. Following the auditor general's report, one public opinion poll conducted in April 2004 showed rising support among Canadians for higher spending on anti-terrorism (55% of those surveyed) and military defence (54%) (Fife, 2004).

8   Such moves are in line with the formation of the Department of Homeland Security in the United States and a similar supranational structure now being designed by the European Union. Notwithstanding this centralizing thrust, there are still elements of organizational separateness within this new department that is arguably more a portfolio of agencies with varying degrees of autonomy. They become unified politically, however, under the clear mandate of a single minister, also the deputy prime minister.

9   Reporting a wide range of federal—provincial—local barriers to coordinated action, the senate report (p.41) states that, "It is imperative that federal, provincial and territorial governments act in common cause, and with common urgency in devising strategies and tactics, and allocating resources and training, to ensure optimal responses to major emergences" (Standing Senate Committee on National Security and Defence, 2004).

10   The thrust of the announced reforms to date mainly envision reduced partisan control within parliament by empowering members to vote more freely and more power to committees to review legislation proposed by government (having just been introduced in February 2004, there is insufficient experience to gauge any impact on such measures, but the hope is a more discursive and bolstered legislative branch to counter the eroding confidence of Canadians in parliament generally (see Coe, 2004) and the more specific assertion of executive branch dominance, notably from the office of the prime minister.

11   As one example, a new consultation portal has been established (www.consultingcanadians. gc.ca), suggestive of online citizen engagement but more a communications tool and clearinghouse to provide information and links to consultations across departments (which vary in online usage).

[12]   This point reflects a tension in the current Canadian system—as public servants are consulting citizens more regularly (more than 30 such initiatives are listed on the consultation portal in April 2004, mechanisms that are examples of public servants reaching out to the public and inviting input. Many parliamentarians (i.e., those outside of Cabinet, within the legislative branch) are uneasy about this trend, since a strict reading of the machinery of government would indicate only they have such authority, and public servants are limited to serving ministers in the executive branch.

[13]   Over the past several years numerous examples have emerged in federal jurisdictions featuring political and operational mismanagement, including gun control registration, human resource assistance programs and most recently, the so-called sponsorship scandal based on government communication spending, primarily in Quebec during the 1990s following the provincial referendum on sovereignty in 1995. The scathing auditor general's report (completed in November, 2003 but released in February 2004) has embroiled the new Martin government in controversy ever since and given rise to a formal public inquiry.

Chapter IV

Motives, Strategic Approach, Objectives and Focal Areas in E-Gov-Induced Change

Hans J. (Jochen) Scholl, University of Washington, USA

Abstract

In its early catalogue and transaction phases, E-Government (e-gov) has been quite successful, although some critics say that it mainly reaped the harvest of relatively low hanging fruits by making paper-based information accessible over the Web, and also by Web-enabling some existing transaction processes. The subsequent horizontal and vertical integration phases of e-gov, those critics hold, present a greater challenge and require more technological sophistication and organizational effort. Business processes may need streamlining, change, and even replacement in order to become more citizen-centric and also increase government internal effectiveness and efficiency (IEE). This exploratory study finds that strategies and objectives for reaching the integration phase vary with focal areas and motives. However, e-gov, it is found, is a main driver of business process change in the public sector. Many practices and lessons learned from private sector reengineering apply in the government context.

Introduction

Practitioners and scholars alike agree that with the advent of Internet-related technologies, which technically underpin the broader movement of organizational streamlining and reorientation in the public sector now known as e-gov (Scholl, 2003a), the business of government has begun to undergo a deep transformation (Balutis, 2001a, 2001b; Fountain, 2001; Layne & Lee, 2001; Traunmueller & Wimmer, 2003), whose future extent is not known (Fletcher, 2003). As Orlikowski (1992) points out, technology-enabled transformations do not unfold deterministically, but rather underlie a complex feedback and interaction between institutional properties, technology, and human agents (see also DeSanctis & Poole, 1994; Fountain, 2001). Through human agents' creation and interaction with technology, institutional properties are engrained, which in turn shape the way in which humans interact with technology (Orlikowski, 1992). Furthermore, in the public sector, human agents interact within multiple institutional settings and with the civil society at large, which leads to repercussions regarding the technologies involved, as well as the institutional and societal settings (Cresswell & Pardo, 2001; Groenlund, 2001). Predictions regarding how this process is going to unfold for e-gov are necessarily vague. Repeating the themes of former technology/growth models (Gibson & Nolan, 1974; Nolan, 1979), some scholars present similar schemes for e-gov (Layne & Lee, 2001).

Others emphasize the relationship between operational and institutional change leading to increased integration and collaboration across agencies (Fountain, 2001). For higher bureaucracy IEE and for more citizen-centric orientation in government to occur (Bush, 2002), a high degree of intra-/interdepartmental, intra-/interagency, and intra-/interbranch integration has been identified as a prerequisite by European (Leitner, 2003; Traunmueller & Wimmer, 2003) and North American scholars and practitioners (Aldrich, Bertot, & McClure, 2002; Bertot, 2003; Forman, 2002). Both physical accessibility and intellectual approachability to information and services matter in this regard (Andersson & Groenlund, 2003).

E-Gov appears to have an impact on government "business processes." A business process can be thought of as a high-level flow of activity and as a set of tasks with a logical relationship geared towards a desired result or product (Davenport & Short, 1990). Business processes such as procurement, taxation, contracting, or licensing can contain up to hundreds or thousands of coordinated and connected workflows (Stohr & Zhao, 1997). Through e-gov projects, those high-level processes, along with their detail-level workflows, seem to undergo increasingly comprehensive changes leading to what has been called "business-process change" (BPC) (Balutis, 2001b; Beaumaster, 2002; Ho, 2002; Layne & Lee, 2001; Relyea, 2002; Scholl, 2003a; Whitson & Davis, 2001), the extent of which has not been documented in the literature. BPC in government may follow paths and patterns similar to BPC observed in the private sector (Scholl, 2003a), in which case the wealth of literature along with the practical lessons learned in that sector could benefit the unfolding of e-gov-induced BPC.

In a comprehensive exploratory study, three main areas were empirically researched: (1) current implementation practices, (2) sourcing approaches, and (3) the strategic thrust of large e-gov projects. While the first two areas have been discussed elsewhere (Scholl, 2003b, 2004), this chapter focuses on the findings in the area of e-gov strategy, objectives, focal areas, and motives, and its relation to BPC. The chapter is organized as follows: First, a short review of the private-sector-related literature in the area of strategic thrust in BPC is recapitulated (Scholl, 2003a). From this literature, eight propositions are derived for further inquiry and assessment within an e-gov context (School, 2003a). Second, the design of the exploratory study is detailed. Then, the findings for each proposition are summarized and discussed in context and relationship to each other. The chapter concludes that empirical evidence exists for assuming e-gov to induce major BPC. Also, by and large, the private-sector-based lessons learned seem to apply. Finally, future quantitative and theory-test-oriented research on the subject is outlined.

Strategic Thrust of BPC in the Private Sector Literature

Strategic Approach and Reach of Objectives in BPC

Systemic Approach. Radical business process change, which has also been known under the term of "reengineering" (Champy, 1995; Hammer & Champy, 1993), marked a caesura from traditional, incremental organizational change and development approaches. It sought immediate and order-of-magnitude process improvement via radical change and was frequently imposed as a revolution from the top (Stoddard & Jarvenpaa, 1995). However, the myths (Davenport & Stoddard, 1994) of its efficacy faded soon in the face of legions of staggering project failures, as well as social and organizational damage (Hammer, 1996). Consequently, BPC has returned to less radical and organizationally and socially more inclusive approaches (Grover, Teng, Segars, & Fiedler, 1998; Kettinger, Teng, & Guha, 1997a; Kettinger, Teng, & Guha, 1997b) employing a systemic view of the organization (Gunasekaran & Nath, 1997; Pardo & Scholl, 2002). If many variables interact and concurrently are subject to change, so the rationale, then the manageability of this process and its ultimate success have to heavily rely on cooperation and collaboration of stakeholders and organizational systems involved (Scholl, 2003a). For a government context, this leads to the following propositions:

Proposition #1: Electronic Government requires a systemic view of the (governmental) organization, its culture, systems, processes, and stakeholders.

Long-Term Orientation and Flexibility in Planning. If an e-gov project (e.g., an interoperability project) predictably leads to significant BPC, such projects expand over longtime horizons and require great flexibility in planning. Such projects also incur relatively high degrees of uncertainty along with relatively high risk. Projects of that caliber typically defy the stringent start-to-finish planning methodologies (Mitchell & Zmud, 1999), since variables may significantly change their values during the course of action, and different detail outcomes than originally envisioned may result. Although the overall course might have remained more or less the same, those projects require more coordination and communication than linear projects. Leadership needs to understand the dynamics of more complex e-gov BPC projects and develop a vision for the long-term and occasionally disruptive processes (Gunasekaran & Nath, 1997). For government, this leads to another proposition.

Proposition #2: Electronic Government requires long-term view and flexible planning due to the iterative and (occasionally) disruptive nature of the change process.

Intertwining of Business and ICT Strategies. In past decades, many organizations have put little emphasis on the synchronization of their information and communication technology (ICT) and business strategies (El Sawy, Malhotra, Gosain, & Young, 1999; Kambil & van Heck, 1998). However, in recent years, that may have changed in favor of tighter co-evolution of those two strategies (El Sawy, Malhotra, Gosain, & Young, 1999; Kambil & van Heck, 1998). It appears as advantageous if business architecture and ICT systems can be co-designed (Giaglis, 1999). However, due to different life cycles of the two components, this may prove a challenge in practice (van Wingen, Hathorn, & Sprehe, 1999). That notwithstanding, empirical evidence suggests improved success rates in change and redesign projects, once those two strategies are intertwined (Mitchell & Zmud, 1999; Teng, Fiedler, & Grover, 1998). Hence, the following proposition in a government context:

Proposition #3: (Government) Agency e-gov programs and ICT strategies must be intertwined.

Modesty in Scope and Objectives. More modest BPC projects (in scope and objectives), it has been found, have higher success rates (Kallio, Saarinen, Salo, Tinnila, & Vepsalainen, 1999). This explicitly dismisses the notion of a clean slate in BPC originally advocated (Hammer & Champy, 1993), which has proven ineffective in various ways (O'Neill & Sohal, 1999). Hence, deep change can be attained by means of a sequence of smaller projects. And yet, even modest BPC can affect any combination and depth of organizational tasks, structure, ICT, and culture (Stoddard & Jarvenpaa, 1995). Transferred to a government context, this yields the following:

Proposition #4: Modest objectives and scope more likely lead to electronic government project success than aggressive objectives and wide scope.

Motives For and Focal Areas in BPC

Gains in Effectiveness and Efficiency. Cost savings, speedups of the business, and service improvements have been used as main arguments in favor of BPC (Ranganathan & Dhaliwal, 2001). While the cost argument presents the weaker line of support, it is frequently used (Laudon & Laudon, 2002). Numerous accounts document that more often than not this argument does not hold (Lyytinen & Hirschheim, 1987). Yet speedups and service improvements may translate into cost savings at some later point, although those are harder to quantify. For government, this leads to the next proposition.

Proposition #5: Speeding up business processes and improving services are among the major motives for launching electronic government projects.

Bounded Rationality and Self-Interest. Decision-making is not grounded in perfect rationality (Simon, 1957; 1979, 1991; Simon, Egidi, & Marris, 1995). Moreover, non-rational and locally rational motives, as well as plain self-interest play important roles in the decision making in any socio-technical context (Markus, 1983; Tillquist, 2002). The human agency problem might be minimized when the various interests have sufficient opportunity to influence the project (Tillquist, 2002). Therefore, also for government is the next proposition.

Proposition #6: Multiple (also personal) interests can affect the development of electronic-government projects.

Core and Cross-Functional Processes. The core of the business has been found to be the most yielding area for reaping BPC benefits. The core processes typically have become fragmented over time (Hammer & Champy, 1993). Departmental and functional fragmentation leaves a high potential for streamlining and redesign (Grover et al., 1998; Harkness, Kettinger, & Segars, 1996; Kettinger et al., 1997a). In a government context, this can be translated into the following:

Proposition #7: Agency core business processes are primary candidates for electronic-government projects.

Proposition #8: Government-to-government (g2g), government-to-business (g2b), as well as cross-functional business processes are primary candidates for electronic-government projects.

In summary, the private sector BPC literature helps formulate a number of propositions, which are expected to help assess whether, and if, yes, to what extent e-gov induces business process change and transformation. The literature suggests that successful BPC projects typically require a systemic strategic approach and that they need to: (1) be long-term oriented while flexible in planning and implementing the change; (2) intertwine business and technology strategies; (3) patiently pursue deep change through small-step projects; (4) focus on both effectiveness and efficiency gains; (5) balance local and overall rationality while acknowledging though checking self-interest; and (6) focus on core and cross-functional processes, which provide the largest leverage.

Research Question and Study Design

Study Question

E-Gov projects, once they involve transaction processing and government-to-public (government-to-business/g2b and government-to-citizen/g2c) application and data integration (i.e., transformational e-gov projects), seemingly induce BPC in the public sector. When this study was designed, e-gov projects with transformational potential were (and still are) relatively scarce. Large sample sizes, hence, could not be expected. Also, the practices employed in such projects were not known by means of previous studies, and no theory had been formulated as to how e-gov-induced BPC would be carried out. Assuming these practices to be identical to those employed in the private sector would be too bold an assumption, in view of the many known differences between the two sectors (Bozeman & Bretschneider, 1986; Rainey, Backoff, & Levine, 1976). Assuming, on the other hand, those practices to be completely idiosyncratic would be an equally bold assumption given the many interactions and exchanges between the sectors. Consequently, an exploratory research design was chosen. The study questions were formulated as follows:

1.   To what extent do strategic approaches, objectives, motives, and focal areas in the context of e-gov-induced BPC differ from those in the private sector?

2.   If those differ between the two sectors, how do they differ?

The eight propositions derived from the private-sector-based literature capture major elements and themes common to strategic approaches, objectives, motives, and focal areas of BPC in that sector. For answering the two research questions, the study would therefore utilize those propositions to probe for similarities and divergences in completed e-gov projects, which involve, at a minimum, transaction processing.

Sampling Method

The purposive sampling (Ritchie, Lewis, & Gillian, 2003) employed in this study initially focused on senior public managers in New York State (NYS) who had supervised at least one major e-gov project. Study participants were recruited by e-mail and/or phone and selected from the State's official list of 75 top-ranked electronic government projects prepared by the NYS Office for Technology (OFT, 2002). Priority was given to those managers who had supervised very large projects. For reasons of availability and proximity, the study was expanded to include another state (Washington State) and other levels of government (King County and the City of Seattle). For the study participants from Washington State, King County (WA), and the City of Seattle, identical sampling principles (senior management with supervisory experience in at least one large e-gov project) were applied. The inclusion of a Washington State-based sub-sample provided access to one of the most advanced e-gov sites in the U.S. (Gant & Gant, 2002; Ho, 2002; Kaylor, Deshazo, & Eck, 2001).

Data Collection

Data were collected via a semi-structured interview format, which allowed for additional probing on the basis of a fixed structure of uniform statements (Arthur & Nazroo, 2003; Denzin & Lincoln, 2000). The eight propositions served as those uniform statements. In a series of 23 semi-structured interviews, 30 senior-level government managers from 13 NYS agencies and, on the West Coast, four Washington State agencies (two King County, WA agencies and two City of Seattle agencies) were asked to comment on the eight statements. Interviews were conducted with single individuals, with groups of two, and, in one case, with a group of three individuals. The interviews were conducted in person or over the telephone. The statements were read to the interviewees one at a time. Interviewees were then asked to comment on those statements from their own experience and involvement in e-gov projects. Probing questions were asked. The interviews, which lasted between 30 minutes and two hours, were audiotaped and transcribed for analysis.

Data Analysis

In four passes, the data collected were analyzed. First, two researchers independently read the transcripts, one statement at a time, assigning levels of agreements or disagreement on a 1-to-5 Likert scale (1=strongly agree, 5=strongly disagree) to each statement of every transcript. The Likert scales were then compared, and discrepancies of magnitude (defined as a variance >1 on the scale) were discussed and resolved. In the second pass, the two researchers read the transcripts again, now one unit of data at time. In an open coding process (Strauss & Corbin, 1998), each unit of data was assigned to a preliminary category or subcategory whose dimensions and properties were developed from the data. New categories and subcategories were introduced in case existing categories did not apply (Gorman, Clayton, Rice-Lively, & Gorman, 1997). Convergence and assignment of categories, which the two researchers had identified independently, were performed at each step of the data analysis. In a subsequent pass, an axial coding process was applied, during which the converged categories (emphasized in SMALL CAPITALS below) and subcategories were analyzed regarding their inherent structures and processes leading to paradigms, whose internal relationships were identified wherever possible (Strauss & Corbin, 1998). In the final pass, a selective coding process was performed in which the resulting concepts and theories were related to each other.

Results

In this section, the results are presented for each proposition, one at a time. For exhibiting the overall tendency of comments, the quantitative distribution of agreement and disagreement is mentioned first. In their majority, the practitioners agreed with seven of the eight propositions indicating support for those propositions developed from the private sector BPC literature. Although one might be tempted to criticize this as an expectable outcome, the reader shall be reminded that this study was not aimed at producing quantitative evidence. The strong general tendency found still is, as the author believes, an interesting and, to its extent, unexpected outcome. Albeit, this research predominantly attempts to qualitatively capture the spectrum of approaches in e-gov BPC projects such that a richer and more robust theory may become available for further testing.

Systemic Approach

Interviewees predominantly agreed (73.9% strongly; 19.6% to some extent), with the notion in this statement (proposition #1), while 6.5% somewhat disagreed. The vast majority of practitioners described a systemic strategic (or "enterprise-type") approach to e-gov projects, particularly those with a BPC impact, as absolutely critical to project success. Only such an approach would allow project teams to understand the interaction of the system components (e.g., multiple agencies), which quite a number of practitioners maintained over time.

Among the various ASPECTS of this approach, many interviewees emphasized that e-gov was about change and about redefining the service portfolio, and not just about automating old processes over the Internet. Hence, for effective change, it was said a deep understanding of the underlying business needs and of the existing business process was critical in any e-gov project. Since processes, business needs, and people were interwoven in many ways, the identification and involvement of salient constituents (STAKEHOLDERS) was seen as an important part of a systemic strategic approach in which citizen orientation had the highest priority. This approach also encompassed establishing the link between stakeholders, their needs, and the technology implemented, it was said. E-Gov leads to more integration requiring more standardization and collaboration between the parties involved, according to quite a few interviewees.

TOP MANAGEMENT SUPPORT was seen as an important aspect of the strategic approach. Some practitioners expressed CONCERNS that the systemic approach might be hampered by the stovepipe structure of government and by personnel and resource cutbacks. Also, some smaller projects might deliberately be flown underneath the radar screen of strategic integration, adding to complexity and impeding integration, it was said.

A prerequisite for e-gov BPC SUCCESS was cross-functional and cross-agency collaboration and a business-need oriented practice, rather than a technology-driven perspective, practitioners maintained. Stakeholders needed to be satisfied as a result of e-gov BPC and, thus, provided the ultimate litmus test for success via utilization rates, it was said.

Long-Term Orientation and Flexibility in Planning

A large number of respondents agreed (67.4% strongly, 10.9% to some extent) with the notion in this statement (proposition #2), whereas some were neutral (13.0%), slightly disagreed, or did not respond (4.3% each).

Many practitioners maintained that in e-gov BPC projects, the long-term view came coupled with small-step projects, and vice versa, as a typical APPROACH. Novelty escaped traditional planning, it was said, and e-gov projects presented a new frontier. Hence, small steps best supported the exploration of the e-gov potential, so was the rationale. E-Gov was not just about "webifying old processes," as the practitioners pointed out, but rather created a strong need for BPC, also providing a broader, more generic and systemic perspective on the business. Some practitioners were amazed at how much they had learned in those projects, including about the existing business processes. Some others saw strong evidence in their practice that through e-gov BPC projects, old information systems and applications would be abandoned in the long run and be replaced by new systems that better supported the new business model.

Arriving at streamlined and redesigned processes was best done by involving stakeholders and by being open to their suggestions, they said. E-Gov BPC projects typically endue an emerging project plan and implementation strategy. A benefit of the small-step approach, it was said, was to show short-term, "opportunistic," and tangible benefits and improvements to stakeholders. Also, dealing with the challenge of cultural resistance to change and building new relationships was easier through the small-step approach, it was noted. Opportunistic wins could be thrown away later at relatively low cost if they did not fit the strategic direction, according to quite a few interviewees. A large number of practitioners emphasized the iterative nature of the change process. The sum of carefully directed and redirected small-step projects would result in an overall sweeping change over time, it was said.

Flexibility was seen as a key prerequisite for e-gov BPC project success by a large number of interviewees. The long-term perspective provided for the tactical flexibility without compromising the direction of change, it was emphasized. Similar projects might advance at different speeds, depending on the particular locale, some interviewees remarked. Through the long-term orientation, important and necessary infrastructure extensions could be provided for early on, it was also highlighted. In some areas, e-gov BPC projects affected a standardization of processes, procedures, and systems, it was reported.

Practitioners also mentioned unexpected discoveries regarding the CHANGE PROCESS. One referred to it as the emerging "wild-west theory of e-gov-induced change," according to which about 5% of the agencies were pioneers who tried e-gov BPC no matter what, 90% were settlers who exposed a "wait-and-see" attitude, and 5% were outlaws who opposed any change no matter what. Quite a few said that e-gov BPC was mostly about organizational and behavioral change, and only partly about technology change. There was disagreement about the extent of disruption through e-gov BPC. While some said that the disruption might be substantial, others held that the change could be done in a non-disruptive fashion.

Practitioners also expressed some CONCERNS regarding the interplay of long-term view and short-term action, in terms of the best balance between the two, for example. If the long-term view was overemphasized, it was said then that the operational short term might be neglected. Or if the tactical aspects received too much attention, the overall direction might be lost, it was noted. Quite a few practitioners mentioned that through the long-term perspective in e-gov BPC, they had learned that successful e-gov BPC posed some serious new challenges with regard to the resulting (1) geographical divide, (2) economical divide, (3) social divide, (4) educational divide, (5) trust issues, and (6) electronic record and document life management issues.

Intertwining of Business and ICT Strategies

Again, the interviewees agreed overwhelmingly (80.4% strongly; 6.5% to some extent) with the notion in this statement (proposition #3), while some (4.3%) were neutral, and others expressed slight disagreement (8.7%).

The ICT strategy should mainly rest on the business STRATEGY, it was repeatedly said. E-Gov projects seemingly played an important role in the intertwining of the two co-evolving strategies. Interestingly, it appeared in a few remarks that the e-gov strategy had been mainly business- and not ICT-driven, and had only recently been better integrated with the overall ICT strategy. In fact, it appeared that in quite many cases, agency e-gov teams operated fairly independently from the IT/legacy departments. Many practitioners acknowledged that since e-gov induced BPC, it would require an enterprise architecture that integrated mission, objectives, information, technology, and outcomes. At the technology side, it was said that the intertwining of strategies also necessitated a set of consistent policies regarding infrastructure, security, firewalls, portal functionality, payments, appearance, and online help.

FRAMEWORKS for interfacing and interoperability, although demanding to develop, paid off after some time, according to many interviewees. While advancing towards transaction processing and interoperability in e-gov BPC projects, three strategies needed intertwining, it was said. The attempts for intertwining those three strategies (ICT/legacy, e-gov, and business strategies), however, apparently also were sometimes impeded by existing, stovepipe-type communication structures and political pressures to rush without thorough strategy development and integration, it was said.

A few practitioners admitted that no strategic plans existed to be integrated. Without a carefully crafted INTEGRATION of the three perspectives, however, resources might be under- or over-utilized, some said. E-Gov projects, by and large, would use the same infrastructure as existing ICT systems, according to the interviewees, which posed a new challenge (e.g., in terms of SECURITY to agencies). With better-integrated strategies, more integrated and usable e-gov systems were expected to emerge. With higher usability, higher user confidence would be a predictable OUTCOME, which, in turn, would increase the value to government and citizens alike, it was said.

Modesty in Scope and Objectives

The notion in this statement (proposition #4) found strong support among interviewees with 73.9% strongly agreeing, 6.5% somewhat agreeing, 13.0% neutral, 4.3% slightly disagreeing, and 2.2% strongly disagreeing.

A foremost argument for advocating modesty in scope and objectives in e-gov projects was MANAGEABILITY, according to a majority of practitioners. Large projects, it was said, were difficult to manage, less specific in scope, and would pose a higher acceptance threshold. In contrast, small projects, it was reported, had a narrow focus, shorter timelines, incremental and modular design, flexibility to act and react quickly, and allowed for gradual learning both internally and externally, resulting in superior manageability compared with large projects. A whole host of tactical considerations favoring small e-gov projects was given, including (1) short completion times to foster the perception of project success, (2) tangible products and benefits to sell the project, (3) demonstrated feasibility, (4) iteratively involved stakeholders, and (5) ownership. One practitioner bluntly held, "When you want to discover America, the first day you just get out of port."

Another important argument in favor of modesty in scope and objectives revolved around the notion of RISK, maintaining that smaller projects (1) had higher success rates, (2) commanded larger support bases, (3) better matched goals to resources, (4) were less costly in case of failure, and (5) were better shielded against scope creep. Finally, although modesty in project scope and objectives was strongly supported, most practitioners pointed at the role of LEADERSHIP in providing vision, direction, and even stretch, while orchestrating the interplay and advancement of smaller projects towards higher aims. It was repeatedly said that a "grandiose vision" that stimulated people's attention and imagination was needed to guide the small projects and provide the context. The tendency towards too modest projects could be mitigated through some higher-level coordination, it was said.

Gains in Effectiveness and Efficiency

Although practitioners mostly agreed (45.7% strongly, 39.1% to some extent) with the notion in this statement (proposition #5), the support was slightly weaker (10.9% of the interviewees reacted neutrally; 4.3% slightly disagreed).

SERVICE IMPROVEMENTS and SPEEDUPS, it was said, were main motives for e-gov projects, since both led to gains in effectiveness and efficiency. For example, many e-gov applications provided novel, extended, or improved service, but at the same time shifted the burden of data entry to citizens, reduced paperwork and double entry, increased data accuracy and recency, allowed for redeployment of workers and resources, and channeled "people and problems away from offices," practitioners explained. However, in times when budgets were stagnant or even shrinking, e-gov applications also helped maintain or increase the service level, according to the interviewees.

Interestingly, COST savings were not mentioned as a prevailing motive when launching e-gov projects, rather cost neutrality or a contribution to cost containment was expected. Some practitioners pointed out that due to inevitable dual-mode operations (i.e., simultaneously offered traditional and new e-gov-based operations), e-gov projects would rather front load additional cost for some time in exchange for back-loaded gains later, once traditional services would be reduced and less requested as a result of increased e-gov utilization.

Besides the measurable internal and external gains, a number of interviewees highlighted, e-gov projects changed the ways government employees understood the business of government in terms of integration, effectiveness, efficiency, and CITIZEN/SERVICE ORIENTATION (i.e., in terms of a cultural change towards a "smarter, better, faster, and cheaper" government) (Brown & Brudney, 1998), which was citizen centric. Citizens, it was noted, increasingly demanded immediate services that matched and exceeded those known from the private-sector e-commerce arena. Finally, it was emphasized that e-gov projects were also motivated by an expected increased ACCOUNTABILITY in government as a result of e-gov implementation.

Bounded Rationality and Self-Interest

The notion in this statement (proposition #6) received by far the most support among interviewees (95.7% strongly agreed, while the remaining 4.3% somewhat agreed).

Interviewees distinguished between GLOBAL, LOCAL, POLITICAL, PERSONAL, and VENDOR INTEREST perspectives in their comments on this statement. A majority of practitioners indicated that they had not observed purely rational decision-making in practice; however, they also pointed out that what might seem to be a non-rational decision from a global perspective might appear completely rational from a local perspective. In the global view, the existence of diverging interests was characterized as the standard case in any project, not only e-gov projects. Multiple-party involvement, it was said, required finding a balanced and large enough intersection of interests on which the project could be couched.

In order to identify this intersection, e-gov projects, like other projects, needed the explicit elicitation of stakeholder interests, which also made possible the definition of common purpose, according to the interviewees. Stepping over interests and downplaying the potential divergence, it was said, had led to project failures. "Investment in the past" was seen as one of the most prominent local interests. Hence, sometimes parochial views prevailed leading to duplicative efforts, it was said.

Among the personal interests, "big egos," anxiety to lose a position, expertise, or a qualification, were the most prominent, it was said. Leadership involvement was said to significantly matter when reconciling global versus local conflicts of interest, as well as containing negative effects of personal interest prevalence in projects. Unsurprisingly, interviewees pointed out that POLITICAL INTERESTS also played a major role in e-gov projects. Those came in the disguise of personal interests, or vice versa, it was noted. Political ambition, some practitioners said, had pushed a few e-gov projects into dimensions that later produced "expensive and ineffective results." Finally, interviewees indicated that VENDOR INTERESTS were part of the overall mix of interests. Vendor interests, it was said, existed and came into play particularly with respect to legacy systems.

Core and Cross-Functional Processes

Interviewees responded differently to the notions in two statements (propositions #7 and #8). Regarding proposition #7 (whether e-gov projects focus on core business processes), agreement and disagreement were fairly distributed with 21.7% of respondents strongly agreeing or agreeing to some extent each, 26.1% assuming a neutral position, 21.7% slightly disagreeing, and 8.7% strongly disagreeing.

Practitioners distinguished various TYPES of core business processes: those with a major administrative component and those without (e.g., a police officer patroling the neighborhood, or a driver maneuvering the public bus). While e-gov in principle might affect every activity, the administrative functions, it was said, were the most immediately addressable. Also, core processes with an interaction component with citizens were distinguished from those without, the former of which were seen as candidates for e-gov.

Those practitioners in disagreement with the notion that core business processes were primary candidates for e-gov indicated that, in their view, changing core processes bore the highest risk. Hence, before those processes were targeted, "fringe" projects targeted at less mission-critical processes needed to demonstrate the feasibility and prepare the mindset, it was said. In other words, the disagreement was of a TACTICAL nature, rather than a matter of principle.

Practitioners in agreement with the notion of the statement mentioned that core business processes provided the greatest potential BENEFITS through productivity gains, process streamlining, resource savings, and overall payback through e-gov. On the DOWNSIDE, even the advocates of e-gov-enabled core processes acknowledged the risk, greater task complexity when overhauling, high cost, and the potential technology and policy limitations. For example, mainframe systems, it was said, mirrored the old processes and were rather hard to replace all at once. Hence, the overhaul required a long-term and phased approach in which e-gov systems were integrated with the legacy systems in some fashion until those systems were finally gone, the interviewees noted.

Adding to the technology problems, practitioners said, was the fact that core business processes involved the highest number of stakeholders and, hence, potentially divergent interests. Those, then, were also the processes for which process knowledge was distributed the most. Hence, resistance to change was observed fiercest regarding core processes, according to the interviewees. Finally, providing dual-mode operation was seen as most expensive and cumbersome for core processes, they said.

With respect to cross-functional processes, interviewees mostly agreed (54.3% strongly, 15.2% somewhat) with the notion in that statement (proposition #8), while 21.7% were neutral, and 8.7% were in slight disagreement.

Beyond G2G and G2B processes, practitioners also added the area of government-to-citizen (G2C) to the list of potential e-gov target processes. The data showed that the city and county agencies were most focused on G2C processes, while state agencies increasingly emphasized G2G and G2B processes. Many practitioners indicated that the initial major driver for e-gov projects had been the procurement process employing a streamlined G2B interface resulting in significant cycle-time savings and more accurate data. In this area, the least extent of a digital divide and the lowest necessity for dual-mode operations had been observed, gleaning the highest initial gains for both government and business.

The interviewees also pointed out that, in their views, the highest potential for productivity and performance gains rested in G2G; however, it was hardest to reap due to (1) diverging legal frameworks, (2) different requirements, (3) complexity in terms of many-to-many relationships, (4) difficulty of sharing control over each others' processes, and (5) relics of stovepipe thinking. Based on their past experiences, practitioners expected the G2G integration to take a long period of time (decades, rather than years) to unfold, requiring new frameworks and methods of interaction, transaction, and information exchange, not just new systems, among all levels and branches of government.

Discussion and Conclusion

Through its exploratory approach, this study has sought rich qualitative data for elucidating and better understanding the strategic approach, objective, motives, and focal areas in e-gov-induced business process change projects. Frameworks and concepts formulated in the context of private-sector BPC guided the study in this effort. With the results regarding those areas in e-gov BPC in hand, those frameworks and concepts may, in turn, now be cautiously assessed for their suitability and applicability to a public-sector context, which was briefly undertaken in the first portion of this discussion. In the second portion, the approaches and practices found are discussed in more detail.

The Suitability of the Private-Sector BPC Literature

Based on the results, a preliminary assessment of the suitability and applicability seems in order, even though the sampling was purposively geared towards a different end, and the sample size (n=23) was relatively small, such that no claim to generalizability can or will be made. If there is some indication that the frameworks and concepts from the BPC literature apply, the utilization of that rich literature in the context of e-gov projects would appear as most recommendable, such that expensive lessons learned elsewhere may not be lost.

Upon analyzing the quantitative results presented above, it is noteworthy that only marginal differences (∂max < 1.1%) were detected between the New York and Washington subsamples. In rank order, there was overall support for propositions #6 (100%), #1 (93.5%), #3 (87.0%), #5 (84.8%), #4 (80.4%), #2 (78.3%), and #7 (69.6%). Fairly weak support was found for proposition #8 (43.5%). In other words, the strategic approach, objectives, motives, and focal areas in e-gov-related BPC are seemingly shaped through the following concepts (Table 1).

The identified approaches and concepts used in private sector BPC appear also to play a significant role in the public sector. If the condition in proposition #7 were relaxed to allow for gaining experience in fringe and new processes first before engaging in changing the core processes, then, as the data show, even this area would be little different between the two sectors. Hence, the private sector literature might be utilized both as a guide and a point of reference in a more systematic fashion in e-gov-related research and practice.

This result also provides a partial answer to the first study question: The extent of differences in BPC strategic approach, objectives, motives, and focal areas ap-

Table 1. Rank order of importance of concepts in e-gov BPC-related projects

Rank	Concept	Degree of Importance in e-Gov-related BPC Projects
1.	Bounded rationality and self-interest	Highest
2.	A systemic approach	Highest
3.	Intertwining business and ICT strategies	Very high
4.	Gains in effectiveness and efficiency (IEE)	Very high
5.	Modesty in scope and objectives	Very high
6.	Long-term orientation and flexibility in planning	High
7.	Cross-functional processes	High
8.	Core processes	Some

pears to reside in details rather than on a grand scale or in principle. As indicated above and fully aware of specifically known differences between the private and public sectors (Bozeman & Bretschneider, 1986; Rainey et al., 1976), this claim is put forth with due caution. However, e-gov projects with a major impact on business processes are well advised when they are reflective of techniques and lessons learned from the private sector, along with the rapidly growing body of knowledge regarding e-gov-induced BPC.

Characteristics and Uniqueness of E-Gov BPC Approaches and Concepts

In this section, it is discussed how the e-gov BPC approaches in the public sector differ from private sector BPC. By and large, the findings of this study show that the differences are minor. However, in e-gov projects, typically a higher number of primary stakeholders with "go/no" powers (Mitchell, Agle, & Wood, 1997; Scholl, 2001) seems to participate as a norm. Power appears to be more distributed in the public sector than in the private sector.

Hence, e-gov BPC projects seemingly necessitate far higher degrees of consensus and support from salient stakeholders than typically in the private sector, leading to higher ownership. Distributed control and accountability, however, come with more distribution in sharing the burden, also leading to more ownership in process, project, and outcome. Due to its mostly consensual nature, and also due to numerous legal, statutory, and regulatory requirements, e-gov BPC projects take longer to complete than similar projects in the private sector.

Obviously, this circumstance greatly benefits the desired e-gov project outcome, leading to far less dramatic failure rates (in fact, reports on e-gov project blunders seem to be still in short supply, if any). Public-sector projects (including e-gov projects) thus may have some insightful lessons in stock, which may help inspire private sector BPC practice as well.

For the following discussion, see Figure 1 for an overview. As opposed to the private sector, where the expectation of cost reduction (Gibson & Nolan, 1974; Laudon & Laudon, 2002; O'Neill & Sohal, 1999) always played an important role in IT-related investments, public sector managers are seemingly not as optimistic in that regard and expect (perhaps more realistically) only a cost containment in the wake of an e-gov-related investment. In the public sector, the motivational emphasis dwells much more on service improvement and speedup. Although not identical, the customer orientation and the orientation on citizens and their needs may be seen as equivalent motives.

In the public sector, the desire to hold public servants and government workers accountable also plays a role. Beyond the rational arguments in favor of e-gov-related

Figure 1. E-gov-induced BPC concepts

investments, public managers were open and clear about non-rational or locally rational arguments, as well as outright self-interest, including political, personal, and vendor interests flavoring investment decisions in e-gov.

Three main objectives in practical e-gov BPC surfaced in the study results: (1) building lean government, (2) building service-oriented government, and (3) building agile government. Lean government, in which tasks and services are more centralized, although in a resource-sharing rather than a hierarchical fashion, require ongoing consensus among stakeholders and well-defined procedures among participating government entities. Also, under e-gov, the trend of rearranging tasks and services through public-private cooperation (Milward, 1994; Savas, 1982) seems to accelerate in some areas, while it reverses in others.

Service-oriented government has been advocated for some time (Osborne & Gaebler, 1992); however, with e-gov, streamlined processes, and a shifting mindset of government workers, this notion obviously begins to become an organizational reality. An improved service orientation towards businesses, citizens, and other government entities was also a clearly identifiable thrust recognized in the study results. Despite its leanness and improved service orientation, as the results indicate, practitioners believe e-gov BPC also helps create an agile government; that is, a government, which is more responsive, more proactive, more effective and efficient, and more quality and performance oriented without increasing the tax bill.

Integration of functions and interoperability of systems was found to be another main thrust of e-gov BPC. While Layne and Lee (2001) suggested that the vertical integration within functional spheres antecedes the horizontal integration across functions, the study results show otherwise. Horizontal/cross-functional integration occurs at least as frequently as vertical/functional integration as first steps.

In a number of cases, they concur. The distinction in Layne and Lee's framework may better serve as an analytical tool rather than suggesting a temporal or logical sequence of integration.

Practitioners were little appreciative of a clean-slate approach to e-gov BPC, as had been suggested in the private sector (Champy, 1995; Hammer & Champy, 1993). Rather, while acknowledging the wide-ranging implications of BPC and the expected transformation of government, they practiced a long-term approach and initially focused on tactical, smaller steps and non-core areas without losing sight of the larger picture. Likewise, rather than radical approaches, incremental approaches were the only ones found by this study.

There was overall agreement that e-gov projects would focus on core and cross-functional processes alike in all three areas (g2b, g2g, and g2c). The greatest gains and transformations were expected in the G 2 B and G 2 G areas, according to the results.

Practitioners were also cognizant of the outcomes of e-gov-induced BPC. Beyond the desired and expected results of transformational benefits and new opportunities, they pointed at major new challenges that would emerge in the wake of successful e-gov BPC: (1) the digital divide in its various forms; (2) continued dual-mode operations for a long time; (3) enormous, not yet well understood requirements in electronic record management (ERM) and document life management (DLM); and (4) the preservation of the constitutionally sanctioned division of powers and the system of checks and balances.

Finally, while technical-functional aspects of BPC in the private and public sectors may be fairly similar (i.e., differences in techniques, tools, technical procedures appear to be minor), e-gov projects with a strong BPC impact seem to be organizationally and socially much better negotiated. This might eventually lead to relatively higher success rates of BPC in the public sector. Hence, lessons learned should be shared between the sectors, and the private sector BPC literature might explicitly benefit from stakeholder approaches as they are practiced in the public sector. Future research will seek more qualitative data regarding current BPC practices in both sectors, in addition to quantitative accounts on the basis of larger samples for a more detailed comparison.

Acknowledgments

I am indebted to my assistant, Thomas K. Richards, at the Information School who helped conduct the interviews, organize the equipment, and prepare the transcripts for numerous hours. He was also instrumental in organizing and conducting the data analysis and coding.

References

Aldrich, D., Bertot, J.C., & McClure, C.R. (2002). E-government: Initiatives, developments, and issues. *Government Information Quarterly, 19*(4), 349-355.

Andersson, A., & Groenlund, A. (2003, September 1-5). *E-society accessibility: Identifying research gaps.* [Paper]. At EGOV 2003, Prague, The Czech Republic.

Arthur, S., & Nazroo, J. (2003). Designing fieldwork strategies and materials. In J. Ritchie & J. Lewis (Eds.), *Qualitative research practice: A guide for social science students and researchers* (pp. 109-137). London; Thousand Oaks, CA: Sage Publications.

Balutis, A.P. (2001a). E-government 2001, Part I: Understanding the challenge and evolving strategies. *The Public Manager,* Spring 2001, 33-37.

Balutis, A.P. (2001b). E-government 2001, Part II: Evolving strategies for action. *The Public Manager,* Summer 2001, 41-45.

Beaumaster, S. (2002). Local government IT implementation issues: A challenge for public administration. [Paper]. At *Proceedings on the 35th Hawaiian International Conference on System Sciences,* Hawaii.

Bertot, J.C. (2003). The multiple dimensions of the digital divide: More than the technology "haves" and "have nots." *Government Information Quarterly, 20*(2), 185-191.

Bozeman, B., & Bretschneider, S. (1986). Public management information systems: Theory and prescriptions. *Public Administration Review, 46*(November, special issue), 475-489.

Brown, M.M., & Brudney, J.L. (1998). A "smarter, better, faster, and cheaper" government: Contracting and geographic information systems. *Public Administration Review, 58*(4), 335-345.

Bush, G.W. (2002). *E-gov: The official web site of the President's e-government initiatives.* Retrieved October 23, 2003 from http://www.whitehouse.gov/omb/egov/

Champy, J. (1995). *Reengineering management: The mandate for new leadership* (1st ed.). New York: Harper-Business.

Cresswell, A.M., & Pardo, T.A. (2001). Implications of legal and organizational issues for urban digital government development. *Government Information Quarterly, 18*(4), 269-278.

Davenport, T.H., & Short, J.E. (1990). The new industrial reengineering: Information technology and business process redesign. *Sloan Management Review, 31*(Summer), 11-27.

Davenport, T.H., & Stoddard, D.B. (1994). Reengineering: Business change of mythic proportions? *MIS Quarterly, 18*(2), 121-127.

Denzin, N.K., & Lincoln, Y.S. (2000). *Handbook of qualitative research* (2nd ed.). Thousand Oaks, CA: Sage Publications.

DeSanctis, G., & Poole, M.S. (1994). Capturing the complexity in advanced technology use: Adaptive structuration theory. *Organization Science, 5*(2), 121-147.

El Sawy, O.A., Malhotra, A., Gosain, S., & Young, K.M. (1999). IT-intensive value innovation in the electronic economy: Insights from Marshall Industries. *MIS Quarterly, 23*(3), 305-335.

Fletcher, P.D. (2003). Creating the front door to government: A case study of the Firstgov portal. *Library Trends, 52*(2), 268-281.

Forman, M. (2002). *E-government strategy: Implementing the President's management agenda for e-government.* Retrieved September 15, 2003 from http://www.whitehouse.gov/omb/inforeg/egovstrategy

Fountain, J.E. (2001). *Building the virtual state: Information technology and institutional change.* Washington, DC: Brookings Institution Press.

Gant, J.P., & Gant, D.B. (2002). Web portal functionality and State government e-service. [Paper]. *Proceedings on the 35th Hawaiian International Conference on System Sciences,* Hawaii.

Giaglis, G.M. (1999). Integrated design and evaluation of business processes and information systems. *Communications of AIS, 2*(1), 1-33.

Gibson, C.F., & Nolan, R.L. (1974). Managing the four stages of EDP growth. *Harvard Business Rev., 52*(1), 76-88.

Gorman, G.E., Clayton, P., Rice-Lively, M.L., & Gorman, L. (1997). *Qualitative research for the information professional: A practical handbook.* London: Library Association Publishing.

Groenlund, A. (2001, January). Democracy in an IT-framed society. *Communications of the ACM, 44,* 23-26.

Grover, V., Teng, J., Segars, A.H., & Fiedler, K. (1998). The influence of information technology diffusion and business process change on perceived productivity: The IS executive's perspective. *Information & Management, 34,* 141-159.

Gunasekaran, A., & Nath, B. (1997). The role of information technology in business process reengineering. *International Journal of Production Economics, 50,* 91-104.

Hammer, M. (1996). *Beyond re-engineering: How the process-centered organization is changing our work and our lives* (1st ed.). New York: HarperBusiness.

Hammer, M., & Champy, J. (1993). *Reengineering the corporation: A manifesto for business revolution* (1st ed.). New York: HapperCollins Publishers.

Harkness, W.L., Kettinger, W.J., & Segars, A.H. (1996). Sustaining process improvement and innovation in the information service function: Lessons learned from Bose Corporation. *MIS Quarterly, 20*(3), 349-367.

Ho, A.T.-k. (2002). Reinventing local governments and the e-government initiative. *Public Administration Review, 62*(4), 434-444.

Kallio, J., Saarinen, T., Salo, S., Tinnila, M., & Vepsalainen, A.P.J. (1999). Drivers and tracers of business process changes. *Journal of Strategic Information Systems, 8*, 125-142.

Kambil, A., & van Heck, E. (1998). Reengineering the Dutch flower auctions: A framework for analyzing exchange organizations. *Information Systems Research, 9*(1), 1-19.

Kaylor, C., Deshazo, R., & Eck, D.V. (2001). Gauging e-government: A report on implementing services among American cities. *Government Information Quarterly, 18*(4), 293-307.

Kettinger, W.J., Teng, J.T.C., & Guha, S. (1997a). Business process change: A study of methodologies, techniques and tools. *MIS Quarterly* (March), 55-80.

Kettinger, W.J., Teng, J.T.C., & Guha, S. (1997b). Business process change: A study of methodologies, techniques, and tools: Appendices 1-8. *MIS Quarterly, 21*(1).

Laudon, K.C., & Laudon, J.P. (2002). *Management information systems: Managing the digital firm* (7th ed.). Upper Saddle River, NJ: Prentice Hall.

Layne, K., & Lee, J. (2001). Developing fully functional e-government: A four stage model. *Government Information Quarterly, 18*(2), 122-136.

Leitner, C. (Ed.) (2003). *E-Government in Europe: The state of affairs*. Maastricht, The Netherlands: European Institute of Public Administration.

Lyytinen, K., & Hirschheim, R. (1987). Information systems failures: A survey and classification of the empirical literature. *Oxford Surveys in Information Technology, 4*, 257-309.

Markus, M.L. (1983). Power, politics, and MIS implementation. *Communications of the ACM, 26*(6), 430-444.

Milward, H.B. (1994). Nonprofit contracting and the hollow state. *Public Administration Review, 54*(1), 73-77.

Mitchell, R.K., Agle, B.R., & Wood, D.J. (1997). Toward a theory of stakeholder identification and salience. Defining the principle of who and what really counts. *Academy of Management Review, 22*(4), 853-866.

Mitchell, V.L., & Zmud, R.W. (1999). The effects of coupling IT and work process strategies in redesign projects. *Organization Science, 10*(4), 424-438.

Nolan, R.L. (1979). Managing the crises in data processing. *Harvard Business Review, 57*(2), 115-126.

OFT (2002, June). *Listing of top 75 e-commerce/e-government services & transactions,* June 2002. Retrieved October 31, 2002 from http://www. oft.state. ny.us/ecommerce/quarterly/june02/top75.htm

O'Neill, P., & Sohal, A.S. (1999). Business process reengineering: A review of recent literature. *Technovation, 19,* 571-581.

Orlikowski, W.J. (1992). The duality of technology: Rethinking the concept of technology in organizations. *Organization Science, 3*(3), 398-427.

Osborne, D., & Gaebler, T. (1992). *Reinventing government: How the entrepreneurial spirit is transforming the public sector*. Reading, MA: Addison-Wesley.

Pardo, T.A., & Scholl, H.J.J. (2002). Walking atop the cliffs: Avoiding failure and reducing risk in large-scale e-government projects. [Paper]. *Proceedings on the 35th Hawaiian International Conference on System Sciences,* Hawaii.

Rainey, H., Backoff, R., & Levine, C. (1976). Comparing public and private organizations. *Public Administration Review, 36*(2), 233-244.

Ranganathan, C. & Dhaliwal, J.S. (2001). A survey of business process reengineering practice in Singapore. *Information and Management, 39,* 125-134.

Relyea, H.C. (2002). E-gov: Introduction and overview. *Government Information Quarterly, 19*(1), 9-35.

Ritchie, J., Lewis, J., & Gillian, E. (2003). Designing and selecting samples. In J. Ritchie & J. Lewis (Eds.), *Qualitative research practice: A guide for social science students and researchers* (pp. 77-108). London; Thousand Oaks, CA: Sage Publications.

Savas, E.S. (1982). *Privatizing the public sector: How to shrink government*. Chatham, NJ: Chatham House Publishers.

Scholl, H.J.J. (2001, October 3-5). *Applying stakeholder theory to e-government: Benefits and limits.* [Paper]. At 1st IFIP Conference on E-Commerce, E-Business, and E-Government (I3E 2001), Zurich, Switzerland.

Scholl, H.J.J. (2003a, January 6-9). *E-government: A special case of ICT-enabled business process change.* [Paper]. At 36th Hawaiian International Conference on System Sciences, Waikoloa, Big Island, HI.

Scholl, H.J.J. (2003b, September 1-5). *Electronic government: Make or buy?* [Paper]. At EGOV 2003, Prague, The Czech Republic.

Scholl, H.J.J. (2004, May 24-26). *E-government-induced business process change (BPC): An empirical study of current implementation practices.* [Paper]. At the 5th Annual National Conference on Digital Government Research: New Challenges and Opportunities, Seattle, WA.

Simon, H.A. (1957). *Administrative behavior: A study of decision-making processes in administrative organization* (2nd ed.). New York: Macmillan.

Simon, H.A. (1979). Rational decision making in business organizations. *The American Economic Review, 69*(4), 493-513.

Simon, H.A. (1991). Bounded rationality and organizational learning. *Organization Science, 2*(1), 125-134.

Simon, H.A., Egidi, M., & Marris, R.L. (1995). *Economics, bounded rationality and the cognitive revolution.* Aldershot, UK & Brookfield, VT: E. Elgar.

Stoddard, D.B., & Jarvenpaa, S.L. (1995). Business process redesign: Tactics for managing radical change. *Journal of Management Information Systems, 12*(1), 88-107.

Stohr, E.A., & Zhao, J.L. (1997, January 3-6). *A technology adaptation model for business process automation.* [Paper]. At the 30th Hawaiian International Conference on System Sciences, Maui, HI.

Strauss, A.L., & Corbin, J.M. (1998). *Basics of qualitative research: Techniques and procedures for developing grounded theory* (2nd ed.). Thousand Oaks, CA: Sage Publications.

Teng, J.T.C., Fiedler, K.D., & Grover, V. (1998). An exploratory study of the influence of IS function and organizational context on business process reengineering project initiatives. *Omega, Int. J. Mgmt Sci., 26*(6), 679-698.

Tillquist, J. (2002). Rules of the game: Constructing norms of influence, subordination and constraint in IT planning. *Information & Organization, 12*, 39-70.

Traunmueller, R., & Wimmer, M.A. (2003, September 1-5). *E-government at a decisive moment: Sketching a roadmap to excellence.* [Paper]. At the EGOV 2003, Prague, The Czech Republic.

van Wingen, R.S., Hathorn, F., & Sprehe, J.T. (1999). Principles for information technology investment in US federal electronic records management. *Journal of Government Information, 26*(1), 33-42.

Whitson, T.L., & Davis, L. (2001). Best practices in electronic government: Comprehensive electronic information dissemination for science and technology. *Government Information Quarterly, 18*(2), 79-91.

This chapter was previously published in the International Journal of Electronic Government Research, 1(1), 59-78, January-March 2005.

Chapter V

E-Government-Induced Business Process Change (BPC):
An Empirical Study of Current Practices

Hans J. (Jochen) Scholl, University of Washington, USA

Abstract

E-government (e-gov) projects have an increasing influence on how government business processes evolve and change. While early e-gov projects focused on government-to-public information and interaction, the second and third wave of e-gov projects also emphasize internal effectiveness and efficiency, along with intra- and interdepartmental as well as intra- and interbranch integration. With these increases in scope and scale of e-gov projects, existing business processes, including core processes, become candidates for improvement and change. While the private-sector-oriented literature on business process change abounds with descriptive and prescriptive accounts, no equivalent has been found in the public-sector-related literature. Although many insights drawn from the private sector may apply, the public sector seems to develop distinct practices. This chapter contributes to the understanding of current practices in e-gov-induced business process change, comparing those practices to prescriptions derived from private-sector experience. Among other factors, the more inclusive approach observed in e-gov business process change may explain the higher success rate of public-sector projects compared to those reported from the private sector.

Introduction

In electronic government (e-government; e-gov), once the service and application potential of the early catalogue and transaction phases has been fully tapped, it is said that the next developmental step leads to the integration of services and processes within and across government agencies and branches (Layne & Lee, 2001). For this integration to happen, however, significant changes to the business logic and, hence, to the business processes, including the core processes, become a necessity (Scholl, 2003). Since the already existing information systems (IS) and applications represent and embody those old processes, they have to be adapted and streamlined, too. Without such redesign of systems and processes, the old fragmented and chapter-based processes, along with their IS mirror images, would be perpetuated electronically, which some scholars have derided as "manumation" (Mohan & Holstein, 1998).

Business processes can be thought of as a high-level flow of activity and as a set of tasks with a logical relationship geared toward a desired result or product (Davenport & Short, 1990). Processes such as procurement, taxation, contracting, or licensing can contain up to hundreds or thousands of coordinated and connected workflows (Stohr & Zhao, 1997). For well over a decade, the streamlining of business processes has been practiced and studied in the private sector. Both radical (Champy, 1995; Grover, Teng, Segars, & Fiedler, 1998; Hammer & Champy, 1993) and moderate, more incremental approaches (Halachmi & Bovaird, 1997; Harkness, Kettinger, & Segars, 1996; Kling & Tillquist, 1998; Martinsons & Revenaugh, 1997) have been observed, yielding mixed results with failure rates of up to 70% (Hammer, 1996) for the more radical and disruptive approaches (Martinsons & Revenaugh, 1997).

The principle of distributed control as a characteristic of democratic governance defies the concept of top-down and disruptive process change, as seen in the private sector in the early 1990s (Mohan & Holstein, 1990). As opposed to the typically monolithic governance structures in private-sector organizations, democratic governance is limited intentionally to relatively small entities of jurisdiction and operational control, which rests on mandates awarded independently. The organization of government into relatively independent levels and branches with built-in procedures of checks and balances further accentuates the principle of distributed control. Hence, change emanates from a complex and typically lengthy process of negotiation among constituents, which effectively safeguards the system against sudden and radical changes. Yet, methods and insights developed in business process change (BPC) in the private sector may inform and even apply, when processes in the public sector need to be changed (Scholl, 2003).

This chapter reports on current practices that project managers and officials use when dealing with BPC, as well as process and information integration in e-gov projects (Klischewski, 2004). For space constraints and since it has been laid out in detail elsewhere, the chapter foregoes the repetition of an elaborate review of the private-sector-related literature on the subject (Scholl, 2003). Also, since this chapter reports on the second part of a research project, whose first part has been published already in a previous issue of this journal (Scholl, 2005), the detailed description of the study design is omitted.

The chapter is organized as follows. First, along with a brief reintroduction of those practices known from the private sector, eight propositions based on the private-sector BPC literature are restated. Then, the qualitative research design, which guided the study's data collection and analysis, is briefly described. Third, the empirical results and observations for each proposition are presented. Finally, the chapter discusses those results and their relationship to each other and presents conclusions regarding the observed BPC practices in the context of e-gov projects, along with suggestions for quantitative testing based on a larger sample size.

BPC Practices Presented in the Private-Sector Literature

Stakeholders

Some scholars in the early reengineering movement suggested that those groups of employees that most likely would impede radical change in business process reengineering projects, should be isolated from those projects until after the fact, with their potential to negatively influence the outcome tightly contained (Stoddard & Jarvenpaa, 1995). The reportedly high failure rate of such BPC projects, however, soon suggested otherwise (Hammer, 1996; Ranganathan & Dhaliwal, 2001). Hence, more inclusive approaches were advocated, which paid more attention to the needs and wants of important (and internal) stakeholders, who potentially would be impacted by or would themselves impact the project's outcome (Freeman, 1984). For a governmental context with its built-in mechanisms of interdependency and distributed control, an even more thorough approach of involving salient constituents was foreseen (Pardo & Scholl, 2002; Scholl, 2001) for business process change projects, suggesting the following proposition:

Proposition #1: The success of electronic government depends on the participation and cooperation of primary stakeholders.

Culture/Change Readiness

Upon looking more closely at internal stakeholders, it becomes obvious that while a certain group of stakeholders may be willing to support a change project in one setting of organizational culture, in a different setting, everything else being equal, the equivalent group of stakeholders may actively oppose the proposed change (O'Neill & Sohal, 1999). In other words, the organizational culture is an important variable, when it comes to any change (Schein, 1969, 1985, 1988, 1992, 1999), including BPC. Upfront assessments of the readiness for change of an organizational culture appears as an instrument for determining the possible extent of change without running into culture-related friction (Douglas, 1999). This, it appears, is very similar in a public-sector setting.

Proposition #2: In order to avoid failure, major electronic-government projects require the upfront assessment of the organizational culture context.

Process and Resource Inventory

BPC obviously produces rippling effects throughout an organization, which seem to increase with the extent of change (Hammer & Champy, 1993). Hence, business processes, before they are changed, have to be carefully analyzed, documented, and assessed for streamlining potential (Hammer & Champy, 1993). Some scholars even suggest the creation of an upfront inventory of all components and elements involved, including existing information and communication technology (ICT) (both hardware and software), related human skills, and internal and external environmental conditions (Mallalieu, Harvey, & Hardy, 1999). In a government context, this, again, should be very similar.

Proposition #3: In order to be successful, before a major electronic-government project is launched, a detailed inventory of business processes, ICT hardware and software, skills, and internal and external conditions needs to be conducted.

Workflow Analysis

While the analysis of high-level business processes may uncover important areas of fragmentation, indicating the potential for streamlining, the full change and stream-lining potential emerges once the analysis drills to the levels of detailed workflow analyses (Alavi, Wheeler, & Valacich, 1995; Kettinger, Teng, & Guha, 1997; Pardo & Scholl, 2002). Business process analysis, workflow analysis, and the evaluation of potential ICT systems, which may embody streamlined workflows, need to go hand-in-hand, because they are interdependent to a certain degree (Giaglis, 1999; Lloyd, Dewar, & Pooley, 1999). In government, a detailed workflow analysis also helps to uncover the exact lines of control and ownership of a given process and workflow.

Proposition #4: In order to be successful, any major electronic-government project requires a detailed workflow analysis beyond the high-level business-process analysis.

Internal Competency and Learning

Developing internal organizational experience and knowledge, although readily complemented with external knowledge and skills, is essential in at least strategic areas of business, since beyond the codifiable elements, the tacit dimensions of knowledge seem to represent an important portion of an organization's capabilities (Kogut & Zander, 1992, 1995; Nelson & Winter, 1982; Spender, 1996). One's own experience is particularly necessary, if change is sought on large scales (Caudle, 1994) in government.

Proposition #5: For electronic-government projects to succeed, organizational knowledge and experience regarding electronic government must be developed internally.

Consensus Among Officials and Citizen

A technology- and change-friendly environment appears necessary for change to happen (Cooper, 2000). Decades ago, it was already observed that users would reject ICT-based systems, not only as a consequence of weak functionality or malfunc-tion, but also for the lack of good communication between system designers and ultimate users (Markus, 1983). Also in the public sector, consensus among salient stakeholders regarding functionality and uses of ICT systems appears to be a major determinant of system acceptance and success (Halachmi & Bovaird, 1997).

Proposition #6: For the success of electronic government, a broad consensus among officials and citizens is necessary.

Senior Leadership Support

Without senior executive sponsorship, no BPC project would have the chance to even be launched, let alone to be completed successfully according to a broad consensus in the private-sector literature on BPC (Kambil & van Heck, 1998; Mallalieu et al., 1999; Poon & Wagner, 2001; Sarker & Lee, 1999; Walston & Bogue, 1999). Since BPC is greatly enabled via ICT, it is noteworthy that this notion is echoed also in the related literature on information systems success (Lyytinen & Hirschheim, 1987). Although ICT literacy still seems to be in short supply among most senior executives, a basic understanding of the intricacies of both areas becomes more important for executives, demanding from them more than just symbolic involvement (Beaumaster, 2002). With the crossing of departmental and other organizational boundaries in e-gov projects, the involvement of and sponsorship by senior executives also appears indispensable in the government context.

Proposition #7: The active involvement and continued commitment of senior government leadership is indispensable to the success of any major electronic-government project.

New Challenges in Record Keeping

While electronic business-induced BPC in the private sector also apparently creates fundamentally new requirements for electronic record management (ERM) and document life-cycle management (DLM) (Barata & Cain, 2003; Symon, 2002; Waldron, 2002), this seems to be even more challenging in the public sector. Laws, statutes, and regulations mandate each government action, transaction, and interaction to be documented for later scrutiny. Ironically, in this regard, while e-gov addresses and overcomes many problems in the traditional, paper-based operations of government and government-to-public interaction (McMullen, 2000), it poses a host of new challenges along every dimension of government record keeping (Relyea, 2002). Government records (including Web sites) and transactional data (including e-mails), unlike their private-sector equivalents, bear the weight of government authority, accountability, and liability. Governments still seem to grapple with understanding the full extent of the challenge and with providing acceptable short- and long-term concepts for meeting those new challenges (Gant & Gant, 2002).

Proposition #8: Electronic government poses a new challenge regarding government records (in terms of creation, maintenance, preservation, security, integrity, and accessibility.

Research Question and Study Design

Study Question

As mentioned in the introduction, this chapter reports on the second portion of a large study, whose design has been detailed in an article published in the previous issue of this journal (Scholl, 2005). In order to avoid unnecessary repetition, this section has been drastically shortened. For further details, the reader is referred to that earlier publication.

Assuming current practices in public-sector BPC to be identical to those employed in the private sector would be too bold an assumption, in view of the many known differences between the two sectors (Rainey, Backoff, & Levine, 1976). Assuming, on the other hand, those practices to be completely idiosyncratic, would be an equally bold assumption, given the many interactions and exchanges between the sectors. Consequently, an exploratory research design was chosen. The study questions were formulated as follows:

1. To what extent do BPC practices related to e-gov projects differ from BPC practices in the private sector?

2. If the practices differ between the two sectors, how do they differ?

The eight propositions derived from the private-sector-based literature characterize current practices in private-sector BPC. For answering the two research questions, the study hence would utilize those propositions to probe for similarities and divergences in completed e-gov projects that involve, at a minimum, transaction processing.

As mentioned earlier, two parallel samples were used, one from New York State (NYS) and the other from Washington State (WAS). With respect to the nature of e-gov projects that were covered, some ancillary details regarding the breakdown

Table 1. E-gov project categories in percent

State	g2c	g2b	g2g	IEE	Multiple
NYS	40%	47%	87%	67%	87%
WAS	100%	75%	88%	50%	88%

of those two samples are worthwhile to be presented here. E-gov projects are categorized as g2g (government-to-government), g2b (government-to-business), g2c (government-to-citizen), and IEE (internal efficiency and effectiveness) projects. Projects, however, in their majority, belonged to more than one category. As shown in Table 1, 40% of the NYS projects had a g2c orientation, while all of WAS had that orientation; 47% of the NYS projects were in the category of g2b, whereas 75% of the WAS project were in that category; in both samples, almost the exact same percentage of projects fell into the g2g category (NYS 87%, WAS 88%); in NYS, 67% were geared at IEE, while 50% in WAS were. As stated previously, the vast majority of projects in both samples had multiple orientations (NYS 87%, WAS 88%).

Given the large differences between the two samples in at least the g2c and g2b categories, one would expect some variation in the quantitative results with respect to overall agreement/disagreement to the statements/propositions. Surprisingly, this was not the case, as discussed in the next section.

Results

In this section, the results are presented for each proposition, one at a time. For exhibiting the overall tendency of comments, the quantitative distribution of agreement and disagreement is mentioned first. In their majority, the practitioners agreed with seven of the eight propositions, indicating support for those propositions developed from the private-sector BPC literature. Although one might be tempted to criticize this as an expectable outcome, the reader is reminded that this study was not aimed at producing quantitative evidence. The strong general tendency found still is, as the author believes, an interesting and, to its extent, unexpected outcome. Albeit, this research predominantly attempts to capture qualitatively the spectrum of approaches and practices in e-gov BPC projects, such that a richer and more robust theory may become available for further testing.

Stakeholders

No other statement (Proposition #1) found a higher rate of overall agreement (97.5% strongly agreed; 2.5% somewhat agreed). Stakeholder involvement and management were seen as absolutely essential for the success of any e-gov project. This result confirms the findings reported in the private-sector-oriented BPC literature. However, our findings suggest that stakeholder management may be even more critical in the public sector. Among the MOST FREQUENTLY CITED REASONS for stakeholder involvement were (1) the experience of past project failure or underutilization; (2) smoother project execution; (3) better need assessment; (4) more focused project orientation; and (5) acceptance of project outcomes, including information systems.

Moreover, due to the distributed control over critical resources, it was argued that stakeholders had to be involved anyway, in order to launch the project and keep it afloat. However, the proper and timely IDENTIFICATION of salient stakeholders occasionally poses a problem, according to the responses. In some cases, for example, particularly in those with high degrees of application and information integration, the number of stakeholders appeared too high, or stakeholder groups were seen as too heterogeneous, such that the involvement posed a serious management problem; in other cases, stakeholder salience had been assessed incorrectly, leading to troublesome situations when the project unfolded. The lack of identifying stakeholders with the power to stall the project was reported as a major mistake in planning and execution.

Interviewees described various aspects of stakeholder INVOLVEMENT, for example, via ongoing communication and participation. Demonstrating a project's potential benefits to stakeholders reportedly increases stakeholder support and mitigates change resistance, it was pointed out. The earlier that stakeholders are involved, it was said, the more deeply the project's impact on process change and its business impact is understood and negotiated among all parties. Piloting and prototyping systems were seen as practical and powerful methods for involving stakeholders, although technically suboptimal; yet, consensus-based systems might be the outcome. Nevertheless, some issues remain with stakeholder involvement. According to the interviewed practitioners, (1) stakeholder involvement alone does not guarantee project success; (2) occasionally decisions are made based on critically incomplete information, even while stakeholders are involved; (3) stakeholders may be over-invested in old systems or not sympathetic to the notion of e-gov; (4) budget and time pressures may preclude the timely and proper involvement of stakeholders, exposing those projects to higher risks of failure; and (5) proof of concepts sometimes may be attainable only through "stealth" projects with limited or no stakeholder involvement. The theme of stakeholder involvement reappeared time and again in respondents' comments to most other statements.

Culture/Change Readiness

Although there was strong support for this statement (Proposition #2) among respondents (54.3% strongly agreed; 21.7% somewhat agreed), neutrality (8.7%), no answer (8.7%), and slight (4.3%) to strong (2.3%) disagreement were also observed.

The *rationale* given by respondents for performing an upfront cultural assessment broke down into three subcategories: (1) textbook wisdom, (2) education, and (3) overcoming resistance. According to the textbooks, with which a number of practitioners seemed to be quite familiar, an upfront culture assessment, so the interviewees said, allows for a better understanding of the project's impact on the culture, which was seen as a major determinant of project success. In that regard, the e-gov project seemed to be no different from any other change project.

The larger the anticipated change, it was also said, the more crucial is an upfront assessment. A cultural change from a bureaucracy-centric to a service-oriented culture, for example, was seen as a major challenge taking a lot of time. E-gov projects with such impacts may be broken up better into smaller chunks in order to avoid clashes, it was felt. For some time, both the traditional and the new way of doing business would co-exist anyway, it was argued. The culture assessment when people are involved may help to educate and to change behaviors regarding the project, it was reported, and may even create the sense of need and of ownership in an e-gov project geared at change.

Foremost, though, the anticipated lines of resistance to change (i.e., "entrenched bureaucracies"), it was believed, become visible in a culture assessment and, hence, inform the project proponents regarding the overall readiness for and likely dynamics of change. According to most practitioners, the assessment is critical, since resistance to the project can become so fundamental that it would be hard to overcome. In this regard, proper identification of STAKEHOLDERS and their needs was seen also as part of the culture/readiness assessment. Some practitioners found the stakeholder identification and particularly the senior executive support to be much more important than upfront culture assessments, which were characterized rather critically as time-consuming and expensive by those respondents. CONCURRENT AS-SESSMENT rather than an upfront assessment was seen as sufficient and even more effective by a number of practitioners who also pointed out that an e-gov project's clearly specified addressing of business needs, its scope definition, budget, scheduling, and resource planning would be more important.

Those practitioners see the culture assessment as an integral part of the project conducted on an ongoing rather than on an upfront basis. Reported OUTCOMES AND INSIGHTS, when upfront assessments had been performed, were that (1) unexpected and valuable results were found, which changed the course of the project; (2) the removal of individuals and groups was inevitable, such that they were unable to contest the project; (3) it was necessary to start the assessment at the top; and (4) the upfront assessment does not guard against failure, particularly if two far different cultures have to be merged. When upfront assessments had not been performed, then projects had a tendency to fail more frequently than when some assessment had been performed, according to some practitioners. While the overall need for cultural or change readiness assessments is not disputed much among practitioners, a variety of approaches seems to exist in practice, ranging from full-scale upfront (for large change projects) over ongoing (for both large and small projects), to little or no assessment (for medium and small projects).

Process and Resource Inventory

Respondents mostly supported (32.6 % strongly agreed; 28.3% somewhat agreed) the notion of inventorying business processes and related resources formulated in this statement (Proposition #3). However, quite a few practitioners were neutral (21.7%) or had certain reservations (8.7% somewhat disagreed), including outright disagreement (8.7% strongly disagreed).

Statement #8 (new challenges in record keeping) provoked more comments than all other statements. The research team identified a total of six categories. Again, practitioners contrasted what they referred to as the TEXTBOOK APPROACH with a CRITIQUE OF THE TEXTBOOK APPROACH. Some practitioners characterized the inventorying of processes and extant resources as indispensable for proper project initiation and planning, not just in e-gov projects. With establishing the current state, a desired state also could be charted, it was said. The building of both shared vision and mission, as proclaimed in many textbooks, and the specifying of business need antecede or accompany this inventorying process, some practitioners said.

Those practitioners also maintained that the more and better analysis and planning that is done upfront, the less time is wasted in later project stages. Where an accurate and current documentation of extant processes and resources exists, some practitioners stated, both analysis and planning for a given project are done more easily. The inventory analysis also was seen as instrumental when pinpointing lacks of functionality. The detailed analysis, however, is routinely performed only when senior executives have signed off on the project and when primary stakeholders are involved, according to the respondents. In critiquing the textbook approach, other respondents said that the analysis is an ongoing, iterative process rather than an upfront, one-time exercise, which quite a few even considered a waste of time and resources. Also, when the process and resource inventory is kept current, project planning and execution unfold hand-in-hand, it was said.

Some practitioners went as far as reporting that the analysis mostly serves the goal to mediate between a "recognized or fabricated problem" and a "projected and desired state." Others pointed at the tradeoffs between strategic project momentum and near-complete analysis, the latter of which had the capacity to lead to "analysis paralysis," to scare away decision-makers, and to stall a project. Still others maintained that many projects are launched without any front-loaded, detailed analysis, and that project success would not hinge necessarily on those analyses, as long as an "awareness of the problem" exists. Also reported were OTHER CONSTRAINTS, which prevent a complete inventorying of extant processes and resources; the most frequently mentioned was the lack of funds, resources, time, or even interest. Further, respondents pointed out that the extent of analysis necessary and executed was related to the size and the perceived risk of a project.

Several respondents emphasized the critical link between process and resource inventorying and the identification and involvement of salient STAKEHOLDERS, as previously discussed. When skipping the detailed analysis and inventory, important stakeholders may remain unidentified, they said. Inventorying and analyzing those practitioners, they held, was part of community building around an e-gov project.

Interviewees also gave the following account on OUTCOMES AND INSIGHTS when inventorying was done or skipped: (1) striking the right balance between the extent of inventorying and analysis, on the one hand, and project drive and dynamics, on the other hand, may determine part of project success or failure, according to quite a few interviewees; (2) while critical gaps may be uncovered through analysis, some projects were continued, while others were cancelled; no account of the failure rate of the former was given; (3) processes may be the foremost target area for inventory and analysis, since they seem to have a high potential for improvement; (4) only through analysis did the complexity of the integration task become clear; (5) the analytical process was seen as ongoing and iterative; (6) proper analysis was not seen as a safeguard against project failure; (7) the results from analysis were found useful when crafting Requests for Proposal (RFPs); (8) rapid prototyping complemented the analysis. In summary, according to the data, inventorying and analysis appears to be conducted in e-gov projects with various levels of detail and intensity, ranging from no to iterative and ongoing detail analysis.

Workflow Analysis

A large number of respondents agreed (63% strongly, 15.2 % somewhat) with the notion in this statement (Proposition #4), while some were neutral (10.9%), some disagreed (2.2% somewhat, 4.3% strongly), and some gave no answer (4.3%).

Some interviewees found that workflow analysis should be part of the overall analysis performed in the context of project management; others were confused whether or not workflow analysis would be equivalent to a user requirements analysis. Practitioners in support of performing the workflow analysis stated the RATIONALE along these lines: (1) "It is a necessary evil" and "the devil is in the detail," especially, when integrating and interfacing workflows that cross organizational boundaries; (2) levers and areas of greatest gains may be identified more easily; (3) through understanding the details, the nature of change may be understood better and conflict may be avoided in e-gov. When describing SCOPE AND DETAIL of workflow analysis in e-gov, quite a few practitioners maintained that workflow scale and scope co-determine the level of analysis.

When individuals who are knowledgeable about a specific workflow are involved in the analysis, the potential for streamlining may raise significantly, some said. To a large degree, project success hinges on the detailed workflow analysis, a few interviewees pointed out. Again, according to a number of respondents, the workflow analysis may vary in extent, from happenstance to too detailed. Others reported on skipping the whole or some parts of workflow analysis, advocating an OPPORTUNISTIC APPROACH as seen previously. According to some respondents, the early e-gov projects just webified existing workflows, while others created completely new methods without expending any detailed analysis. Also, it was said that with outsourcing e-gov systems, old workflows were obliterated with no need for ex-post scrutiny.

Again, it also was reported that workflow analyses were skipped for reasons of overwhelming workload. Several times, it was stated that workflows would not change through the advent of e-gov, suggesting that no detailed analysis was necessary. As in the previous section, so also for workflows, quite a few practitioners suggested that an iterative approach was applied also to workflow analysis. Among the reported OUTCOMES AND INSIGHTS from performing or not performing a detailed workflow analysis were the (1) better understanding through matching workflows with business needs and requirements; (2) increased accountability and transparency through matching tasks to workers and workers to tasks; (3) better understanding when troubleshooting; (4) users' increased project acceptance; and (5) a lower rate of nasty surprises while the project unfolded. In one case, the detailed workflow analysis was found disappointing, since no new insight had been derived. In e-gov projects overall, workflow analysis also seems to be performed with varying degrees of detail, again ranging from no analysis to detailed and ongoing/iterative analysis, apparently depending on the project's or agency's developmental stage in e-gov.

Internal Competency and Learning

Agreements (30.4% strong; 15.2% somewhat) and disagreements (2.2% strong; 23.9% somewhat), along with neutral responses (23.9%) and no answers (4.3%) were distributed regarding this statement (Proposition #5), although agreement was relatively strong among practitioners.

Respondents pondered the value of INTERNAL KNOWLEDGE UTILIZATION versus EXTERNAL SOURCES OF KNOWLEDGE. Quite a few respondents bluntly stated that e-gov is a government core function and, hence, must be seen as internal. While not opposed to using external sources in some capacity, internal expertise would be needed to solidly manage e-gov projects over long periods of time. Also, it was felt that availability of internal expertise keeps both consultants and vendors from inflating bids. Quite a few practitioners identified internal experts as having better understanding of government culture, structure, and process, leading to higher gains and a higher commitment to desirable outcomes than external experts.

While onsite learning from external subject field experts (e.g., advanced Web techniques) or component outsourcing were found appropriate, leaving "our core and destiny to strangers" was seen as unacceptable. Critical knowledge, hence, was to be maintained and built inside, it was said. As an obstacle to this goal, a number of practitioners quoted what they called the knowledge drain through either early retirement programs in the wake of continued budget pressures over the years or more attractive professional opportunities and remuneration in the private sector. Proponents of using external expertise in e-gov highlighted the productive role external experts and change agents had played as coaches when developing internal expertise. Others pointed out that outsourcing e-gov systems had been considered only for as long as e-gov had not touched the core processes. On the downside of using external expertise, even advocates of external expertise cited those external experts' long and expensive learning curves regarding government processes.

When pointing to OUTCOMES AND INSIGHTS, respondents reported that (1) a mix of internal and external expertise was used; (2) the business expertise was seen as the most important element in e-gov and, hence, had never been outsourced, while technology components may or may not have been outsourced, depending on their relative importance; (3) sufficient internal expertise also regarding the technology needed to be maintained; and (4) knowledge transfer from external technical experts to internal experts had been sought and observed.

Consensus Among Officials and Citizens

Respondents were overwhelmingly in disagreement (47.8% strongly, 28.3% somewhat) with the notion in this statement (Proposition #6), while some were neutral (13%), others strongly agreed (6.5%), and yet others gave no answers (4.3%).

Practitioners' answers were seen to fall into two broad categories of describing an IDEAL WORLD, as opposed to the "real world" of ORGANIZATIONAL PRACTICE. Within the former category, interviewees said more consensus most likely would breed more success, and it was known that force-fitting services would be detrimental; however, no formal process for creating such consensus regarding e-gov had been set in place. Moreover, even the few proponents admitted broad consensus between officials and citizens not to be essential, but rather more like "motherhood and apple pie." Talking about the realities of organizational practice, many respondents pointed out that broad consensus between officials and citizens regarding e-gov was neither achievable nor necessary; on the contrary, seeking broad consensus could be detrimental to the progress of e-gov. What was sought, according to a majority of practitioners, was consensus among important stakeholders, including government officials and senior executives, regarding e-gov project objectives, opportunities for improvement, priorities, needs, and the functionality of e-gov systems.

A number of interviewees pointed out that government agencies have substantial discretion when choosing among e-gov project avenues to follow. They also distinguished government-perceived need for a service from consensus building with citizens regarding that particular need. Some other respondents also maintained that whether or not they were appointed or elected officials, they were held responsible by their seniors and not by the citizens. Citizens would have their say through the elected legislators and other representatives. Most consensus-seeking activities would be conducted after the fact, once favorable results could be shown, it was said. Also, since the traditional way of doing business would not go away for a long time, new approaches such as e-gov were not subjected to broad consensus building anyway, some respondents held. In summary, according to the broad majority of practitioners, e-gov projects do not hinge upon the broad consensus between officials and citizens.

Senior Leadership Support

Practitioners overwhelmingly supported the notion in this statement (Proposition #7) (82.6% strongly agreed; 10.9% somewhat agreed; there was no disagreement), while some were neutral (2.2%) or did not respond to the statement (4.3%). The respondents qualified the NECESSITY AND EXTENT of senior executive support in e-gov projects as follows: (1) in a context in which resources are typically scarce and competition for them is stiff, funding and resource allocation was seen as an important aspect of senior executive support; (2) the senior executive leans his or her authority to the project, which helps establish legitimacy and accountability along the line of command, especially, in non-routine business situations such as change projects; (3) the senior executive is indispensable for overcoming resistance to change and bureaucratic inertia along with maintaining stakeholder commitment and focus; (4) the larger the project (in terms of span of control and time horizon) and the more government entities are involved, the more senior executive support and involvement (e.g., via steering committees) is necessary for synchronization and mediation; (5) souring projects may only be turned around if senior executives weigh in; and (6) while reassured via periodic update reports, a senior executive's support of the e-gov project needs to be continuous, whereas the frequency of the executive's involvement may vary.

The practitioners also pointed at certain LIMITS of senior executive support. Some respondents said that executives seem to lose interest in a subject after a while. Also, executives appear to have a limited tolerance and capacity of understanding for technical and other details in e-gov projects, such that they rely on their subject experts, anyway, it was pointed out. Overall, the criticality of continued senior executive support for the success of any e-gov project was strongly confirmed.

New Challenges in Record Keeping

Among practitioners, there was very high support for the concept formulated in this statement (Proposition #8): 78.3% of interviewees strongly agreed; 10.9% somewhat agreed; 2.2% were neutral; 6.5% somewhat disagreed; and 2.2% strongly disagreed. This statement produced a plethora of comments and practical examples.

Many interviewees emphasized the expected and observed BENEFITS of electronic record keeping as opposed to paper-based archiving and preservation. E-government, it was said, presents an opportunity to find and access all types of records quickly (at least at some future point in time). Also, access to electronic records was seen as easier, less duplicative, and less costly than with paper records, particularly for handicapped individuals. Some practitioners expected that the days were numbered for huge archival warehouses in an e-government-oriented environment. Pervasive electronic record keeping also would allow for secondary uses at a later date. Further, access to electronic records would curtail the role of middlemen who have traditionally provided newsletters and compiled services for dispersed paper records. While most practitioners acknowledged the numerous potential benefits of both electronic record management (ERM) and document life cycle management (DLM), they also were cognizant of many challenges in terms of record accessibility, preservation, retention, maintenance, ERM/DLM technology, ERM/DLM evolution, and security, as well as with respect to the policy and the legal implications in the context of ERM and DLM.

Among the major challenges, the practitioners emphasized the following: With respect to ACCESSIBILITY, the future needs were hard to define in advance; likewise, it was difficult to clearly identify and articulate the level of access to the archived information; access even might become too easy over the Internet; government, it also was feared, might lose control over who has access to records and information, which would lead to unforeseen legal and other consequences.

According to the interviewees, the PRESERVATION of electronic records might pose a new challenge of its own kind: First, electronic records appeared to be potentially foilable, including information represented on a government Web site; hence, the preservation must make sure that the documents would not be altered when and while preserved. Further, since keeping separate paper-based and electronic records would not be desirable in the long run, from the current perspective, it was unclear to most interviewees what amount of paper records needed electronic preservation. However, even the current documentation of electronic sources was problematic, it was said, since it was done mainly by preserving electronic images, which were only searchable via indices and keywords rather than full text. Finally, the electronic preservation of government records had to meet longest-term archiving needs, while technology generations of media and hardware are rather short-lived, it was said. Consequently, the electronic preservation of records had to provide for an ongoing migration of the ever-growing stock of electronic documents from one technology generation to the next over the decades to come.

An important role in this context, the interviewees said, would fall on the proper definition of rules of electronic record RETENTION. Most practitioners assumed that rules for paper-based records and for electronic records might differ. For example, practitioners had diverging opinions about whether or not a change in an informational government Web site would require a particular documentation. In general, it seemed unclear and unaddressed what electronic information needed to be retained and for what stated purpose it was maintained, the interviewees said. Some practitioners were very concerned that the standards for preserving paper and electronic records would be incongruent. While shorter-term archival requirements (some seven years and longer) were seen as well met via contemporary ERM/DLM procedures, the requirements for longest-term historical electronic archiving were rather undetermined, it was said. Also, when and for what reason electronic records were to be destroyed was still an unresolved issue. If records were destroyed prematurely, this could lead to troublesome legal issues in future times, it was maintained.

Practitioners were very much in agreement that paper retention periods should not be applied to electronic records without thorough prior assessment. An interesting side note on the issue of record retention was the current treatment of E-MAIL by many government workers and agencies: Most workers, it was said, still misunderstood e-mail (casual and informal, much like a phone conversation) as a personal and even private communications device, which might be treated and deleted at will. Consequently, many government workers and agencies alike grossly ignored the official character and the need for archiving, the interviewees said. The challenge would be to educate workers that e-mail exchanges via government computers and networks were just like any paper-based exchange.

The practitioners also maintained that standards and procedures for short- and long-term ERM/DLM would undergo an EVOLUTION, since most requirements were still not known. Most interviewees acknowledged that the enormity of the challenge of record management in e-government had caught them by surprise. One major element in the more demanding management of records and documents was seen in the "higher degree of integration and higher number of participating entities." On the other hand, certain transaction types, it was emphasized, had proved to be documentable and loggable in e-gov just as in the paper-based organization by "adding a small layer." Ironically, in the absence of proper electronic archiving standards, some agencies had reverted to documenting every e-gov transaction on paper, some interviewees indicated.

With the expected evolution of ERM/DLM standards and procedures, it was also foreseen that additional requirements and safeguards for the SECURITY of network, access, records, and documents would emerge. Constraining unauthorized access with traditional means such as "the walk-in only method" as a powerful de-facto safeguard when accessing paper records would no longer exist and would limit accessibility to records and documents in e-government, it was maintained.

Some interviewees also pointed out that the greatly unresolved issue of ERM/DLM in e-gov was a classical example of the unforeseen and unanticipated consequences of introducing new TECHNOLOGY. "Technology factually drives the business problem," one interviewee held. Apart from the rapid sequence of technology changes and the introduction of new system generations mentioned previously, which would lead to an ongoing and most likely costly migration of archives from one generation to the next, it was also the sheer number and variety of data sources, systems, and business processes that puzzled most interviewees in the context of ERM/DLM. In other words, although the architecture for this huge undertaking was required from the outset, its requirements only would become fully understood over time. Developing and maintaining metadata for the ever-vaster number of ERM/DLM sites, however, was seen as an immediate necessity. Still, documenting an electronic trail for a transaction or a document from one end to the other was seen as insufficiently implemented with current technology.

With the lack of understanding of ERM/DLM architectures and requirements, it came as no surprise, interviewees said, that the LAW has not provided the necessary framework either. Case law has not developed yet, it was said. It was not clear what legal standards were to be met for accepting electronic record and document integrity as well as nonrepudiability. A tactical approach currently used, some interviewees said, was the "piggy-backing" of ERM/DLM on existing paper-based procedures, although with dubious success. In some states, paper records could be destroyed if imaging systems were used for preservation. Record and document ownership and custodial obligations were distributed among various levels and branches of government; hence, in many cases, unifying ERM/DLM standards was not easy to agree upon or could not be imposed. Eventually, different authorities and legislations, other practitioners felt, might govern ERM/DLM.

Almost all interviewees stressed the urgency and necessity of developing a robust POLICY that includes guiding principles for creation, retention, migration, preservation, accessibility, and maintenance; that addresses the risks of record and document forging, privacy breaches, and information misuses, and also that enforces the emerging ERM/DLM legislation. Some practitioners found that e-record standards may be even higher than paper record standards. Despite those enormous challenges, most interviewees emphasized that effective ERM/DLM would make government less paper-intensive, more effective and efficient, and more agile.

Discussion

Through its exploratory approach, this study has sought rich qualitative data for elucidating and better understanding the current practices in e-gov-induced business process change projects. Frameworks and concepts formulated in the context of private-sector BPC guided the study in this effort. With the results regarding those areas in e-gov BPC in hand, those frameworks and concepts in turn may now be cautiously assessed for their suitability and applicability to a public-sector context, which is briefly undertaken in the first portion of this discussion. In the second portion, the salient themes and factors embodied in those approaches and practices found are discussed.

Suitability of the Private-Sector BPC Literature

Based on the results, a preliminary assessment of suitability and applicability seems in order, even though the sampling was purposively geared toward a different end, and the sample size (n=23) was relatively small so that no claim to generalizability can and will be made. If there is some indication that the frameworks and concepts from the BPC literature apply, the utilization of that rich literature in the context of e-gov projects would appear as most recommendable such that expensive lessons learned elsewhere may not be lost.

Upon analyzing the quantitative results presented, it is noteworthy that only marginal differences ($\partial < 1.1\%$) were detected between the New York and Washington subsamples. In rank order, there was overall support for propositions #1 (100%), #7 (93.5%), #8 (89.1%), #4 (78.2%), #2 (76%), and #3 (60.9%). Weak support was found for proposition #5 (45.6%). Proposition #6 was rejected by 76.1% of the respondents. In other words, the current practices in e-gov-related BPC are seemingly shaped through the following concepts (Table 2).

Identified practices and approaches in private-sector BPC play a significant role in seven of eight instances also in the public sector. If the condition in proposition #7 were relaxed to the property of salient stakeholder consensus, then, as the data show, even this practice would be little different between the two sectors. From this preliminary assessment, it appears that the private-sector-based literature is highly relevant to e-gov BPC practice and might be utilized in a more systematic fashion in both academia and practice. This also provides a partial answer to the first study

Table 2. Rank order of importance of concepts in e-gov BPC-related projects

Rank	Concept	Degree of Importance in e-Gov-related BPC Projects
1.	Stakeholder involvement	Highest
2.	Senior executive commitment	Highest
3.	New challenges in record keeping	Very high
4.	Workflow analysis	High
5.	Culture/change readiness assessments	High
6.	Process and resource inventorying	Some
7.	Internal competency and learning	Some
8.	A broad consensus between officials and citizens	Does Not Matter

question: The extent of differences in BPC practices appears to reside, if so, in details and in emphasis rather than on a grand scale or in principle.

Salient Themes and Factors Embodied in Current E-Gov BPC Practices

The emphasis with which the practices are employed may differ between the two sectors. In the absence of a parallel study for e-commerce-induced BPC in the private sector, one only can speculate which practices carry more weight than others in the private sector. Interestingly, the least important factor in e-gov process change was found to be the broad consensus between government officials and citizens. Also, process and resource inventorying as well as internal competency building and learning were not among the highly emphasized practices. This, indeed, could be different in private-sector settings, where intimate process knowledge and focused resource development are prerequisites for sustained competitiveness. On the other hand, the private sector literature seems to mention few accounts, if any, where the ongoing involvement of internal and external stakeholders appears as the most important factor in securing a successful project outcome. This strong emphasis on stakeholder involvement and participation seems directly related to the project environment of distributed control, as previously discussed, where carefully prene-gotiated outcomes are the result of numerous checks and balances.

Within e-gov BPC, it seems that those practices that address social and organizational themes receive much more attention than those addressing technical themes. Actually, the two most prominent technical themes (ERM/DLM) and workflow analysis encompass important organizational aspects rather than just technical ones. Figure

Figure 1. Most prominent themes and factors in current e-gov BPC practices

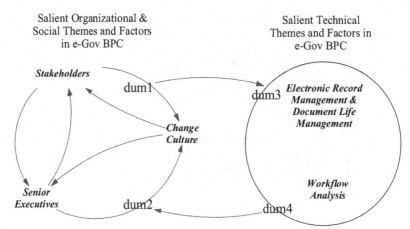

1 depicts the interaction between the most prominent themes and factors within the practices of e-gov BPC. The involvement of stakeholders impacts the cultural change processes in the organization; at the same time, both stakeholders and the cultural context are influenced by senior executives: With strong and continuing senior executive support, the prospects for culture change and stakeholder commitment were reportedly far better than without. However, in turn, the stance of senior executives also is influenced significantly by the various stakeholder groups as well as by the (changing or resisting) cultural context of the organization. The prominent technical themes and factors of ERM/DLM and workflow analysis are embedded into the organizational and social context; however, they likewise shape that context (DeSanctis & Poole, 1994; Orlikowski, 1992).

From the empirical data in this study, an exemplar of an e-gov BPC project (see Appendix) has been synthesized, which captures and delineates typical practices and their concurrent use within a project. This synthesized exemplar may be of particular value for practitioners of e-gov BPC.

Conclusion and Future Research

Although e-gov BPC projects seem to follow patterns and employ techniques similar to their private sector counterparts, the different principles of governance in the public sector make e-gov BPC projects intrinsically more complex. Due to the distribution of powers, e-gov BPC projects seemingly necessitate far higher degrees of consensus among salient stakeholders as well as pre-negotiated outcomes than is typical in the private sector. Distributed control and accountability, however, comes with more distributed sharing of burden also leading to more ownership in process, project, and outcome. Due to its mostly consensual nature and also due to numerous legal, statutory, and regulatory requirements, e-gov BPC projects take longer to complete than similar projects in the private sector, obviously with the benefit of much less staggering failure rates (Hammer, 1996). In fact, reports on e-gov project blunders still seem to be in short supply. So far, major failures in the public sector appear to be related mostly to more traditional information system projects, where huge cost overruns (e.g., the NYS PaySR initiative) (*Senate Budget Report: Section Four*, 2002) or a combination of cost overruns, project delays, and user dissatisfaction (e.g., the California DMV project) (Dawes et al., 2004) were reported. Although a comparative study on the success rates of e-gov projects as opposed to private-sector e-commerce projects also is still missing, public-sector projects (including e-gov projects) may have some insightful lessons in stock, which may have the capacity to inspire private-sector BPC practice, as well.

Future research will seek more qualitative data regarding current BPC practices in both sectors, as well as quantitative accounts on the basis of larger samples for a more detailed comparison. The following research projects may have the capacity to advance our knowledge in this regard:

1. As mentioned, a study on the key factors and the interplay between those factors leading to e-gov/e-commerce project success and failure is still missing. Such a study would try to establish a quantitative account of sector-related differences in the success and failure rates. It also would study pairs of cases of similar sizes and characteristics in both sectors in order to derive a deeper understanding of differences and similarities between the sectors; that is, (a) to what extent the key factors for success and failure are similar/different, (b) to what extent the interaction between the key factors is similar/different, and (c) how the differences/similarities can be related to the respective outcomes.

2. The theoretical elements developed through this study need to be tested with a far larger sample of e-gov projects across the nation. For this purpose, a survey instrument, which captures the main theoretical elements presented here, needs to be developed. A stratified sample, which reflects the different levels and branches of government as well as the geographical distribution, appears appropriate. The analysis of those data may hold many more fine-grained insights regarding the speed, extent, and effects of BPC through e-gov.

3. BPC, as already outlined, will be more imminent as more vertical and horizontal integration occurs through e-gov. A longitudinal exploratory study or an action research study, which accompanies a multi-year integration and interoperability project, would provide data and insights on the (a) technical, (b) organizational, (c) social process, (d) legal/regulatory/statutory, and (e) other challenges and complexities in the context of a large-scale interoperability project.

Acknowledgment

I am indebted to my assistant Thomas K. Richards at the Information School, who helped conduct the interviews, organize the equipment, and prepare the transcripts for many hours. He also was instrumental in organizing and conducting the data analysis and coding.

References

Alavi, M., Wheeler, B.C., & Valacich, J.S. (1995). Using IT to reengineer business education: An exploratory investigation of collaborative telelearning. *MIS Quarterly, 19*(3), 293-312.

Barata, K., & Cain, P. (2003). Records management toolkits from across the pond. *Information Management Journal, 37*(4), 40-47.

Beaumaster, S. (2002). Local government IT implementation issues: A challenge for public administration. *Proceedings of the 35th Hawaiian International Conference on System Sciences*, Hawaii.

Caudle, S.L. (1994). *Reengineering for results: Keys to success from government experience.* Washington, DC: Center for Information Management, National Academy of Public Administration.

Champy, J. (1995). *Reengineering management: The mandate for new leadership.* New York: HarperBusiness.

Cooper, R.B. (2000). Information technology development creativity: A case study of attempted radical change. *MIS Quarterly, 24*(2), 245-276.

Davenport, T.H., & Short, J.E. (1990). The new industrial reengineering: Information technology and business process redesign. *Sloan Management Review, 31*(Summer), 11-27.

Dawes, S.S., et al. (2004). *Making smart IT choices: Understanding value and risk in government IT investments.* Albany, NY: Center for Technology in Government, University at Albany/SUNY.

DeSanctis, G., & Poole, M.S. (1994). Capturing the complexity in advanced technology use: Adaptive structuration theory. *Organization Science, 5*(2), 121-147.

Douglas, C. (1999). Organizational redesign: The current state and projected trends. *Management Decisions, 37*(8), 621-627.

Freeman, R.E. (1984). *Strategic management: A stakeholder approach.* Boston: Pitman.

Gant, J.P., & Gant, D.B. (2002). *Web portal functionality and state government e-service.* Proceedings of the 35th Hawaiian International Conference on System Sciences, Hawaii.

Giaglis, G.M. (1999). Integrated design and evaluation of business processes and information systems. *Communications of AIS, 2*(1), 1-33.

Grover, V., Teng, J., Segars, A.H., & Fiedler, K. (1998). The influence of information technology diffusion and business process change on perceived productivity: The IS executive's perspective. *Information & Management, 34,* 141-159.

Halachmi, A., & Bovaird, T. (1997). Process reengineering in the public sector: Learning some private sector lessons. *Technovation, 17*(5), 227-235.

Hammer, M. (1996). *Beyond reengineering: How the process-centered organization is changing our work and our lives.* New York: HarperBusiness.

Hammer, M., & Champy, J. (1993). *Reengineering the corporation: A manifesto for business revolution.* New York: HapperCollins Publishers.

Harkness, W.L., Kettinger, W.J., & Segars, A.H. (1996). Sustaining process improvement and innovation in the information service function: Lessons learned from Bose Corporation. *MIS Quarterly, 20*(3), 349-367.

Kambil, A., & van Heck, E. (1998). Reengineering the Dutch flower auctions: A framework for analyzing exchange organizations. *Information Systems Research, 9*(1), 1-19.

Kettinger, W.J., Teng, J.T.C., & Guha, S. (1997, March). Business process change: A study of methodologies, techniques and tools. *MIS Quarterly,* 55-80.

Kling, R., & Tillquist, J. (1998). *Conceiving IT-enabled organizational change.* Retrieved January 20, 2002: *www.slis.indiana.edu/kling/orgsci98h.html*

Klischewski, R. (2004). *Information integration or process integration? How to achieve interoperability in administration.* Proceedings of the EGOV04 at DEXA, Zaragoza, Spain.

Kogut, B., & Zander, U. (1992). Knowledge of the firm, combinative capabilities, and the replication of technology. *Organization Science, 3*(3), 383-397.

Kogut, B., & Zander, U. (1995). Knowledge and the speed of the transfer and imitation of organizational capabilities: An empirical test. *Organization Science, 6*(1), 76-92.

Layne, K., & Lee, J. (2001). Developing fully functional e-government: A four stage model. *Government Information Quarterly, 18*(2), 122-136.

Lloyd, A.D., Dewar, R., & Pooley, R. (1999). Business process and legacy system reengineering: A pattern perspective. *Communications of AIS, 2*(4), Article 24.

Lyytinen, K., & Hirschheim, R. (1987). Information systems failures–A survey and classification of the empirical literature. *Oxford Surveys in Information Technology, 4*, 257-309.

Mallalieu, G., Harvey, C., & Hardy, C. (1999). The wicked relationship between organizations and information technology (industry trend and event). *Journal of End User Computing, 11*(4), 40-50.

Markus, M. L. (1983). Power, politics, and MIS implementation. *Communications of the ACM, 26*(6), 430-444.

Martinsons, M.G., & Revenaugh, D.L. (1997). Re-engineering is dead; Long live re-engineering. *International Journal of Production Economics, 17*(2), 79-82.

McMullen, S. (2000). US government information: Selected current issues in public access vs. private competition. *Journal of Government Information, 27*(5), 581-593.

Mohan, L., & Holstein, W.K. (1990). EIS: It can work in the public sector. *MIS Quarterly, 14*(4), 434-448.

Mohan, L., & Holstein, W.K. (1998). *Decision support systems: An applications perspective* [unpublished].

Nelson, R.R., & Winter, S.G. (1982). *An evolutionary theory of economic change.* Cambridge, MA: Belknap Press of Harvard University Press.

O'Neill, P., & Sohal, A.S. (1999). Business process reengineering: A review of recent literature. *Technovation, 19*, 571-581.

Orlikowski, W. J. (1992). The duality of technology: Rethinking the concept of technology in organizations. *Organization Science, 3*(3), 398-427.

Pardo, T.A., & Scholl, H.J. (2002). Walking atop the cliffs: Avoiding failure and reducing risk in large-scale e-government projects. *Proceedings on the 35th Hawaiian International Conference on System Sciences*, Hawaii.

Poon, P., & Wagner, C. (2001). Critical success factors revisited: Success and failure cases of information systems for senior executives. *Decision Support Systems, 30*, 393-418.

Rainey, H., Backoff, R., & Levine, C. (1976). Comparing public and private organizations. *Public Administration Review, 36*(2), 233-244.

Ranganathan, C., & Dhaliwal, J.S. (2001). A survey of business process reengineering practice in Singapore. *Information and Management, 39*, 125-134.

Relyea, H.C. (2002). E-gov: Introduction and overview. *Government Information Quarterly, 19*(1), 9-35.

Sarker, S., & Lee, A.S. (1999). IT-enabled organizational transform: A case study of BPR faliure at TELECO. *Journal of Strategic Information Systems, 8*, 83-103.

Schein, E.H. (1969). *Process consultation: Its role in organizational development.* Reading, MA: Addison-Wesley.

Schein, E.H. (1985). *Organizational culture and leadership.* San Francisco: Jossey-Bass Publishers.

Schein, E.H. (1988). *Organizational culture.* Cambridge, MA: Alfred P. Sloan School of Management, Massachusetts Institute of Technology.

Schein, E.H. (1992). *Organizational culture and leadership.* San Francisco: Jossey-Bass.

Schein, E.H. (1999). *The corporate culture survival guide: Sense and nonsense about culture change.* San Francisco: Jossey-Bass.

Scholl, H.J. (2001). Applying stakeholder theory to e-government: Benefits and limits. *Proceedings of the 1st IFIP Conference on E-Commerce, E-Business, and E-Government (I3E 2001)*, Zurich, Switzerland.

Scholl, H.J. (2003). E-government: A special case of ICT-enabled business process change. *Proceedings of the 36th Hawaiian International Conference on System Sciences*, Waikoloa, Big Island, Hawaii.

Scholl, H.J. (2005). Motives, strategic approach, objectives & focal areas in e-gov-induced change. *International Journal of Electronic Government Research, 1*(1), 58-77.

Senate Budget Report: Section Four (2002). *New York State Senate.* Retrieved October 07, 2003: *www.senate.state.ny.us/docs/sfc02d.pdf*

Spender, J.C. (1996). Making knowledge the basis of a dynamic theory of the firm. *Strategic Management Journal, 17* (winter special issue), 45-62.

Stoddard, D.B., & Jarvenpaa, S.L. (1995). Business process redesign: Tactics for managing radical change. *Journal of Management Information Systems, 12*(1), 88-107.

Stohr, E.A., & Zhao, J.L. (1997). A technology adaptation model for business process automation. *Proceedings of the 30th Hawaiian International Conference on System Sciences,* Maui, Hawaii.

Symon, J. (2002). Records management across Europe. *AIM E-Doc Magazine, 16*(4), 46-47.

Waldron, M. (2002). The new business necessity. *AIM E-Doc Magazine, 16*(2), 50-53.

Walston, S.L., & Bogue, R.J. (1999). The effects of reengineering: Fad or competitive factor? *Journal of Healthcare Management, 44*(6), 456-476.

Appendix

E-Gov BPC Project Exemplar

An e-gov project exemplar with a BPC impact (in this definition) at least would situate in the transaction phase or higher (Layne & Lee, 2001). It also would span across at least two lines of command (interdepartmental, interagency, interlevel, or interbranch). Depending on who initiated it, the project initially would launch differently. If it is a bottom-up, grass-roots project (initiated, for example, by Web or IS groups, user groups, or line departments), it may live a "stealth" life for a while until the proof of concept could have been demonstrated. Once this milestone is passed, sponsorship and support from senior executives from both "sides of the channel" are sought. If the project proponents manage to win over the necessary executive sponsorship, the project inherits similar authority and legitimacy to a top-down initiated project, which marks the other case for an e-gov BPC project. As soon as the hypothesized exemplar project has obtained the executive mandate, a core project team with members from both entities involved forms. The team would engage in a project scope discussion focusing on understanding the specific business needs to be addressed. When a preliminary, joint understanding of scope and business needs within the core project team is reached, a stakeholder analysis is performed. Salient stakeholders are identified, whom the team subsequently involves in the project. Other important senior executives may be identified among those salient stakeholders, whose sponsorship also may turn out to be indispensable in the unfolding of the project. As a next step, a more detailed stakeholder-needs analysis in the context of the project's scope definition is performed. An initial change readiness assessment might or might not become part of this stakeholder-needs assessment. Change readiness assessments are not done routinely upfront in e-gov BPC projects but rather concurrently, unless evidence for their necessity appears. Equally concurrent, the project team performs assessments of business processes and resources. Along with salient stakeholders, the team charts out and presents a high-level project plan (including project objectives, problems/constraints/assumptions, chosen strategy, sequence of activities, estimate of costs and resource requirements) to senior management. Once the project is formally funded, the project team engages in a detailed workflow analysis (whereever and whenever necessary), helping raise user awareness and involvement and craft a request for information (RFI), if necessary. Since the project spans at least two separate lines of command, different perspectives and requests need to be reconciled and renegotiated throughout the project. The team also involves external expertise for knowledge transfer purposes and for complementing existing skills. With the responses from the RFI process and with the results from the internal workflow analysis in hand, the team develops a more detailed plan in which alternative solutions are presented and recommendations for a sourcing approach are formulated. Again, senior executive signoff is sought. Once the detailed project phase is funded, the recommended sourcing approach is taken and e-gov system components are deployed. At each and every step of the project, salient stakeholders remain actively involved players throughout the project's lifespan, which mitigates the risk of later non-acceptance. Sponsoring executives are periodically updated. The challenges of ERM/DLM would be addressed in a tactical fashion, since the project otherwise could stall due to the enormity of the consequences (and cost). As soon as the project concludes, and the e-gov system has become operational, the team conducts a project evaluation followed by a formal debriefing involving salient stakeholders and senior executives.

This chapter was previously published in the International Journal of Electronic Government Research, 1(2), 27-49, April-June 2005.

Chapter VI

Computer Security in Electronic Government:
A State-Local Education Information System

Alison Radl, Iowa Department of Human Services, USA

Yu-Che Chen, Iowa State University, USA

Abstract

As e-government projects proliferate at all levels of government, and as they transition from voluntary to mandatory participation, close examination is required, particularly the examination of security issues. The CIA (confidentiality, integrity, availability) model offers a framework for examining e-government projects. This study examines the factors impacting security, using as a case study an education information system in the 2003-2004 school year. The study focuses on how CIA factors relate to a host of variables, such as school district size, software selection, technology staffing, technical competence and support, awareness of security issues, and project commitment. For the organizations participating in the project, typical factors of district size and software selection are found to be insignificant, and technical support is identified as one of the key factors promoting security.

Introduction

E-government refers to the use of information and communication technology to carry out government operations such as delivering government information and services. E-government has grown in the past decade. E-government efforts can vary from Web portals to online license renewals to experimentation with online voting. E-government is generally recognized as a means of making government more efficient while allowing it to be more responsive to customer needs. The growth in e-government has been rapid. For example, in the United States, the percentage of local governments with Web sites increased from 8.7% in 1995 to over 80.0% in 2000 (Holden, Norris, & Fletcher, 2003). The numbers reached 87.7% in 2002 (Norris & Moon, 2005). Advances in information and communication technology are helping to make the growth in e-government a global phenomenon. A United Nations report shows that governments around the world are moving towards higher levels of e-government to better serve their citizens (United Nations and American Society for Public Administration, 2002). By 2004 93.0% of United Nations (U.N.) member states had a Web site and a third provided public services on-line (United Nations, 2004).

For the evaluation of e-government projects, there are a number of approaches grounded in the information systems research literature. One method calls for examining e-government projects in terms of the factors promoting implementation (Brown, O'Toole, & Brudney, 1998; Brown & Brudney, 2004; DeLone & McLean, 2003; King et al., 1994; Shaw, 2003). Adoption and user acceptance constitute another approach (Brown, 2003; Davis, 1989; Ho & Ni, 2004; Venkatesh & Davis, 2000). Some scholars focus on various aspects of administrative reform, focusing on impacts on efficiency, transparency, and accountability arising from the use of information and communication technology (Brown & Brudney, 1998; Danziger & Andersen, 2002; Ho, 2002; Moon, 2002; Pandey & Bretschneider, 1997; West, 2004).

Moreover, a wealth of studies on e-government initiatives around the world offers opportunities for comparative understanding. The United Nations has issued a report consisting of a comprehensive country-by-country account of e-government activities. The report offers advice on building institutional foundations for continuing success (UN-ASPA, 2002). The Cyberspace Policy Research Group examines the transparency, democratization, and accountability of e-government projects. Since 1995, it has examined national government Web sites around the world. Working with scholars and practitioners around the world, Heeks (2001) proposed a generic framework for developing and implementing e-government projects. He offers detailed country and project-specific case studies.

And yet among the current studies of e-government, a common theme recurs: Despite the increasing need for such research, there is a lack of comprehensive evaluations of information and computer security. Comprehensive evaluation involves assessing the confidentiality, integrity, and availability of the information under government control. While several studies have attempted to examine computer security issues (Ives, Walsh, & Schneider, 2004; Karr, Dobra, & Sansil, 2003; Pierce, 2004), they have focused only on a single aspect of computer security.

Two concurrent trends underlie the need to evaluate the security of e-government projects. First, a growing amount of confidential citizen data is being gathered through e-government projects. One prominent example in Europe is the modernization of National Health Services in England. The data spine of this e-government project will have all critical medical information of every citizen in the country. Online tax filing and employment applications are also examples of e-government initiatives that collect personal and financial information. The increase in the collection of confidential data arises in part due to the transition from voluntary to mandatory participation and requirements that lower-level governments submit electronic data to higher-level governmental offices. Second, increasing cyber-crime activities poses greater risks for e-government information systems. Statistics from the Carnegie Mellon CERT Center indicate an approximately 13-fold increase in security incidents from 1999 to 2003. Such identified widespread weaknesses pose a threat to government information systems (U.S. General Accounting Office, 2000). A 2004 survey of government and business found that over 70.0% of the respondents experienced at least one e-crime or intrusion (CERT, 2004). As more and more government and commercial activities take place online, nations around the world grow increasingly concerned about cybersecurity.

There are two main reasons why this study focuses on an education information system that requires vertical integration of government operations. First, education is one of the prominent government service areas amenable to computer security studies. Compromises in the security of confidential student information can result in dire consequences for students and their families. The reach of the education information system is far greater than that of other services covering a much smaller population segment, such as a welfare system. This study will have implications for countries around the world as more countries begin to store and disseminate student information electronically.

Second, the integration of state and local information systems is a growing focus of attention for all nations striving to provide seamless e-government services at the most mature stage of e-government. One main way to provide this kind of seamless service is through collaboration among different levels of government.

This article begins with a definition of computer security in the context of e-government, then it proposes a model for understanding how various factors affect computer security. Next, the study examines the impact of these factors on an education information system that requires vertical government collaboration. Background information about the system is also provided. These are the two main research questions: How does the information system measure in terms of confidentiality, integrity, and availability (CIA)? What are the impacts of various organizational and policy factors on CIA?

The study methodology employed in data collection and analyses followed by research findings are then detailed. This article concludes with discussions and policy recommendations.

Computer Security for E-Government

Defining Computer Security

In general, computer security has three dimensions: confidentiality, integrity, and availability, also known as the CIA model (Pfleeger, 2000; Bishop, 2002). The CIA model is a generic model for various types of organizations, and it is applicable to e-government projects. *Confidentiality* requires that information be disclosed only to authorized parties at the authorized time and in the approved manner (Denning, 2001). An authorized user who accesses a system in a manner that violates the system-use policy breaches confidentiality. Authorization policies are governed by contracts, regulations, and law. For example, the Social Security Administration of the United States is required to block unauthorized access to individual social security numbers. *Integrity* includes both the trustworthiness of the content, as well as the origin of the information (Bishop, 2002). Though content may be free from corruption, information coming from a false source can still prove problematic. Integrity can be ensured by preventing unauthorized modification of data and verifying the authenticity of information sources. For instance, the Department of Education needs access control and data verification protocols to protect the integrity of the financial data of students applying for and receiving student loans through the government.

Availability refers to the ability to access and use information or resources as desired. On the surface, availability may be excluded from the security picture. However, availability is still an important part of a secured system that is able to guard itself against denial-of-service attacks and that is able to maintain uninterrupted access to information resources. Business continuity, as embodied in the notion of availability, is particularly relevant in emergency management and critical infrastructure protection. Data should be readily available when an authorized data request has been made. Failure in this respect can result in loss of life and property on a grand scale.

Computer security should be treated holistically as a multi-dimensional construct and a comprehensive organizational endeavor. Yet, discussions on security issues in e-government projects have been limited and have tended to focus on only one aspect of security. Lauer (2004) examines the security of e-voting. Karr et al. (2003) review the importance of the confidentiality of individual identity in federal data collection systems. System-design issues with table servers have been examined in relation to the dissemination of federal data to data users. Ives et al. (2004) discuss weakness in access control due to password reuse in password protection schemes, focusing on the potential for compromised data confidentiality. Pierce (2004) discusses data integrity issues for all systems, not just e-government projects, and examines methods for reviewing data quality using control matrixes. Rees, Bandyopadhyay, and Spafford (2003) propose a framework for information security known as the policy framework for interpreting risk in e-business security (PFIRES). However, this framework was developed according to private sector experiences, and it narrowly focuses on policy development.

Model for Computer Security in E-Government

Computer security in e-government is a neglected research topic. The United States government publishes technical and evaluation reports on computer security issues, and it did so even before September 11, 2001. For instance, the information assurance directorate has published a report on the national information assurance acquisition policy. Moreover, the general accounting office has published several reports on computer information security in federal government. However, much less rigorous research has been done on the *organizational determinants* of computer security. A survey of this topic in leading peer-reviewed journals of research on information systems and public administration yields very few entries.

To fill this knowledge gap and to remedy the lack of pertinent previous research, this study draws broadly from research literature on information systems and e-government, seeking to identify key factors for computer security. The factors affecting implementation of information systems, as suggested by the literature, are particularly relevant since security can be treated as an integral part of well-functioning systems. The factors discussed below include size of organizations, technology use, staffing, security awareness, management commitment, technical competence, and technical support (Figure 1).

The first factor is the *size of organizations*. At the local government level, size plays an important role in determining the kind of e-government service and information that can be provided (Norris, Fletcher, & Holden, 2001). This may be attributed to the relation between size and availability of technical staff and resources, both of which are critical for e-government services (International City/County Manage-

Figure 1. Organizational determinants of computer security

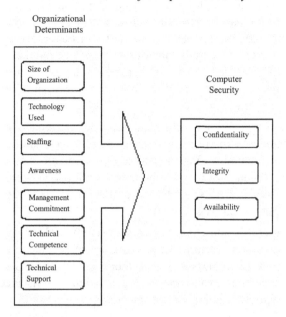

ment Association, 2001, 2002). It is hypothesized that the greater the size of an organization, the higher the level of computer security needed, due to variation in comparative resource availability.

Technology use, particularly associated with level of complexity, has been identified as one main determinant in the adoption of new information and communication technologies (Venkatesh & Davis, 2000; Venkatesh, 2000). If the technology is easier to use and has built-in security functions, it is likely that a higher level of computer security will be implemented.

Staffing is another possible source of increased computer security. Technical staff members knowledgeable in computer and cyber security are likely to bring that knowledge to their organization. The lack of technical staff has been identified as one of the main challenges for local e-government efforts (International City/County Management Association, 2002).

The organization's *awareness* of computer security issues is another critical factor. The security of information systems depends on the level of awareness of the organization and its employees, particularly in terms of the degree to which they can learn and apply critical security policies. Thus, a standard security plan usually emphasizes education and training. A high level of awareness is likely to denote a high level of computer security.

Commitment of the management is another key ingredient for success in government computer security. Top management support has been identified as one critical factor for successful adoption and implementation of information systems, particularly in the contexts of forming partnerships and outsourcing arrangements (Brown et al., 1998; Chen & Perry, 2003). Management support is critical in the implementation of changes necessary for the introduction of new practices and the maintenance of vital resources during the transition from old to new systems. Securing an information system requires that management is committed to bringing forth the change necessary for new security practices.

Technical competence is another factor that can make an impact on computer security. Lack of technical expertise is one of the main barriers to using information and communication technology in government (Melitski, 2003; Nedovic-Budic & Godschalk, 1996). Technical expertise increases confidence. It also enhances the understanding of involved risks, while, more importantly, facilitating the implementation of computer security solutions.

As a promoter of usability and security, *technical support* is likely seen as a higher level of information system security. Ease of use is a critical factor in the adoption of new information systems (Davis, 1989). Technical support eases the difficulty novice users may face in using a new system, and technical assistance may include on-site real-time support, training, or documentation.

A State-Local Education Information System

U.S. state and local governments are under increasing pressure to provide education information to the federal government. A driving legislation is the No Child Left Behind Act of 2001 that mandates states to expand their data collection. States are looking at electronic ways of collecting data to reduce the reporting requirements on school districts. State and federal laws protect against unauthorized disclosure of data collected by e-government projects, data such as individual student information. Attention to security concerns and protection of citizen data is paramount.

This midwestern state is one of the first states in the U.S. to electronically collect individual student information from districts. It therefore must address a variety of security concerns associated with such a collection. The Department of Education e-government effort requires that school districts send individual student data electronically to the department to fulfill federal and state reporting requirements. For the districts, the project is not voluntary. All public school districts in the state are required to send data through the project.

Lessons learned may be applied to states that may go through similar processes in the future. Also, the collaboration between state and local governments may prove instructive to other nations attempting to increase computer security for information systems that require teamwork among regional and local government units.

The Project: Background and Policy Issues

The project is an effort to provide the state's 370 public school districts an alternate method of completing some of their state reports. The data collected through the project used to fulfill state and federal reporting requirements, such as those stipulated by No Child Left Behind, Performance Based Data Management Initiative, and Common Core Data reports. Most districts/schools in the state use some form of student information system (SIS) to store and organize student data. Under the project, a district extracts a file from their SIS and sends it to the Department of Education to be used to complete the district's state reports.

Collecting data on students from pre-kindergarten through grade 12 presents unique privacy concerns. Since data is being collected on minors, state and federal laws are invoked. At the federal level, student data is protected by the Family Educational Rights and Privacy Act (FERPA). FERPA protects the privacy of students and parents by limiting disclosure of certain information. Schools may not disclose personally identifiable information, such as social security numbers or personal characteristics easily traceable to the student, without the consent of parents and students. There are exceptions for federal or state program purposes, but the receiving governmental agency must protect the information and not permit personal identification of students. In addition, the data must be destroyed by the collecting agency when no longer needed. Other federal laws grant additional protection to students. The Individuals with Disabilities Education Act (IDEA) protects the confidentiality of data on special education students. The National School Lunch Act of 1994 protects student information collected in conjunction with the free and reduced-price lunch program (National Forum on Education Statistics, 2004). At the state level, personal information in records regarding a student must be kept confidential.

Because of privacy regulations covering student data, strong limitations restrict who can access the data. The data may be submitted by local school districts, but the collective district data stored on the project's database, becomes the responsibility of the Department of Education. For these reasons, the Department of Education began work on creating a privacy policy in Spring 2004.

Implementation and Security Issues of the Project

The current process involves extracting a file and uploading it to the Department of Education (hereafter "Department"). If the file had been produced through Vendor

A, Vendor B template, or Vendor C information systems, then a Web-based system processes the file. If the file had been produced by another student information system, project staff processes the file manually (see Figure 2).

There are a number of weaknesses in the current system. The current data collection and project processor Web sites are encrypted by 128-bit secure-socket layer (SSL) encryption. Users must activate an updated version of a browser with appropriate security certificates. Some districts bypass the SSL encrypted upload utility and e-mail unencrypted files to the department.

The Web site is also password protected, with each district receiving a unique login and password. District passwords are not randomly generated. They follow a pattern and use existing data about the district. Passwords for department staff are less rigorous. The department does not provide security training for district or Department of Education staff. Also, programming errors have surfaced in the new project Web-based processing system. The vendor C sub-processor contained coding errors. One error changed the race variable for some students. The other error assigned courses to the wrong students in the file.

Human interaction with technology is a key factor in ensuring the security of the project system. Security features of student information systems vary from software package to software package, but the implementation of the features still depends on the user. Some student information systems are Web-based, allowing parental access to the system, while other systems are stand-alone, accessed via a single PC within the district administrative office. Some SIS systems require a login and password for access. Local districts may circumvent this feature by sharing a single login and password with all users, or by creating weak passwords. District staff may be unaware that antivirus software and firewalls are needed for the machines running

Figure 2. Current project process

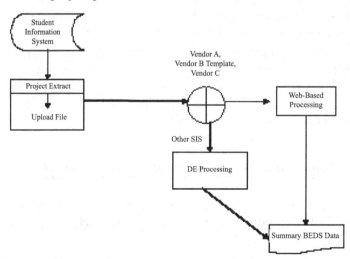

student information systems. Lack of training may make district users unaware of problems resulting from bypassing security features built into the project process, such as the SSL encrypted upload utility.

Research Model and Methodology

Research Model and Operationalization of Variables

This study of the project follows the conceptual model illustrated in Figure 1. Consequently, the selection of key factors is grounded in research literature on information systems and public administration. This section will begin with a general discussion of the three dimensions of computer security, particularly pertaining to state/local e-government education information systems. Then, specific measures for operationalizing each of the three constructs are provided. Next is a discussion on how policy and organizational characteristics are associated with computer security. These policy and organizational characteristics are then operationalized and captured by data collected from the survey.

Several main features of computer security reflect the core concepts of confidentiality, integrity, and availability. The formulation of a privacy policy would show the recognition that confidentiality is an important concern of students and their families, and would indicate the recognition that confidentiality should be protected by district staff. The implementation of confidentiality would be seen in computer security training and implementation of access control; district staff members would be able to acquire the tools necessary for helping to protect the confidentiality of student data. As for data integrity, the project would have to meet its goal of providing accurate data sets that can be used to guide educational policy. Availability refers to whether the project is able to offer comprehensive data to school districts, the state education department, and the national education agency.

Based on the previous discussion, the three dimensions of the CIA model are captured by survey questions aimed at operationalizing these factors. More specifically:

1. *Confidentiality* is measured by:
    a. whether the district had a written privacy policy regarding electronic student data;
    b. whether the district provided computer security training to district staff; and
    c. whether the district implemented additional access control to the fall 2003 data collection Web site using the Department's security utility.

2.   *Integrity* is measured by whether the district modified its fall 2003 summary data after its project file had been submitted and processed.

3.   *Availability* is measured by whether the district submitted project data for all school buildings in the district for fall 2003. If school districts submit data for all school buildings, they make all student data available.

The research model illustrated in Figure 1 suggests that size of organization, technology used, staffing, awareness, management commitment, in-house technical competence, and technical support are relevant to the three dimensions of computer security. One would expect that larger districts have resources to better meet the security requirements of confidentiality, integrity, and availability. Such districts would also be more visible and responsive to public concerns about information system security.

For such a highly technological effort as project, one expects that the type of technology used (in this case, software for student information systems) would play a key role in the participation success of the districts and their success in the security process. Some software vendors took a hands-off approach, requiring the department of education to develop the extracting features needed to pull data from the student information systems. Other vendors, such as vendor A, actively participated in the project by adding new data fields to their software and building an extracting feature to simplify the process of pulling data from SIS for transmission to the department.

Having a specialized IT staff in-house is likely to be associated with better handling of computer security requirements. The existence (or not) of a technology coordinator is used as a measure of staffing. Technical competence would be critical for district participation and successful implementation of security. Technical support helps school district staff that would otherwise have no technology training, to understand and implement information system security measures. Management commitment should be commensurate with the level of resources being devoted to ensuring computer security. A district lacking awareness of security issues would seem less likely to devote resources and time towards implementing security.

These policy and organizational characteristics are operationalized below, according to corresponding data elements and/or survey questions.

1.   *Size:* district size based on fall 2003 certified enrollment.

2.   *Software:* the student information system used in the district.

3.   *Technology coordinator:* whether district reported a technology coordinator (position code 638, on the fall 2003 Licensed Staff Detail reports).

4. *Awareness:* sum of points assigned as responses to the following prompts on sharing information with the state (maximum possible points: 15). Users rated their level of concern with certain aspects of the project system:

    a. The sharing of individual student data (i.e., student names or social security numbers) with the Department of Education;

    b. The security of a statewide student identification system; and

    c. The tracking of students over time.

5. *Commitment:* the perceived level of commitment for the district's continued participation in the project, based on the response to the following prompt: "My district was reluctant to join the project."

6. *Technical competence:* the degree of preparedness for participation in the project among district staff, based on their response to the following prompt: "I have the computer/technical knowledge needed to work with the project."

7. *Technical support:* the level of technical support perceived to be available to district staff for the project, based on the following prompt: "A district technology person is available, when needed, to assist the project team in my district."

Data Collection and Analysis

This section discusses the data collection methods and the practical aspects associated with conducting a survey of public school districts. The Department of Education has some basic information on school districts and students. However, some district data are not available from the state and can be gathered only through a district survey. Information regarding district security policies, training, awareness, commitment, and technical support are some examples of data available only at the local level.

For this project, all public school districts in the state were surveyed. A total of 388 surveys were mailed, with each district receiving at least one survey. The person responsible for submitting project data and completing state reports were designated a survey respondent. Respondents included superintendents, building administrators, district administrative staff, and technical staff. Effort has been made to send the survey to the person responsible for completing the project submission and state reports, rather than the district's official project contact person.

A paper survey has been utilized, rather than a Web-based survey, because district school staff members are often uncomfortable using the Internet, and more assistance would be required for completion of a Web-based survey. Confidentiality of answers is also easier to maintain with a paper survey. The survey has been conducted independently of the Department of Education. Surveys were returned to the Political Science Department at the State University. The survey incorporated different aspects of the project data process, using the perspectives of the school districts. The survey covers system design, ease of use, user experience, institutional incentives, management support, resource commitment, and privacy and security issues. Staff at the Center for Survey Statistics & Methodology at the State University reviewed the survey instrument and provided feedback.

Two rounds of surveys (March and April 2004) generated 246 responses out of the 388 district staff receiving the survey. This was a 63.4% response rate. Respondents included 232 districts out of a possible 370, with 12 anonymous responses. Also, the degree of involvement in the project varied among the districts responding to the survey. Some districts had been involved with the project from its inception, while others were joining it for the first time in 2004. As a result, some districts did not have experience with all aspects of the project process and, therefore, they did not respond to all survey questions.

The data analysis follows two general strategies: descriptive and statistical. First, the descriptive analysis of the survey responses helps to generate summary level results, providing a view of the education information system as a whole. Also, when organized into categories, the descriptive statistics help show the level of computer security measures implemented according to various organizational characteristics. Second, statistical testing ascertains whether a relationship exists between these factors and computer security. Since the pertinent variables are either ordinal or nominal, Chi-Square tests based on contingency tables are more appropriate than other tests that try to pinpoint relationships among variables (Meier & Brudney, 2002). Cramer's V is also calculated for all nominal variables to check the strength of associations.

Summary Level Results

The responding districts reflected the geography of the state, comprising both urban and rural districts. Districts in each of the state's 12 area education agencies were included in the responses. The responding districts varied by the size category of the district and the type of software used. All size categories were represented in the responses. The 2,500-7,499 size category produced the highest percentage of responses, and the 7,500+ category the lowest percentage of responses. There were 12 anonymous responses, and it is unclear to which size category those districts belonged.

Different student information system software packages were also reflected in the survey responses. At least one district from each of the different software categories responded to the survey. Some districts were in the process of joining the project for the first time in the 2003-2004 school year. These districts either did not have a student information system or the system information had not been entered into the project's software tables. Some districts used more than one software package. For example a district might use vendor D at the high school level and Vendor A at the elementary school level. Some districts did not have a student information system for every school in the district. For example, some alternative schools did not have a student information system in place.

Confidentiality

Confidentiality measures for the project included existence of a privacy policy, security training for staff, and password creation. Overall, 78 of the respondents (31.7%) indicated that their districts have a written privacy policy regarding electronic student data. However, 27 respondents left the question blank, and 141 respondents (57.3%) indicated that their districts do not have a written privacy policy regarding electronic student data. If the respondents that had not answered the policy question were included with the negative responses, assuming that lack of awareness of the policy is similar to having no policy, then the ratio of responding districts without a privacy policy increased to 68.3%.

Respondents who disagree or strongly disagree with the statement that their districts have provided computer security training to staff were grouped together as districts without training. Overall, 37.8% of respondents indicated that their districts did not offer computer security training. Most districts did not use the Department of Education security utility to create additional passwords, particularly for the fall 2003. Only 56 districts had created additional passwords.

Integrity

Data integrity, or accuracy, is the second feature of computer security. It can be measured in terms of the accuracy of the data collected and stored by an e-government system. Project data accuracy was measured by whether the school district made changes to the summary level data produced from their project transmission. For fall 2003, 333 districts submitted project data and 282 districts (84.7%) reported changing their summary level data for at least one report. Of the 232 survey respondents, 180 made data changes, 34 made no changes, and 18 did not submit data through the project for the fall 2003. Some districts that had not made data changes later discovered inaccuracies in the data after the deadline for making corrections had passed.

Availability

Data availability in computer security traditionally refers to the availability of the system. Are authorized users able to access the system when they need to? For the purposes of this research, availability is defined in terms of the availability of data within the system. For the project, availability refers to whether a district is sending data for all schools within the district. The fall 2003 report shows that 63.0% of the total possible schools had submitted student data through the project.

Ninety-seven of the survey respondents submitted project data for all the schools in their district. However, 118 districts had not, and 18 districts had not submitted any data through the project for fall 2003. Elementary and alternative schools were typically among those that had not sent data through the project.

Results by Organizational Characteristics

Discussion of the study results was organized according to statistical analysis. Each characteristic of the school districts was analyzed according to the three dimensions of computer security; namely, confidentiality, integrity, and availability. There are seven tables in total because each table summarizes one of seven characteristics. As discussed above, three separate measures were used to gauge confidentiality. Thus, each table consists of five columns covering three measures of confidentiality, one indicator of integrity, and one measure of availability.

Statistical tests were conducted to attempt to associate each organizational characteristic with each of the five measures of computer security. Since most of the measures are either ordinal or nominal, the Chi-square test was used to determine whether various categories are able to classify dimensions of computer security with confidence. All statements in this section on degrees of associative significance are grounded in statistical tests.

Size and CIA

Size does not have a significant relationship with any of the district characteristics. The size of the enrollment of the district does not appear to play a part in whether the district has a written privacy policy (Table 1). Over half of the responding districts in each size category did not have a written privacy policy. The largest and smallest categories have roughly equal percentages of districts without a written privacy policy.

Table 1. Size of school districts and CIA

Size	Districts Without A Privacy Policy	Districts Without Training	Districts Without Passwords	Districts with Inaccurate Data	Districts with Incomplete Data
<250	70.6%	46.7%	83.3%	81.8%	27.3%
250-399	56.7	45.5	78.8	87.5	43.8
400-599	62.5	42.2	76.1	86.1	53.5
600-999	67.2	34.4	78.5	75.0	59.4
1,000-2,499	63.6	34.0	76.0	87.0	65.2
2,500-7,499	62.5	42.1	63.2	94.1	52.9
7,500+	66.7	33.3	33.3	100.0	33.3
Total	63.9	38.9	76.1	83.8	54.6

Source: Project Survey and Certified Enrollment 2003

Similarly, district size is not significantly related to whether computer security training is offered to the district staff. Though there is no significant relationship between the size of the district and the creation of passwords, larger districts in the survey did demonstrate a higher percentage of password creation. However, additional passwords created by districts were sometimes less rigorous than those created by the Department of Education. Some passwords were common words or names that can be easily guessed.

Data accuracy and completeness are not directly linked to district size. The largest enrollment category had the highest percentage of districts changing data (100%), but each enrollment category shows at least 50.0% of districts making data changes. The largest and smallest size categories experienced a higher percentage of complete data than the other size categories. This is especially worth noting, considering that the districts in the 7,500+ category had substantially more school buildings than districts in the <250 category. For districts in the <250 category, this is intuitive. These districts typically only have one school building in their district and either send data or do not. The 1,000-2,499 category had the highest percentage of incomplete data.

Technology (Software) Use and CIA

Technology (software) also did not appear to play a factor in the district performance in the areas of confidentiality, integrity, and availability. Nearly 20 different software packages are used by school districts for student information systems. The three main systems used by districts are vendor A, vendor B, and vendor C. The remaining systems have only a small number of users. For this analysis, these systems are grouped together in the "Other" category. The software type is not

Table 2. Technology (software) use and CIA

Software	Districts without a Privacy Policy	Districts without Training	Districts without Passwords	Districts with Inaccurate Data	Districts with Incomplete Data
Vendor A	63.0%	36.1%	72.5%	82.8%	54.3%
Vendor B	71.8	43.2	81.8	81.8	61.4
Vendor C	61.9	40.9	95.7	86.4	63.6
Other	56.7	36.1	69.4	87.9	39.4
Unknown	70.0	62.5	72.7	100.0	100.0
Total	63.9	38.9	76.1	83.8	54.6

Source: Project survey and project software tables

available for a handful of districts; these districts were classified as "Unknown." The breakdown of software programs used by each of the five measures of CIA is presented in Table 2.

There is not a strong relationship between the software used in the student information systems and whether the district has a privacy policy. More than half of the districts in each category did not have a privacy policy. The difference in the percentage of school districts having a privacy policy, compared to variations in software programs used, is not statistically significant. Additionally, training does not show a significant relationship with the use of a particular software program. The percentages are very close, rendering them statistically insignificant.

While districts for all software types are unlikely to have established additional passwords, Vendor C districts stand out as the most unlikely. Only 4.3% of the vendor C districts had created additional passwords. Most software types showed roughly 80% of districts changing data after transmission. The "Unknown" category was the exception. However, this category contained the fewest responding districts.

Data accuracy is not associated with the use of a particular software program, at least based on the Chi-square test. Neither is software use statistically related to completeness of data reported to the central system. The "Other" software category is worth noting. It shows the lowest percentage for incomplete data. The larger school districts fall into this category since they tend to use specialized systems rather than the three main off-the-shelf packages. These specialized systems seem to give their users more complete data.

Staffing: Technology Coordinator

Districts were examined to determine if they had reported a technology coordinator in their fall staff reports. It was hypothesized that a technology coordinator, with

Table 3. Technology coordinator and CIA

Technology Coordinator	Districts without a Privacy Policy	Districts without Training	Districts without Passwords	Districts with Inaccurate Data	Districts with Incomplete Data
Coordinator	74.4%	41.7%	77.8%	93.0%	60.5%
No Coordinator	61.5	38.1	75.6	81.5	53.2
Total	63.9	38.9	76.1	83.8	54.6

Source: Project survey and staff file

specialized technical training and skills, would help promote computer security within the districts and facilitate participation in the project.

Interestingly, there is no statistically significant relationship between staffing a technology coordinator and various dimensions of CIA; namely privacy policy, training, passwords, and data completeness. The relationship between districts with a technology coordinator and data accuracy is significant. Districts with technology coordinators are more likely to make changes to the summary level data after their project transmission. In districts with a technology coordinator, the coordinator often extracts and sends the data, but other district staff reviews the final data for accuracy. The explanation lies in the nature of the process. Perhaps communication between the coordinator and the staff members responsible for review is limited. This would explain why staff members' corrections after data transmission were more likely.

Awareness and CIA

District awareness is measured by the total number of points scored on survey questions pertaining to the sharing of individual student data with the Department of Education. The maximum points total 15. The relationships among awareness and passwords, inaccurate data, and incomplete data are not significant. As shown in Table 4, the percentages are close for two different awareness levels.

Table 4. Awareness and CIA

Awareness (Total Points)	Districts without a Privacy Policy	Districts without Training	Districts without Passwords	Districts with Inaccurate Data	Districts with Incomplete Data
1-8	69.7%	34.8%	74.0%	86.4%	57.6%
9-15	61.3	40.6	77.0	82.7	53.3

Source: Project survey

One significant relationship is between awareness and training, but this is rather counter-intuitive. Districts with lower points for awareness are more likely to have security training for staff. Perhaps top management intervenes to counter lower levels of awareness. In contrast, the relationship between awareness and having a privacy policy seems to go in an intuitive direction. Districts scoring low on awareness are more likely to lack a privacy policy than districts receiving higher points.

Commitment and CIA

Commitment represents the district's desire to remain in the project. There is a strong relationship between commitment and training. As shown in Table 5, districts with higher levels of commitment are more likely to offer computer security training to staff. This is confirmed by a Chi-square test. Moreover, there is also a strong relationship between commitment and the creation of passwords. Perhaps such activities fall into the domain of management. Managers have a strong influence on providing security training and implementing password protection.

Technical Competence and CIA

Technical competence shows a significant relationship to security training. As illustrated in Table 6, the districts indicating adequate technical competence are more likely to offer computer security training. Perhaps technical competence can

Table 5. Management commitment and CIA

Commitment	Districts without a Privacy Policy	Districts without Training	Districts without Passwords	Districts with Inaccurate Data	Districts with Incomplete Data
Committed	62.2%	32.7%	74.8%	82.0%	53.3%
Not Committed	75.9	58.1	74.2	84.6	46.2

Source: Project survey

Table 6. Technical competence and CIA

Competence	Districts without a Privacy Policy	Districts without Training	Districts without Passwords	Districts with Inaccurate Data	Districts with Incomplete Data
Competent	62.2%	33.9%	76.4%	84.9%	54.2%
Not Competent	78.6	73.3	73.3	71.4	42.9

Source: Project survey

Table 7. Technical support and CIA

Technical Support	Districts without a Privacy Policy	Districts without Training	Districts without Passwords	Districts with Inaccurate Data	Districts with Incomplete Data
Support	66.0%	31.0%	78.4%	82.3%	57.3%
No Support	62.1	68.8	68.8	89.7	44.8

Source: Project survey

be translated into recognition of the importance of security training. If so, more computer security training would be provided. The relationships among competence and policy, passwords, and inaccurate/incomplete data are not significant.

Technical Support and CIA

The availability of technical support within the district has a significant relationship to all but one of the CIA components, based on the Chi-square test. Districts with technical support are more likely to offer computer security training. The training may be provided by the IT support personnel. The districts with technical support show a higher percentage of lack of a privacy policy and passwords. They also are more likely to have incomplete data.

Discussion and Policy Recommendations

Discussion and Future Research

Computer security is still at a relative low level of maturity in school districts. Only eight districts out of the 233 responding to the survey during the 2003-2004 school year reported having a security policy, implemented access control, and agreed/strongly agreed that their district offered computer security training. These eight districts varied in size, their awareness levels varied, and all but one did not have a technology coordinator.

Technical support appears to be an important factor for districts and computer security. Districts are facing tightened budgets and staff reductions. Non-teaching positions are often the first to be eliminated in the face of budget decreases. Alternatives for technology support for districts should be explored. Management commitment seems to play an important role in both computer training and the creation of additional passwords. This suggests the importance of management in increasing needed computer security.

The results do not offer strong statistical proof that certain other hypothesized factors have made an impact on computer security. Size of district and the actual student information system utilized by the district do not appear to relate to confidentiality, integrity, and accessibility. The exception is password creation, since larger districts are more likely to have implemented additional access control. Awareness does not appear to lead districts to taking actions that enhance computer security. Districts need assistance in converting their awareness of security issues into actions that will improve computer security.

Any generalization beyond the case presented here needs to be made with caution. Care needs to be given to similarity of information systems configuration, as well as the makeup of school districts. The state studied is a locally controlled state, and districts are allowed to select the student information system that best fits their needs. Other states have a stronger state education department that may utilize a standard or centralized student information system. The findings may be more relevant to a state-local information system with local control than to one that is centralized. Moreover, care also needs to be given to the measurement of key factors. Factors measured should be conceptually equivalent to ensure cross-case comparison.

This study is a first step in conducting empirical investigations of computer security in e-government settings, particularly in the context of a state-local information system. To develop a more general model, future research can examine similar state-local arrangements in other public service areas and other states. The goal should be to identify the organizational and policy variables that are critical for enhanced computer security. Another research avenue involves collecting longitudinal data to shed light on how computer security matures over time. Such a study would not only provide a snapshot view, but also longitudinal data that would offer insight into which factors can move computer security to higher levels of maturity. For all future studies, there should be a common effort at gaining meaningful comparisons and accumulation of knowledge. There must be careful treatment, development, and measurement of key factors.

Policy Recommendations

Policy recommendations should be understood in the context of the project. Yet, the recommendations may also prove relevant for other e-government projects similar in system configuration and organizational characteristics. In the area of security and privacy, a general privacy/data management policy would be quite useful. Since most of the school districts do not have a privacy policy, a standard policy developed by the state for the school districts would be helpful. The policy should outline the appropriate uses of student data and the protections implemented to ensure confidentiality, integrity, and availability. In addition, the department should develop a draft privacy policy for use by school districts.

State governments need to make sure that technical support is available to local government for computer security. The research findings suggest that technical support is arguably the most important factor in computer security at the district level. Various actions can make the level of technical support higher in school districts. First, there can be collaboration with intermediaries such as regional education organizations. This can offer support to small school districts lacking funding to hire internal staff. Second, there can be training via teleconferencing, with online documentation support. For example, the Bureau could work with the Information Technology Unit to develop a computer security-training program that can be used internally at the Department of Education and within school districts.

To raise awareness and technical competence, education and training are critical. One possibility is to have school district teleconferences dedicated to computer security training. Included in the training topics should be access control and the creation of addition passwords for district staff. Emphasis should be placed on the importance of using the SSL encrypted upload utility, as preferable to e-mailing unencrypted data to the department.

Integrity of data is an important aspect of computer security. State government can stress the incentives for quality control at the local government level. For student information systems, state governments can emphasize the link between funding and data accuracy. Data accuracy is becoming increasingly important. Moreover, state governments can improve district data accuracy by providing directions on ways to improve data accuracy. By illustrating to the districts how data sent through the project compares to final data certified by the districts, the department can help districts better understand the relationship between what gets entered into the student information system and what gets reported to the department.

Postscript

The original study covered the 2003-2004 school year and the project continued to adapt and change since that time. By the 2005-2006 school all student information system extracts were processed using the Web-based processing system. Although districts utilized the Web-based processor manual intervention by Department of Education staff was still necessary for many extracts to successfully complete processing. Districts continued to modify their student level data after it was sent to the Department of Education to correct errors and omissions in the original data submissions. The Department of Education formed an advisory group with the regional education organizations in the state to discuss data quality. The Department of Education offered a computer security training session to districts for the first time in spring 2006.

References

Bishop, M. (2002). *Computer security: Art and science*. Boston: Addison-Wesley.

Brown, M. M. (2003). Technology diffusion and the "knowledge barrier": The dilemma of stakeholder participation. *Public Performance and Management Review, 26*(4), 345-359.

Brown, M. M., & Brudney, J. L. (1998). A "smarter, better, faster, and cheaper" government: Contracting and geographic information systems. *Public Administration Review, 58*(4), 335-345.

Brown, M.M. & Brudney, J.L. (2004). Achieving Advanced Electronic Government Services Opposing Environmental Constraints. *Public Performance and Management Review, 28*(1), 96-113.

Brown, M. M., O'Toole, L. J., & Brudney, J. L. (1998). Implementing information technology in government: An empirical assessment of the role of local partnership. *Journal of Public Administration Research and Theory, 8*(4), 499-525.

CERT Coordination Center (2004). *2004 E-Crime Watch Survey Summary of Findings*. Pittsburgh, PA: CERT Software Engineering Institute.

Chen, Y-C., & Perry, J. (2003). Outsourcing for e-government: Managing for success. *Public Performance & Management Review, 26*(4), 404-421.

Danziger, J., & Anderson, K. (2002). The impacts of information technology on public administration: An analysis of empirical research from the "golden age" of transformation. *International Journal of Public Administration, 25*(5), 591-627.

Davis, F. (1989, September). Perceived usefulness, perceived ease of use, and user acceptance of information technology. *MIS Quarterly, 13*(3), 319-339.

DeLone, W., & McLean, E. (2003, Spring). The DeLone and McLean model of information systems success: A ten-year update. *Journal of Management Information Systems, 19*(4), 9-30.

Denning, D. (2001). *Information warfare and security*. New York: Addison-Wesley.

Heeks, R. (Ed.). (2001). *Reinventing government in the information age: International practice in IT-enabled public sector reform*. London; New York: Brunner-Routledge.

Ho, A. T -K. (2002). Reinventing local governments and the e-government initiative. *Public Administration Review, 62*(4), 434-44.

Ho, A. T -K., & Ni, A. Y. (2004). Explaining the adoption of e-government features: A case study of Iowa County treasurers' offices. *American Review of Public Administration, 34*(2), 164-80.

The Family Educational Rights and Privacy Act (FERPA), 20 U.S.C. §1232g. Family Educational Rights and Privacy Act Regulations, 34 CFR Part 99. FERPA Online Library, U.S. Department of Education: http://www.ed.gov/offices/OM/fpco/ferpaonline.html

Holden, S., Norris, D., & Fletcher, P. (2003, June). Electronic government at the local level progress to date and future issues. *Public Performance & Management Review, 26*(4), 325-344.

International City/County Management Association (2001). *Electronic Government 2000 Survey Dataset.* Washington, DC: International City/County Management Association.

International City/County Management Association (2002). *Electronic Government 2002 Survey Dataset.* Washington, DC: International City/County Management Association.

Ives, B., Walsh, K., & Schneider, H. (2004, April). The domino effect of password reuse. *Communications of the ACM, 47*(4), 75-78.

Karr, A., Dobra, A., & Sansil, A. (2003, January). Table servers protect confidentiality in tabular data releases. *Communications of the ACM, 46*(1), 57- 58.

King, J. L., Gurbaxani, V., Kraemer, K., McLean, W., Raman, K. S., & Yap, C. S. (1994). Institutional factors in information technology innovation. *Information Systems Research, 5*(2), 139-169.

Lauer, T. W. (2004). The risk of e-voting. *Electronic Journal of e-Government, 2*(3), 177-186.

Meier, K., & Brudney, J. (2002). *Applied statistics for public administration.* Belmont, CA: Wadsworth Group/Thomson Learning.

Melitski, J. (2003). Capacity and e-government performance: An analysis based on early adopters of Internet technologies in New Jersey. *Public Performance and Management Review, 26*(4), 376-90.

Moon, M. J. (2002). The evolution of e-government among municipalities: Rhetoric or reality. *Public Administration Review, 62*(4), 424-33.

National Forum on Education Statistics (2004, March). *Forum guide to protecting the privacy of student information: State and local education agencies.* Washington, DC: National Forum on Education Statistics.

Nedovic-Budic, Z., & Godschalk, D. R. (1996). Human factors in adoption of geographic information systems: A local government case study. *Public Administration Review, 56*(6), 554 67.

Norris, D. F., Fletcher, P. D., & Holden, S. H. (2001). *Is your local government plugged in? Highlights of the 2000 electronic government survey.* University of Maryland, Baltimore County.

Norris, D. F., & Moon, M. J. (2005). Advancing e-government at the grassroots: Tortoise or hare? *Public Administration Review, 65*(1), 64-75.

Pandey, S. K., & Bretschneider, S. (1997). The impact of red tape's administrative delay on public organizations' interest in new information technologies. *Journal of Public Administration Research and Theory, 7*(1), 113-30.

Pfleeger, C. (2000). *Security in computing* (2nd ed.). Upper Saddle River, NJ: Prentice Hall.

Pierce, E. (2004, February). Assessing data quality with control matrixes. *Communications of the ACM, 47*(2), 82-86.

Rees, J., Bandyopadhyay, S., & Spafford, E. (2003, July). PFIRES: A policy framework for information security. *Communications of the ACM, 46*(7), 101-106.

Shaw, N. (2003). Identifying relationship among factors in IS implementation. *Communications of the Association for Information Systems, 11*, 155-165.

United Nations. (2004). *Global E-Government Readiness Report 2004 towards access for opportunity*. New York: United Nations.

United Nations and American Society for Public Administration (2002). *Benchmarking e-government: A global perspective*. New York: United Nations and American Society for Public Administration.

United States General Accounting Office (2000). *Federal information security: Actions needed to address widespread weaknesses*. Statement of Jack Brock, Jr., Director, Governmentwide and Defense Information Systems; Accounting and Information Management Division. Washington, DC: United States General Accounting Office.

Venkatesh, V. (2000). Determinants of perceived ease of use: Integrating control, intrinsic motivation, and emotion into the technology acceptance model. *Information Systems Research, 11*(4), 342-65.

Venkatesh, V., & Davis, F. (2000, February). A theoretical extension of the technology acceptance model: Four longitudinal studies. *Management Science, 46*(2), 186-204

West, D. (2004). E-government and transformation of service delivery and citizen attitudes. *Public Administration Review, 64*(1), 15-27.

Endnote

[1]   We express gratitude to Dwight Ink for the generous award that covered the cost of the project survey.

Chapter VII

Measuring and Explaining the Quality of Web Sites in the (Virtual) House of Representatives

Kevin M. Esterling, University of California, Riverside, USA

David M. J. Lazer, Harvard University, USA

Michael A. Neblo, Ohio State University, USA

Abstract

To date, research on e-government has devoted relatively little attention to how legislators use the Internet to enhance the representative function. In this chapter, we develop a general method to evaluate the quality of legislative Web sites and apply the method to the Web sites of members of the U.S. House of Representatives. We use a dichotomous latent variable model that combines a measurement model with a structural model to explain the variation in the quality of Web sites. We find the correlates of high quality Web sites include shorter tenure in office and closer electoral margin; the percentage of constituents who are connected to the Internet; and higher socio-economic status of the district. We propose this latent variable measurement approach as a general method for estimating the quality of Web sites for e-government research.

Introduction

As Richard Fenno demonstrates in his landmark work, *Home Style: House Members in Their Districts*, Members of Congress tend to be very good at interacting with constituents face-to-face. Digital interaction, however, is inherently new terrain for many Members, and any new activity entails uncertainty and risk. Furthermore, implementing and making effective use of innovations requires new knowledge and new operating procedures. As a consequence, adoption of Web technologies is neither automatic nor effortless. As Dawes, Bloniarz, and Kelly (1999, p. 21) write, "Throughout our history, developments in technology have emerged much faster than the evolution of organizational forms."

Communication between legislators and constituents is fundamental to effective democratic representation, and devising the institutional means for citizen/legislator communication stands as one of the core and persistent problems in the practice of democracy. A legislator needs information about the preferences, ideals, norms, and beliefs of her constituents in order to do her job well. Similarly, citizens need information about the actions and decisions of their representative in order to maintain appropriate accountability. But as national problems become more complex, and as the political process grows more and more dominated by experts and organized groups, it is becoming more difficult for interested citizens to understand the very meaning of government action, much less to find an effective voice in the process.

Recent developments in interactive information technology create new possibilities for establishing communication links between citizens and their representative. Bianco (1994) has shown that when citizens have better knowledge of the hard choices Congress often has to make, and the rationale legislators have for making them, many citizens may reinvest their trust in government. The widespread adoption and use of Web-based technologies among citizens creates the potential for greater citizen participation in, and knowledge and trust of, their government (Chadwick, 2006; Hamlett, 2002; Shane, Muhlberger, & Cavalier, 2004). Web technologies in principle allow citizens access to the government irrespective of their geographic proximity to the seat of government, and increasingly, irrespective of their wealth and educational level (Thurber & Campbell, 2003). Wisely used, the Internet may re-connect citizens and Congress in very meaningful ways.

Much of the scholarly research on e-government throws a cautionary light, however, on strong assertions of techno-optimism. Studies of politics and the Internet, for example, suggest the impact of the Internet has been to reinforce existing tendencies of citizens (Norris, 2002), and to create a "winner take all" system of information dissemination to citizens (Hindman, 2004). Further, e-government rarely reaches its theoretical potential, in large part because of the constraints of existing processes in government (Fountain, 2001; West, 2005). A recent study by the Congressional Management Foundation (CMF, 2003) found that over the past few years many representatives in the U.S. Congress have greatly improved the quality of their official Web sites in a variety of ways, but there is still a large disparity among the offices. Some members of Congress have high quality Web sites, while others have yet to take full advantage of the capabilities for communication that the Internet has to offer (CMF, 2003). It is thus an open question how much the Internet can affect the representative process, and whether members will seize this opportunity even if it can.

In this chapter, we examine the correlates of the adoption of effective Web sites in the U.S. House of Representatives. Our central question focuses on the determinants of the quality of legislators' Web sites. One major challenge in the study of online representation, and for e-government research of Internet practices more generally, is devising a measure of the intrinsic quality of Web sites useful for statistical analysis. In the next section, we outline a measurement model approach that makes use of relevant coded indicators of the quality of sites, and combine this measurement model with a structural model to uncover the political and institutional correlates for the adopting best practice Web sites among members of Congress.

Statistical Analysis: Measuring and Explaining the Quality of Web Sites

The House of Representatives is a unique laboratory for understanding the effective use of information technologies in the public sector. Congressional offices are 440 small, functionally identical, public organizations with a set of policy and procedural outputs (Salisbury & Shepsle, 1981). This enables a large N statistical study of innovation adoption and Internet practices of representatives. In this section, we develop measurement models to uncover the intrinsic quality of legislators' Web sites. We combine the measurement models with a structural model to test standard political science expectations that the behaviors of Members of Congress can be explained by recent electoral experience, district characteristics, and institutional resources (e.g., Fenno, 1978). The statistical study yields a portrait of the incentives for the adoption of best practice Web page innovations in the online legislature.

It is a common problem in social science that researchers wish to examine theoretical constructs that are difficult if not impossible to measure directly. It is difficult to directly measure the intrinsic quality of a Web site, but it is relatively easy to code attributes that one would expect a high quality legislative Web site to have. A measurement model is useful when one has several measured or observed indicators of a latent or unmeasured trait. In this chapter we develop measurement models of Web site quality that rely on latent variable modeling techniques, where we regress a set of related indicator variables on an unobserved latent quality factor. The measurement model estimates weights (or factor coefficients) that link the observed indicators to the unobserved trait. In turn, in the structural model we regress the latent variable on exogenous correlates to test hypotheses regarding the determinants of legislators' Web site quality. Figure 1 illustrates the measurement and structural models.

We first introduce the variables that we use for the measurement models and the structural models, and then we describe the statistical methods for estimation.

Figure 1. Specification of the measurement models

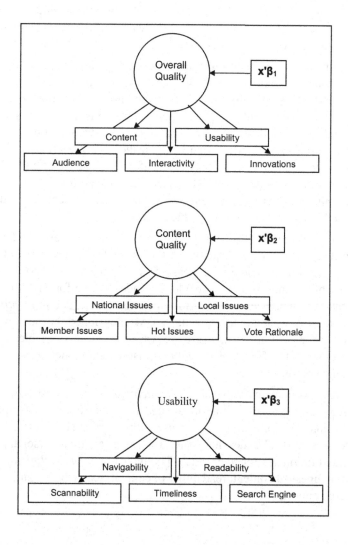

Measurement Model Variables

In 2002, the Congressional Management Foundation (CMF) evaluated each Web site of the U.S. House of Representatives based on 37 operational criteria (see Johnson 2004). The criteria tapped into what makes for a high quality legislative Web site in the normative sense—whether the Web site performs basic representative functions of communicating information that citizens want to see on Web sites, and information the member wants constituents to know. CMF identified the criteria using a number of sources: asking focus groups of citizens to spend time on a sample of sites, interviews and surveys with office staff and citizens, as well as Web industry research on usability. (For more detail on the coding see Appendix 1.) Some criteria, for example rationales for key votes and issue information, were measured on a 0–5 point ordinal scale, while others like voting records and the presence of a search engine were measured on a binary scale, receiving a "1" if the site had the feature, and a "0" if it did not. These coded variables are described in the Appendix.

CMF grouped substantively related criteria into five categories relevant to the online representative function: *audience*, *content*, *interactivity*, *usability*, and *innovations*. The *audience* indicators tap into whether the Web site provides information in a manner appropriate to different groups of citizens, both constituents and DC elites. The *content* indicators include voting records and rationales for important votes, substantive issue information, and information about the district. *Interactivity* includes such things as e-townhalls, bulletin boards, Webforms, email newsletter signups, and the like. *Usability* includes items like navigability, readability, and scannability (see www.usability.gov), and *innovation* is based on an assessment of whether the site has unusual features that provides value to the site.

We use these data to construct three separate measurement models. We first wish to create a measure of the overall quality of Web sites, but a measurement model with 37 indicators is too unwieldy. To measure overall quality, we first reduce the dimensionality of the indicators to five additive indexes, one for each of the five quality dimensions, *audience, content, usability, interactivity,* and *innovations*. To construct the indexes, we make use of weights CMF developed for the importance of each attribute for each dimension (see the Appendix for the variables for each and the priority weights). The *overall quality* measurement model takes these five indexes as indicator variables.

We then create measurement models for the *content quality* and for the *usability* of members' Web sites making use of the unweighted indicator variables corresponding to each dimension. The indicators of *content quality* were the extent to which the member discusses national issues, hot issues, issues that are their personal priority, local issues, and rationales for their votes. The indicators of *usability* are ease of navigation, timeliness of content, readability of content, scannability, and the presence of a search engine.

Structural Model Variables

The explanatory variables in the model are derived from the behavioral literature on the incentives and constraints for members of the U.S. Congress, including measures of the electoral situation, the local district situation, and the intra-institutional situation. Table 1 provides the summary data for the independent variables.

It is well known that members of Congress generally seek re-election (Mayhew, 1974). In the model we include two variables that tap into the member's electoral situation. *Tenure in office:* Members gain greater electoral security with longer tenure in office due to the well-known incumbent advantages (Jacobson, 1987). Members with longer tenures in office have fewer incentives to seek out innovative ways to interact with constituents than those with shorter tenures. In addition, Members with longer tenures are more likely to have well-established ways of communicating with constituents (Arnold, 2004). *Margin of previous electoral victory:* Those with narrower victories have more powerful incentives to reach out to constituents in every manner possible (Arnold, 2004).

The institutional context within Congress also can create advantages and disadvantages for members to undertake new initiatives. The political parties in Congress help to organize and promote the adoption and use of IT among their members. We expect that for historical reasons the two parties in the House will have different capacities to promote the adoption of Web-based technologies among their members, and we include the political party variable to capture any difference. *Political party:* This is a dichotomous variable coded 1 if the Member is a Republican, and 0 otherwise.

Representation inherently requires attention to district needs and interests. In the model we use state level measures for these variables, which will serve as rough measures of district characteristics. *Percent of households in the state with Internet connections* measures the capacity and the interest of citizens to use online services and to contact their member through Web sites, where for the average state, 50% of the households have an Internet connection as of 2002 (NTIA, 2002). *Manufacture of electronic equipment in the state (dollars per capita).* Organized interest group politics often drives members' choices (Jacobson, 1987), and the amount of production of electronic equipment serves as a proxy for industry demand for technology-driven, online representation.

We also include measures of the demographics of the district. Here we are interested in seeing if the digital divide is reproduced in Congress. We include *Median income of the district* to measure the relative income of the district (Arnold, 2004). We also include *Per capita gross state product* (in millions of dollars for year 2000) to capture contextual effects on the assumption that districts located in wealthier states benefit from positive externalities and redistributive polices. We also include a measure of the *Percentage of the district that is African American.*

Table 1. Summary statistics for the independent variables

	N.	Mean	SD	20th percentile	80th percentile
Tenure (# of terms)	436	5.52	3.83	2	9
Margin in Previous Election	437	68.88	13.55	58	77
Percent of State Households Connected to the Internet	433	50.43	5.17	46.9	55.3
Elec. Equip. Manuf. ($ per capita)	433	802	785	321	1364
Political Party (Republican = 1)	440	.497	.500	---	---
Gross State Product ($ per capita)	433	35602	11466	31182	39267
Percent of District African American	435	11.8	15.7	2.1	17.8
Median Income of District	435	36020	9306	28591	43375

Statistical Method

The statistical models combine a measurement model for Web site quality with a structural model that regresses measured quality on exogenous covariates. For each measurement model, we specify a link function and distribution for regressing the indicator variables on the latent variable, with the constraint that the latent variable can take on one of two values or "classes": low quality and high quality. Simultaneously, we regress the dichotomous latent variable on a vector of exogenous covariates in a structural model using a logit distribution. In the analysis, the parameters of the measurement model and the structural model are estimated simultaneously in a single likelihood function (see Skrondal & Rabe-Hesketh, 2004).

More formally, for the *Overall quality* model, label the observed variables as follows: audience O_1, content O_2, usability O_3, interactivity O_4, and innovations O_5. We specify the following identity link functions for each indicator:

$$O_i = d_i + \lambda_i \eta_1 + \varepsilon_i \quad \text{for i = 1 to 5} \tag{1}$$

Assume that each O is distributed normally. We set $\lambda_1 = 1$ for identification. In addition, only one level 1 error variance is identified, so assume

$$\varepsilon_i \sim N(0,\theta) \quad \text{for i = 1 to 5}$$
$$E(\varepsilon_i \varepsilon_{i'}) = 0 \quad \text{for i} \neq i' \tag{2}$$

Assume the latent variable can take on one of two values, e_1 for low quality Web sites and e_2 for high quality Web sites, with corresponding prior probabilities π_1 and π_2. Set

$$\sum_{c=1}^{2} \pi_c e_c = 0$$

for identification. Further assume that the prior probability that a legislator's Web site falls into the higher class follows a logistic distribution

$$\pi_c = \frac{1}{1 + e^{x\beta}}$$

To ease interpretation of the estimated coefficients β, we standardize all continuous variables with zero mean and unit variance, so that a one unit change for a continuous variable is a standard deviation, and a one unit change for a dichotomous variables compares the zero to the one category. In this case, the marginal percent change in probability for a one unit difference for any variable is given by $1-\exp(\beta)$, where the difference is from the mean for continuous variables.

The structural coefficients $\{\beta\}$, latent class locations $\{e\}$, and latent class probabilities $\{\pi\}$ are estimated using maximum likelihood estimation. We estimate all models using the GLLAMM software (available at gllamm.org). The standard errors for all marginal percent changes and linear combinations are approximated using the delta method as implemented in the Stata statistical software.

The estimation of the *usability* and the *content quality* models proceeds in a similar fashion, with two exceptions. First, we dichotomize the 6-category indicator variables to reduce measurement error, with the cut point in each case between 3 and 4. We then specify a binomial distribution with probit link for each dichotomous indicator. While dichotomizing the indicator variables reduces variability, there is a net increase in efficiency since dichotomizing allows us to substitute a probit for an ordered probit link function, reducing the number of estimated parameters by 25 in each model. Second, each equation in the measurement model has probit variability rather than an additive error term.

Results

Tables 2 and 3 give the results of the statistical estimations.

Table 2. Intercepts and factor coefficients for the measurement models

	Intercept	Factor Coefficient
Overall Model		
Audience	-0.082* (0.068)	1 (0)
Content	-0.083* (0.065)	0.941* (0.076)
Usability	-0.073* (0.061)	0.838* (0.074)
Interactivity	-0.047* (0.053)	0.649* (0.075)
Innovations	-0.057* (0.057)	0.738* (0.075)
Usability Model		
Ease of Navigation	-0.724* (0.105)	1 (0)
Timeliness of Content	-0.479* (0.078)	0.614* (0.097)
Readability	-0.924* (0.175)	1.526* (0.232)
Scannability	-1.259* (0.254)	1.596* (0.297)
Search Engine	-0.639* (0.068)	0.252* (0.085)
Content Model		
Member Issues	-0.825* (0.113)	1 (0)
Hot Issues	-1.548* (0.137)	0.780* (0.119)
National Issues	-1.337* (0.151)	1.118* (0.163)
Local Issues	-1.223* (0.121)	0.824* (0.108)
Vote Rationale	-1.870* (0.163)	0.644* (0.118)

*$p<0.05$

Table 2 reports the intercepts and the factor coefficients for all three measurement models. The factor coefficients are all positive and statistically significant, and most are of similar magnitude. This indicates that each indicator variable has similar weight in determining quality along the different dimensions. The reliability of the overall quality measurement model is 0.43. The intercepts are all statistically significant and negative, which shows that Web sites of average quality ($\eta=0$) tend to score relatively low on the indicator variables. In other words, the average quality of Web sites tends to be low by the CMF coding standards.

Table 3. Marginal percent change in probability of high quality Web site

	Overall	Usability	Content
Percent Households Connected to Internet	0.170 (0.136)	0.114 (0.131)	**0.341°** (0.107)
Previous Margin of Victory	-0.142 (0.159)	**-0.274°** (0.169)	0.042 (0.140)
Tenure	**-0.635°** (0.241)	**-0.319°** (0.161)	**-0.512°** (0.257)
Median Income	0.142 (0.126)	-0.063 (0.147)	0.033 (0.147)
Republican (1=yes, 0=otherwise)	0.232 (0.203)	-0.019 (0.249)	0.292 (0.194)
Percent African American	-0.447 (0.306)	-0.137 (0.165)	-0.234 (0.238)
Electronic Equipment Manuf. (dollars per capita)	**0.273°** (0.121)	**0.210°** (0.102)	0.046 (0.111)
Gross State Product (dollars per capita)	-0.157 (0.216)	0.044 (0.171)	-0.106 (0.213)

°$p<0.05$

Cells give the percent change in probability from changing the row variable by one unit (one standard deviation from the mean for continuous variables), holding all other variables constant. Standard errors of percent changes in parentheses, approximated using the delta method

Table 3 reports the estimated effects from the structural models. The cells give the marginal percent change in the probability that a typical member has a high quality Web site that counterfactually would occur if one were to change the row variable one unit from the mean (one standard deviation for continuous variables), holding all other variables constant at their mean.

The variables measuring members' electoral situation, not surprisingly, generally have a strong and robust effect on the overall quality of members' Web sites. The most robust finding is the effect of tenure, or years of service, on the quality of Web sites across all three measurement dimensions. Increasing tenure by one standard deviation from the mean, approximately four terms or eight years, decreases the probability of a member falling into the high quality class for overall quality by nearly 64%, for content quality by over 50%, and for usability by over 30%. The result is robust and is largely expected since seniority helps to confer a member an incumbency advantage, and at the same time members with a longer tenure in office will have established standard operating procedures for communicating with constituents.

In addition, we find that margin of victory affects usability. Decreasing the margin of victory by one standard deviation from the mean (or by about 14%) increases the probability that a member has a highly usable Web site by about 27%. This result also is not surprising since the re-election incentive is strong, and one would expect members desire to improve communication with their constituents if they are in competitive districts. Perhaps more surprising is that having a narrow margin of victory does not appear to affect the quality of the issue-based content on a member's site; the coefficient in the content quality model is positive but is swamped by its standard error. Combining these two results suggests that members with narrow margins are risk averse: they attempt to improve communication through better usability without risking communication that offends potential voters by posting specific content. A distinctive but important feature of Web sites is, currently, the content cannot be tailored to individual audiences, and members with narrow margins may wish to exercise the virtues of ambiguity when it comes to issue content.

We include several variables in the model that measure the demand and the capacity for local constituents to gain access to their member's Web site. The percent of households in the state that are connected to the Internet is a measure of the individual-level constituent capacity to access the member's Web site, and also a proxy for the demand among constituents for Web-based information and services. We find this measure, controlling for the member's margin of victory, tends to drive issue-based content. Increasing the percent of citizens connected by one standard deviation (or about 5%) increases the probability that the member's Web site has high quality content by about 34%. To measure the demand for technology-based communication among local organized interests and firms, we include a measure of the total output in the electronic equipment manufacturing sector, normalized by the state population. We find that increasing the per capita production of electronic equipment (our proxy for high tech local industry) by one standard deviation above the mean increases the probability that the member has an overall high quality Web site by about 27% and increases usability by about 21%.

Adler, Gent, and Overmeyer, (1998) found that Republicans are more likely to have setup homepages in the early days of adoption on the Hill. Thus, we had expected to find that Republican have an advantage in quality given their longer experience with e-government. We find that the party variable has a large and positive point estimate in the overall and the content quality models, consistent with the Adler findings, but there is insufficient power in the statistical model to distinguish the effects from zero.

We assumed that we would find the digital divide reproduced in Congress, and indeed we find some evidence that the Web sites for poor and minority districts are of relatively worse quality. The point estimates for district median income and percent African American are large in several of the models but not significant at conventional levels in any of the models. Given that race and income go hand-in-hand, there is some collinearity among these variables, and the joint effect of the two variables combined reaches statistical significance in the overall quality model. Increasing the percent black and decreasing median income, each by one standard deviation from the mean, decreases the overall quality of members' Web sites by a whopping 69%, although the statistical evidence for this remains weak (p = 0.09).

In the other two measurement models, he combined effect of race and income is not nearly as dramatic and does not reach statistical significance.

Discussion

These cross sectional findings confirm the expectations given in the political science literature (see Arnold, 2004) on U.S. congressional behavior: the quality of members' Web sites, as in other decisions, is heavily dependent, in predictable ways, on the member's political and institutional situation.

On "the electoral connection" side, necessity appears to be the mother of invention when it comes to adopting Web-based innovations among members of Congress. It seems quite natural that a narrow victory would intensify a member's incentives to extend his or her "advertising, position-taking, and credit-claiming" activities to a high quality Web presence (Mayhew, 1974). Nearly all of the Web sites carry the member's picture and biography, the beginning of any good campaign to advertise a person. We find however that members with narrow margins tend to improve the usability of their Web sites, but do not necessarily increase the amount of issue-related content. Taken together, the estimates suggest a dilemma for members with narrow margins: these members likely wish to improve communication with constituents, but are reluctant to place content on their Web site that may offend potential voters. This calls attention to the distinctiveness of the Web site as a forum for representation, since members cannot tailor the content of the Web site to different audiences as they can when meeting with constituents in a face-to-face setting.

Shorter tenure contributed to higher quality Web sites in all three measurement models, even controlling for margin of victory. There are several possible interpretations of this result. First, it is possible that there is still a kind of electoral security connection beyond margin of victory. That is, there may be more variance in margins of victory early in one's career (or just less information) leading to a kind of risk-averse discounting of a freshman's wide margin of victory. Second, the tenure effect might be driven by institutional factors. Since members with lower seniority have fewer institutional roles and powers, they tend to focus more on constituent services. Such services are featured prominently on many Web sites. Third, new members will be setting up their Web sites from scratch and thus may benefit from more recent "best practices" before routinization and office inertia set in. Finally, tenure may be proxying for some mechanisms associated with age (e.g., younger people being more comfortable with technology). Because of co-linearity issues, this last possibility is difficult to tease out, but in future research we plan to identify the precise mechanism or mechanisms driving the significant tenure effect.

So far we have discussed "supply side" determinates of high quality sites. Turning to the "demand side," we find local determinants of the demand for computer-mediated interaction with one's elected representatives. First, we find that increasing high tech industry presence enhances the usability of Web sites, with members possibly meeting technical expectations or standards of local industry. Second, we find that controlling for margin of victory and tenure, increasing the percent of citizens with Web connections enhances the quality of the issue-based content of members' sites. The dynamics around this latter variable should become more interesting over time. As Web connections go the way of the telephone—i.e., from a luxury to a nearly universal household feature—the decrease in variance for this variable will presumably cause it to lose predictive power. However, it is possible that the effect is capturing something more than merely the raw possibility for accessing Web sites, such as the characteristics of individuals and districts that adopted technology early (controlling for income and local tech industry). The search will then be on to find indicators for these other possible effects.

The evidence for the reproduction of the digital divide within Congress is somewhat mixed. We find weak evidence that districts that are disproportionately poor and minority have lower quality Web sites, but we do not find evidence for this difference in any of the measurement models. If the divide indeed does exist in Congress, it appears to operate at only in a diffuse manner or at very general levels.

Conclusion

In sum, we argue that the determinants of Web-based innovations among congressional offices presented in this chapter generally comport well with predictions generated out of previous research into "pre-Web" domains of congressional behavior (exemplified by Mayhew [1974] and Fenno [1978]). It also integrates nicely with research into the very early days of congressional e-government (Adler et al., 1998; Owen, Davis, & Strickler, 1999). Both "supply side" variables that tap members' motivational incentives, such as tenure and the margin of victory, and "demand side" variables that tap constituent and industry interests behave as predicted.

Thus, the cross sectional study shows that adoption of Web site features that enhance the quality of online representation is not haphazard, but is often a purposeful response to a member's political situation. So where do we go from here? The static nature of our cross-sectional analysis, while interesting and informative, does not answer other important questions regarding the diffusion and use of digital technologies inside of Congress. What is the specific process of diffusion of Web-based innovations? Do members with better quality Web sites also make better use of feedback from constituents in their offices? Do members themselves monitor and evaluate the effectiveness of their Web sites, and further, do they use such feedback to modify and improve the quality of their Web-based representation?

These considerations suggest that future studies of Web-based innovations require combined quantitative/qualitative and dynamic analyses to identify the mechanisms behind, and impact of, adopted technologies. In combination with the research presented here, such studies will help political scientists and e-government researchers better understand what is rapidly becoming the most common mode of interaction between citizens and their elected representatives. And this academic knowledge can, in turn, be deployed by practitioners to facilitate more and better representation. Thus, we can say, without hyperbole, that the Web and its progeny are almost certain to prove a key nexus for any normatively ambitious 21st-century democracy.

Acknowledgments

An earlier version of this chapter was presented at dg.o2004, the National Conference on Digital Government Research, Seattle, Washington, May 24-26, 2004, and subsequently published in "Home (Page) Style: Determinates of the Quality of House Members' Websites," *International Journal of Electronic Government Research*, 1(2), 50-63, 2005. The authors would like to thank the Congressional Management Foundation and Scott Adler for the use of their data; Michael Hannon, a graduate student at OSU for research assistance; Kathy Goldschmidt and Rick Shapiro for their direct intellectual contributions to this chapter; for insightful comments from Paul Herrnson; Richard Niemi; three anonymous reviewers from the program committee for the dg.02004 conference; and three additional anonymous reviewers for the *International Journal of Electronic Government Research* review process. We also acknowledge generous support for this research from National Science Foundation grants 0131923 and 0429365. Any opinions, findings, and conclusions or recommendations expressed in this chapter are those of the authors and do not necessarily reflect the views of CMF or the NSF. For updates on this research, visit http://www.ksg.harvard.edu/netgov/html/

References

Adler, E. S. (1997). *Congressional district data file, 1997*. University of Colorado, Boulder. Retrieved from http://sobek.colorado.edu/esadler/districtdataWebsite/congressanddistrictdatasetWebpage.htm.

Adler, E. S., Gent, C. E., & Overmeyer, C. B. (1998). The home style homepage: Legislator use of the World Wide Web for constituency contact. *Legislative Studies Quarterly, 23*(4), 585-595.

Arnold, R., & Douglas (2004). *Congress, the press, and political accountability.* Princeton, NJ: Princeton University Press.

Bianco, W. (1994) *Trust: Representatives and constituents.* University of Michigan Press.

Chadwick, A. (2006). *Internet politics: States, citizens, and new communication technologies.* New York: Oxford University Press.

Congressional Management Foundation. (2003). *Congress Online 2003: Turning the corner on the information age.* Congress Online Project, Washington, DC.

Dawes, S. S., Bloniarz, P. A. & Kelly, K. L. (1999). *Some assembly required: Building a digital government for the 21st century.* SUNY Albany Center for Technology in Government.

Fenno, R. F. (1978). *Home style : House members in their districts.* Boston: Little, Brown.

Fountain, J. (2001). *Building the virtual state: Information technology and institutional change.* Washington, DC.

Hamlett, P. W. (2002, June 6-8). *Adapting the Internet to citizen deliberations: Lessons learned.* In Proceedings of the 2002 International Symposium on Technology and Society, Social Implications of Information and Communication Technology, Raleigh, North Carolina.

Hindman, M. (2003). *Googlearchy: How a few heavily-linked sites dominate politics online.* Midwest Political Science Association Annual Conference.

Jacobson, G. C. (1987). *The politics of congressional elections* (2nd ed.). Boston.

Johnson, D. W. (2004). *Congress online: Bridging the gap between citizens and their representatives.* New York: Routledge.

Mayhew, D. R. (1974). *Congress: The electoral connection.* New Haven: Yale University Press.

National Telecommunications and Information Administration/Department of Commerce. (2002). *A nation online: How Americans are expanding their use of the Internet.*

Norris, P. (2002). Revolution, What revolution? The Internet and U.S. elections, 1992-2000. In *Governance.com: Democracy in the information age.* Washington, DC: Brookings.

Owen, D., Davis, R., & Strickler, V. J. (1999). Congress and the Internet. *Press/Politics, 4*(2), 10-29.

Rabe-Hesketh, S., & Skrondal, A.. (2005). *Multilevel and longitudinal modeling using Stata.* College Station, TX: Stata Press.

Salisbury, R. H., & Shepsle, K. A. (1981). Congressional staff turnover and the ties-that-bind. *American Political Science Review, 75*(2), 381-396.

Shane, P., Muhlberger, P., & Cavalier, R. (2004, May 24-26). *Developing and testing a high telepresence virtual agora for broad citizen participation: A multi-trait, nulti-nethod investigation.* Paper presented at dg.02004, The National Conference on Digital Government Research, Seattle, Washington.

Skrondal, A., & Rabe-Hesketh, S. (2004). *Generalized latent variable modeling: Multilevel, longitudinal, and structural equation models.* Boca Raton, FL: Chapman and Hall.

Thurber, J. A., & Cambell, C. C. (Eds.). (2003). *Congress & the Internet.* Upper Saddle River, NJ: Prentice Hall.

West, D. (2005). *Digital government: Technology and public sector performance.* Princeton: Princeton University Press.

Appendix: Data and Sources

CMF Codes

In this section, we list the criteria CMF used in evaluating the Web sites, with the level of priority each criteria received listed in parentheses. All variables are dichotomous except those with an asterisk are measured on an ordinal 0 to 5 scale.

Audience: Constituent interests* (1) Recruit interests* (2) Press interests* (2)

Content:

- *Issue information*: Member's key issues* (1) "Hot" issues* (1) National issues* (1) State/local issues* (1)

- *Casework and Constituent Services*: Casework guidance or answers to frequently asked questions* (1) Casework initiation instructions* (2) Information and links for key agencies for casework* (2) Grant information* (3)

- *Accountability Information:* Vote rationale* (2) Voting record (1) Sponsorships and co-sponsorships (1)

- *Educational Information*: Information about the legislative process

- *Press Information*: Press contact information (2) Press releases by date (1) Press releases by topic (1)

- *Legislative Information*: Member's committee service (1) House and/or Senate schedules (2) Link to Thomas or Thomas search box (2)

- *District/state Information*: Member's district schedule or schedule of district events (2)
- *Member Information*: Member's biography (1) Member's photo (3)
- *Privacy Information*: Privacy statement (1)

Interactivity: E-mail updates (1) Office hours (2) Web form or public e-mail address (1) Postal addresses (1) Phone numbers (1) Guidance on how to communicate with the office

Usability: Navigation* (2) Timeliness* (1) Readability* (2) Scannability* (2) Search engine (2)

Innovations: To what degree does the site provide innovative features or content that makes the site easier or more interesting to use?* (1)

Data Sources for the Exogenous Variables

The gross state product and electrical equipment manufacturing variables come from census data from the calendar year of 2000. The district level variables, percent African American, and median district income, are from Scott Adler's Web site, department of political science, University of Colorado (Adler, 1997).

Chapter VIII

Electronic Democracy at the American Grassroots[1]

Donald F. Norris, University of Maryland, Baltimore County, USA

Abstract

In this chapter, I examine the delivery of electronic democracy (e-democracy) by U.S. local governments through their e-government activities. In particular, I examine three issues related to local e-democracy through data from focus groups with officials from 37 municipal and county governments across the U.S. The issues are: (1) why local governments decided to adopt e-government, and whether e-democracy was among the reasons for its adoption; (2) whether e-government has produced or affected local e-democracy; and (3) what plans, if any, local governments have with respect to e-democracy in coming years. My principal findings are that e-government at the local level was adopted principally to deliver governmental information and services and to provide citizen access to governmental officials; that e-government does not operate in a manner that either produces or impacts local e-democracy (at least as the term is broadly defined herein); and that e-democracy is not on the radar screens of most American local governments for future deployment.

Introduction

Electronic government (e-government) has been defined as the electronic delivery of governmental information and services 24 hours per day, seven days per week (Norris, Fletcher, & Holden, 2000). This is a broad definition and, as such, would include a wide variety of activities undertaken electronically by governments.

In this chapter, I focus on only one aspect of e-government and at only one level of government in the U.S. I examine the delivery of e-democracy among U.S. local governments through their e-government efforts. E-democracy, which I will define, can be part of a government's initial deployment of e-government, a subsequent development within an e-government deployment, a consequence (intended or unintended) of the deployment of e-government (e.g., e-democracy may be demanded by citizens' organizations), or possibly a combination of two or more of these.

However it may arise, e-democracy is viewed by many observers as a potentially significant phenomenon with far-reaching consequences. In recent years, scholars and political observers in the U.S. and Europe have argued that new forms of public participation in government and politics are necessary to rejuvenate what they believe to be a stagnating, if not failing, democracy. The evidence that these critics offer to support their claim includes at least the following: declining citizen participation in national and local elections and decreasing citizen trust in and feelings of efficacy toward government (Westin, 2004). These critics also argue that e-democracy (essentially the ability of citizens to participate in government and politics via various electronic means, including electronic voting) has the potential to reverse these trends and to breathe new life into democracy (Clift, 2004).

If these claims are true (and nearly all observers agree that voter turnout and citizen trust in government have declined substantially in the recent past), then e-democracy may be an important option that governments might find worth adopting in order to increase citizen participation in government and improve citizen trust in government. Additionally, scholars should find e-democracy worth careful study, particularly to learn how e-democracy arises, to examine the role that governments play in deploying and supporting e-democracy, to understand the forms that e-democracy actually takes on the ground, to identify what impacts e-democracy may have, and to forecast what the future may bring with respect to e-democracy.

In this chapter, I address three questions related to e-democracy through data from focus groups with officials from 37 municipal and county governments across the U.S. The questions are:

1.   why local governments decided to adopt e-government and whether e-democracy was among the reasons for its adoption;

2.   whether e-government has produced or affected local e-democracy; and

3.   what plans, if any, local governments have with respect to e-democracy in coming years.

In the following pages, I first discuss and define e-democracy. Next, I explain the methodology that I employed to gather data for this study. Then, I present findings with respect to each of the three previous questions. Finally, I draw conclusions about e-government and e-democracy at the American grassroots.

What is E-Democracy?

E-democracy can be defined in a number of ways (Gabardi, 2001). For example, it can be something as simple as electronic access by citizens to governmental information. E-democracy can also be more complex and can involve far greater interaction between citizens and government, including: the ability of citizens to reach and interact with governmental officials (e.g., via e-mail or other electronic means); online review of and comment on government proposals (budgets, land use plans, etc.) and regulations; citizen participation in governmental actions and decisions through such things as online forums, online consultations, and electronic town hall meetings; online referenda; online registration; e-voting; and more.

Kakabadse et al. (2003) discuss four models of e-democracy. The first, the electronic bureaucratic model, is essentially a paradigm for service delivery in which governments provide information and transactions electronically to improve governmental operations and to reduce costs. The second, the information management model, involves greater levels of interactivity between citizens and governments, especially in terms of access to governmental information and contact with officials. These two models of e-democracy are consistent with what I and others call e-government, the electronic delivery of information and services to citizens.

According to Kakabadse et al. (2003), in the third, or populist, model, citizens can make known their preferences on a range of issues through mechanisms such as electronic town hall meetings. Their final, or civil society, model assumes that e-government is transformational. This is where (or so it is argued) the use of information and communications technologies (ICTs), especially the Internet, will transform political cultures and "strengthen connections between citizens and promote a robust and autonomous site for public debate," which, in turn, will strengthen democracy (Kakabadse et al., 2003, p. 48). Kakabadse et al.'s (2003) third model is consistent with my broad definition of e-democracy (which follows), while their fourth model goes beyond description and prescribes outcomes from e-democracy. Indeed, the prescribed outcomes are consistent with the claims that many proponents of e-democracy make for its curative capacity (i.e., e-democracy will fix democracy by bringing citizens back into government and politics).

These and other models of e-democracy may or may not be descriptively accurate. That is, they may or may not accurately portray the actual practice of e-democracy. Nevertheless, the models provide useful theoretical insights into how ICTs may affect and indeed, may enhance democracy, especially democratic participation. However, to fully understand e-democracy, it is necessary to begin with a clear definition of the term, something that is often missing from models and other discussions of e-democracy that are not grounded in empirical evidence.

In this chapter, I offer a two-part definition of e-democracy. The first part of the definition is a minimalist conception of e-democracy that includes the following three components:

1. electronic access to governmental information and services;

2. electronic access to and the ability to interact electronically with governmental officials; and

3. online transactions with governments (e.g., to conduct business with and provide information and opinions, etc., to governments).

Nearly all local government Web sites in the U.S. provide the first two of these capabilities, and a small but slowly growing fraction is providing online transactions (Holden, Norris & Fletcher, 2003; Moon, 2002; Norris, Fletcher & Holden, 2000; Norris & Moon, 2005; West, 2003).

These components of e-democracy—the minimalist definition—are not sufficient, at least from an American perspective, to fully encompass the concept of democracy. What are missing are more active citizen involvement components that infuse democracy with both theoretical and practical meaning. To Americans, the term *democracy* means self-government, and local self-government is perhaps the quintessential form of American democracy (Syed, 1966). Democracy means that citizens have the ability to act both directly and through their chosen representatives to govern themselves and their communities. Any meaningful definition of e-democracy—at least from an American perspective—must therefore include elements of citizen involvement (direct and indirect) in democratic self-governance.

A broader and, I believe, more satisfactory definition of e-democracy and the one that I adopt for this chapter includes expressions of self-governance that go beyond the electronic availability of governmental information, contact, and transactions. My broader definition of e-democracy adds the following three components to the three previously articulated:

Table 1. Definition of e-democracy (all via electronic means)

A. Minimal Definition – Three Components

1. Citizen access to information and services
2. Citizens' ability to contact and interact with officials
3. Citizens' ability to conduct online transactions with government

B. Meaningful Definition – Six Components
Includes the three components of the minimal definition and adds:

4. Citizen participation in governmental activities and programs
5. Citizen participation in governmental decision making
6. Voting

---

4. citizen participation via electronic means in routine governmental activities and programs;

5. citizen participation via electronic means in governmental decision-making; and

6. citizens' ability to vote electronically (both on-site and remotely) in elections (see Table 1).

The expressions of self-governance subsumed under the final three definitional components can include a variety of specific mechanisms, including e-issues forums, e-town halls, e-consultations, e-policy dialogues, e-public hearings, e-comment periods (e.g., on proposed regulations), e-referenda, e-voting, and perhaps many more. Furthermore, the electronic means that support these expressions of self-governance include a government's Web site but can go beyond it to encompass such things as telephone, IVR, kiosks, television, video conferencing, video texting, extranets, and other electronic technologies.

Methodology

The data presented in this chapter are from four focus groups that I conducted in the fall of 2002 with officials from 37 American city and county governments. The focus group locations were Boston, Massachusetts (northeast), Chicago, Illinois (midwest), Atlanta, Georgia (south), and San Francisco, California (west). The focus groups ranged in size from seven to 12 participants. The focus group is a well-recognized method of qualitative data collection, best known for its use in marketing research but also increasingly used by scholars from the disciplines of psychology, sociology, education, political science, public health, and communication (Morgan, 1996). The focus group is a research method involving researcher-facilitated data collection from group interaction on a predetermined topic. This methodology involves three components: data collection, interaction through group discussion, and active participation by the researcher in shaping the discussion (Morgan, 1996).

Focus groups have relative strengths and weaknesses compared to other research methods, such as surveys and individual interviews (Merton, 1987; Merton & Kendall, 1946; Morgan, 1993, 1996). For example, survey data collection is best for breadth and for questions with discrete answers. Focus groups and individual interviews are best for depth and for questions where detail and explanation are sought. An important advantage of focus groups can be found in the choice of participants. For this research, I wanted to gather data from knowledgeable informants—persons who knew their governments' decisions, rationales, and actions regarding e-government. Thus, I selected chief information officers (CIOs) or their equivalents and top administrative or policy officials from local governments that had adopted official sites on the World Wide Web[2]. These persons constitute a body of key informants with critical knowledge of and insights into their governments' adoption of e-government and issues related to it.

A weakness of the focus group methodology, even focus groups with key informants, however, is that the respondents are not selected randomly. Therefore, the respondents are not representative of the broader population from which they were selected (i.e., local governments that have adopted e-government). Moreover, even if selected randomly, the number of local governments (in this case, 37) is so small that it would not permit the use of quantitative analysis beyond simple descriptive statistics. For these reasons, it is not possible to generalize or extrapolate the results of the focus groups to the broader population of local governments that have adopted e-government.

Nevertheless, the focus group results represent the actual experiences, opinions, and perceptions of knowledgeable officials from U.S. local governments that, for the most part, were on the leading edge of e-government in the U.S. As such, the results will be valuable additions to the contemporary knowledge about local e-government and local e-democracy.

I selected participants only from larger local governments (i.e., cities and counties over 100,000). This was because of consistent findings in the literature that size (as measured by population) is directly related to the adoption of IT in general, and e-government, in particular, by local governments (Holden, Norris & Fletcher, 2003; Norris & Demeter, 1999; Norris & Kraemer, 1996; Norris & Moon, 2005). As it turned out, I was successful using this criterion except for two governments (Portland, Maine, pop. 64,257; and Roanoke, Virginia, pop. 94,911). They were selected both because of the quality of their Web sites and in order to provide for regional diversity.

In order to assure further diversity among selected governments (e.g., so that no single category of government could dominate the discussion), I included both cities and counties, professionally managed and elected executive-led governments, and those from the four major regions of the nation (see the Appendix for a list of participating jurisdictions). So that technology specialists did not dominate the focus group proceedings, I chose both CIOs or their equivalents and top administrative and policy officials.

I employed a semi-structured instrument covering six broad areas to guide the focus group meetings. These areas were adoption of e-government, barriers to e-government adoption and expansion, strategies to overcome the barriers, problems and impacts from e-government, financing and managing e-government, and future plans. The instrument also permitted the participants to address other issues that they felt might be relevant.

The focus group participants consented to having the sessions on the record and tape-recorded. The tape-recordings were transcribed by a professional transcriptionist. A graduate research assistant and I listened to the tape-recordings, reviewed the transcriptions, and made corrections (for accuracy only), where necessary. We transmitted the transcripts to the respective focus group participants and asked for their comments. Six of the participants submitted corrections to the transcripts. After making all corrections, we produced final versions and transmitted them to all of the participants.

Next, the graduate research assistant and I coded the data from the transcripts. We coded them based on the verbatim words of the participants or reasonable inferences from those words. (We achieved a 90% or greater degree of intercoder consistency. Where we did not agree, we discussed our differences and, relying on the participants' verbatim words, reached consensus on the final coding.) When in doubt about a response, we coded conservatively and created separate response categories. This produced a large number of disaggregated results, which I then aggregated around consistent themes.

The CIOs and other top local officials who participated in the focus groups were highly cooperative, and their participation was open, reasoned, candid, and straightforward. Indeed, some were quite enthusiastic, and nearly all indicated that their participation had permitted them to learn from their colleagues, and that they would endeavor to apply those lessons in their own jurisdictions. Finally, readers should note that, although 37 local governments participated in the focus groups, two of them sent two representatives. Hence, there was a total of 39 participants.

Findings

In the following pages, I discuss the results of the focus groups, insofar as they permit me to address the three questions raised earlier (i.e., why local governments deployed e-government and whether e-democracy was a reason for its deployment; whether e-government has produced or affected local democracy; and what local governments plan with respect to e-democracy in coming years). Finally, I draw conclusions about the relationship between e-government and electronic democracy at the American grassroots and suggest a likely future trajectory for e-democracy practice among U.S. local governments.

E-Democracy and the Deployment of E-Government

The first question that I asked the focus groups was why their local governments adopted e-government. The question was open-ended and permitted participants to answer without the limitations of closed-ended questions. The principal finding here is that e-democracy figured hardly at all into these governments' reasons for adopting e-government.

The most frequently cited reason that the focus group participants gave for why their governments decided to adopt e-government was the delivery of information and services (25 responses) (see Table 2). The second most frequently cited reason (13 responses) was for efficiency, economy, effectiveness, and related reasons. Other

Table 2. Reasons for e-government (number of responses—not number of respondents)

Responses	Total
Information and Services	25
(Information)	(15)
(Services)	(10)
Efficiency, economy, and related	13
Citizen contact, access, oriented, centric	10
Demand Total	7
(Elected officials demanded)	(2)
(Citizens, businesses demanded)	(2)
(Perceived expectations/demand)	(3)
IT department led or pushed	7
Economic development, tourism, advertising the city or county	6
Keeping up with the Joneses	6
Other	9
Total reasons given	83

responses, in order of frequency, included: demand by elected officials, businesses, and citizens (7); leadership by the IT department (7); economic development and tourism (6); and "keeping up with the Joneses" (6). None of the participants gave e-democracy, per se, as a reason for adopting e-government, nor could e-democracy be reasonably inferred from the participants' verbatim words or from the discussion among them. Thus, only those components of e-democracy that conform to the minimalist definition of the term (e.g., citizen access to governmental information, services, and officials) can be deduced from these governments' reasons for adopting e-government.

When I probed to get beneath these responses and to discover deeper meaning from them, what emerged was a portrait of local governments endeavoring to join the bandwagon of e-government adoption, to use e-government to improve service delivery, to promote internal efficiencies, and to serve their citizens better. Again, these are essentially information provision and service delivery reasons that fit the minimalist definition of e-democracy. Furthermore, the notion of better citizen service was almost always connected to information and service delivery. It was not connected to a broader concept of e-democracy. Even those participants who said that their jurisdictions had deployed e-government mainly or partly because of demands from citizens, businesses and elected officials (10 responses) were clear that the demands that they heard were for information and services, greater governmental efficiencies, and the like, and not for e-democracy as defined more broadly herein. Moreover, as I will report later, the focus group participants perceived few, if any, current demands (circa fall 2002) from their elected officials or local residents for any greater deployment of e-democracy.

The closest that the participants came to offering reasons related to e-democracy for their governments' deployment of e-government came from responses about providing citizen access (e.g., to information, to government, to officials) and making government more citizen-centric. What the respondents meant in this regard were such things as governmental openness; ensuring that the provision of services and information served the needs of citizens rather than the needs of government; and providing another avenue to contact public officials. No one mentioned citizen participation in governmental activities, programs and decisions, or e-voting as reasons for establishing e-government.

Part of the reason the participants did not indicate that e-democracy was a reason that their governments adopted e-government can be found in their operational definitions of e-democracy. Their definitions of e-democracy were primarily, if not solely, related to information and service provision with an added dash of access to and communication with governmental officials. Thus, operationally, they did not separate e-democracy from e-government.

Except for the occasional and infrequent e-forum or e-town hall meeting, the participants did not cite electronic citizen participation in governmental activities, programs, decisions, or e-voting as reasons for or elements of their e-government deployment. Nor, for the most part, did their governments offer these further elements of e-democracy through their Web sites or other e-government initiatives.

E-Government and E-Democracy Impacts

It is quite possible that, although e-government was adopted by these governments without conscious consideration of e-democracy (except at a minimalist level), e-government could produce or affect e-democracy. For example, citizen demands for information and access could escalate into citizen demands for more active participation, and governments could react by making provisions for more forms of e-participation. Here, I asked a series of open-ended questions about e-government impacts. In particular, I asked what these officials had perceived were the biggest impacts resulting from their adoption of e-government.

Table 3 lists the responses from the focus groups. I divided the responses, based on whether they expressed negative or positive impacts from e-government. Based on these responses, it is clear that few, if any, of the participants perceived that e-government had produced or had impacted e-democracy. Their responses concerning negative impacts mainly had to do with difficulties adopting e-government. These included: internal governmental issues impeding e-government (19 responses); the length of time required to go live with e-government applications (time to mar-

Table 3. E-government impacts

Negative Impacts	
Impact	**Total**
Internal governmental issues impeding e-government	19
Time to market	8
Vendor problems	7
Workload and cost	7
Show citizen uptake	6
Legacy system problems	5
Marketing difficulties	5
Privacy and security issues	4
Other	30
Total	91
Positive Impacts	
Citizen centric, openness, responsiveness, popularity	28
BPR, productivity, efficiency, effectiveness	7
Improve government image	6
Speed or ease of e-government implementation	6
Services 24/7	4
Other	21
Total	**73**

ket, 8 responses); lack of vendor readiness or vendor failure (7 responses); added workload or cost imposed by e-government (7 responses); slow citizen uptake of e-government (6 responses); difficulty with legacy systems (5 responses); issues around marketing e-government internally and externally (5 responses); and privacy and security issues (4 responses). The remaining responses were fairly random and were coded "other" (30).

The responses concerning positive impacts from e-government mainly reflected these officials' perceptions that e-government was citizen-centric, had opened up government, had made government more responsive, and had become popular (i.e., the Web site or particular Web site applications) (28 responses). Efficiency and effectiveness reasons came next (7 responses). Then came improving government image (6 responses), speed or ease of implementing e-government applications (6 responses), and the availability of services 24/7 (4 responses). All other responses (21) were scattered and not amenable to further aggregation.

With the exception of six responses indicating slow citizen uptake, the negative impacts responses mainly concerned internal governmental operations and had little to do with e-democracy. Among the positive impacts, a large number (28) had to do with positive consequences for information and service delivery to citizens (e.g., greater governmental responsiveness, citizen centricity of government, governmental openness, Web site popularity, etc.). Here again, these officials' perceptions of the impacts of e-government had little to do with e-democracy, except in the minimalist definition.

The Future: Is E-Democracy on Local Governments' Radar Screens?

Next, I inquired about these local governments' future plans regarding e-government. For the most part, future plans involved functions, services, and transactions (37 responses); specific technologies (33 responses); integration (16 responses); or transforming Web sites into portals (8 responses). Plans to address economy, efficiency, and business process reengineering and to make e-government more citizen-centric both received six (6) responses. Only one respondent mentioned e-democracy, per se (Table 4).

Because so few responses to the open-ended question about future plans for e-government involved e-democracy, I specifically asked what plans, if any, these governments had regarding e-democracy. I allowed the participants to fill in the blanks around the specific meaning of the term e-democracy by describing whatever they believed their governments' future e-democracy plans to be. The responses were revealing — mainly in showing the paucity of any plans at all for deploying e-democracy (Table 5).

Table 4. Future plans for e-government

Plans	Total
Functions, services, transactions	37
Specific technologies	33
Integration	16
Portal	8
Economy, efficiency, BPR	6
Citizen centric, oriented, etc.	6
E-democracy	1
Other	19
Total	126

Table 5. Future plans for e-democracy

E-Democracy Plans	Total
Information	9
TV, video	8
E-participation (e-forums, e-hearings, etc.)	4
Communication	4
Functions, services, transactions	2
Total	27

The 37 governments provided a total of only 23 specific responses regarding future e-democracy plans and initiatives. Nine mentioned providing information online to citizens; four said communication with governmental officials; four listed some form of e-participation (e.g., e-forums); two said additional sources; and eight talked about specific additional technologies (specifically television or streaming video).

All of the participants in the southern focus group said that e-government is not on local radar screens, except for e-mail and citizen access. Participants in the western group were somewhat more divided about whether e-government was on the agenda. But, as they described it, e-democracy was also clearly service-oriented. As one participant put it:

"There is a push for what I call citizen engagement in government; [to] try to get more citizen involvement with government, input, ideas, have easier access to information, subscribe to services. And, it's related to services, a lot of it. It improves services. Citizens have better access to government."

Similarly, all of the members of the northeast focus group concurred that e-government is about services and service delivery. A subset of this group, however, felt that increasing citizen participation and citizen engagement was also a goal of e-government. The members of the midwest group were split between e-democracy as functions and services and those with no future plans. Finally, when asked, nearly all of the respondents felt that e-voting is off the table (not under consideration and not likely to be considered anytime soon).

In all, the participants made clear that their governments viewed e-democracy as the provision of governmental information and services and access to governmental officials (the minimalist definition of e-government) and that their governments and elected officials perceived few, if any, demands for e-democracy from citizens. Finally, the participants noted that, for the most part, their local elected officials would likely be opposed to e-democracy if they felt that it would become e-referenda. Elected officials, being elected to represent citizens, do not want government by keystroke.

Conclusion

The focus group methodology that I employed for this chapter does not permit generalization to broader populations (in this case, the broader population of U.S. local governments). However, it is reasonable and proper to draw conclusions from focus group data that may be suggestive of behavior among the broader population and may inform what limited theory there is about e-democracy (Yin, 1994) and to suggest avenues for further research on the subject of e-democracy.

Evidence from focus groups clearly shows that Web sites and other local e-government efforts among the participating 37 U.S. local governments were adopted and operate principally to deliver governmental information and services and to provide citizens greater access to governmental officials. The sites were not adopted to be nor do they operate as agents of e-democracy, at least insofar as they either enable or promote e-citizen participation in government activities, programs, or governmental decision making or permit e-voting. Thus, these e-government efforts are service and information oriented and, as such, are consistent with the first and second stages of the model of e-democracy proposed by Kakabadse et al. (2003).

The focus group data also show that e-democracy, at least as defined in this chapter, is not on the radar screens of the participating local governments. Few, if any, of the focus group governments had plans to deploy components of e-democracy that were consistent with the broader definition of that term. In other words, there is little—if any—evidence that these governments are moving toward the third or fourth stages of that model in which Kakabadse, et al. (2003) predict citizen participation in all aspects of government, and vigorous public debate will be encouraged and facilitated. An obvious question is why is e-democracy not more central to e-government at the American grassroots? Part of the answer is found in the definition of e-democracy provided by the focus group participants. Theirs is a grounded or an in-practice definition in which e-democracy operationally and functionally means the electronic delivery of governmental information and services and the ability of citizens to contact and interact with governmental officials. Another part of the answer is that, at the end of the day, the participating local governments did not want to go too far with e-democracy. That is, they did not want e-democracy to supplant the roles of elected officials and their appointed subordinates.

Nearly all American local governments of any size have official sites on the World Wide Web that constitute their principal method of providing e-government. The sites are mainly informational but are slowly growing more sophisticated and are adding interactive and transactional capabilities (Norris & Moon, 2005). They are also moving slowly in some, but not all, of the directions predicted by the principal normative models in the field; that is, toward horizontal and vertical integration, toward true portalness, and toward seamlessness around the concept of life events (Baum & Di Maio, 2000; Hiller & Belanger, 2001; Layne & Lee, 2001; Ronaghan, 2001; Wescott, 2001).

These models appear to suggest a linear, step-wise path from adoption of the most basic e-government offerings to governmental transformation and full-fledged e-democracy. In other words, once the "E" (i.e., the technology necessary to support e-government) is in place, the predicted evolution and positive outcomes will follow. Evidence from this study suggests, to the contrary, that although the "E" is surely a necessary condition for e-government, it is not a sufficient one for the evolution of e-government into e-democracy.

At the very least, these findings (from governments at the leading edge of local e-government) would suggest that other American local governments may be similarly inclined (or disinclined, as the case may be) regarding e-democracy. Although there is considerable practice of local e-government in the U.S. there is little emphasis on and little support for e-democracy (as broadly defined here). Few American local governments have plans for e-democracy deployment in the near future.

Whether American grassroots governments' minimalist approach to e-democracy is normatively good or not is beyond the purview of this chapter. Regardless, however, the minimalist approach represents the philosophy and the practice of e-democracy by local governments in the U.S. today and suggests what these governments are likely to do (or not do) regarding e-democracy for at least the next few years. Among other things, this suggests that few American local governments will be likely to take significant steps to extend or implement greater forms of e-democracy, such as those that are emerging in the UK and Europe, for example (Coleman, 2003; Coleman & Norris, 2005; Coleman & Spiller, 2003). Of course, further study will be required to confirm or refute these suggested findings.

Scholars should continue to monitor the practice of e-government and e-democracy and should employ a variety of methodologies to do so. They should continue to study e-government in order to identify and examine future developments, to compare these developments against the predictions of normative models, and to compare e-government and e-democracy developments among nations and regions of the globe. These studies should ascertain whether and the extent to which predicted e-government and e-democracy outcomes have occurred, and whether new and altogether unanticipated consequences have appeared (as is likely). Another fruitful, although certainly not final, avenue of exploration is to begin the search for the sufficient conditions for the predicted evolution of e-government to full-fledged e-democracy, assuming that such an evolution is more than the wishful thinking of e-government and e-democracy proponents.

References

Baum, C., & Maio, A.D. (2000). *Gartner's four phases of e-government model.* Gartner Group.

Clift, S.L. (2004). E-government and democracy. Retrieved August 10, 2004, from: *http://www.publicus.net/articles/cliftegovdemocracy.pdf*

Coleman, S. (2003). *Connecting Parliament to the public via the Internet: Two case studies of online consultations* (unpublished paper). Oxford, UK: Oxford Internet Institute.

Coleman, S., & Norris, D.F. (2005). *A new agenda for e-democracy.* Oxford, UK: Oxford Internet Institute.

Coleman, S., & Spiller, J. (2003). *Exploring new media effects on representative democracy* (unpublished paper). Oxford, UK: Oxford Internet Institute.

Gabardi, W. (2001). Contemporary models of democracy. *Polity, 33*(4), 547-568.

Hiller, J.S., & Belanger, F. (2001). Privacy strategies for electronic government. In M.A. Abramson, & G.E. Means (Eds.), *E-government 2001.* Lanham, MD: Rowman and Littlefield.

Holden, S.H., Norris, D.F., & Fletcher, P.D. (2003). Electronic government at the local level: Progress to date and future issues. *Public Productivity and Management Review, 26*(3), 1-20.

Kakabadse, A., Kakabadse, N.K., & Kouzmin, A. (2003). Reinventing the democratic governance project through information technology? A growing agenda for debate. *Public Administration Review, 63*(1), 44-60.

Kaylor, C.H., Deshazo, R., & Van Eck, D. (2001). Gauging e-government: A report on implementing services among American cities. *Government Information Quarterly, 18*, 293-307.

Layne, K., & Lee, J. (2001). Developing fully functional e-government: A four stage model. *Government Information Quarterly, 18*, 122-136.

Merton, R.K. (1987). The focused interview and focus groups: Continuities and discontinuities. *Public Opinion Quarterly, 51*(4), 550-566.

Merton, R.K., & Kendall, P.L. (1946). The focused interview. *American Journal of Sociology, 51*(6), 541-557.

Moon, M.J. (2002). The evolution of e-government among municipalities: Rhetoric or reality. *Public Administration Review, 62*(4), 424-433.

Morgan, D.L. (1993). *Successful focus groups: Advancing the state of the art.* Thousand Oaks, CA: Sage Publications.

Morgan, D.L. (1996). Focus groups. *Annual Review of Sociology, 22*(1), 129-152.

Norris, D.F., & Demeter, L.A. (1999). Computing in American city governments. In *The 1999 municipal yearbook.* Washington, D.C.: International City/County Management Association.

Norris, D.F., & Moon, M.J. (2005). Advancing e-government at the grassroots: Tortoise or hare? *Public Administration Review.*

Norris, D.F., Fletcher, P.D., & Holden, S.H. (2001). *Is your local government plugged in? Highlights of the 2000 electronic government survey.* Washington, D.C.: International City/County Management Association.

Ronaghan, S.A. (2001). *Benchmarking e-government: A global perspective.* New York: United Nations Division for Public Economics and Public Administration and American Society for Public Administration.

Syed, A. (1966). *The political theory of American local government.* New York: Random House.

Wescott, C.G. (2001). E-government in the Asia Pacific Region. *Asian Journal of Political Science, 9*(2), 1-24.

West, D. (2001-2003). Surveys with appropriate Web addresses. Retrieved October 1, 2003.

Westen, T. (2000). Comments at international forum on e-government at the Oxford Internet Institute. Oxford: Oxford University.

Yin, R.K. (1994). *Case study research: Design and methods.* Thousand Oaks, CA: Sage Publications.

Endnote

[1] This research was funded by award No. EIA0131554 from the Digital Government Program of the National Science Foundation.

Appendix: Participating Jurisdictions

Name	Gov. Type	Region	Name	Gov. Type	Region
Albuquerque, NM	City	W	Milwaukee, WI	City	MW
Bellevue, WA	City	W	Minnehaha County, SD	County	MW
Boise, ID	City	W	Mobile, AL	City	S
Boston. MA	City	NE	Montgomery County, MD	County	S
Broward County, FL	County	S	Nashville, TN	City/ County	S
Buffalo, NY	City	NE	Philadelphia, PA	City	NE
Charlotte, NC	City	S	Phoenix, AZ	City	W
Colorado Springs, CO	City	W	Plano, TX	City	S
Dauphin County, PA	County	NE	Portland, ME	City	NE
Denver, CO	City/ County	W	Provo, UT	City	W
Des Moines, IA	City	MW	Roanoke, VA	City	S
Fairfax County, VA	County	S	San Diego County, CA	County	W
Hamilton County, OH	County	MW	San Francisco, CA	City/ County	W
Indianapolis, IN	City/ County	MW	Seattle, WA	City	W
Kansas City, MO	City	MW	Sedgwick County, KS	County	MW
Lane County, OR	County	W	Stamford, CT	City	NE
Lincoln, NE	City	MW	Tampa, FL	City	S
Manchester, NH	City	NE	Westchester County, NY	County	NE
Middlesex County, NJ	County	NE	**Total**		37

This chapter was previously published in the International Journal of Electronic Government Research, 1(3), 1-14, July-September 2005.

Chapter IX

A Brave New E-World?
An Exploratory Analysis of Worldwide E-Government Readiness, Level of Democracy, Corruption, and Globalization

Zlatko J. Kovačić, The Open Polytechnic of New Zealand, New Zealand

Abstract

This chapter reports research results on the relationship between e-government readiness and its components and the level of democracy, corruption and globalization for 191 countries. A supply-side approach to e-government analysis using data about national government Web sites, telecommunication infrastructure and human capital was taken rather than a demand-side approach, which is based on the real use of e-government Web sites by citizens, businesses and government, or their perceptions of the online services delivery. Statistically significant differences in the level of e-government readiness and its components between three groups of countries classified according to the level of democracy were identified using ANOVA. It was also shown, using correlation and regression analysis, that e-government readiness indices are related to the level of democracy, corruption and globalization.

Introduction

This chapter aims to contribute to empirical research literature in the area of electronic government, focusing on socio-economic and political factors that might have an impact on the country's readiness for e-government. Before identifying these factors and setting up a theoretical framework for the analysis, we must begin by defining the core concepts and identifying the main issues.

The concepts of electronic governance (hereafter labeled e-governance), electronic government (e-government), and electronic democracy (e-democracy) have not been uniquely defined and used in literature. The term e-government is sometimes confused with e-governance and the two terms are often used interchangeably (Fountain, 2004). However, e-governance is a broader concept, which includes the use of information and communication technology (ICT) by government and civil society to promote greater participation of citizens in the governance of political institutions. Though most of the e-government definitions focus more on use of technology, and management, and delivery of public services (Edmiston, 2003), the strategic aspect of e-government initiative is even more important (Grönlund, 2003). We have accepted the definitions provided by Okot-Uma (2004). He uses the "good governance" concept to clearly explain the relationships between e-governance, e-government and e-democracy. E-governance includes all processes and structures by means of which the new ICTs can be used by government to enable: administration of government and delivery services to the public (e-government); all forms of electronic communications between government and citizen with the aim of informing, representing, encouraging to vote, consulting and involving the citizen (e-democracy); and transact business with its partners, clients, and the markets (government electronic business).

A country's overall readiness to adopt, use and benefit from using ICTs is called a country's e-Readiness. Knowledge of the factors that make a significant contribution to e-readiness and the country's position on the e-readiness scale would help the country's leaders to identify the strengths and weaknesses of the country's current position and to concentrate on the areas where improvement and further integration of ICT could be made (Bridges.org, 2001). The label 'e-government readiness' is used to describe government readiness to adopt, use and benefit from ICT. Why is it important to study e-government readiness at the national level? Fountain (2001) argued that innovation often begins at the state level and diffuses to federal and local government. In other words, a country's e-Readiness shows the country's potential for future diffusion of ICT to lower levels. The concept of e-government readiness is also important because of the opportunities it creates for each country in terms of benefiting from e-commerce activities, openness to globalization, potential to strengthen democracy and make governments more responsive to the needs of their citizens.

The main objective of this chapter is to identify whether there are empirical links between e-government readiness at the country level and the level of democracy, corruption, and globalization. More specifically the data gathered for this chapter was used to address the following four questions:

- Has a country's position changed in regard to e-government readiness from year 2001 to 2003?
- What are the empirical links between e-government readiness, participation, democracy, corruption, and globalization?
- What is the contribution of each component of the e-government readiness index: Web measure index, telecommunication infrastructure index and human capital index described in Table 1, to the level of democracy worldwide?
- How robust is the relationship between democracy and e-government readiness to the change of the e-government readiness and democracy index definition?

It is worth emphasizing that this chapter has a limited scope because of the nature of the methodological approach used. It belongs to the corpus of exploratory studies resulting in "stylized facts" about the observed phenomena and therefore does not provide evidence of a causal relationship between e-government readiness and other variables.

The theoretical arguments and framework for empirical analysis are briefly outlined in the next section. Previous empirical research related to e-government readiness, democracy, participation, corruption, and globalization are also discussed. Data and methodology are discussed in the following section. The results are presented in the subsequent section, along with critical comments. Concluding remarks including the limitations of the analysis finish the chapter.

Outline of the Theoretical Arguments

The factors that might affect e-government readiness can be classified into two broad groups, pushing and pulling factors. Pushing factors are those factors that appear within governments or politics. Pulling factors are societal forces that promote and facilitate advances in e-government. The factors we consider in this chapter belong to both of these groups.

E-Government Readiness

E-government readiness is defined as the aptitude of a government to use ICTs to move its services and activities into the new environment. While the e-readiness assessment indicators vary, most tend to measure ICT connectivity, ICT use and integration, training, human capacity, government policies and regulations, infrastructure, security, and economy. The most complete assessments of e-government readiness were undertaken by the United Nations in 2001 and 2003. There were also other assessments of e-government readiness worldwide (West, 2001, 2004; Kirkman, Osorio, & Sachs, 2002), at different levels of federal, state or local governments (Holden, Norris, & Fletcher, 2003) and regions of the world (Altman, 2002). Choucri, Maugis, Madnick, and Siegel, (2003) critically considered these, what they called "first generation" e-readiness models and set up a theoretical framework for the "next generation" where emphasis in the e-readiness framework is on value creation opportunities. The main reason for not using one of proposed "next generation" models is a lack of the full set of data for most of the countries.

Democracy

The advent of the Internet and recent developments of ICTs have opened the gate for greater democracy, inviting at the same time the reconsideration of our democratic processes (Shi & Scavo, 2000). New ICTs also raise expectations of increasing the participation of citizens in public affairs and bring new promises of improving our democratic processes (Jakob, 2003; Lidén & Avdic, 2003). However, Kraemer and King (2003) are more skeptical since they did not find any empirical evidence which would support the claim that IT has the potential to dramatically change organizations. What does the term e-democracy mean? Grönlund (2003) describes e-democracy as a term usually used to mean IT applied to enhance public participation in democratic processes. E-democracy should be assessed in terms of its defining processes, not in terms of the extent IT artifacts used.

Beside the almost traditional relationship between economic development and democracy there have been a few attempts to link the development of new ITs with democracy (Kedzie, 1997). A strong correlation between democratization and interconnectivity was found, even controlling for economic development, though the causality direction of this relationship is unclear. What is more important for this research is the significant contribution he made by discussing why information, access to it and emerging IT in general are so important for the democratic process (see also Tsagarousianou, 1999; Lidén & Avdic, 2003; Oates, 2003). However, optimism raised by those writing about the potential that ICTs might have to enhance and improve democracy was rarely backed up with solid evidence. Kampen and Snijkers (2003) concluded that a lot of problems in both representative and direct democracies remain unsolved and that e-government even can create new problems.

The literature does not provide a definitive statement about the possible causality relationship between ICTs and democracy. E-government and bureaucracy impact upon each other in reciprocal, quite complex ways (Jain, 2004) with a continuous process of mutual adjustment and adaptation (La Porte, Demchak, & Friis, 2001). However, empirical research did not support the hypothesis that democracy has a significant impact on the openness of government Web sites (La Porte, Demchak, de Jong, & Friis, 2000) or that democracy and bureaucracy have significant impact on e-government readiness (Moon, Welch, & Wong, 2005). Contrary to these results Norris (2003) found significant impact of democracy on e-government readiness, while West (2004) reported a weak link between democratization and e-government performance, claiming that authoritarian governments are as likely to rank highly on e-government readiness as democratic countries.

Corruption

In this chapter the Huntington (1989, p. 377) definition of corruption which emphasizes social constructivism ("behavior of public officials which deviates from accepted norms in order to serve private ends") is adopted. We focused on the first group of theories of corruption, among six groups identified by Graaf (2004), which highlights certain social, political, organizational, or individual factors. The empirical findings are not very explicit on the causality of corruption. For example, "income" and "corruption" are often correlated, which means that the lower the income of a country, the more occurrences of cases of corruption. However, due to correlation between "income" and "political system" it is not clear whether relationship between "income" and "corruption" is of a causal nature (Huberts, 1998). Even when there are some doubts about the direction of causality, it is true that corruption is negatively correlated with most fundamental economic variables. However, economic factors are not the only causes of corruption; political institutions (Lederman, Loayza, & Soares, 2001), country's legal origins (La Porta, Lopez-De-Silanes, Shleifer, & Vishny, 1999) and more ethnically or linguistically fractionalized countries (Mauro, 1995) could also affect corruption. We would expect that the e-government might reduce corruption by taking away the discretion of officials in decision-making process, thereby reducing opportunities for arbitrary action. Also, by keeping detailed data on transactions the e-government application could reduce the probability of corruption. On the other hand, we could argue that there is a link from corruption to the level of e-government readiness. Namely it would not be reasonable to expect the promotion and implementation of an e-government initiative from a government in a country with a high level of corruption, simply because it would take away an almost certain source of income from officials.

Globalization

Globalization is a multifaceted phenomenon which represents one of "the most influential forces" (Intriligator, 2001) shaping the future perspective of the whole world. It includes not only economic aspects, but also political, social, cultural and ideological ones. Globalization is generally regarded as the increasing interconnectedness of the world through flows of information, capital, and people facilitated by trade and political openness as well as ICT. Overall, GDP and the degree of globalization in domestic economic structure seem to strongly correlate with the level of e-government readiness, though some countries have a more advanced Web presence, despite the fact that their national income is at a lower level (La Porte et al., 2001). National income and degree of globalization are also positively correlated with not very strong impact of globalization on the national openness score (La Porte, de Jong, & Demchak, 1999). This was attributed to the relationship between globalization and national income, since the world's wealthier countries tend to have more liberal trading regimes. It could also be argued that processes of globalization are driving all countries toward the adoption of e-government initiative, a national version of "keeping up with the Jones" and thus having a positive impact on the country's e-government readiness. However, the causality link from e-government readiness to a country's openness and integration in the world is not ruled out. It can be argued that though the basic social values such as openness and democracy are deeply affected by ICTs, they also have an impact on them or at least on the way we use them. Countries that adopt more free-market trade policies may also adopt free-market domestic policies and stable fiscal and monetary policies, which could potentially increase their output per capita. These countries would also push towards the implementation of an e-government initiative because they would see e-government Web sites as another channel for attracting foreign investors to invest in their economy.

The ongoing theoretical discussion of the factors such as democracy, corruption and globalization that might have an impact on the attitude of the government toward increasing the level of e-government readiness and the summary of the previous empirical findings leads to the following hypotheses:

Hypothesis H1: The government of a more democratic country would have a more positive attitude toward increasing the level of e-government readiness.

Hypothesis H2: The government of a country with less corruption would have a more positive attitude toward increasing the level of e-government readiness.

Hypothesis H3: The government of a country with a high integration in the world economy would have a more positive attitude toward increasing the level of e-government readiness.

Hypothesis H4: The government that actively works on increasing the level of e-government readiness would be rated higher on the democratic scale.

Data and Methodology

Data for this chapter were collected from various sources as described in Table 1. GDP per capita was included as a control variable. When the effects of "hard variables" such as economic variables on dependent variable are significant, then the political variables may be redundant. If the political variables are still significant in spite of included economic variables, then the effect of political variable could be confirmed.

A few methodological issues face researchers interested in studying specific phenomena using data at the national level. It is a common practice in empirical research such as this, to use national data compiled from various data sources. However, use of such data could cause problems because of the inconsistency in the definitions of the raw data used in the calculation of the composite indicators for different countries. Consequently, in such cases a good portion of the observed country differences in e-government readiness may simply reflect measurement artifacts. In this chapter it would be reasonable to expect that this problem would be minimized by the fact that the same prescribed United Nations methodology was used for gathering and calculating e-government readiness index. However, it is still not clear how much error this heterogeneity in the initial data used for the calculation of composite indicators could introduce into the results. Also, including some countries in a worldwide analysis while excluding others could cause a selection bias. For example, including the globalization variable in the correlation/regression analysis would result in the exclusion of more than 130 country's e-government readiness data because only 62 countries have globalization data. Usually more advanced countries with much better developed data collection procedures would be among included countries. It is not clear how much bias this selection introduces into the results.

The conceptual frame of the UN (2001) project, postulates that the state of e-government readiness is a function of the combined level of a country's state of readiness, economic, technological development, and human resource development; a final product is a synthetic indicator eGOV(UN)2001. Two years later the UN (2003)

Table 1. Description of data used

Acronym	Description, Data Source and Availability
eGOV(UN)2001	*E-government Index* is a composite index based on the Web presence measure, infrastructure measure (includes: PCs/100; Internet hosts/10,000; % Population online, Telephone lines/100; Mobile phones/100; and TVs/1,000) and human capital measure (includes: UNDP human development index, information access index and urban/rural ratio) (Source: UN [2001]) Available for 133 countries.
eGOV(UN)2003	*E-government Readiness Index* is a composite index based on the Web Measure Index, the Telecommunication Infrastructure Index and the Human Capital Index. (Source: UN [2003]) Available for 191 countries.
WMI	*Web Measure Index* is a quantitative index based on a theoretical "Web presence measurement model," which measures the generic aptitude of governments to employ e-government as a tool to inform, interact, transact and network. The five stages are theoretically ascending in the level of maturity or sophistication of e-government presence online (Source: UN [2003]) Available for 191 countries.
TII	*Telecommunication Infrastructure Index* is a composite, weighted average index of six primary indices, based on basic infrastructural indicators that define a country's ICT infrastructure capacity. These six indices are: PCs/1,000; Internet users/1,000; Telephone lines/1,000; Online population/1,000; Mobile phones/1,000; and TVs/1,000. (Source: UN [2003]) Available for 191 countries.
HCI	*Human Capital Index* is based on the UN Development Programme "education index." This is a composite of the adult literacy rate and the combined primary, secondary and tertiary gross enrolment ratio, with two thirds of the weight given to adult literacy and one third to the gross enrolment ratio. (Source: UN [2003]) Available for 191 countries.
ePART	*E-participation Index* is a qualitative measure which employs proxy indicators for the quality, relevance, usefulness and willingness of government Web sites to provide on-line information and participatory tools and services to people. (Source: UN [2003]) Available for 191 countries.
eGOV(WM)2001	World Markets Research Centre *E-government Index* is a composite index based on 28 features of the governmental Web sites such as information availability, service delivery and public accessibility. (Source: West [2001]) Available for 191 countries.
eGOV(WM)2003	World Markets Research Centre *E-government Index* is a composite index based on 28 features of the governmental Web sites such as information availability, service delivery and public accessibility. (Source: West [2001]) Available for 198 countries.
eGOV(NRI)	*Network Readiness Index* is a composite index which assesses countries' capacity to exploit the opportunities offered by ICTs. Two components are considered: network use and enabling factors. (Source: Kirkman et al. [2002]) Available for 74 countries.
GDPPC	*Gross Domestic Product* per capita in equal purchasing power parity. (Source: U.S. Central Intelligence Agency [2002, 2003]) Available for 192 countries.
DEMOCRACY	*Freedom House Index* (measure of the state of freedom) is the combined average of each country's political rights and civil liberties ratings which were assessed by selected experts. (Source: Freedom House [2004]) Available for 192 countries.
POLITY2	*Revised Combined Polity Score* is a composite index calculated by subtracting the AUTOC (Institutionalized Autocracy) score from the DEMOC (Institutionalized Democracy) score. Obtained score was further modified to facilitate the use of this variable in time-series analysis. (Source: Marshall & Jaggers [2004]) Available for 159 countries.
POLYARCHY	*Vanhanen's Index of Democratization* is a composite index comprising two dimensions of democracy: competition and participation. (Source: Vanhanen [2000, 2002]) Available for 191 countries.
CORRUPTION	*Corruption Perceptions Index* is a composite index to measure the perceived level of corruption in each country by business people and risk analysts. (Source: Transparency International [2004]) Available for 131 countries.
GLOBALIZATION	Kearney's *Globalization Index* is a composite index comprising the following four components: economic integration, personal contact, technology and political engagement. (Source: Kearney [2003]) Available for 62 countries.

slightly changed the definition of the e-government index eGOV(UN)2003, adding also a new measure of participation. The second alternative measure of e-government readiness (West, 2001, 2004) focuses on the features national government Web sites are offering. Most other e-government readiness measures, following the Choucri, Maugis, Madnick, and Siegel (2003) recommendation also include a component which captures the potential of e-government, in other words, opportunities that the implementation of an e-government initiative could be expected to create. eGOV(WM)2003 takes a snap-shot of the current state of e-government in each country, focusing only on the government Web sites. It may be said that this index tries to capture the same phenomenon as the WMI. In the next section an assessment is made on whether data confirms this statement. The last e-government readiness measure included in the analysis is the *Network Readiness Index* (eGOV(NRI)) (Kirkman et al., 2002). Two components were taken into consideration in the computation of eGOV(NRI): network use, such as a measure of increase in the use of ICT and enabling factors such as network access, network policy, networked society, and networked economy.

According to Munck and Verkuilen (2002) the most frequently used measures of democracy are Freedom House index (Freedom House, 2004), Polity IV (Marshall & Jaggers, 2004) and Polyarchy, in other words, Index of Democratization (Vanhanen, 2000, 2002). Freedom House and Vanhanen appear to represent the two "extremes" of measuring political freedom and democracy. Freedom House index is based on raw scores assigned by experts, and hence, seem to be subjective. Vanhanen's Index of Democratization relies on observables, and attempts to avoid subjective judgments. Other indices are discussed in Casper and Tufis (2002) and Munck and Verkuilen (2002). Since Polyarchy dataset is not available for the period we considered (2001-2003) and Polity IV dataset is available for 159 countries only (Freedom House index is available for 192 countries) we decided to use Freedom House index (DEMOCRACY) in further analysis. The high correlations between alternative measures of democracy suggest they may be used interchangeably because they code countries in similar ways. However, as Casper and Tufis (2002) show, this could be far from the truth. To assess the robustness of the results concerning regression models of democracy both POLITY2 and POLYARCHY measures of democracy were used instead of DEMOCRACY in these models.

A few alternative measures for corruption were used in literature (Mauro, 1995; Kaufmann, Kraay, & Zoido- Lobatón, 1999). Unfortunately, these measures are not updated regularly and were not available for the period we considered. The most often used corruption indicator is the Transparency International (2001) *Corruption Perceptions Index*, labeled CORRUPTION, which measure the perceived level of corruption by business people and risk analysts (Lambsdorff, 2003). High values of the index represent good governance, that is, low corruption. We multiplied the index by -1 so that countries with a high value of CORRUPTION are indeed more corrupt. Kearney's (2003) *Globalization Index*, labeled GLOBALIZATION, is a composite index comprising the following four components: economic integration, personal contact, technology and political.

The list of factors that might affect a country's e-government readiness considered here is different from the list used in the Moon et al. (2005) study. TII and HCI variables capture the educational and technological aspects of the e-government readiness and as such are already embedded in the e-government readiness measure, in other words, eGOV(UN)2003. For the same reason we did not consider including the equivalent variables from their study, such as human development index, Internet penetration, or social capital.

To answer the questions raised in the Introduction, a graphical representation of relevant data and descriptive statistics was used, along with ANOVA for testing the difference between mean values. Correlation and regression analysis were also used for testing the four hypotheses stated in the previous section.

Results

To answer the question whether a country's position with regard to e-government readiness has changed from 2001 to 2003, the scatterplot with an accompanying 45^0 line in Figure 1. was created. The scatterplot is based on eGOV(WM)2001 and eGOV(WM)2003 variables.

The 45^0 line is the dividing line which separates countries that improved their position from those whose progress with an e-government initiative was not so successful. Changes in a position of each country are relative to the e-government readiness framework used, which is the World Markets e-government framework (West, 2001, 2004). Any country whose position has worsened would be below this line, all the others, whose position has improved, would be above this line. Also a regression line which lies below the 45^0 line was added. The fact that this regression line has slope less than 1 would suggest that in general all the countries did not progress well in this two-year period. Those countries that made significant leap, increasing their e-government readiness, lie above 45^0 line. It is encouraging that among them are a few developing countries (such as Somalia and Uganda) which means that they can improve their e-government readiness in a short time and that e-government is not a tool limited to richer countries. Another interesting point is that variability in eGOV(WM)2003 data reduced almost two times when comparing it with variability in eGOV(WM)2001 data (standard deviation dropped from 8.3 to 4.6). This result would suggest that the differences between countries' e-government ratings become smaller.

To see whether there are differences in e-government readiness, integration with other countries and level of corruption among countries with different democratic

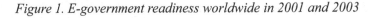

Figure 1. E-government readiness worldwide in 2001 and 2003

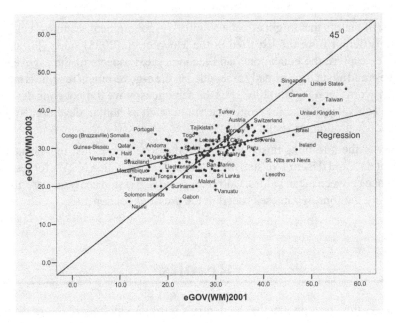

status we have used a one-way ANOVA. Since all the data in Table 1 are interval level data ANOVA method could be applied. The mean value for each variable across all countries, grouped by democracy status was computed and presented in Table 2. The table also contains a figure which shows the number of countries that belong to each of the three groups (columns labeled N). Levene's test of equality of error variance indicated that the variances for each group were significantly different at the 5% level, i.e., the homogeneity-of-variance assumption was violated for most of dependent variables. Additional nonparametric Welch and Brown-Forsythe tests of equality of means were conducted and were significant for all variables at 5% level, i.e., the results of each test confirmed the finding of the test based on F-ratio.

Value of the F-ratio suggests that we should reject a hypothesis that there are no differences in the mean values in between "Free", "Partly Free", and "Not Free" group of countries for each variable. There is the following general tendency in the mean values: the "Free" group has the highest mean value for each variable, followed by the "Partly Free" group, and finally the "Not Free" group has the lowest mean value among three groups. While the difference in mean value for each variable between "Free" group and other two groups are easily distinguished, for most of variables the differences in mean value between "Partly Free" and "Not Free"

Table 2. Mean values by democratic status

Variable	Free		Partly Free		Not Free		Total		F-ratio*
	Mean	N	Mean	N	Mean	N	Mean	N	
eGOV(WM)2001	31.2	88	26.0	54	24.9	49	28.6	191	18.2
eGOV(WM)2003	30.5	88	28.4	55	28.2	49	29.3	192	5.9
eGOV(NRI)	4.42	51	3.22	19	2.88	4	4.03	74	19.7
eGOV(UN)2001	0.59	62	0.40	38	0.38	33	0.48	133	23.4
eGOV(UN)2003	0.49	87	0.31	55	0.27	49	0.38	191	30.9
WMI	0.38	87	0.19	55	0.11	49	0.26	191	34.9
TII	0.30	87	0.08	55	0.06	49	0.18	191	37.4
HCI	0.77	87	0.66	55	0.64	49	0.71	191	5.5
ePART	0.25	87	0.10	55	0.04	49	0.15	191	23.7
GDPPC	13,483	88	3,929	55	4,179	49	8,372	192	33.5
DEMOCRACY	91.6	88	52.3	55	16.2	49	61.1	192	916.3
CORRUPTION	5.62	61	2.96	40	2.98	30	4.20	131	33.1
GLOBALIZATION	37.6	42	21.7	14	11.5	6	31.5	62	10.8

* P-value for each F-ratio is <0.001.

groups are quite small. Finally, the smallest difference in mean values between the three groups is for HCI and eGOV(WM)2003. In case of the eGOV(WM)2003 variable this would mean all governments, including governments in authoritarian countries performing well on e-government.

To test the hypothesis that the e-government readiness correlates with the level of democracy, the level of corruption and globalization, the Pearson's correlation coefficients were calculated and presented in Table 3. All the correlation coefficients are highly significant and with the expected positive sign (CORRUPTION has the expected negative sign). Though correlation does not imply causation, these significant correlation coefficients allow us to say that in a country where the government is willing to utilize the full potential of e-government it is more likely that the level of democracy would be higher, the level of corruption would be lower and the country would be more integrated with the other countries worldwide. A less democratic country's government would not perceive the political benefits of the further development of the e-government initiative. In these countries it would be expected that the level of corruption would be higher and the integration of the country with the rest of the world would be lower. Finally, it would be less likely that the citizens in a less democratic country would be engaged in any form of participation and communication with the government.

Generally all the correlation coefficients for ePART are less than the corresponding coefficients for eGOV(UN)2003. This may due to the fact that even in democratic countries, less corrupted and more integrated with other countries, facilities that support citizens' participation, consultation and two-way communication are not widely advertised or implemented on the government Web sites.

Table 3. Pearson's correlation coefficients *

	(2)	(3)	(4)	(5)	(6)	(7)	(8)	(9)	(10)	(11)	(12)	(13)
eGOV(WM)2001 (1)	.53	.62	.64	.68	.66	.58	.48	.59	.56	.38	-.58	.45
eGOV(WM)2003 (2)		.66	.63	.60	.61	.55	.37	.54	.50	.21	-.61	.46
eGOV(NRI) (3)			.85	.93	.69	.97	.68	.62	.93	.66	-.92	.85
eGOV(UN)2001 (4)				.90	.77	.85	.74	.70	.82	.52	-.77	.63
eGOV(UN)2003 (5)					.87	.84	.81	.77	.76	.50	-.83	.74
WMI (6)						.71	.51	.86	.65	.51	-.67	.52
TII (7)							.45	.66	.94	.55	-.91	.84
HCI (8)								.45	.37	.23	-.55	.55
ePART (9)									.59	.46	-.61	.53
GDPPC (10)										.52	-.89	.82
DEMOCRACY (11)											-.57	.63
CORRUPTION (12)												-.82

Note: Column labeled (13) is related to GLOBALIZATION variable;
* P-value for every correlation coefficient is < 0.01

The correlation coefficient of GLOBALIZATION with CORRUPTION is -0.84 in 2000 (Transparency International, 2001), which illustrates that countries integrated more into world markets developed political, social and legal institutions that deter corruption. Calculation of the same correlation coefficient three years later gives almost the same value (-0.82). This suggests that economic, social, and technological integration is associated with perceptions of less corrupted government. Almost the same value, -0.83 for correlation coefficient between eGOV(UN)2003 and COR-RUPTION suggests that wider information access and more online services offered by the government are strongly associated with the citizen's perception of more transparent government. According to the UN (2003) report the most sophisticated Web sites even in the countries with a small e-government readiness index were those where the information for potential foreign investments were presented. Taking into account that one of the key components of the globalization index is the inflow and outflow of foreign direct investment it seems that making a better online presentation of the country's attractiveness for investors will eventually increase its level of economic integration. In other words, increasing the WMI will increase the e-government readiness index, which will probably trigger an increase in the country's globalization index.

In order to answer the question of how robust the relationship between e-government readiness and other variables is, in an analysis of the changes in the e-government readiness index definition, two alternative measures were used (West, 2001, 2004; Kirkman et al., 2002). Firstly, these three measures of e-government readiness are highly significantly positively correlated. To check whether the three e-government readiness measures are measuring the same construct the Cronbach's alpha was calculated. The value obtained (0.905) suggests that these three e-government readiness indicators are indeed measuring the same phenomenon. Secondly, eGOV(NRI) and eGOV(WM)2003 measures also show a positive and significant linear relationship with all other variables. This suggests that the relationships between e-government readiness and other variables might be stable under changes in the e-government readiness index definition. However, the use of the eGOV(UN)2003 would be rec-ommended, because it takes into account not just the government Web site features that eGOV(WM)2003 did, but also other important factors such as the telecom-munication infrastructure and human capital and is available for more countries than eGOV(NRI).

We assumed previously that eGOV(WM)2001/eGOV(WM)2003 might capture the same phenomenon as WMI. Inspection of the correlation coefficients in Table 3 shows that eGOV(WM)2001/eGOV(WM)2003 are indeed more positively cor-related with WMI than with TII and HCI variables.

Finally a regression analysis was used to get further insight into the relationship between the variables. Based on correlation coefficients and theoretical consideration in the second section, we cannot assume that the e-government readiness, corruption or globalization are truly exogenous, in other words, that there is one-way causation between democracy and e-government readiness, corruption and globalization. We could argue equally well that the level of democracy could have a positive influence on a government's willingness to support an e-government initiative, which would eventually increase the e-government readiness index. Therefore if we have a two-way causation in a function such as democracy, this implies that the democracy function cannot be treated in isolation as a single equation model, but belongs to a wider system of equations that describe the relationships between the relevant variables. This system of equations, known in econometrics as a simultaneous equation system, would be more appropriate to use. However, at this stage we have estimated single regression equations for e-government and democracy in spite of the fact that the estimation method used (ordinary least squares) will produce a biased estimate of the effects that e-government readiness, corruption and globalization might have on democracy. This result is due to a violation of the assumptions of the estimation method used, which creates what is known as simultaneous equations bias.

Initial specification of the regression model for the eGOV(UN)2003 variable, which includes GDPPC, DEMOCRACY, CORRUPTION, and GLOBALIZATION, was estimated. The result is not presented here because of a serious problem with multicol-linearity (CORRUPTION and GDPPC and CORRUPTION and GLOBALIZATION correlation coefficients are -0.89 and -0.82 respectively). The same problem occurred when the other two e-government readiness indices instead of eGOV(UN)2003 were used. A variance-inflation factor (VIF) was calculated and was well above 4 for each regression model indicating that the multicollinearity is really a problem. The most frequently used remedy for coping with multicollinearity is to drop the variables suspected of causing it. Therefore the CORRUPTION variable was excluded from the initial model. However, the CORRUPTION variable is one of those variables whose impact we would like to measure and excluding it from the model could cause a specification problem—a case of missing a variable. The model with three

Table 4. Regression models for e-government readiness

Left hand side variable	Regression Model					
	eGOV(UN)2003	eGOV(WM)2003	eGOV(NRI)	eGOV(UN)2003	eGOV(WM)2003	eGOV(NRI)
	Standardized β (*t*-ratio)					
GDPP	0.786 (8.15)**	0.810 (4.41)***	0.772 (7.54)**	0.680 (12.5)**	0.532 (7.25)**	0.870 (16.2)**
DEMOCRACY	0.254 (3.57)**	-0.140 (-1.03)	0.049 (0.45)	0.151 (2.78)*	-0.061 (-0.83)	0.100 (1.866)
GLOBALIZATION	-0.063 (-0.66)	-0.116 (-0.64)	0.156 (1.60)	-	-	-
R^2	0.84	0.41	0.89	0.59	0.25	0.88
adjusted R^2	0.83	0.38	0.88	0.58	0.24	0.87
F-ratio	100.6**	13.4**	126.7**	135.6*	32.0*	257.1**
Sample size	61	62	51	191	192	74

* P-value < 0.01; ** P-value < 0.001

independent variables, otherwise known as GDPPC, DEMOCRACY, and GLO-BALIZATION, was estimated using the three alternative e-government readiness measures and the results are shown in Table 4. The model in the last three columns contains GDPPC and DEMOCRACY as the only two independent variables. In all reported regression models (Table 4) VIF values were below four, which mean that the multicollinearity does not seem to be a problem.

In the both specified models (with and without the GLOBALIZATION variable) the most significant variable was GDPPC. In other words, a "hard" economic variable is the most significant predictor of the country's e-government readiness. This result is robust across the three alternative e-government readiness indices. The GLOBALIZATION variable was not significant in the first three regressions and was dropped (the last three regressions in Table 4). The other reason to drop the GLOBALIZATION variable was because it limits the data set to 62 countries only. Without it a full data set with over 190 countries' data could be used.

The DEMOCRACY variable was highly significant with an expected positive sign in both models, with eGOV(UN)2003 as dependent variable. However, in the model with the other two e-government readiness measures DEMOCRACY was not significant, or only weakly significant at the 6.6% level in the case of eGOV(NRI) measure. Furthermore, the regression coefficient did not have the expected positive sign as in the in case of eGOV(WM)2003. The main reason for such variation in the estimated models is the structure of the sample when the GLOBALIZATION variable was included. With inclusion of GLOBALIZATION our sample size drops from 191 to just 62 countries. Most countries among 62 retained countries are classified as "Free" countries (42 countries), while only 6 "Not Free" countries are included. Also, most of the "Free" countries scored the maximum score on the Freedom House scale which means that the variation among these countries is quite small. Consequently DEMOCRACY would not explain most of the variation in the dependent variable. Therefore, the more reliable result was obtained in the larger sample in the model with eGOV(UN)2003 as dependent variable, where GDPPC and DEMOCRACY account for 59% of the variation. Among these two factors GDPPC seems to be the most influential factor as it has the highest standardized β coefficient.

Table 5 displays results from regression analysis in which DEMOCRACY is regressed on different e-government readiness variables. The model with eGOV(NRI) variable is not displayed because of its poor statistical quality. In the first model GDPPC was the only significant factor. In the second model both factors, i.e., e-government readiness and GDP per capita, were highly significant but accounted only 29% of variation in the country's democratic scores. The third regression model was used to answer the question about the contribution of each component of U.N. e-govern-

Table 5. Regression models for democracy

Left hand side variable	Regression Model		
	DEMOCRACY	DEMOCRACY	DEMOCRACY
	Standardized β (*t*-ratio)		
GDPPC	0.545 (7.58)**	0.262 (2.78)**	
eGOV(WM)2003	-0.060 (-0.83)		
eGOV(UN)2003		0.315 (3.35)**	
WMI			0.273 (3.08)**
TII			0.400 (4.68)**
HCI			-0.090 (-1.28)
R^2	0.27	0.29	0.34
adjusted R^2	0.26	0.28	0.33
F-ratio	34.6**	38.9**	32.0**
Sample size	192	191	191

* P-value < 0.01; ** P-value < 0.001

ment readiness index to the level of democracy. The three factors included, explain 34% of variation in the democracy level, among them WMI and TII have positive significant coefficients, while TII has a greater influence on the level of democracy than WMI. This suggests that from the perspective of supporting democratic processes in some countries it would be more important to build telecommunication infrastructure and increase the sophistication of the government online presence than trying to increase the value of the human capital index. A small R^2 would suggest reconsidering the specification of the regression model, such as including the factors that might affect democracy, but are missing in the current specification.

To assess the robustness of results in Table 5 two alternative measures of democracy have been used: POLITY2 and POLYARCHY.

The results for the first two models in Table 6 are consistent with the result of the first model in Table 5. Namely, only GDPPC is statistically significant, while eGOV(WM)2003 is not. The last two models in Table 6 are consistent with the result of the second model in Table 5. Both variables: GDP per capita and UN e-government readiness index were highly significant and accounted 32% and 51% of variation in the country's democratic scores (POLITY2 and POLYARCHY measures respectively). Thus, we may conclude that the regression model for democracy is robust enough to the changes in the measures of democracy used.

Returning to the four postulated hypotheses, it could be said that the hypothesis H1 was moderately supported, in other words, the government of a more democratic country does have a positive attitude toward increasing the level of e-government readiness. Hypothesis H2 was moderately supported via correlation analysis, for

Table 6. Regression models for democracy (alternative democracy indices)

Left hand side variable	Regression Model			
	POLITY2	POLYARCHY	POLITY2	POLYARCHY
	Standardized β (*t*-ratio)			
GDPPC	0.455	0.613	-0.189	0.141
	(4.89)**	(8.86)**	(-1.36)	(1.48)
eGOV(WM)2003	-0.012	0.050		
	(-0.13)	(0.73)		
eGOV(UN)2003			0.722	0.594
			(5.21)**	(6.24)**
R^2	0.200	0.413	0.319	0.512
adjusted R^2	0.190	0.406	0.310	0.507
F-ratio	19.0**	63.6**	35.3**	94.6**
Sample size	154	183	153	182

* P-value < 0.01; ** P-value < 0.001

example, the government of a country with less corruption does have a positive attitude toward increasing the level of e-government readiness. However, because of the multicollinearity problem detected in the regression model with the CORRUPTION variable included, was not possible to separate the impact of corruption from the other variables (GDPPC in particular). Hypothesis H3 was not supported—the country's integration in the world economy has nothing to do with the attitude toward increasing the level of e-government readiness. Hypothesis H4 was mildly supported—the government of a country that actively works on increasing the level of e-government readiness would be rated higher on the democratic scale.

Concluding Remarks

Our review of the recent literature discloses that at the theoretical level there are indications of a positive relationship between e-government readiness, democracy, and globalization and a negative relationship between these three variables and corruption. Though there have been a few empirical studies on these relationships the evidence remains contradictory. For example Norris (2001, 2002) suggests that there is a relationship between e-government readiness and democracy, while West (2004) and La Porte et al. (2000) suggest that no such relationship exists. Other authors, such as Moon et al. (2005), found some evidence of a weak relationship between e-government readiness and democracy. Similar inconclusive results were achieved for the relationship between e-government readiness and globalization, and e-government readiness and corruption.

The research reported here demonstrates moderate support for the propositions developed in this chapter. First, there has been change in countries' positions measured on World Markets e-government readiness scale. An overall trend is that countries did not improve their position in 2003 in comparison to 2001. There is a significant increase in the quality of the features offered on the government Web sites in the underdeveloped and developing countries, which moved them higher on the e-government readiness list. Also, a reduction in the gap in the quality of government Web sites between wealthiest and poorer countries has been identified. Second, contrary to expectation, globalization does not appear to contribute to a country's e-government readiness. This result is due to the bias in the sample structure when the globalization variable is included. Third, the inclusion of an economic variable, such as GDPPC, induces a multicollinearity problem (high correlation between the economic variable and corruption) which was reduced by dropping the corruption variable. Fourth, the government of a more democratic country appears to be more enthusiastic to pursue an e-government initiative than an authoritarian government. However, this research finding is not robust across the different e-government readiness constructs, only eGOV(UN)2003 shows a strong relationship with DEMOCRACY. We believe these inconsistencies could be partly attributed to selection bias and to the conceptual differences in the definition of an e-government readiness measures. Namely, eGOV(WM)2003 only captures the features of government Web sites, while the two other indicators encompass the technological and human components of overall e-government readiness.

The study shows also the robustness of regression models for democracy using alternative democracy measures, such as Freedom House, Polity and Polyarchy, confirms the impact that democracy has on the e-government readiness has on democracy.

This study has implications both for practice and for theory. It shows that the DEMOCRACY variable is moderately relevant to the worldwide e-government readiness. Indeed, the empirical analysis found that the model with both economic and democracy variables explains the differences in intra-country e-government readiness accounted for about 60% of the variability in eGOV(UN)2003. In addition to this empirical finding, the study also has implications for the adoption of a new technology theory. Empirical results justify the inclusion of political variables and demonstrate the need to broaden the adoption of the new technology theory in the area of the influence of political factors. On the other hand, countries that do extremely well in implementing an e-government initiative will be more democratic and liberal. The three factors included: WMI, TII, and HCI, explain 34% of variation in the DEMOCRACY, but the first two components make the most important contribution.

There are a few main limitations which constrain the conclusiveness and generalizability of this research.

1. We have examined e-government readiness at the national level. This approach based on the highest level of data aggregation, could partly distort results in case of federal states as was suggested by one of reviewers. Since in federal states e-government solutions are primarily offered on the subnational level in such cases e-government readiness measures or at least component which is related to the Web presence might indicate lower level of overall country's e-Readiness despite the fact that the Web presence at the subnational level might be very sophisticated. In future research, the introduction of an indicator such as "form of government" in the analysis should probably be able to capture this effect.

2. The globalization and corruption indices were derived from Kearney (2003) and Transparency International (2004). Since the other globalization and corruption indices are available it would be necessary to assess whether these indices based on alternative definitions, confirms the impact that globalization and corruption might have on the e-government readiness and vice versa.

3. Beside a few economic and political factors we have considered, other factors such as social and cultural and a full list of economic and political variables that might affect e-government readiness should be considered as candidates for inclusion in the model. The current model of e-government readiness might be mis-specified. This may prove important in future research.

Acknowledgments

This chapter in its original form was published in the inaugural issue of the *International Journal of Electronic Government Research, 1*(3), 15-32. I take this opportunity to thank three anonymous journal reviewers for their time and extremely valuable work which helped me to improve the final version of this chapter. However, the author should be held responsible for any remaining errors.

References

Altman, D. (2002). Prospects for e-government in Latin America: Satisfaction with democracy, social accountability, and direct democracy. *International Review of Public Administration, 7*(2), 5-20.

Bridges.org (2001). *Comparison of e-readiness assessment models.* Retrieved April 1, 2004, from http://www.bridges.org/ereadiness/report.html

Casper, G., & Tufis, C. (2002). Correlation versus interchangeability: The limited robustness of empirical findings on democracy using highly correlated datasets. *Political Analysis, 11*(2), 1-11.

Choucri, N., Maugis, V., Madnick, S., & Siegel, M. (2003). Global e-Readiness: For what? *MIT Sloan School of Management Research Paper 177.*

Edmiston, K. D. (2003). State and local e-government: Prospects and challenges. *American Review of Public Administration, 33*(1), 20-45.

Fountain, J. E. (2001). The virtual state: Transforming American government? *National Civic Review, 90*(3), 241-251.

Fountain, J. E. (2004). Digital government and public health. *Preventing chronic disease: Public Health Research, Practice, and Policy, 1*(4), 1-5.

Freedom House. (2004). *Freedom in the World Country Ratings 1972 through 2003.* Retrieved May 10 2004, from http://www.freedomhouse.org

Graaf, G. d. (2004). *Portraits of corruption: Towards a contextual theory of corruption*. EGPA 2004 Annual Conference, Four months after: Administering the New Europe, Ljubljana, Slovenia.

Grönlund, Å. (2003). Emerging electronic infrastructures: Exploring democratic components. *Social Science Computer Review, 21*(1), 55-72.

Holden, S. H., Norris, D. F., & Fletcher, P. D. (2003). *Electronic government at the grass roots: Contemporary evidence and future trends*. Proceedings of the 36th Hawaii International Conference on System Sciences.

Huberts, L. W. J. C. (1998). What can be done against public corruption and fraud: Expert views on strategies to protect public integrity. *Crime, Law & Social Change, 29*, 209-224.

Huntington, S. P. (1989). Modernization and corruption. In A. J. J. Heidenheimer, M. Johnson, & V. T. LeVine (Eds.), *Political corruption. A handbook* (pp. 377-388). New Brunswick NJ: Transaction Press.

Intriligator, M. D. (2001). *Globalization of the world economy: Potential benefits and costs and a net assessment*. Center for Globalization and Policy Research, School of Public Policy and Social Research, Working Paper No 2. UCLA.

Jain, A. (2004). *Using the lens of Max Weber's theory of bureaucracy to examine e-government research*. Proceedings of the 37th Hawaii International Conference on System Sciences, Big Island.

Jakob, G. (2003). Electronic government: Perspectives and pitfalls of online administrative procedure. *Proceedings of the 36th Hawaii International Conference on System Sciences*.

Kampen, J. K., & Snijkers, K. (2003). E-democracy: A critical evaluation of the ultimate e-dream. *Social Science Computer Review, 21*(4), 491-497.

Kaufmann, D., Kraay, A., & Zoido-Lobatón, P. (1999). Governance matters. *World Bank Policy Research Working Paper No. 2196*, Washington.

Kearney, A. T. (2003). Measuring globalization: Who's up, who's down? Globalization at Work. *Foreign Policy*, 60-72.

Kedzie, C. R. (1997). Communication and democracy: Coincident revolutions and the emergent dictator's dilemma. *RAND, RGSD-127*.

Kirkman, G. S., Osorio, C. A., & Sachs, J. D. (2002). The network readiness index: Measuring the preparedness of nations for the networked world. In S. Dutta, B. Lanvin, & F. Paua, (Eds.), *The global information technology report 2001-2002: Readiness for the networked world* (pp. 10-29). New York: Oxford University Press.

Kraemer, K. L., & King, J. L. (2003). *Information technology and administrative reform: Will the time after e-Government be different?* Paper prepared for the

Heinrich Reinermann Schrift Fest, Post Graduate School of Administration, Speyer, Germany.

Lambsdorff, J. G. (2003). *Framework document: Background paper to the 2003 corruption perceptions index*. Transparency International and University of Passau.

La Porta, Lopez-De-Silanes, R. F., Shleifer, A., & Vishny, R. (1999). The quality of government. *Journal of Law, Economics, and Organization, 15*, 222-279.

La Porte, T. M., de Jong, M., & Demchak, C. (1999). Public organizations on the World Wide Web: Empirical correlates of administrative openness. *The National Public Management Research Conference*, Texas A&M University.

La Porte, T. M., Demchak, C., de Jong, M., & Friis, C. (2000). Democracy and bureaucracy in the age of Web: Empirical findings and theoretical speculations. *The International Political Association*, Québec, Canada.

La Porte, T. M., Demchak, C. C., & Friis, C. (2001). Webbing governance: Global trends across national level public agencies. *Communications of the ACM, 44*(1), 63-67.

Lederman, D., Loayza, N., & Soares, R. R. (2001). Accountability and corruption: Political institutions matter. *World Bank Policy Research Working Paper 2708*.

Lidén, G., & Avdic, A. (2003). *Democracy functions of information technology*. Proceedings of the 36th Hawaii International Conference on System Sciences. Big Island.

Marshall, M. G., & Jaggers, K. (2004). *Polity IV Project: Political regime characteristics and transitions, 1800-2003*. Retrieved July 10, 2005, from http://www.cidcm.umd.edu/inscr/polity/polreg.htm

Mauro, P. (1995). Corruption and growth. *Quarterly Journal of Economics, 110*, 681-712.

Moon, M. J., Welch, E. W., & Wong, W. (2005). *What drives global e-governance? An exploratory study at a macro level*. Proceedings of the 38th Hawaii International Conference on System Sciences.

Munck, G. L., & Verkuilen, J. (2002). Conceptualizing and measuring democracy: Evaluating alternative indices. *Comparative Political Studies, 35*(1), 5-34.

Norris, P. (2001). *Digital divide? Civic engagement, information poverty and the Internet worldwide*. Cambridge: Cambridge University Press.

Norris, P. (2003). Deepening democracy via e-governance. *World Public Sector Report*, United Nations.

Oates, B. J. (2003). The potential contribution of ICTs to the political process. *Electronic Journal of e-Government, 1*(1).

Okot-Uma, W'O R. (2004). *Building cyberlaw capacity for e-governance: Technology perspectives.* The Commonwealth Centre for e-Governance, London.

Shi, Y., & Scavo, C. (2000). Citizen participation and direct democracy through computer networking. In G. D. Garson (Ed.), *Handbook of public information systems* (pp. 247-263). New York: Marcel Dekker.

Transparency International. (2001). *Global corruption report 2001.*

Transparency International. (2004). *Global corruption report 2004.*

Tsagarousianou, R. (1999). Electronic democracy: Rhetoric and reality. *Communications: The European Journal of Communication Research, 24*(2), 189-208.

United Nations. (2001). *Benchmarking e-government: A global perspective. Assessing the progress of the UN member states.*

United Nations. (2003). *UN global e-government survey.*

U.S. Central Intelligence Agency. (2002). CIA World Factbook 2002. Retrieved July 10, 2005, from http://www2.cia.gov/2002/factbook2002.zip

U.S. Central Intelligence Agency. (2003). CIA World Factbook 2003. Retrieved July 10, 2005, from http://www2.cia.gov/2003/factbook2003.zip

Vanhanen, T. (2000). A new dataset for measuring democracy, 1810-1998. *Journal of Peace Research, 37,* 251-265.

Vanhanen, T. (2002). The Polyarchy dataset: Vanhanen's index of democracy. Retrieved July 10, 2005, from http://www.prio.no/page/Project_detail//9244/42472.html

West, D. M. (2001). *World Markets Research Centre Global E-Government Survey 2001.* Retrieved May 10, 2004, from http://www.worldmarketsanalysis.com/pdf/e-govreport.pdf

West, D. M. (2004). *Global perspectives on e-government.* Annual Meeting of the American Political Science Association, Chicago.

Chapter X

Scenarios for Future Use of E-Democracy Tools in Europe

Herbert Kubicek, University of Bremen, Germany

Hilmar Westholm, Institute for Information Management Bremen, GmbH, Germany

Abstract

Many ICT-based tools for supporting democratic participation that have been developed with public funds and applied in pilot projects have not yet achieved large-scale outreach. Optimists still believe this will happen; sceptics doubt. This chapter starts from the assumption that technological development and diffusion are largely influenced by socioeconomic conditions. It develops a contingency model for e-democracy tools and applies the scenario method for differentiating the future context of these tools. It is based on the results of a research project that described possible futures of European e-government in general and e-democracy in particular on a 10-year time horizon by using the scenario method and inputs from European experts on e-government. Out of three different scenarios, possible and plausible futures of e-democracy are described in order to analyse robust technologies that are expected to be used in all three scenarios.

The Research Question and Approach

Recently, former EU Commissioner Erkki Liikanen expected new information and communication technology (ICT) to provide a great push for the participation of citizens in political decision processes (2004). These technologies can make participation cheaper and more effective on the side of the citizens as well as on the side of the administration or political bodies. Others are more sceptical about the impact of technologies and stress the relevance of societal, economic, and cultural factors for the future development of democratic participation (Coleman, 2003). There have always been technological utopians and optimists and social science-based technological sceptics. When governments are requested to invest in platforms and tools for e-democracy and/or to launch funding programs for technical support of local processes, these scholarly differences are not very helpful. Of course, nobody is able today to predict the use of ICT in democratic processes 10 years from now with a high degree of certainty. Technological predictions have turned out more often to be false than true.

In this chapter, a more differentiated approach is chosen to analyze the future use of e-democracy tools. Instead of applying a yes or no dichotomy, we develop a contingency model with a set of context factors that are considered to have some influence on these developments. Assumptions about the future constellation of these context factors are derived by the scenario method. These scenarios are not predictions. They have been developed to contrast different developments and, thus, to define a space of possible futures. In order to analyze the future use of ICT in democratic processes, the use within each of the scenarios can be compared. By identifying communalities and differences in the use of ICT, finally we can analyze the robustness of the technological tools (i.e., their context sensibility) and provide a more profound answer to the question of whether, depending on different social and economic conditions, the kinds of e-democracy tools will vary in the future or only the kind of application of basically the same tools. In the latter case, investment and program definition decisions would be less risky today.

The concept of a contingency approach was developed in organisation theory in the late 1960s and stressed the fact that organisations develop differently and adopt different structures, according to differences in their environments and other characteristics, such as size, technology, and so forth (Kieser & Kubicek, 1983; Lawrence & Lorsch, 1967; Pugh, Hickson, Hinings & Turner, 1969). A contingency model starts with defining the dependent variables that are to be explained or predicted, then looks for the relevant factors influencing their development, and finally, checks whether relevant contextual factors might intervene or influence both sets of variables. The dependent variables in our subject area are e-democracy tools and their use, which are described in the following section. The influencing or context variables are differentiated into the specific context for democratic participation and the broader socioeconomic context for which the scenario method has been applied. The contingency model, the scenario approach, and the role of e-democracy tools within these scenarios are presented in later sections. This article also discusses the robustness of the e-democracy tools by comparing the three scenarios.

E-Democracy Tools

Electronic democracy and digital democracy are rather recent terms for which a generally agreed definition has not yet been found (Coleman & Gøtze, 2001; Hague & Loader, 1999; Jankowski & van Selm, 2000; Tsagarousianou, Tambini & Brian, 1998). We define e-democracy in this context similar to Hacker & Van Dijk's (2000) definition of digital democracy, as the use of ICTs (mainly the Internet, and mobile technologies) and CMC (computer mediated communication) to enhance active participation of citizens and to support the collaboration between actors for policy-making purposes without the limits of time, space, and other physical conditions in democratic communication, whether acting as citizens, their elected representatives, or on behalf of administrations, parliaments, or associations (i.e. lobby groups, interest groups, NGOs) within the political processes of all stages of governance. According to Tsagarousianou (1999), electronic democracy consists of three components: information provision, deliberation, and participation in decision making.

A wide range of ICT applications for citizens' participation has emerged over the last decade. These applications or tools can be distinguished by their func-tionality in three categories (OECD, 2001):

- information, such as Web sites and portals with elaborated search functions, frequently asked questions (FAQs), Web-casting of meetings, newsletters, and so forth;
- communication and consultation, such as online forums, chats, and newsgroups, petitions and complaint management systems; and
- active participation, such as online mediation, voting in elections and referenda, and so forth.

These electronic tools substitute or complement analogue formal and informal means that serve the same functions. Table 1 lists different analogue means of citizens' involvement, assigns corresponding electronic online tools, and gives some recent examples of application.

These tools are applied at different stages of the policy cycle, in the phase of prob-lem perception, agenda setting, decision-making, implementation, and evaluation,

Table 1. Means of citizen involvement and corresponding e-democracy tools

Analogue means of citizens' involvement (examples)		Online
Formal	*informal*	*Electronic tool*
Information		
Access to information according to national (Freedom-of-information-) acts	Brochures, flyers	Web sites of governments, local communities and politicians providing textual and illustrative (GIS) information
		Information management systems / Knowledge Management systems
		Search function for information access
		Online-glossary
	Hotlines	FAQ
TV-Broadcasting of council or parliament sessions		Webcast of meetings
Announcement of council meetings Announcement of legislation in selected newspapers and journals		Instant messaging, newsletter
Communication and consultation		
Legally binding planning procedures		Online forms
Participation of representatives of NGOs in council committees		
Citizen meetings, Hearings	Focus groups, Neighbourhood committees	Online-forum
Citizen request sessions within council meetings	Complaint management	Web-based complaint management
Petitions		Online petition
	NGO's / interest groups' campaigning + protests: letters to members and sympathizers	Email
		Newsgroups
	Surveys	Polling
		Interactive web-based city-planning game
		Chat with single political and administrative representatives or about specific issues
		Citizen's comments on draft bills
		NGO's: online protests, campaigning
Active participation		
Elections, referenda, ballots		e-voting at elections, ballots or referenda
Involvement of representatives of NGOs in legislation and planning procedures	Consensus conferences, Mediation, Round tables, Advocacy planning	Online mediation, CSCW

most often in combination with the established traditional means and procedures (for a compilation of these tools, see Kubicek, Westholm, & Winkler, 2003). In technical terms, many of the existing applications are prototypes or rather simple systems. However, the more binding the information collected by these tools has to be, the more demanding are the technical requirements with regard to scalability and, in particular, security. For example, to run a survey on the Internet for which it is not important whether some people fill in two or more questionnaires, makes quite different demands than using the Internet for legally-binding referenda. Scalability refers to the number of users and interactions that a platform has to deal with. We assume that the functionality, the degree of binding force, and the scale of e-democracy tools in 10 years are dependent on a number of factors, which are combined in a contingency model.

A Contingency Model of E-Democracy

As mentioned before, a contingency model defines a set of independent or context variables that are assumed to influence the dependent variables in focus. Of course, the use of e-democracy tools depends on the kind and number of democratic processes in society. During the past 10 years, we have learned that the Internet only provides a platform for supporting democratic procedures and that the use of such provisions is still determined by the standard model of political participation (Dalton, 1988) and by the political culture, which influences the extent and the direction of civic engagement. This is in line with the basic assumption developed in technology assessment research in the late 1970s, arguing that ICT is an amplifier of existing or emerging social trends (Reese, Kubicek, Lange, Lutterbeck, & Reese, 1979). The crucial question, then, is what the relevant trends with regard to e-democracy look like. We propose a multi-layer conceptual framework to answer this question. The dependent variables in our case are the offerings of e-democracy tools. These offerings depend directly on the kind of participation offered by public administrations and political bodies, as these tools have to be embedded into these institutions. The choice of which tools are used and which share of the whole information and communication offerings e-democracy tools will have in relation to other media and forms (e.g., print media, physical meetings) varies, depending on the subject, the scope and range, and the addressees of the participation offering in question.

This participation setting establishes the immediate context for e-democracy tools. In addition, the extent and frequency of offered e-democracy tools is influenced by the use of these tools by citizens and NGOs and may also be a response to demands for participation by citizens and/or NGOs.

The demand for and the offering of participation are dependent variables themselves. According to the proposed multi-layer framework, we distinguish between a specific and a broader context (see Figure 1). The broader context refers to the broad and general socioeconomic and sociocultural trends, which are also relevant to explain the use of ICT in e-government, e-business, e-learning, and other areas. They are covered by the scenarios developed in the EU-funded project PRISMA (Providing Innovative Service Models and Assessment). Besides or rather within these broader trends, there are subtrends specific to different application areas. As a specific context for e-democracy, we suggest looking at four trends or conditions that influence the offering of and the demand for participation. By analyzing these factors, it should

Figure 1. A "contingency model" of e-democracy tools

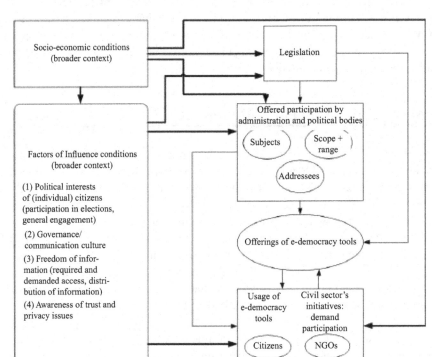

be possible to explain differences in the kind and scope of participation between countries but also to make predictions about offerings and their acceptance as they may establish a more or less favourable and supportive environment.

1.   The most frequently mentioned factor is the political interest and the resulting civic engagement. Since citizens have become less deferential and dependent, and more consumerist and volatile, old styles of representation have come under pressure to change, and the traditional affiliation to established mass institutions, such as churches and trade unions, gets lost (Putnam, 2000). In many democracies, not only participation rates in elections in the long term are decreasing, but there is also a decline of membership in civil networks and long-term political engagement, in general, with less commitment to the political process and less trust in government (Coleman & Gøtze, 2002). Nowadays, citizens prefer selective, focused, and limited involvement in political processes and transparency of political-administrative procedures. But there are still differences between countries and variations, depending on how controversial issues are and how the voters assess the importance of an election (Forschungsgruppe Wahlen, 2004).

Similar differences exist as to what extent direct democratic procedures are appropriate to support and supplement representative democracy, sometimes combined with deliberative elements; citizens' initiatives, referenda, and ballots become part of the constitutional law, mostly on the local level. "Legislatures are increasingly squeezed between the general public and the executive; the new technologies make plebiscite democracy more feasible and this possibility is putting pressure on representative democracy" (OECD, 1998, p. 8). But these forms of votes are often criticised, because they reduce complex political problems to simplifying yes/no alternatives (Bellamy & Taylor, 1998), and ICT-supported voting by pressing the button amplifies this risk, as well.

2.   Communication culture covers a whole bundle of different trends, such as the openness of political discourse, tolerance for minorities, the existence of common values, and so forth, which vary to a large extent among EU-member states. New means of cooperation are emerging, such as consensus-building strategies with mediation and covenants as results. One decisive but still rather open trend is the future role of non-governmental organisations (NGOs). Given the alienation of parts of society toward politics on the one hand and the globalisation of economic activities, standards of human rights, ecological risks, and ICT-networks on the other hand, new political organisations are emerging, which act increasingly independent from the borders of nations and seem to be a symptom of globalisation as well as an answer to it.

Meanwhile, interest groups are also better informed, better linked through networks, and, according to a survey in eight OECD-countries, better able to bring pressure to bear, especially on the middle level of bureaucracy (OECD, 1998). NGOs have used the advantages of the Internet as one of the first political stakeholders. Practices of representation are of extreme importance for these groups, because contact to target groups normally can be provided only via media channels. Electronic mailing (lists) is a good example for cheap dissemination of specific information over far distances.

3.   Many countries have launched freedom of information acts providing access to government information for citizens. In particular, NGOs are making use of these access rights. However, at the same time, public administrations are required to act like enterprises and to look for new kinds of revenues. One idea is to sell the information that is gathered for administrative purposes. A prominent example is geographical information. This is in line with a more general trend of commodification of information. There are not only chances of new revenues for administrations, but the administrations themselves suddenly have to pay for information that was available for free before. New intellectual property rights are requiring payments for providing information to citizens, raising costs of public libraries, and so forth. Partly due to the Internet, many citizens expect that information that is available within government is made

available to the public, as well, and a large majority expects that this information is provided for free without any special charges. This expectation collides with the economic pressure for cost effectiveness in public administration and with the trend toward commodification of information described previously.

4.   Awareness of trust and data privacy issues concerning ICT also has a strong influence on participatory processes and the use of e-democracy tools. But this attitude varies throughout Europe, as also does the general trust in governmental bodies. Citizens and companies want to know how their data are used and how personal (and business) data and privacy are protected. Governmental agencies are insisting on strong data protection regulations, while these tendencies could interfere with enhancing ICTs. Transparency may become an even stronger demand because of concerns of corruption and spending of taxpayers' money.

This description of the specific context of e-democracy shows that these factors or conditions depend on a broader context of general socioeconomic conditions and developments. They shall be considered in the form of scenarios.

The Scenario Approach

A scenario describes a possible future and is one of the tools that is used in foresight exercises and for policy analysis. This instrument incorporates developments both within the system (endogenous) and outside the system (exogenous) that affect the system under consideration (Botterman et al., 2001). It presents an analytic tool to identify uncertainties of a policy decision and aims at enabling decision makers to make more rational decisions, considering the unpredictability of the future (Riet, Loo, Kahan, & Europe, 2002). As such, a scenario has to fulfil the following criteria:

•   It should be plausible, but it does not have to be probable. Given the uncertainty of the future, it needs to be explicitly stated that the scenario is not a prediction, but only a possibility, as likely as many other possibilities.

•   It should be internally consistent in order to be plausible and in order to enable a coherent discussion.

•   It should not describe the developments that led to the described picture of the future.

•   It should contain enough information to describe the functioning of a system.

In the research on which this chapter is based, the process of scenario building was designed as a two-stage process. Stage one was devoted to developing exploratory scenarios by a team of RAND Europe, Leiden (The Netherlands), the Danish Technological Institute, Copenhagen and Arhus, and the Institute of Technology Assessment within the Austrian Academy of Science, Vienna, mainly based on existing work, including the European Commission's Forward Studies Unit "Scenarios for Europe 2010" (1999) and the ISTAG "Scenarios for Ambient Intelligence in 2010" (2001). In this stage, five drivers and important dimensions of change were identified out of a total of 75 trends and drivers by discussing the major trends in the areas of sociocultural, economic, political, technical, and ecological changes over the next 10 years within the whole research consortium, which was composed of e-government experts from academia, a think tank, and consultants in 12 European states. These trends and drivers were then consolidated and assessed according to four criteria:

- importance (i.e., importance for e-service delivery: low, medium, high);
- certainty (i.e., likelihood of occurrence: low, medium, high);
- controllability (i.e., ability to manage if high; ability to determine outcome, if not: low, medium, high); and
- significance (global and European: yes, no).

Using assessments of the project-involved experts on all trends and drivers, four dimensions were identified upon which the scenarios could be built:

1. prosperity of the economy and society;
2. power of government;
3. degree of innovation of information technology; and
4. consideration of sustainable development.

All drivers considered important to any sector were included in at least one of the four dimensions. In addition, some drivers, especially those considered important with high certainty, were used in all of the scenarios as context-setting materials. These include, among others, population growth and migration. These dimensions were treated as variables that could have different (i.e., positive, negative, etc.) values. Using them to arrive at scenarios, at least eight possible scenarios were considered before a set of three was selected (Prisma, 2002a).

Stage two integrated the external scenarios from stage one and sketched plausible effects on e-administration and e-democracy as important sections of e-government.

Figure 2. Overview on scenarios of future e-government

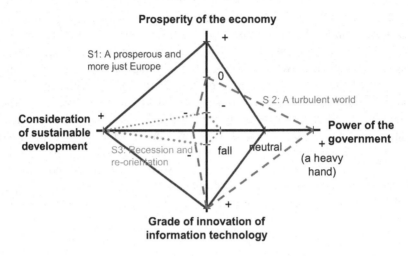

This stage was undertaken with important inputs from 15 internal and external experts in e-government in group discussions in a specifically designed scenario workshop. Given each external scenario, their expertise was used to determine future-oriented good practice related to e-administration and e-democracy, based on fundamental European values (normative standards) and in consideration of circumstances and requirements of service provision in 2010. For this chapter, only the results for e-democracy were extracted.

Three Scenarios for E-Democracy

The main results are full descriptions of three alternative scenarios that represent realistic, internally consistent, and plausible pictures of alternative futures, while probability is not the focus but the covering of a wide range of principally possible futures.

Scenario 1: A Prosperous and More Just Europe

The first decade of the 21st century has been beyond everyone's expectations. The world is at peace and has experienced widespread economic and social progress. It is possible to combine economic growth with a reduction in the environmental burden on the planet. Moore's Law is still in force, and ICT continues to contribute to the prosperity of Europe. The scenario assumes positive economic development, a neutral (i.e., less regulating) role of government, a positive contribution by ICT technologies, and increasing sustainable development.

By 2010, governments will be re-organized at all levels and enable horizontal (among different agencies on the same level) as well as vertical (among different levels of government) integration of services, which then will be delivered at one-stop sites with flexible front offices. They are gaining enough tax revenues to invest in ICT infrastructure, such as public access points. E-government is well funded and attracts more and more users. People trust technological systems; government becomes "big brother" and "invisible," but people will be happy with it. Technological devices have become indispensable, and most homes have turned into e-homes. Good co-operation with the private and third sectors provides a combination of private and public services according to special life events and commercial issues.

The ongoing privatisation of the public sector helped to balance the public budget of most member states. In 2010, they will be able to increase their public spending on social policy and provide public services, together with non-profit organisations and private corporations to EU citizens.

E-democracy becomes less state-centred (e.g., political parties lose large numbers of their supporters), while many NGOs register an increase in (passive) member-ship. Consequently, co-operation and highly integrated network building among stakeholders from all edges of the political triangle (state, market, civil society) are improved.

Despite increased contacts as consumers of services, citizens all over Europe have low political interest, because they are largely satisfied with the status quo and feel very comfortable. A smug population will just vote, but does not participate in deliberative affairs. On the information stage, administrations will continue to publish their information at one-stop e-portals, while some of these services, mainly economically attractive information like geographical data, are being commercialised by private enterprises. Public access to information about com-panies will increase, as freedom-of-information acts have been extended and include information that nowadays is not available, because it is considered as business secrets. Extensive freedom of information rights increased the trust in the political system and its institutions, in particular because pro-active information delivery has become the rule, and inter-governmental knowledge management systems are performing well.

"Online-consultations" are broadly provided but rarely used. They offer procedures to discuss political and planning issues, but mainly so that citizens can comment on planning issues electronically. The social exclusion issue in participation will still continue, due to the circumstance that citizens on the lower income and educa-tion level are not very interested in deliberative participation processes. "Active participation" in the form of groupware-based "communities of practice" will only be used frequently by (growing) networks of experts (e.g., in issue-related consensus-oriented mediation and moderation processes). "E-voting" will be applied in many areas but will not substitute for traditional voting in political elections, as basic security issues have not been solved.

Scenario 2: A Turbulent World

In this scenario, economic growth has not been sustained. After an initial trend toward privatisation and outsourcing, there has been a shift back toward strong central government capacities. At the same time, the market power of the private sector has increased significantly. The two forces are frequently in severe conflict. Driven by market incentives, information technology has continued to grow, while the concern for sustainability has been abandoned in favour of economic volatility. The scenario assumes slow but unstable economic development, an intervention-ist role of government, a positive contribution by ICT technologies, and a loss of sustainability.

By 2010, the market will be characterised by ruthless competition in a winner-take-all environment. As a result of privatisation and outsourcing in the first half of the first decade in this century, a growing proportion of public tasks will be provided by private enterprises, and e-government will have to compete with private orga-nizations offering similar services. Digital exclusion has become a big issue both worldwide (the developed vs. the developing world) and on the local level. Society has become more fragmented than ever; the individual reigns supreme. Internet access, although widespread, is inefficiently organised and relatively expensive for anything other than e-mail and information services. Due to pervasive applica-tions, people do not think any longer about when and how they are interacting with computers. Although turbulent, the IT sector will expand in this scenario.

Government is politically strong, but its economic basis is poor due to decreasing tax revenues. Most European countries were forced to consolidate their national budgets by severe cuts. In this scenario, there is pressure for rapid change within governmental organisations. Governments' main task becomes taking care of the "losers" of the economic development. Therefore, a flexible development of various delivery channels is necessary—Internet access for the richer and individualised face-to-face contacts for the "have-nots."

By 2010, nation states and regional identities are still the most meaningful reference points for citizens. The trend away from globalisation is reinforced by the growing influence of anti-globalisation movements that organize protests throughout the world against increasing investment liberalisation and the widening gap between rich and poor countries. Economic and social turbulence has heightened the politi-cal interest of voters. People can now access information when, where, and how they want, but government will only provide information for money under this scenario. Government increasingly intervenes and attempts to return a number of privatised services to some form of public ownership. The private sector resists. Concurrent with the privatisation of marketable functions of the state, the role of the third sector becomes more important; associations support e-democracy through provision of links from and to e-government. This education in citizenship leads to a stronger civil society; e-democracy becomes less state-centred. As international governance becomes more and more important, there is a need for international cooperation. The Internet has become the medium of choice for political discussions, developing strategies, and planning action on this level as well. In a turbulent world there is a greater need for accurate information than ever before. Therefore, administrations are considered reliable institutions by most user-groups. Only a small new source of revenue for administrations will have been generated by charging fees for information delivered according to FOI law. IT business takes over development of those e-democracy tools and applications, which are expected to become profitable (e.g., development of online-voting tools and the provision of platforms for e-democracy toolkits).

Scenario 3: Recession and Reorientation

In the decade up to 2010, people favoured decentralisation, environmentalism, and local markets, whereas they have become more sceptical toward technology, government, and global market forces. The scenario assumes only slow economic development, a smaller role of government, a slow development of ICT technologies, but an increasingly sustainable development. Citizens have turned to non-materialism, and more emphasis has been put on spiritual values. Environmentalism has become in vogue again, and NGOs have seized control of the agenda.

After an economic crash in the mid-2000s, Europe's economy recovered slowly. Most Western EU countries successfully consolidated their public budgets due to significant reduction of public expenditure. Introducing lean administration models and privatising public functions have downsized most European public administrations. Budget shifts enabled the reorganisation of the European welfare systems. The Central and Eastern European countries (CEEC) became the focal point of growth in Europe; however, cuts in EU subsidies slowed down the economic development process there. The European internal market becomes more important; the clientele of government will not be mainly its citizens, but business and third sector to a higher degree than today.

Increasing liberalisation of investment flows caused worldwide protests organised by grassroots organisations. This deprivation of political power has resulted in extremely low voter turnouts, but has also led to a resurgence of political interest from the bottom up. Citizens were enabled to set up local community associations in which a third of the population is involved. NGOs have become progressively more important for policy making, while the membership and influence of political parties decreased. Large multi-national NGOs have become equal to their industrial counterparts in terms of political influence on government. Thus, governments consider these developments in their information strategies and outsource main parts of democratic tasks to the third sector and local communities. Simultaneously, more emphasis will be put on face-to-face meetings. Mediation with NGOs through combined delivery channels becomes an often-used procedure to solve conflicts.

Digital divide issues play a very important role in this scenario. However, in this context, most people are not unable to deal with technology; they are just unwilling to do so. People have become increasingly sceptical concerning technology and have lost faith and interest in technological devices. It has become fashionable to be unreachable by mobile phone or e-mail. Nevertheless, people will frequently be forced to use e-government services, since there is no alternative and most of the public services can only be accessed electronically. Neighborhood access points ensure that as many citizens as possible have access to these services.

Data protection has become more important. Personalised systems enable citizens and businesses to choose on which issue they want to get informed and to whom the information shall be delivered.

The potential of new media to provide easier and better access to government services for citizens and businesses has not been fully exploited. Although there is a strong demand for topical, correct, and easy-to-find information, the quality of public information provision is very poor under this scenario. Public authorities do not have the financial means to prepare well-structured and accurate information in all areas of governmental action, as this still requires a high degree of personnel resources. Therefore, their information strategies will concentrate on the subject areas relevant for the business sector and professional intermediaries (e.g., geographical information). Companies and NGOs use direct contact to offices to receive relevant information. Access to government-held information by citizens is still largely restricted either by data-protection law or by administrative culture.

The Role of ICT in Different Scenarios

The robustness or the sensitivity of e-democracy tools over the three scenarios is summarised in Table 2 according to three main categories of political involvement: information, communication and consultation, and active participation.

A main function of ICT over all scenarios is the electronic delivery of information that is relevant for all three sectors of the society: government, industry, and civic.

The scenarios differ with regard to FOI rights, privacy, and intellectual property rights issues. The discriminating criteria are content and costs. For instance, in the prosperous scenario, citizens expect reliable and quick information from public

Table 2. Implications of the scenarios on the robustness of tools—societal and market-related

Scenarios and robustness / Electronic tool	S 1: Prosperous and more just Europe	S 2: Turbulant world	S 3: Recession and re-orientation	Robustness over the scenarios and sensitivity analysis
Information				
Web sites *of governments, local communities and politicians providing textual, and illustrative information* *Information management systems (IMS) / Knowledge Management Systems (KMS)*	Important tools – most important providers are PA's (public administrations) Economically attractive information delivery is commercialised 3-D technologies are promoted; Intergovernmental IMS / KMS.	Civic sector demands for access to information and databases. PA's are reliable institutions – government provides information only for money. For specific areas, civic-sector organisations provide information.	Information services are not much improved. Access to government-held information is largely restricted either by law or by administrative culture. Public sector concentrates on good and reliable information for the business sector, intermediaries and NGO-work. IMS used between the market and civil sector.	*Technically and economically robust but providers vary over scenarios.* *Data are stored centrally with de-central access depending on the task of the agency and the issue. (In the recession scenario, some data such as information on health and income are stored de-centrally).*
Search function for information access, FAQ	Promoted, FAQ's also supported by natural language processing (NLP)	Used - prerequisite to sell information services, increasing demand for FAQ's, hardly maintained	NGOs' job (voluntary or "outsourced") and targeted to their members	*Partially technically and economically robust, varying addressees over the scenarios; NLP only in the first*
Instant messaging, newsletter	Pro-active information delivery and citizen relationship management	Newsletter subscription	Targeted to multiplying groups and mediators because of financial restrictions	*Technically and economically robust (but different target groups and conditions)*
Webcast of meetings	Promoted		Hardly offered because of high cost and low demand	*Not robust*
Complaint management	Promoted (back-office integration by sophisticated routing technologies)	Used	Rarely used	*Not robust*
Communication and consultation				
Online petition	(Technically) promoted	Promoted	Rarely used, analogue means preferred	*Not robust* *Strongly related to online-voting because of authentication*
Email	Strongly used (new technologies developed for management)	Strongly used (new technologies developed for management)	NGOs specifically are using it for online protest and campaigning	*Robust;* *Strongly used (new technologies demanded and developed for management)*
Newsgroup	Used	Used	Used	*Robust*
Polling	Promoted	Rarely used for political communication	Not relevant because less representative	*Not robust*
Forum/ Consultation	Normally procedures to discuss political and planning issues but hardly used	People increasingly use the Internet to discuss matters of European and global concern	Less public political e-consultations but mainly for internal use (e.g. within NGOs)	*Robust but different means of use*
Interactive web-based city-planning game	Promoted	Not relevant	Not relevant	*Not robust*
Chat	Promoted, rarely used for political communication	Not relevant	Not relevant	*Technically robust, but no political relevance over the scenarios*

Table 2. continued

Scenarios and robustness / Electronic tool	S 1: Prosperous and more just Europe	S 2: Turbulent world	S 3: Recession and re-orientation	Robustness over the scenarios and sensitivity analysis
Active participation				
Online mediation	Promoted (civil servants as mediators)	Promoted (facilitation by "third parties")	With NGOs through various channels (face to face and ICT supported- often-used procedure to solve conflicts	*Robust*
Online-voting at elections, ballots or referenda	Realised (juridical and financial rather than technical problems)	Not promoted due to cost reasons – implementation only in side-areas (e.g. local level)	Not relevant, extremely low voter turnouts; but online-elections within NGOs	*Not robust* *Realisation of ballot voting via the Internet not robust, too.*
Groupware (CSCW)	Frequently used	Interest groups are using it at least for internal affairs as a (virtual) working platform.	Governments invest in networking strategies; interest and lobby groups are using it at least for internal affairs.	*Technically and economically robust, socially used in different circumstances over the scenarios.*

administrations rather than from other stakeholders. Public administrations are reliable institutions in the turbulent scenario, too. But for specific areas, especially the civic sector, organisations provide information. In the recession scenario, public sector concentrates on good and reliable information for the business sector, professional intermediaries, and NGO work. Meanwhile, in this scenario, environmental information as well as governmental permits and licenses become more important government services. Here, the civil society and especially NGOs are trustworthy organisations; and information tasks that today are fulfilled by the government are taken over by third sector organisations.

However, the increasing amount of information will promote the demand for information management strategies and systems (IMS). IMS and knowledge management systems will be technically and economically robust, but the providers vary over scenarios. In the prosperous world especially, good intergovernmental IMS are required, and in the recession scenario, IMS are mainly used "internally" within the market and civil society sector.

Both in the prosperous and in the turbulent scenario, a lot of information will be delivered for money. Besides Web casting of meetings, information delivery systems are both technically and economically robust; only the providers (for information management systems), the user-conditions (for instant messaging and pro-active information via newsletters), or the addressees (for search-function tools and FAQs) vary in the scenarios.

In the prosperous scenario, information can be tailored to a large number of specific target groups. In the turbulent world, e-government in general and e-democracy in particular can only be served selectively according to two criteria, important basic needs, and financial sustainability. In the recession scenario, a sophisticated mechanism of selection of target groups (e.g., students, due to their IT-skills and openness) is installed and combined with incentive-systems. Data are stored centrally with decentralised access, depending on the task of the agency and the issue. In the recession scenario, some data, such as information on health and income, are stored decentrally.

New means of democratic communication are being introduced, influenced both by societal changes like good governance and by technological innovations; the Internet will not only be used as a network of knowledge, but more and more as a (virtual) working and communication platform based on a huge organisational performance (Lenk, 1999). This implies more than tele-working and will influence opinion-making, especially on the local level.

Online consultations have been the beginning and are technically robust over the scenarios, although they are used in different ways in the scenarios. In the prosperous world, they are becoming normally provided procedures to discuss political and planning issues, although citizens are not very interested in deliberative participation processes. In the turbulent world, people increasingly use the Internet to discuss matters of European and global concern. In the recession scenario, they are mainly used internally (e.g., by NGOs). One challenge over all scenarios is to renovate procedures by structuring debates about controversial issues with Issue Based Information Systems (IBIS).

Meanwhile, newsgroups and e-mail are robust tools. Although technically and economically robust, chats will not be relevant for political communication in all scenarios. Not robust are communication tools such as complaint management, online petition, polling and interactive Web-based city planning games. Online supported mediation as a tool in the category of "active participation" for conflict negotiation will gain increasing importance. Only the facilitators will vary: In the first scenario, it will be government (e.g., local councils), while in the recession scenario, on the one hand, government supports mediation, but moderators have to be neutral and cannot be members of government or public administration. Meanwhile, mediation with NGOs through combined delivery channels (face-to-face and supported by ICT groupware technologies, such as in-service communities) becomes an often-used procedure to solve conflicts. Also, groupware (CSCW-) applications are technically robust over the scenarios but used socially in different ways; in the turbulence-scenario, interest and lobby groups are using it at least for internal affairs. Here, the Internet is used not only as a network of knowledge, but as a (virtual) working platform. In the recession scenario, governments invest in networking strategies; interest and lobby groups are using it at least for internal affairs.

Meanwhile, tools like online voting and ballot voting are not robust. Particularly, questions of security (e.g., the arising scepticism in scenario 3), usability, usefulness, and costs (problem in scenarios 2 and 3) will limit application. There will be differences among countries as well as among local and national elections. In scenarios

2 and 3, the driving force behind these developments, the IT-industry, will succeed in elections for special political bodies, respectively, within NGOs.

Conclusion

The scenario method offers the opportunity to describe different futures and to try to understand what might happen in the framework of specific variables. The scenarios partly include ("external") inputs that normally might not happen, but, generally speaking, cannot include all these possibilities (e.g., a terrorist attack or a new disease). Nevertheless, they are fruitful to understand many circumstances and framework conditions under which something may or may not happen.

Several tools are likely in the three scenarios and, therefore, are assessed as "robust." This is assumed for sophisticated information and knowledge management systems for information delivery. They can be seen as a counterweight to the increasing influence of the industrial sector on policy making. Further, robust e-democracy tools are, for example, groupware applications that provide the opportunity of improved (remote) communication within groups over all scenarios, independent from the issue, and characterise the Internet as a working platform.

The scenario technique clarifies very uncertain future developments. Online voting, chat, and interactive Web-based planning games, for instance, are tools that do not seem robust over all three scenarios. On the other hand, there are tools that are technically robust but either will be addressed to different target groups, depending on the broader context (online mediation), or offered by different stakeholders (pro-active information delivery, such as newsletters).

In all three scenarios, ICT is not the key to solving the problem of political apathy. Therefore, the risk of disproportionate expectations from technical innovations remains. Citizens' involvement is not mainly a question of technology, but rather of the individual political efficacy anticipated and resources, such as income. Before a method of information, communication, or participation is chosen, the target groups (the stakeholders and their roles within government or parliamentary consultation procedure) and the issue (substance, topics, situation of the decision, reach) have to be clarified. With regard to technological development and design of tools, the results support a tendency toward generic applications and platforms that separate functionality, presentation, and content and, therefore, allow changes of content for new target groups without changing the functionality.

Acknowledgment

The chapter is based upon research within the IST project PRISMA (Providing Innovative Service Models and Assessment), funded by the European Commission. External scenarios (the "broader context") were constructed mainly by a development team of RAND Europe, Leiden (The Netherlands), the Danish Technological Institute, Copenhagen, and the Institute of Technology Assessment within the Austrian Academy of Science, Vienna. The authors also would like to thank the external experts who joined the scenario workshop.

References

Bellamy, C., & Taylor, A. (1998). *Governing in the information age*. Buckingham, Philadelphia: Open University Press.

Botterman, M., et al. (2001). *Selected scenarios for networking evolutions*. Leiden: RAND Europe and ULB/STC.

Coleman, S. (2003). *Democracy in the age of the Internet. Proceedings of the CISCO Public Services Summit at Nobel Week Explore the Possibilities*, Stockholm, Sweden.

Coleman, S., & Gøtze, J. (2002). *Bowling together: Online public engagement in policy deliberation*. London: Hansard Society.

Commission of the European Communities. (2001). *European governance* [white paper]. Brussels, Belgium: COM(2001) 428 final (25.7.2001).

Dalton, R.J. (1988). *Citizen politics in Western democracies. Public opinion and political parties in the United States, Great Britain, West Germany, and France*. Chatham, NJ: Chatham House Publishers.

Forschungsgruppe Wahlen Telefonfeld GmbH. (2004). *Politische Partizipation in Deutschland. Ergebnisse Einer Repräsentativen Bevölkerungsumfrage*. Mannheim: Bertelsmann Foundation.

Forward Studies Unit of the European Commission. (1999). *Scenarios Europe 2010. Five possible futures for Europe*. Brussels, Belgium: European Commission.

Hacker, K.L., & van Dijk, J. (2000). *Digital democracy: Issues of theory and practice*. London: Sage.

Hague, B., & Loader, B. (Eds.). (1999). *Digital democracy: Discourse and decision making in the information age*. London: Routledge.

ISTAG. (2001). *Scenarios for ambient intelligence in 2010. Final report.* Brussels, Belgium: European Commission, Community Research.

Jankowski, N.W., & van Os, R. (2002). *Internet-based political discourse: A case study of electronic democracy in the city of Hoogeveen. Proceedings of the Euricom Colloquium: Electronic Networks & Democracy.* Nijmegen, The Netherlands.

Jankowski, N.W., & van Selm, M. (2000). The promise and practice of the public debate. In K.L. Hacker, & J. van Dijk, *Digital democracy: Issues of theory & practice* (pp. 149-165). London: Sage.

Kieser, A., & Kubicek, H. (1983). *Organisation.* Berlin: de Gruyter

Kubicek, H., Westholm, H., & Winkler, R. (2003). *E-democracy.* Prisma Strategic Guideline 9. Brussels: Self-published.

Lawrence, P.R., & Lorsch, J.W. (1967). Differentiation and integration in complex organizations. *ASQ, 12,* 1-47.

Lenk, K. (1999). Electronic democracy—Beteiligung an der kommunalen Willensbildung. In H. Kubicek, et al. (Eds.), *Multimedia@Verwaltung. Jahrbuch Telekommunikation und Gesellschaft 1999* (pp. 248-256). Heidelberg: Hüthig.

Liikanen, E. (2004). Reinforcing eDemocracy. *Proceedings of the eDemocracy Seminar,* Brussels, Belgium.

OECD. (1998). *Impact of the emerging information society on the policy development process and democratic quality* [PUMA Policy Brief (15)]. Paris: OECD.

OECD. (2001). *Engaging citizens in policy-making: Information, consultation and public participation* [PUMA Policy Brief no. 10]. Retrieved November 2002 from http://www.oecd.org/pdf/M00007000/M00007815.pdf

PRISMA. (2002a). *Report on pan-European scenario-building* [Deliverable 4.1 to the Commission of the European Communities within the IST-project Prisma (Providing Innovative Service Models and Assessment)]. Brussels, Belgium: Self-published.

Pugh, D.S., Hickson, C.R., Hinings, C.R., & Turner, C. (1969). The context of organisational structures. *ASQ, 14,* 91-114.

Putnam, R. (2000). *Bowling alone: The collapse and revival of American community.* New York: Simon and Schuster.

Reese, J., Kubicek, H., Lange, B.-P., Lutterbeck, B., & Reese, U. (1979). *Gefahren der Informations-Technologischen Entwicklung.* Frankfurt: Campus.

Riet, O.A.W.T., Loo, M.V.H., Kahan, J.P., & Europe, R. (2002). *Using scenarios in interactive policy analysis: Experiences from two policy analysis studies.* Leiden, The Netherlands: RAND Europe.

Tsagarousianou, R. (1999). Electronic democracy: Rhetoric and reality. Communications. *The European Journal of Communication Research, 24*(2), 189-208.

Tsagarousianou, R., Tambini, D., & Bryan, C. (1998). *Cyberdemocracy: Technology, cities and civic networks*. London: Routledge.

This chapter was previously published in the International Journal of Electronic Government Research, 1(3), 33-50, July-September 2005.

Chapter XI

The Quest for Advocates:
Exploring the Missing Political Good Will for E-Democracy in Europe

Harald Mahrer, Vienna University of Economics and Business
Administration & METIS Institute for Economics and Political Research,
Austria

Abstract

Throughout the world, democratic countries, whether old, new, or in transition, are facing innovations in communications and information technology. Especially within developed economies, the challenge toward e-democracy through the digital transformation of democratic institutions has become increasingly evident. With the identification of the notion of the "middleman paradox," recent research findings have added a new dimension to existing theories on the hesitant evolution of e-democracy, which clearly identifies politicians as an inhibiting factor. Consequently, the research in this chapter attempts to explore further this newly discovered phenomenon by presenting theoretical and empirical evidence. The findings of a multiple case study carried out in all 25 EU member countries, based on an adopted exploratory research design are presented. These findings give more detailed insights on the nature of the middleman paradox and on the ambiguous role of politicians in the further evolution of e-democracy.

From the Agora to the Internet

For more than 2,000 years, the idea of democracy, which had been originally invented in ancient Greece, had not found favorable conditions to evolve and endure its contests with political systems like centralized monarchy, hereditary aristocracy, and oligarchy. During the European Enlightenment, the 18th century philosophic movement rejected traditional social, religious, and political ideas, and the intellectual foundations of modern constitutional and representative democracy were laid. The promotion of democratic institutions were strongly supported by the ideas of John Locke and Charles Louis de Secondat, Baron de Montesquieu, who both believed in a republican government based on the consent of the governed (Locke, 1963; Montesquieu, 1952). Montesquieu's concept of separated and balanced powers among the executive, legislative, and judicial branches of government helped to form the philosophical basis for the U.S. Constitution and, consequently, became a role model for constitutional representative democracies throughout the world.

During the last 250 years, a variety of theoretical models of democracy has been introduced, discussed, supported, and opposed by political scientists and philosophers (Barber, 1984; Dahl, 1956; Held, 1996; Pateman, 1970; Przeworski, 1999; Rousseau, 1968; Schumpeter, 1942). Among the more prominent theoretical concepts of democracy, the concept of deliberative democracy has gained enormous public attention parallel to a declining trust in democratic governments in Western democracies and the global wide-spreading of the Internet (Ackerman & Fishkin, 2004; Dryzek, 2000; Elster, 1998; Fishkin, 1991; Habermas, 1996; Shapiro, 2003; Van Aaken, List, & Luetge, 2004).

Linking theories of further evolution of information and communication technology with contemporary theories in the area of democratic governance and democracy created the concept of e-government, describing the use of technology by government agencies to enhance the access to and the delivery of governmental services for the benefit of citizens, business partners, and employees (Heeks, 2001). Around the globe, various different definitions of e-government can be found that generally contain goals of more efficient operations, of better quality of services, and increased and better quality of citizen participation in democratic processes (Andersen, 2004; Grönlund, 2002; Kraemer & King, 2006). Looking at definitions in use, there currently seems to be a shift from government to governance, which rather implies a wider and more social and political view than government electronic services to citizens (Council of Europe, 2004b; Norris, 2005). In this chapter we follow the approach that clusters e-government research into two different fields.

E-administration refers to the transformation of governmental services in order to meet the needs and expectations of citizens and to optimize the internal processes of public administration. This should lead to a reduction of internal processing time, an enhancement of internal communications in the administration, together with cost reduction, the identification of new outsourcing opportunities, the generation of more flexibility, and lower response times of administrative bodies (Heeks, 2002; Mahrer, 2002; Osborne & Gaebler, 1992).

E-democracy (also referred to as digital democracy or Internet democracy) addresses the transformation of political systems by means of technology (Agren, 2001; Gisler, 2000; Goulandris, 2005; Grönlund, 2002; Kyriakou, 2005; Merz, 2001; Schedler, 2000) and is generally regarded as a tool for abandoning the representative system for one with a more direct citizen engagement (Becker, 2001; Browning, 2002; Coleman, 2005; Davis, Elin, & Reeher, 2002; Grönlund, 2001).

By providing substantial empirical evidence, previous research demonstrates that, contrary to the success of projects in the field of e-administration proposed by e-government strategies around the globe, there is a fundamental lack of empirical evidence concerning the effects or even the progress of proposed e-democracy projects (United Nations, 2003). To date, the total amount of e-democracy projects compared to the total amount of e-administration projects within different e-government initiatives is negligible (Agren, 2001; Anttiroiko, 2001; Betz & Bargmann, 2003; Wilhelm, 2000). Facing this imbalance, it is questioned why, with all these initiatives, politicians are only addressing e-democracy as a rhetorical promise as the implementation of e-democracy projects is undertaken at a much slower pace and with dramatically less support than the implementation of other so-called e-administration activities in the public sector (Anttiroiko, 2001; Coleman, 1999; Moore, 1999).

Recent research findings add a new dimension to existing theories on the hesitant evolution of e-democracy, which clearly identifies politicians as an inhibiting factor (Mahrer & Krimmer, 2005). After the identification of the notion of the middleman paradox, the research in this chapter consequently attempts to explore further this newly discovered phenomenon. By widening the research focus from the Austrian national level (where the middleman paradox has been observed for the first time) to the national level of all 25 EU member countries, we significantly add to this new dimension existing theories on the limping evolution of e-democracy. We have structured the chapter in the following way: First, our theoretical framework concerning the fields of political science, e-government, and e-democracy is discussed. Second, after describing our research objectives and the adoption of an exploratory research design, we present the findings of our multiple case study and the cross-case analysis. Third, we discuss our findings and relate them to contemporary theories of democracy and e-democracy evolution.

E-Democracy in Its Early Stages

Commonly, democracy is defined as a form of government in which ordinary citizens may take part in governing (Held, 1996). Besides various ideal models of democracy, contemporary democratic theory sometimes describes the modern type of large-scale democratic government as polyarchal democracy (Dahl, 1956, 1971, 1989). The concept of polyarchal democracy qualifies a political system with six democratic institutions in place, which are considered as the minimal requirements for a democratic country: elected officials; free, fair, and frequent elections; freedom of expression; alternative sources of information; associational autonomy; and inclusive citizenship. As the size of a political unit to be governed matters, these six democratic institutions are necessary for large-scale democracies to guarantee effective participation, control over the political agenda, voting equality, enlightened understanding, and full inclusion (Dahl, 1989).

History has shown that these institutions do not arrive in a country all at once and that, over time, some of these institutions remain highly fragile and vulnerable. Democracy seems to require underlying conditions to guarantee its survival and further evolution. Dahl (1998) describes three essential conditions for polyarchal democracy—control of military and police by elected officials; democratic beliefs and political culture; and no strong foreign control hostile to democracy—as well as two favorable conditions for democracy—a modern market economy and society and weak subcultural pluralism.

Depending on more or less favorable conditions and their individual histories, polyarchal democracies throughout the world are facing an array of different challenges. Especially in Western countries, more people than ever have the right to vote, but fewer than at any time in the history of universal suffrage choose to do so. Declining popular faith in parliaments and other institutions of democratic representation is observed more frequently as citizens' participation is reduced to a few seconds of power in the polling booth (Coleman, 2003). The whole portfolio of severe and complex challenges and opportunities that democracies are facing is much more diverse. The Council of Europe (2004a) has identified globalization, European integration, intercultural migration, demographic trends, economic performance, technological change, state capacity, individuation, mediatization of politics, and sense of insecurity to have significant influence on the following question: How well do the well-established formal institutions and informal practices of democracy fit with the much more rapidly changing social, economic, cultural and technological arrangements that surround it and upon which democracy depends both materially and normatively?

The Internet has been the subject of many discussions on how to deal with these challenges and how to further influence the evolution of modern large-scale representative democracy. Expectations range from the development of a virtual agora to involving citizens (Barber, 1998a, 1998b; Gilder, 2000; Rheingold, 1993) to the fact that the Internet appears to enlarge the inequalities of the digital divide within information-rich and information-poor environments (Golding, 1996; Haywood, 1995). At present, the effects of the Internet on different western democracies are still in their very early stages. Nevertheless, political observers raise an ever- increasing number of challenging questions concerning the impact the Internet could have on the concept of polyarchal democracy: Toying with the idea of deliberation, is there still a need for experts (politicians) to balance society's different interests? Will direct democracies replace representative democracies? Will we experience a broadening of the spectrum of the politically engaged population? Will we experience a fragmentation of the sense of community and legitimacy that underpins central governments and central parliaments (Applebaum, 2002; Levin, 2002; Morris & Ogan, 1996; Nugent, 2001; Nye Jr., 2002; Schlosberg & Dryzek, 2002; Thompson, 2002)? Empirically grounded and theoretically-satisfying insights addressing these questions remain elusive.

However, the concept of e-democracy seems to offer a feasible path to further explore these questions, as it is founded on the idea of streamlining political communications and altering aspects of political decision making in order to improve the effectiveness and efficiency of democracy (Gross, 2002; Hague & Loader, 1999; Mahrer & Brandtweiner, 2004; Schuler, 2001; Watson & Mundy, 2001). Currently, governments are following a "services-first-and-democracy-later" approach to e-government (Clift, 2002), as digital citizen participation remains patchy and uneven in all countries around the globe, with its full potential under-utilized according to recent research findings (United Nations, 2003). An OECD report published in 2003 on promise and problems of e-democracy has identified an array of barriers and has defined a set of future challenges (Macintosh, 2003): coping with the problem of scale; building capacity and active citizenship; ensuring coherence throughout the policy-making progress; evaluating the benefits and impacts of offering digital citizen engagement; and ensuring government commitment.

Most recent research findings on the further advancement of e-democracy have identified a phenomenon called the "middleman paradox" (Mahrer & Krimmer, 2005), which opened a new perspective in addition to existing literature and theory in the area of e-democracy and political support and commitment for e-government (Chadwick & May, 2003; Coleman & Norris 2005, Jensen, 2003; Macintosh, 2003; Margetts & Dunleavy, 2002; Norris, 2005; Øystein & Hallgeir, 2004).

The middleman paradox illustrates that there are different levels of support for a variety of concepts within e-government with politicians explicitly and implicitly fostering all activities in the area of e-administration but otherwise interfering explicitly and implicitly in the advancement of e-democracy. More precisely, these findings show that the more citizen participation specific concepts of e-democracy that were suggested, the less support for these concepts would be provided by politicians. Possibly, reasons for the politicians' approach can be grouped into two clusters: collective opposition to change and personal fear of change. These attitudes come with a strong belief in the concept of representative democracy and political elitism, with a firm opposition to further political deliberation and a widespread collective, distinctive skepticism concerning all forms of direct and/or digital political participation of the common citizen. In addition, a rejection of any change in the current balance of power as well as a prevalent concern in possible future dispensability could be identified among the politicians (Mahrer & Krimmer, 2005).

As the emergent concept of the middleman paradox had been based exclusively on Austrian data, the next step consequentially was to expand the research focus to all 25 member countries of the European Union. In order to be consistent with the research framework and the overall design of the study, the research question remained unchanged: Are politicians promoting the further evolution of e-democracy to a much lesser extent than they are promoting the evolution of e-administration, and, if so, why?

Research Methodology and Design of the EU-25 Study

Widening the focus of our research from the Austrian perspective to cover all 25 member countries of the European Union, the research team decided to continue with the exploratory research approach. We continued, following a case research design that provided us with the opportunity to engage in theory building in an area in which there has been little prior research (Benbasat, Goldstein, & Mead, 1987). At this stage of our research, having observed the middleman paradox only in one country, we were still as close as possible to the ideal of no theory under consideration and no hypotheses to test (Eisenhardt, 1989).

Focusing on parliamentarians as members of the political system, we set up a multiple case study design using a theoretical replication logic (Yin, 1994). As the case study approach refers to an in-depth study or investigation of a contemporary phenomenon using multiple sources of evidence within its real-life context, it would be the most appropriate method of collecting data within the political system to find answers to our research question.

During the data collecting phase for all national cases, we used multiple methods, including documentation, archival records, protocols, minutes, reports, speeches, and interviews, as well as in some cases internal discussion papers of different political parties. As our main source of information, we carried out 220 semi-structured, open-ended interviews to provide for focus, reliability, and increased validity (Yin, 1994). These interviews were conducted with members of 25 national unicameral or bicameral parliaments.

We selected parliamentarians from both government and opposition parties. The participants were informed about the research team's understanding of e-government and its separation into the fields of e-administration and e-democracy using the definitions described in the introduction of the chapter. Afterward, the participants were encouraged to share their personal views, experiences, and interpretations of the current e-government discussion. During the interview, the participants were also asked to focus on the relationship of e-administration and e-democracy, their reflection on the further evolution of these concepts, and its influences on the basically required democratic institutions. The interviews lasted between 60 and 120 minutes with a majority lasting 90 minutes. Two-person teams conducted the interviews in English, with one researcher handling the interview questions and the other recording notes and observations. We used this common and successful procedure for undertaking interviews in case study research to obtain valid data, since a lot of members of parliament would not permit recording (Eisenhardt & Bourgeois, 1988). The research team built a case study database after it had transcribed the

Figure 1. Multiple case study design

interviews to be able to manage the voluminous data and to allow all members of the research team to review all data collected directly.

Given the size of this pan-European research project, the research team employed multiple investigators. Their employment enhanced the creative potential of the study and enhanced confidence in our findings by the convergence of their observations, knowing that conflicting views could deter our research from premature closure (Eisenhardt, 1989). In order to add richness and depth to our research findings, we tried to combine as many methods as possible. The collection of written or printed data was hindered by the problem that a lot of minutes, protocols, and internal notes were only available in native languages (the European Union currently has 20 official languages).

In an attempt to produce persuasive and insightful conclusions, the research team combined different techniques during the analytical phase. Analytical memos, based on our researchers' field notes that recorded the results of the tentative analyses, were written at regular intervals (Barley, 1990). For the initial data analyses we separated the research team into two groups. One group used open coding procedures and the other group used template analysis coding procedures in order to make sure that one part of the research team had no idea what the data categories would be (Strauss & Corbin, 1990). The other group started their coding using the research template (King, 1998). The material on hand was coded separately by both groups and their analyses were compared afterwards.

After having finished the within-case analyses of the different national parliaments, a cross-case analysis was carried out to cover all 25 cases to search for cross case patterns using divergent techniques. The usage of multiple and different types of data from a wide selection of sources provided triangulation and increased the overall reliability of our study (Miles & Huberman, 1984). We looked for similarities and differences among the 25 cases during one stage of the cross-case analysis. During a second round, we tried another analysis and divided the data by data source to go beyond primarily impressions (Eisenhardt, 1989). Maneuvering within a grounded theory framework, the research team iterated between the empirical data and possible theoretical conceptualization (Glaser & Strauss, 1967). The development of conjectures gave us the opportunity to compare systematically our emergent concept with the evidence from each of the 25 cases in order to assess how well or how poorly it fit with the data. In confirmation of our findings, we started to compare our emergent concept with existing literature on different models of democracy and the evolution of e democracy in order to enhance internal validity and to further sharpen our final concept.

Case Background: Democracy in the EU Member Countries

Initiated by the fall of the Berlin Wall in 1989, democracy's "third wave" (Huntington, 1991) spread out over the Iron Curtain. By 1990, most of the states of Eastern Europe held competitive elections. Following a period of 14 years, during which these post-Communist countries had institutionalized democracy, a large majority joined the European Union in May 2004. As the new Eastern European democratic constitutions were modeled on the constitutions of their Western neighbor countries, only small variations regarding the democratic institutions can be identified. Basically, by the advent of the 21st century, all 25 EU member countries had, to a large extent, established the six political institutions of modern representative democracy, as described in our polyarchal democracy research framework, even though these institutions have not arrived all at once in several countries. Even in some western European countries, for example, universal suffrage was not introduced until after World War II or even later.

Regardless if the political system is a parliamentarian democracy (as in 18 EU member countries) or a parliamentarian democracy under a hereditary monarchy (as in seven EU member countries), all 25 EU countries have employed a nearly similar type of large-scale polyarchal democratic government. These systems of checks and balances among executive, legislative, and judicial branch are based on a written constitution, with the exception of the United Kingdom. Although all 25 EU countries operate on a representative parliamentarian system, due to the constitutional design of their parliaments, the total number of inhabitants, and the number of parliamentarians, the proportion of inhabitants per parliamentarian varies greatly among these countries, as shown in Table 1.

Forms of direct democracy through participation in referenda on the national level can be found in 20 member countries, ranging from obligatory referenda based on the constitution to only consultative referenda, if proposed by the parliament. At least one form of direct participation can be found within all 25 countries. Throughout the EU, citizens can elect their national legislative branches by popular vote in a unicameral system. In all 12 countries with a bicameral parliamentarian system, popular vote is established for the chamber with the significant legislative powers. A comparison of the major elements of direct participation on the national level in the 25 EU member countries is presented in Table 2.

Within these differently operating political systems, which are based on older as well as much younger democratic pillars, the e-government programs of the member countries of the EU are embedded. All e-government efforts are dominated by the European Commission's e-Europe initiative and its predecessors, focusing nearly entirely on the field of e-administration (EC, 1994, 1997, 1999, 2002).

Table 1. Parliamentarian systems of the 25 EU members countries

Country	Political System	Parliament	Population	MPs	Inhabitants per MP
Austria	Parliamentary democracy	Bicameral	8.000.000	183	43.716
Belgium	Parliamentary democracy under a hereditary monarchy	Bicameral	10.300.000	212	48.585
Cyprus	Parliamentary democracy	Unicameral	660.000	80	8.250
Czech Republic	Parliamentary democracy	Bicameral	10.300.000	200	51.500
Denmark	Parliamentary democracy under a hereditary monarchy	Unicameral	5.300.000	179	29.609
Estonia	Parliamentary democracy	Unicameral	1.400.000	101	13.861
Finland	Parliamentary democracy	Unicameral	5.100.000	200	25.500
France	Parliamentary democracy	Bicameral	59.000.000	577	102.253
Germany	Parliamentary democracy	Bicameral	82.000.000	601	136.439
Greece	Parliamentary democracy	Unicameral	10.600.000	300	35.333
Hungary	Parliamentary democracy	Unicameral	10.100.000	386	26.166
Ireland	Parliamentary democracy	Bicameral	3.700.000	166	22.289
Italy	Parliamentary democracy	Bicameral	57.300.000	630	90.952
Latvia	Parliamentary democracy	Unicameral	2.350.000	100	23.500
Lithuania	Parliamentary democracy	Unicameral	3.690.000	141	26.170
Luxembourg	Parliamentary democracy under a hereditary monarchy	Unicameral	400.000	60	6.667
Malta	Parliamentary democracy	Unicameral	400.000	65	6.154
Netherlands	Parliamentary democracy under a hereditary monarchy	Bicameral	15.700.000	150	104.667
Poland	Parliamentary democracy	Bicameral	38.610.000	460	83.935
Portugal	Parliamentary democracy	Unicameral	9.800.000	230	42.609
Slovakia	Parliamentary democracy	Unicameral	5.400.000	150	36.000
Slovenia	Parliamentary democracy	Bicameral	2.000.000	90	22.222
Spain	Parliamentary democracy under a hereditary monarchy	Bicameral	39.600.000	350	113.143
Sweden	Parliamentary democracy under a hereditary monarchy	Unicameral	8.900.000	349	25.501
UK	Parliamentary democracy under a hereditary monarchy	Bicameral	59.200.000	659	89.833
Total			*449.810.000*	*6.619*	*1.214.855*
Average			*17.992.400*	*264,8*	*48.594*

Even in the most current e-government communiqués of the European Commission—including the recent i2010 information society agenda—e-democracy is addressed, but only very vaguely; it states that the Internet has enabled new forms of citizen involvement in policy-making and that citizens throughout Europe are calling for more transparency and democratic involvement (EC, 2003, 2005). Whereas,

Table 2. Forms of direct participation on federal level in EU member countries

Country	Popular vote for parliament	Popular vote for head of state	Direct participation in referenda
Austria	For chamber of representatives	Yes	Yes - mandatory, facultative & consultative
Belgium	For chamber of representatives	No	No
Cyprus	For parliament	Yes	No
Czech Republic	For both chambers	No	No
Denmark	For parliament	No	Yes - mandatory, facultative & if ceding powers
Estonia	For parliament	No	Yes - mandatory, facultative & consultative
Finland	For parliament	Yes	Yes - consultative
France	For national assembly	Yes	Yes - facultative & if ceding powers to EU
Germany	For the federal assembly	No	No
Greece	For parliament	No	Yes - facultative & consultative
Hungary	For parliament	No	Yes - mandatory
Ireland	For house of representatives	Yes	Yes - mandatory
Italy	For both chambers	No	Yes - facultative & consultative
Latvia	For parliament	No	Yes - mandatory
Lithuania	For parliament	Yes	Yes - mandatory & facultative
Luxembourg	For parliament	No	Yes - facultative & consultative
Malta	For parliament	No	Yes - based on special bill
Netherlands	For the federal chamber	No	No
Poland	For both chambers	Yes	Yes - mandatory & facultative
Portugal	For parliament	Yes	Yes - facultative
Slovakia	For parliament	Yes	Yes - mandatory & facultative
Slovenia	For national assembly	Yes	Yes - mandatory & facultative
Spain	For whole congress of deputies and partly for senate	No	Yes - mandatory & consultative
Sweden	For parliament	No	Yes - facultative & consultative
UK	Popular vote for House of Commons, Scottish, Welsh, and Northern Ireland Parliament	No	Yes - based on special bill

for the area of e-administration, detailed action plans can be found for the area of e-democracy, these action plans are missing completely.

Case Findings

In the following section of this chapter, we are primarily analyzing the findings of the cross-case analysis. In presenting evidence through specific examples and individual comments that we have gathered during the interview process, we explain our research findings. These findings are related to the two opposing aspects of the research question as well as to the phenomenon of the middleman paradox in order to make the discussion more meaningful.

Parliamentarians and E-Administration

Members of parliaments throughout all member countries of the EU are well in-formed about e-government. Nearly all of them are aware of the EU's e-Europe program. They know a lot about its e-administration focus, the opportunities it is offering, and the challenges that have to be faced in order to reach its full potential. The majority of the parliamentarians view limited Internet access, low level of computer literacy, and security problems as the main barriers to e-administration. Still, all across Europe politicians are confident that, in the long run, these problems will be solved by combined pan-European and national efforts. However, beside these unison praises for the positive effects of e-administration, differences among motives of the parliamentarians coming from old and new democracies could be observed.

For parliamentarians coming from older democracies (all of them have at least been established prior to the fall of the Iron Curtain), e-administration is primarily a tool to improve the overall performance of public administrations and to reduce very old and unnecessary bureaucracy. With the exception of the Scandinavian EU member countries, these goals seem only to be secondary to the majority of parliamentar-ians in Western Europe. Their prior interest is not to improve the system of public administration but to regain popular faith.

A member of the Italian chamber of deputies described the situation representa-tively:

To meet the demands of the citizens in an area where for decades the political system was unable to accomplish any reform could mean to reduce the citizens' dissatisfaction with their political representatives. Logically we are addressing e-administration projects enthusiastically.

In Eastern Europe's young democracies, different motives for supporting e-admin-istration could be observed. Nearly all parliamentarians mentioned very clearly that the use of information technology in public administration was highly welcomed, because it would create transparency. For them, transparency is necessary to fight cor-ruption, which still seems to be widely spread in the new EU member countries.

A member of Poland's parliament noted:

Transparency and access to information have always been big problems in the old communist bureaucracy. We are still battling these communist structures which are promoting and protecting corruption. You will still find this type of bureaucracy around every corner you go. Digital government gives us hope to keep our young democratic government institutions healthy and to do away with this sleaze.

A large number of parliamentarians from the Baltic states, Poland, the Czech Republic, Slovakia, and Hungary commented that e-administration offered their governments the opportunity to totally rebuild administrative processes right from scratch.

A Hungarian member of parliament noted more straightforwardly:

If the public sector wants to be competitive we need competitive public institutions and processes. For us this means that we need totally new institutions and processes. We have to abandon old communist torpor by introducing a fast, efficient, and cost saving Internet-based administration.

Comparing parliamentarians from Western Europe to their colleagues from Eastern Europe, e-administration relates primarily to organizational and cultural change within the administrative system. For them, the support of e-administration is an opportunity for finally leaving behind Communist bureaucracy and corruption. Naturally for the parliamentarians in Eastern Europe, the transformation of their public administrations is not only reasonable but necessary.

Parliamentarians and E-Democracy

Generally, parliamentarians across Europe notice that they are "very much interested in the concepts of e-democracy," that these concepts are "promising" and "should be further explored in the future." They praise the EU's and their national governments' official e-government white papers and strategies and their remarks on e-democracy. When discussing the merits of e-democracy during the interviews, only parliamentarians from former communist countries explicitly stated that, for them, it is "a noteworthy concept" but "far away from implementation."

A member of the Czech parliament noticed:

Leaving the dark age of communism behind us we have already made fantastic progress towards a brighter future. We have established democracy only within a few years. But still it is young—a baby to say so—and it needs practical instruments to strengthen its institutions. Currently information technology is no such practical instrument.

The rationale behind this view was described with other more important tasks waiting on the political agenda.

A Polish member of parliament stated:

E-democracy is Science Fiction for us. All these e-services in Western Europe have gone as far as they have because of the Internet. In Eastern Europe we are several years behind the west in Internet usage. Access is mostly based on dial-up connections. Broadband? Are you joking—it is still as rare as water in the desert. So I say: New highways and railroads first. I would also like to have reliable power grids. And of course we need modern hospitals and so on. E-democracy? To be honest, right now it has no priority for us at all. Voters are first and foremost interested in secure jobs and more appealing living conditions. That's what will stabilize our democratic institutions in the near future. Or else the citizens will demand our heads.

A member of the Slovakian parliament, being less elegant in his argument, noted:

With e-democracy maybe you can bring our parliamentarians home to the people and the other way round. But will this really improve their living conditions? No, it will not. First we have to care for new and stable jobs, for better education of our youngsters and so on ... otherwise they [citizens] will chase us away like dogs.

When it comes to discussing more direct citizen participation by digital means, the parliamentarians throughout Europe would name a lot of reasons and barriers that would hinder the implementation of e-democracy. During the interviews, the majority described the same barriers they had already noticed when discussing barriers for e-administration. Contrary to the previous discussion, in the case of e-democracy, the parliamentarians viewed that there were little chances to overcome these barriers. When asked about the reasons for the change in their path of argumentation, the politicians were very reserved about sharing their true position. A significant number of parliamentarians tried to argue that they strongly believed in representative democracy and its institutions and that more direct citizen participation "would erode these institutions." Moving down the path of the interviews, the majority of parliamentarians noticed that "people really do not want to be informed"; "they are not interested in political discussion"; "citizens are unqualified"; and "they are not able to handle complexity." Another set of arguments addressed the topic of balance of power. The majority of parliamentarians strongly opposed any changes in the balance of power toward the "uninformed" and "ignorant" citizen. They argued that in such a case, a well-educated and informed minority would dominate digital decision making. Furthermore, parliamentarians noticed that with more direct digital participation, they would have to question their own role as "democracy's experts" and "elites." In the end, the majority of parliamentarians also admitted that they were concerned about their personal roles in the future in e-democracy scenarios with direct digital citizen participation. For them, "concepts of e-democracy that are highlighting the displacement of political representation are threatening."

The Middleman Paradox

Summarizing the findings of our interviews, it is evident that throughout the European Union, the majority of parliamentarians are opposing e-democracy. Our observations confirmed all findings that had been presented when the notion of the middleman paradox was introduced for the first time (Mahrer & Krimmer, 2005):

- There are different levels of support for different concepts of e-government.
- Parliamentarians are explicitly and implicitly fostering all e-administration activities.
- Parliamentarians are explicitly and implicitly interfering in the advancement of e-democracy.
- The more direct citizen participation in specific concepts of e-democracy is suggesting less support for these concepts will be provided by politicians.
- In addition to these findings, we observed particular variations, depending on the age and actual state of different democracies.
- The longer democratic institutions have been established in a country, the more opposition against different concepts of e-democracy could be observed.
- The longer democratic institutions have been established in a country, the more parliamentarians seem to believe that a maximum level of democracy has already been accomplished and that these institutions have served the country quite well and need no further evolution.
- The longer democratic institutions have been established in a country, the more widespread the opinion of parliamentarians seems to be that the future challenges of democracy will be best faced with the democratic institutions at hand.

Also, some type of north-south difference regarding the geographic regions in Europe was observed. It seems that parliamentarians in the Scandinavian and Baltic states as well as in Ireland and Great Britain are opposing concepts of e-democracy to a lesser extent than their colleagues from all other EU member countries:

- Only in these countries did we notice that the parliamentarians recognized at least some basic need to stimulate further development of democratic institutions in order to strengthen these very same institutions.
- Parliamentarians from these countries also noted that they were observing a substantial and widespread discussion about their country's democratic institutions in the press.

- Only in Scandinavian countries did parliamentarians suggest to very actively look into e-democracy and its benefits as well as to look into the opportunities more direct citizen participation would offer.

Although this study did not focus on business drivers and technology drivers for the further evolution of e-democracy, it should be mentioned that underlying economic conditions, which are linked to these drivers and are of critical importance for the stability of democratic institutions, have been intensely associated by parliamentarians with their support for e-administration throughout the interviews in all EU member countries. In direct association with e-democracy, these drivers and underlying economic conditions were hardly ever mentioned.

Concerning the possibly true motivations and reasons for the significantly lower level of support for concepts of e-democracy than for concepts of e-administration, we made the same observations on the national level of all other 24 EU member countries that had been made on the Austrian level before. Parliamentarians believe that they are much more qualified to participate in political decision making than ordinary citizens. In addition, they fear a lasting loss of power for the political elite when supporting e-democracy. But the main driver for interfering with the further evolution of e-democracy appears to be fear of change. These possibly true motivations are generally much more distinct in older democracies than in younger democracies. While some countries have experienced and strengthened democratic traditions and institutions for at least three generations or even longer (e.g., the United Kingdom), the Eastern European countries had to establish and secure a democratic development within a much shorter period. Naturally, parliamentarians in the 25 EU countries draw on very different extrinsic and intrinsic democratic values, some of them having lived under communist dictatorship for the majority of their lifetime. Observing the differences between the parliamentarians' main interest in power, influence, and control in Western Europe and improvement of economic conditions in Eastern Europe provides good examples for different democratic values.

Given these insights and based on our findings, we want to add a new conjecture linked to the middleman paradox. The longer democratic institutions in a country have been established, the less support for changing these institutions will be provided by politicians.

Finally, we wanted to note that, even without explicitly covering aspects of political morale during our research, it seems quite obvious that our findings are interconnected to these aspects, as one set of interests will be served above all others; that is, the interests of those actually in charge (Schumpeter, 1942).

The concept of democracy is more than 2,500 years old but may not be static. Rather, it may demand dynamic adaptability (Hurley, 1999). For polyarchal democracies, it may prove essential to adapt its current democratic institutions in order to successfully face the challenges ahead. The gap between democratic ideals and democratic realities, already large, will grow even greater if democracies fail to rise to these challenges (Dahl, 1998; Held, 1996). E-democracy concepts offer a lot of ideas to avoid this gap. The ideas are not only about direct participation in decision making, but also are about more democratic inclusion in general, drawing on concepts of deliberation and more participatory politics (Åström, 2001).

Regardless of which scenario of e-democracy would be introduced, it would require the support of the political elites. Naturally, without their cooperation and commitment, a reform of democratic institutions is impossible to achieve. Considering our research findings, the notion of the middleman paradox may apply not only on the further evolution of e-democracy, but on the further evolution of democracy as well. In accordance with the Green Paper of the Council of Europe (2004a) on the future of democracy in Europe, "The key problem will be finding the will to reform existing rules with the very rulers who have benefited by them and who usually cannot be compelled to do so by an overriding external threat to their security or tenure in office."

Limitations and Future Research

The findings that are presented in this chapter suffer from the usual limitations of interpretative case studies in terms of generalization. As with any empirical investigation, our methodology and procedures affect our findings. Two limitations, in particular, should be mentioned. First, our observations could not be compared with an extensive pool of knowledge of previously consolidated findings, as we wanted to engage in theory-building in an area in which there has been relatively little prior research. Second, the data utilized in this study were collected exclusively within the European Union. Even though these 25 parliaments may be representative of others throughout the world, this is by no means certain. As a result of these limitations, our findings should be approached with some amount of skepticism. However, further interdisciplinary investigation of the middleman paradox and of the politicians' ambiguous roles for the future of democracy seems appropriate. For a final thought, we note that further research on the notion of the middleman paradox should also focus on the underlying conditions that are forcing democracies to change its institutions as well as making such changes possible at all.

References

Ackerman, B., & Fishkin, J. S. (2004). *Deliberation day*. New Haven, CT: Yale University Press.

Agren, P. O. (2001). Is online democracy in the EU for professionals only? *Communications of the ACM, 44*(1), 36-38.

Andersen, K. V. (2004). *E-government and public sector rebuilding*. Dilettantes, Wheel Barrows, and Diamonds. Boston: Kluwer.

Anttiroiko, A -V. (2001). Toward the European information society. *Communications of the ACM, 44*(1), 31-35.

Applbaum, A. I. (2002). Failure in the cybermarket of ideas. In E. C. Kamarck & J. S. Nye Jr. (Eds.), *Governance.com: Democracy in the information age*. Washington, DC: Brookings.

Åström, J. (2001). Should democracy online be quick, strong or thin? *Communications of the ACM, 44*(1), 49-51.

Barber, B. R. (1984). *Strong democracy: Participatory politics for a new age*. Princeton, NJ: Princeton University Press.

Barber, B. R. (1998a). Three scenarios for the future of technology and democracy. *Political Science Quarterly, 113*(4), 573-589.

Barber, B. R. (1998b). *A passion for democracy*. Princeton, NJ: Princeton University Press.

Barley, S. R. (1990). Images of imaging: Notes on doing longitudinal field work. *Organization Science, 1*(3), 220-247.

Becker, T. (2001). Rating the impact of new technologies on democracy. *Communications of the ACM, 44*(1), 39-43.

Benbasat, I., Goldstein, D. K., & Mead, M. (1987). The case study research strategy in studies of information systems. *MIS Quarterly, 11*(3), 532-544.

Betz, F., & Bargmann, M. (2003). Electronic government in Austria: Between post-feudal and neo-liberal governmentality. In A. Prosser & R. Krimmer (Eds.), *E-democracy: Technology, law and politics*. Report of the Austrian Computer Society Working Group. Vienna: Austrian Computer Society.

Browning, G. (2002). *Electronic democracy: Using the Internet to transform American politics*. Witton: Pemberton.

Chadwick, A., & May, C. (2003). Interaction between states and citizens in the age of the Internet: "E-government" in the United States, Britain, and the European Union. *Governance: An International Journal of Policy, Administration and Institutions, 16*(2), 271-300.

Clift, S. (2002). *The future of e-democracy: The 50 year plan*. Retrieved December 10, 2003, from http://www.publicus.net/articles/future.html

Coleman, S. (1999). Cutting out the middle man: From virtual representation to direct deliberation. In B. N. Hague & B. D. Loader (Eds.), *Digital democracy: Discourse and decision making in the information age* (pp. 195-210). London: Routledge.

Coleman, S. (2003). The future of the Internet and democracy beyond metaphors: Towards policy. In OECD Report, *Promise and problems of e-democracy, challenges of online citizen engagement*. Paris: OECD.

Coleman, S. (2005). *Direct representation: Towards a conversational democracy*. London: Institute for Public Policy Research.

Coleman, S., & Norris, D. (2005). Report from the field: A new agenda for e-democracy. *International Journal of Electronic Government Research, 1*(3), 69-82.

Council of Europe. (2004a). *The future of democracy in Europe* (green paper). Strasbourg, France: Council of Europe

Council of Europe. (2004b). *Electronic governance*. Recommendation Rec(2004)15 adopted by the Committee of Ministers of the Council of Europe. Strasbourg, France: Council of Europe

Dahl, R. A. (1956). *A preface to a democratic theory*. Chicago: University of Chicago Press.

Dahl, R. A. (1971). *Polyarchy: Participation and opposition*. New Haven, CT: Yale University Press.

Dahl, R. A. (1989). *Democracy and its critics*. New Haven, CT: Yale University Press.

Dahl, R. A. (1998). *On democracy*. New Haven, CT: Yale University Press.

Davis, S., Elin, L., & Reeher, G. (2002). *Click on democracy*. Boulder, CO: Westview Press.

Dryzek, J. S. (2000). *Deliberative democracy and beyond: Liberals, critics, contestations*. Oxford, UK: Oxford University Press.

EC. (1994). *Europe's way to the information society*. An action plan. Brussels, Belgium: European Commission.

EC. (1997). *The Bangemann Report*. Retrieved November 10, 2003, from http://www.egd.idg.fhg.de:10555/WISE/globals/ecinfo/general_information/bangeman.html

EC. (1999). *Information society eEurope*. Retrieved November 10, 2003, from http://europa.eu.int/comm/information_society/eeurope/background/index_en.htm

EC. (2002). eEurope 2002. *An information society for all*. Action plan prepared by the council 19-20 June. Brussels, Belgium: European Commission.

EC. (2003). *The role of eGovernment for Europe's future*. Retrieved May 5, 2004, from http://europa.eu.int/information_society/eeurope/2005/doc/all_about/egov_communicatin_en.pdf

EC. (2005). *i2010 – A European Information Society for growth and employment.* Retrieved February 26, 2006, from http://europa.eu.int/information_society/ eeurope/i2010/docs/communications/com_229_i2010_310505_fv_en.pdf

Eisenhardt, K. (1989). Building theories from case study research. *Academy of Management Review, 14*(4), 532-550.

Eisenhardt, K., & Bourgeois, L. J. (1988). Politics of strategic decision making in high velocity environments: Toward a mid-range theory. *Academy of Management Journal, 31*, 737-770.

Elster, J. (1998). Deliberation and constitution making. In J. Elster (Ed.), *Deliberative democracy.* Cambridge, MA: Cambridge University Press.

Fishkin, J.S. (1991). *Democracy and deliberation.* New Haven, CT: Yale University Press.

Gilder, G. (2000). *Telecosm: How infinite bandwith will revolutionize our world.* New York: Free Press.

Gisler, M. (2000). Einführung in die Begriffswelt des eGovernment. In M. Gisler & D. Spahni (Eds.), *eGovernment—Eine Standortbestimmung.* Bern, Germany: Verlag Paul Haupt.

Glaser, G., & Strauss, A. (1967). *The discovery of grounded theory: Strategies of qualitative research.* London: Wiedenfeld and Nicholson.

Golding, P. (1996). World wide wedge: Division and contradiction in the global information infrastructure. *Monthly Review, 48*(3), 70-85.

Goulandris, V. (2005). E-democracy: From theory to practice. In Council of Europe (Eds.), *Reflections on the future of democracy in Europe* (pp. 121-126). Strasbourg: Council of Europe.

Grönlund, A. (2001). Democracy in an IT-framed society. *Communications of the ACM, 44*(1), 22-26.

Grönlund, A. (2002). Electronic government: Efficiency, service, quality and democracy. In A. Grönlund (Ed.), *Electronic government: Design, applications & management* (pp. 23-50). Hershey, PA: Idea Group.

Gross, T. (2002). e-Democracy and community networks: Political visions, technological opportunities and social reality. In A. Grönlund (Ed.), *Electronic government: Design, applications & management* (pp. 226-248). Hershey, PA: Idea Group.

Habermas, J. (1996). *Between facts and norms: Contributions to a discourse theory of law and democracy.* Cambridge, MA: MIT Press.

Hague, B. N., & Loader, B. D. (1999). Digital democracy: An introduction. In B. N. Hague & B. D. Loader (Eds.), *Digital democracy: Discourse and decision making in the information age* (pp. 3-22). London: Routledge.

Haywood, T. (1995). *Info-rich, info-poor: Access and exchange in the global information society*. London: Bowker-Saur.

Heeks, R. (2001). *Building e-governance for development: A framework for national and donor action*. Manchester, UK: Institute for Development Policy and Management.

Heeks, R. (2002). Information systems for public sector management. Manchester, UK: Institute for Development Policy and Management.

Held, D. (1996). Models of democracy. Stanford, CA: Stanford University Press.

Huntington, S. P. (1991). *The third wave: Democratization in the late twentieth century*. Norman, OK: University of Oklahoma Press.

Hurley, S. L. (1999). Rationality, democracy, and leaky boundaries: Vertical vs. horizontal modularity. *Journal of Political Philosophy, 7*(2), 126-146.

Jensen, J.L. (2003). Public spheres on the Internet: Anarchic or government-sponsored: A comparison. *Scandinavian Political Studies, 26*(4), 349-374.

King, N. (1998). Template analysis. In G. Symon & C. Cassell (Eds.), *Qualitative methods and analysis in organizational research: A practitioner's guide* (p. 118-134). Thousand Oaks, CA: Sage.

Kraemer, K., & King, J. L. (2006). Information Technology and Administrative Reform: Will e-government be different? *International Journal of Electronic Government Research, 2*(1), 1-20.

Kyriakou, D. (2005). A prospective view of the political-economic implications of e-democracy. In Council of Europe (Eds.), *Reflections on the future of democracy in Europe* (pp. 73-75). Strasbourg: Council of Europe.

Levin, Y. (2002). Politics after the Internet. *Public Interest,* 80-94.

Locke, J. (1963). *Two treaties of government*. Cambridge, MA: Cambridge University Press.

Macintosh, A. (2003). Using information and communication technologies to enhance citizen engagement in the policy process. In OECD report: *Promise and Problems of e democracy, challenges of online citizen engagement*. Paris: OECD.

Mahrer, H. (2002). *E-government report 2002*. Vienna: Legend Research.

Mahrer, H., & Brandtweiner, R. (2004). Success factors for implementing e-government services. *International Journal of Information Technology and Management, 3*(2/3/4), 235-245.

Mahrer, H., & Krimmer, R. (2005). Towards the enhancement of e-democracy: Identifying the notion of the 'middleman paradox'. *Information Systems Journal, 15*, 27-42.

Margetts, H., & Dunleavy, P. (2002). *Cultural barriers to e-government*. London: National Audit Office, House of Commons.

Merz, F. (2001). Demokratie per Mausklick? "Virtuelle Demokratie" als Teil par-lamentarischer Demokratie. In K.   Joos, A. Bilgeri, & D. Lamatsch (Eds.), *Mit Maus und Tastatur. Wie das Internet die Politik verändert* (pp. 201-219). München: Olzog Verlag.

Miles, M., & Huberman, A. M. (1984). *Qualitative data analyses*. Beverly Hills, CA: Sage.

Montesquieu. (1952). *The spirit of laws*. Chicago: William Benton.

Moore, R.K. (1999). Democracy and cyberspace. In B. N. Hague & B. D. Loader (Eds.), *Digital democracy: Discourse and decision making in the information age* (pp. 39-59). London: Routledge.

Morris, M., & Ogan, C. (1996). The Internet as mass medium. *Journal of Communication Quarterly*, 46(1), 39-50.

Norris, P. (2005). The impact of the Internet on political activism: Evidence from Europe. *International Journal of Electronic Government Research*, 1(1), 20-39.

Nugent, J. D. (2001). If e-democracy is the answer, what's the question? *National Civic Review*, 90(3), 221-233.

Nye Jr., J. S. (2002). Information technology and democratic governance. In E. C. Kamarck & J. S. Nye Jr. (Eds.), *Governance.com: Democracy in the information age*. Washington, DC: Brookings.

Osborne, D., & Gaebler, T. A. (1992). *Reinventing government: How the entrepreneurial spirit is transforming the public sector*. New York: Penguin Books.

Øystein, S., & Hallgeir, N. (2004). The support for different democracy models by the use of a Web-based discussion board. *Proceedings of the EGOV 2004 Conference,* Zaragoza, Spain.

Pateman, C. (1970). *Participation and democratic theory*. Cambridge: Cambridge University Press.

Przeworski, A. (1999). Minimalist conception of democracy: A defense. In I. Shapiro & C. Hacker-Cordon (Eds.), *Democracy's value*. Cambridge, MA: Cambridge University Press.

Rheingold, H. (1993). *The virtual community: Homesteading on the electronic frontier*. Reading, MA: Addison Wesley.

Rousseau, J. J. (1968). *The social contract*. Harmondsworth: Penguin.

Schedler, K. (2000). eGovernment und neue Servicequalität der Verwaltung? In M. Gisler & D. Spahni (Eds.), *eGovernment — Eine Standortbestimmung*. Bern, Germany: Verlag Paul Haupt.

Schlosberg, D., & Dryzek, J. S. (2002). Digital democracy: Authentic or virtual? *Organization & Environment*, 15(3), 332-335.

Schuler, D. (2001). Computer professionals and the next culture of democracy. *Communications of the ACM, 44*(1), 27-30.

Schumpeter, J. R. (1942). *Capitalism, socialism, and democracy.* New York: Harper Brothers.

Shapiro, I. (2003). *The state of democratic theory.* Princeton, NJ: Princeton University Press.

Strauss, A., & Corbin, J. (1990). *Basics of qualitative research: Grounded theory procedures and techniques.* Newbury Park, CA: Sage.

Thompson, D. (2002). James Madison on cyberdemocracy. In E. C. Kamarck & J. S. Nye Jr. (Eds.), *Governance.com—Democracy in the information age.* Washington, DC: Brookings.

United Nations. (2003). *World public sector report 2003: E-government at the crossroads.* New York: United Nations.

Van Aaken, A., List, C., & Luetge, C. (2004). *Deliberation and decision: Economics, constitutional theory and deliberative democracy.* Aldershot: Ashgate.

Watson, R. T., & Mundy, B. (2001). A strategic perspective of electronic democracy. *Communications of the ACM, 44*(1), 27-30.

Wilhelm, A. G. (2000). *Democracy in the digital age: Challenges to political life in cyberspace.* New York: Routledge.

Yin, R. K. (1994). *Case study research: Design and methods.* Beverly Hills: Sage.

Chapter XII

E-Gov Research 2003-2006:
Improvements and Issues

Åke Grönlund, Örebro University, Sweden

Annika Andersson, Örebro University, Sweden

Abstract

This chapter follows up on an earlier study (Grönlund, 2004) by assessing the nature of 117 papers from two e-gov (electronic government) conferences, EGOV 05 and HICSS 06, in terms of rigor and relevance criteria using a straightforward maturity model. The study uses the same method as the 2004 one and makes comparisons between the results. We find that however still focusing overwhelmingly on descriptions and little on theory testing and creation, paper quality appears much better in that references to literature have increased grossly, there are very few dubious claims, philosophical research and theoretical arguments are virtually extinct, and the number of case stories is vastly reduced. However, the number of product descriptions is doubled. We also find that there is no particular focus on specific government and society issues, but rather on traditional information systems ones; IT, method and organization.

Introduction

Grönlund (2004) made a survey of 170 papers at three main (2003) electronic government (e-gov) conferences for the purpose of measuring the maturity of the field as a research area, and at the same time, at a general level, the quality of papers. Maturity, we proposed, could be assessed by charting the nature of the research done. A scientific field should be characterized, we suggested, by not just a common object of study, but also a set of theories which can be used to understand the general conditions of the field. As a field matures, there would then be more of theory generating and testing, whereas more of pure description and case story telling would be signs of a less mature field.

Paper quality was measured at a principal level by some rigor and relevance-oriented criteria. In the 2004 study we found that as concerns rigor, theory generation and theory testing were not frequent, whereas case stories (no theory, no data) and product descriptions (no analysis or test) were very frequent. Worse, dubious claims (beyond what is reasonable given the method used) were also frequent, appearing in 29% of the papers

As concerns relevance, we found that only a few of the cases where theories were either tested or generated concerned the role and nature of government, most concerned general organizational issues which could well find a place within traditional IS conferences. Further, only 11 papers (of 170) involved shared authorship involving government practitioners.

On the positive side we found contributions from a number of disciplines, both social science and technically oriented, and international outreach beyond the North Atlantic shores was good with contributions from some 30 countries.

In this chapter we repeat the 2004 study, however for reasons of availability this time only with papers from two conferences, (DEXA) EGOV 05 (80 papers) and HICSS 2006 (37 papers)—a total of 117 papers. This time the EGOV featured some design changes, motivated by quality concerns, dividing the conference into two categories published in two different proceedings—30 papers were "research papers" and 50 "workshop papers".

The chapter proceeds as follows: After a brief discussion about the motivations for this chapter we present the investigation model and procedures. Then follows a relatively thorough presentation of data after which we discuss the findings and present some hypotheses which might be worth following up for those who seek an explanation to the findings, which are a bit ambiguous.

E-Gov History Update

In the previous study (Grönlund, 2004), we expressed some concerns about the area of electronic government (e-gov), both in terms of relevance—is there a distinct field worth pursuing?—and rigor—are we doing good research? Since then, a few things have happened. One is that the number of journals publishing e-gov research has grown. This includes both dedicated ones and those publishing special issues on e-gov. This is in itself a quality mark as journals have more rigorous review processes than conferences. At the same time, e-gov practice has expanded, most conspicuously to include the developing world, but also in the developed countries the field has grown both in terms of number of services, number of users, and complexity of services. Such changes may have introduced new challenges to e-gov research. In assessing the nature of the field, we therefore think it is still worthwhile studying conference proceedings, for at least the following reasons:

- Conferences publish new research and hence signal where the field is going.
- Conferences more quickly than journals reflect changes in research directions. They pop up more quickly when new research fields emerge, and decreasing attendance signals that a field is not that interesting anymore. Because journals tend to publish reworked conference papers and also have higher publication status, there tends to be papers coming in even as conference attendance goes down.

For this chapter we wanted to follow the development over time, and hence we selected the same conferences as in the 2004 study. As things evolved, the ECEG proceedings did not show up for several months after we ordered them, in fact not until the day of this writing, so we had to make do with the other two. This reduces the possibilities to make generalizations, in particular as the findings from EGOV and HICSS are disparate in some respects. However, even if we had included the ECEG, we would not have completely covered the field as it has grown into a huge number of conferences. We believe that even this limited review gives some interesting food for thought and discussion about the status and future directions of our field.

Research Questions

Just like in the 2004 study, the basic question asked in this chapter is, what is the e-gov field like in terms of what constitutes a scientific fields? This is operationalized by questions concerning rigor and relevance, with an emphasis on the former.

Relevance: To what extent is the e-gov field distinct from other fields? This could be assessed by investigating what are the questions asked—what (kind of) theories are used, or sought in an inductive manner? If e-gov is indeed a specific field, at least some of these issues and theories would be different.

Rigor: What methods are used? Who are the researchers? What are the results so far? How well are the claims founded in the method used? What disciplines do they come from? Given the nature of the e-gov field many disciplines should be involved. To what extent is research collaborative involving more than one of the involved triad of organizations: academia, government, and IT industry?

The main question asks to what extent the field is mature as a research field. Maturity would mean there would be a critical amount of methodologically sound examination of relevant issues, be they related to technological quality, user understanding, extent and qualities of use, or other. Maturity could be measured by a longitudinal study—comparison with the past—or by comparison with some other field, such as the IS one. In this article we compare the results with our 2004 study—what differences in maturity can we see? We measure maturity according to the following rather intuitive model, based on the probably uncontroversial assumption that research fields mature over time, incorporating successively roughly the following phases:

Philosophical: ("What will the world be like when everyone has a computer?"). When new phenomena occur, people start wondering about them. As there are no or few theories in the field and empirical data is scarce or uncertain as the object of study is changing rapidly, studies will at this stage be mainly speculation based on philosophy, properties of technology, world view, and so on.

Anecdotal case stories: ("Look what I found"). At this stage there is an increasing amount of data, but there is still no clear focus in the field so studies focus on "emerging" features, usually grounded in the researchers field of origin, personal interest, and commercial focus of the IT development. Focus is still on exploration, finding new exciting traits of the development. The researcher is a Vasco da Gama exploring new territory.

Clustering: (grouping according to similarities among cases). At this stage cases abound and people start looking for similarities. The new continent is found physically, now we try to understand life on it. Benchmarking is a commonly used concept in this phase.

Theory creating: (similarities more strictly modelled). When similarities are found, people start looking for more stable relationships, models and theories so as to more credibly inform further research, product development, and organizational remodelling.

Theory testing: (using theories found by inductive methods or borrowed from other fields pertinent to government and/or IT). This stage generally appears slightly after stage 4, as theory creating is usually qualitative and builds on smaller but richer data sets than theory testing and hence is more suitable to earlier stages of development where radical changes are about, but thereafter they continue in parallel.

This model should not be used strictly. For one thing, the nature of the objects of study will influence the development, as do traditions and cultures in different research communities. But although vitality in a field probably requires that even mature fields contain some component of each of the above "stages", we propose that a new, immature, field would contain more of the early stages while a mature field would contain more of the latter ones.

There is a debate as to what is important in research, in particular there has been a long-standing debate in the IS field on rigor and relevance, often juxtaposed: move towards one and you get further away from the other (see for example the debate in MISQ, December 1998). There is also the opinion that claims for more rigor may be used tactically in domain or hegemony struggles rather than for the purpose of actually promoting better research (King & Lyytinen, 2004). This debate is important, and in the context of this chapter it might also be discussed whether the open nature of the field makes stories equally interesting as theories. After all, governments look very different in different countries and there is no one best model of government beyond basic limitations including global agreements such as human rights and democratic values. Given also the new unexplored field of e-gov in developing countries with vastly different preconditions than the developed world, perhaps storytelling and interpretation allowing for a number of views should be rather encouraged.

This is not the place to continue this debate, but the findings may give some food for thought. Rather, the model above suggests taking a neutral stance simply saying that while case stories represent the "new", theory testing and creation represent "later" stages of the development of a field, and any mature and vital field should include all.

Method

The design of the research model started from similar studies previously conducted. As for rigor, Dubé and Paré (2003) list attributes used to assess IS positivist case studies (p. 606) based on earlier work by Benbasat, Goldstein, and Mead (1989); Eisenhart (1989); Lee (1989); and Yin (1994). These criteria fall into the categories of Research design, Data collection, and Data analysis. While the Dubé & Paré study concerns just one type of research—positivist case studies—most of the criteria could be used also for other research methods. For example "clear research question", and "multiple data collection methods" are qualities honoured in most methods. But as e-gov research includes all kinds of methods and it is very hard to directly compare quality across methods—for example comparing qualitative and quantitative methods on how, in detail, a research question should be formulated—we wanted to use criteria that assessed rigor and relevance in a more general way. We also wanted to best possible avoid interpreting articles but rather try to find objectively measurable criteria. Also, as e-gov is currently moving from practice to research, a primary concern was to distinguish between papers that at all met academic standards and those which were merely practitioner-oriented case stories. This resulted in using the following rigor categories: research type, method, claim, number of pages, and number of references (to be described).

Relevance is perhaps even harder to assess, in particular as the e-gov research field lacks a clear definition but rather is very widely conceived, and hence have several target groups with many and often conflicting views of what is relevant (e.g., De', 2005). What should be quite clear is that the e-gov research field should include some societal aspects, going beyond organizational ones, hence the "focus unit" criterion. As societal issues clearly involve more disciplines than those directly IS and IT focused, the criterion "discipline" was used to see if the whole set of papers would cover a broad enough spectre of disciplines. Further, as there is a practice field of e-gov, research should be directed towards, and reflect, that field, hence the criteria "target audience" and "institution". "Target audience" later had to be dropped because it was impossible to assess in a reliable way. Both for reasons of societalness and coupling to practice, the criterion "collaborative" was introduced. Finally, as e-gov projects can be found in most countries on earth, the criterion "country" was used to investigate how large geographical part of the e-gov practice field was covered by the conferences. Relevance criteria, then, include focus unit, target audience, discipline, collaborative, and country.

The categories were designed so as to involve a minimum of interpretation. Both category definitions and interpretation were "generous". As our original hypothesis was that the e-gov field is indeed immature, we wanted to avoid this bias to guide the interpretation, and so a generous approach was applied. Any evidence of actually using previous research in any systematic way was actively searched for and appreciated in the classification.

The categories were defined as follows.

Research Type

Category	Description
Descriptive	Describes a phenomenon in its appearance without any use of theory
Philosophical	Reflects upon a phenomenon without data or reference to any theory
Theoretical	Reflects upon a phenomenon based on some theory but without empirical data or with only anecdotal and particular such
Theory generating	Attempts to analyse/interpret quantitative or qualitative data in a systematic manner for the purpose of model building
Theory testing	Attempts to test a theory using quantitative or qualitative data in a systematic manner, i.e., not just strict theory testing

Method

The categories used are a mix of the wish to keep the number as low as possible, to include any quantitative and qualitative method while being specific enough to not hide the fact that sometimes very specific methods are used. The latter is the reason for including GT as a separate item. The former motivates including both

Category	Description
Argument	Logical argument but not based on any particular theory or relating explicitly or by clear implication to any theory
Case story	Tells about a case but as opposed to a case study there is no strict data collection method. Usually own experiences or anecdotal evidence
Ethnography	Any attempt to understand actions by systematic observation and interpretation
Experiment	Field experiments included
GT	Grounded theory
Interpretative	Any kind of more strictly performed data collection than "case story" but not necessarily strictly explained or spelled-out method for interpretation. A case study belongs here, but also more limited studies where qualitative or quantitative data is analysed. Multi-method studies are also included here
Literature study	Only documents used, be they scientific, policy documents or other. Not necessarily strict method or even explicitly labelled as literature study
Product description	IT product, method, or similar, described by the manufacturer
Survey	This covers also qualitative overviews of several documents or cases
Unclear	Not even the widely defined categories above fail to capture the method

quantitative and qualitative methods under the category "interpretative". "Product description" was not preconceived but during the first study it emerged as necessary to properly describe some papers.

There were some papers using more than one method, for example a survey complemented with case studies. Such a paper was classified as "interpretative". This makes this category a bit of a garbage can, and the alternative of creating a separate category "multi-method" was considered. This was not pursued, for two reasons. First, the number of multi-method papers was quite small. Second, often only the first step was completed anyway, for example an interpretative case study to gauge the situation before setting up a survey.

Focus Unit

Focus unit employed largely categories used to define other fields, such as HCI, CSCW, and IS: individual, group, method, and organization. We added "society", as government is not just any organization, and e-gov research should consider not just internal efficiency but also societal role.

Target Audience

Target audience was a category we used in the 2004 study, but we dropped it this time. It concerned whether results explicitly or implicitly primarily aim at guiding "researchers" or "practitioners". In the previous study we found it impossible to measure this reasonably well. It was rarely explicitly mentioned, and it proved futile to interpret from language and way of writing.

Claim

Claim concerns what validity the authors claim for their results:

- **Normative:** The paper claims generality beyond case.
- **Descriptive:** Claims validity but not generality. The authors claim to have described the situation correctly and/or credibly.
- **Lessons:** Only claims anecdotal value, e.g., "we learned that we need a champion and we weren't prepared for that". Those claims may or may not be candidates for generalization, but the point here is what validity the authors actually claim.

- **Ongoing:** Research is not completed and the paper does not make any claim as to the validity or the scope of application of the findings, not even in principle.

In cases when the claim was not explicitly stated, it was often very clearly implied by the way findings were formulated. When the claims were not possible to discern, the paper was classified as "ongoing/no claim".

Validity

As is clear from the above method and research model description, some interpretations had to be made. There are intersections between criteria where a line has to be drawn. How much empirical data, and how much additional analytical structure is needed to turn a "case story" into an "interpretation", for example? In the clear-cut cases there should be no problem, but in many papers the methods used were not clearly described and so interpretations had to be made. One general choice could have been to discard everything that was not clearly stated. This method was deemed to be too harsh and would throw out some babies along with the bathing water. One reason is that EGOV explicitly targets practitioners and invites project reports, and with that follows less strict demands for academic rigor for at least those sections of the conferences. Another reason is that we looked not only for rigor but also for relevance, and given our assumption that e-gov is a nascent field in development towards becoming a research field with the more rigorous demands that this requires, it might be unwise to unduly disrepute highly relevant projects, topics and developments on basis of them being not yet rigorously described. Third, as even a strict research model would involve interpretations, we did not want to unnecessarily impose a too narrow definition of what is good research. After all, the opinions of that differ across disciplines, and there is no apparent need to promote one of these views in this context. Not even within the IS field there is agreement, even less so can be expected given the multitude of disciplines involved in e-gov.

For all these reasons, we choose a "generous" interpretation of the criteria. This meant that when in doubt we choose a more "positive" category, one that suggests more maturity in terms of our above model. For example, when in doubt whether a report from a case would be a "case story" or an "interpretative" analysis, we would choose the latter whenever we could find some evidence of analysis, even if not that clearly structured or that well exemplified by reference to empirical findings. This is a difference from for example Dubé and Paré (2003) who claim to know exactly what a "clearly formulated" research question is as they do not question their own interpretations.

Our main goal, hence, was to look for interesting developments that might turn into more rigorous research over time, and in particular, contribute to the e-gov field as a whole improving. This means that what we end up with is an account on the positive side, as we made positive interpretations wherever uncertain. The advantage of this approach is that it makes our conclusions more credible. Any negative conclusion can be defended, as the use of positive interpretations means that we can claim that there are, for example, *at least* this large number of case stories, *at the most* this limited amount of theory testing and creating, and *at least* this high number of product descriptions. For the positive conclusions, our method could lead to underestimation. As this time we make comparisons with the earlier study, using the same main reviewer and a different co-reviewer, we believe the differences found should be fairly reliable. Possible groupthink from last time should not remain as there were changes in reviewers. Keeping the same main reviewer should make interpretations consistent across studies. As our conclusions mainly draw on the differences, not on the absolute numbers, also the positive conclusions should be credible if possibly understated.

We made some checks to ensure that the above reasoning was supported by the method used. Fifty papers (43%) were coded by both researchers independently on the criteria that involved interpretation: research type, method, focus unit, target audience, and claim. We did this works in chunks of 10 papers. After reviewing the first 10 papers we compared assessments and discussed differences to arrive at a shared interpretation. For the initial 10 papers there were in total 16 discrepancies (32%). The percentage of discrepancies gradually decreased for each chunk of papers, and by papers number 40-54 there were only six (9%). At this point we decided that we had sufficient agreement about interpretation, so the rest of the papers were coded by the first author only.

Many of the discrepancies concerned distinctions, such as between focus on "organization" and "method", which sometimes is a subtle matter of choice—when developing a new method for systems development, what is more in focus, the organizational issues which are dealt with by the method or the method itself? Such differences are not important for the discussions of rigor. They are of importance, however, for the discussion of the focus of the field, so in that respect the findings must be treated with some caution.

Findings

In the following, we compare data from EGOV 2003 and HICCS 2003 with the new survey covering EGOV 2005 and HICCS 2006. For comparison with the field more generally, we also display 2003 results from ECEG. "EGOV 2005" refers to the "conference" (Wimmer, Traunmüller, Grönlund, & Andersen, 2005), "EGOV workshop refers to the "workshop proceedings (Andersen, Grönlund, Traunmüller, & Wimmer, 2005). The HICSS papers were collected from the HICSS Web (http://csdl2. computer.org/persagen/DLAbsToc.jsp?resourcePath=/dl/proceedings/&toc=comp/ proceedings/hicss/2006/2507/04/25074toc.xml).

Research Type

As shown in Tables 3a and 3b, the share of descriptive research has increased at all conferences. The difference is greatest at HICSS, from 24% to 38%. Theory generating has increased at EGOV 2005 compared to the 2003 EGOV total, but decreased by 7% at HICSS. There is no trend to be spotted as developments seem to go different ways at the different conferences. Theory testing has increased slightly at EGOV and considerably at HICSS, but the numbers are very small—only two papers in 2003 and six in 2006. Theoretical research has decreased to the point of extinction—only three papers 2005 as compared to 17 in 2003. Philosophical research has decreased, but from a low level.

Table 3a. Research type 2003

	EGOV 03		HICSS 03		ECEG 03		Total	
Descriptive	57	61%	6	24%	27	53%	90	53%
Philosophical	3	3%	0	0%	2	4%	5	3%
Theoretical	12	13%	5	20%	9	18%	26	15%
Theory generating	12	13%	12	48%	7	14%	31	18%
Theory testing	10	11%	2	8%	6	12%	18	11%

Table 3b. Research type 2005

	EGOV 05		EGOV workshop 05		Total	
Descriptive	20	67%	34	68%	54	68%
Philosophical	0	0%		0%	0	0%
Theoretical	1	3%		0%	1	1%
Theory generating	5	17%	9	18%	14	18%
Theory testing	4	13%	7	14%	11	14%
Total	30	100%	50	100%	80	100%

Table 3c. Research type HICSS 2003 and 2006

	HICSS 03		HICSS 06	
Descriptive	6	24%	14	38%
Philosophical	0	0%	0	0%
Theoretical	5	20%	2	5%
Theory generating	12	48%	15	41%
Theory testing	2	8%	6	16%
Total	25		37	

To support our maturity model, philosophical and theoretical research has largely disappeared. We also predicted a more mature field would include more of theory testing and creation, and indeed theory generating and theory testing research has increased, but not much. Finally, we predicted less of description, but this category has instead increased at all conferences. This suggests that either our maturity model is incorrect or the field is for some reason taking some other direction. We will return to this issue as we present more data below.

In the following tables, the complete set of conferences in 2003 is presented for reasons of completeness.

Method

As shown in Tables 4a, b and c, "argument" has in 2005 become almost extinct. Case stories are down from 34% to 8% at EGOV, most so at the conference (3%). Interpretative research has increased considerably, from 12% to 35% at EGOV and from 32% to 57% at HICSS. As "interpretative" includes also multi-method studies, some other categories show a lower number than the actually conducted studies. A finding that seems to contradict our maturity model is that "product descriptions" have increased from 14% to 31% at EGOV. Also at EGOV, literature studies have on the total increased slightly, but most remarkable (as for product descriptions) is the differentiation—increase to 23% at the conference and decrease to 3% at the workshop.

At HICSS, there are more surveys, but small numbers defy trend spotting.
In all, this still supports our maturity model, provided a modification concerning the object of study. This time we find more rigorous descriptions and less of stories, which is a quality improvement. We find a clear differentiation between the EGOV conference and the workshop, which is expected given the conference redesign. However, we also find product descriptions being increasingly common, which seems to call for some investigation as it does not fit with the model. We will return to this issue in the concluding discussion.

Table 4a. Method 2003

	EGOV 03		HICSS 03		ECEG 03		Total	
Argument	19	20%	6	24%	11	22%	36	21%
Case story	32	34%	2	8%	8	16%	42	25%
ethnography	0	0%	1	4%	0	0%	1	1%
Experiment	4	4%	1	4%	2	4%	7	4%
GT	0	0%	2	8%	0	0%	2	1%
Interpretative	11	12%	8	32%	5	10%	24	14%
Literature study	10	11%	1	4%	13	25%	24	14%
Product description	13	14%	3	12%	6	12%	22	13%
Survey	5	5%	1	4%	6	12%	12	7%

Table 4b. Method 2005

	EGOV 05		EGOV workshop 05		Total	
Argument	1	3%	4	8%	5	6%
Case story	1	3%	5	10%	6	8%
ethnography		0%	1	2%	1	1%
Experiment	1	3%		0%	1	1%
GT		0%		0%	0	0%
Interpretative	10	33%	18	36%	28	35%
Literature study	7	23%	3	6%	10	13%
Product description	9	30%	16	32%	25	31%
Survey	1	3%	3	6%	4	5%
Total	30	100%	50	100%	80	100%

Table 4c. Method, HICSS 2003 and 2006

	HICSS 03		HICSS 06	
Argument	6	24%	1	3%
Case story	2	8%	2	5%
ethnography	1	4%	0	
Experiment	1	4%	2	5%
GT	2	8%	1	3%
Interpretative	8	32%	21	57%
Literature study	1	4%	1	3%
Product description	3	12%	4	11%
Survey	1	4%	5	14%
Total	25		37	

Focus Unit

As shown in Tables 5a, b, and c, the already in 2003 strong focus on IT has increased at EGOV, from 33% in 2003 to no less than 60% in 2005. This is not only due to the invention of the workshop, also the conference has a high score (43%). "Society" scores marginally higher, counting all conferences but considerably higher for the EGOV conference. "Individual" is dropping, but from a low number. At HICSS, the focus on IT is down considerably. The focus here in 2006 is almost exclusively on organization and method.

This is only partially in line with our maturity model. If the field were about to mature in the sense of creating a distinct set of theories, we should see more focus on all the criteria that have to do with the relation between government and citizen, that is, "individual" and "society". While the increasing focus on Method and Organization at HICSS seems reasonable from the perspective of putting IT in context, which is a sign of maturity, is does not signal a new field, rather an extension the traditional IS field's domain to also encompass government.

What about the strong IT focus at EGOV, then? Are we here looking at a work distribution among conferences with EGOV retaining the practitioner focus and

Table 5a. Focus unit 2003

	EGOV 03		HICSS 03		ECEG 03		Total	
Individual	6	6%	7	28%	3	6%	16	9%
Group	0	0%		0%		0%	0	0%
Organization	20	21%	8	32%	20	39%	48	28%
Society	12	13%	2	8%	6	12%	20	12%
Method	25	27%		0%	16	31%	41	24%
IT	31	33%	8	32%	6	12%	45	26%

Table 5b. Focus unit 2005

	EGOV 05		EGOV workshop 05		Total	
Individual	1	3%	1	2%	2	3%
Group		0%		0%	0	0%
Organization	5	17%	3	6%	8	10%
Society	8	27%	3	6%	11	14%
Method	3	10%	8	16%	11	14%
IT	13	43%	35	70%	48	60%
Total	30	100%	50	100%	80	100%

Table 5c. Focus unit, HICSS 2003 and 2006

	HICSS 03		HICSS 06	
Individual	7	28%	3	8%
Group		0%		
Organization	8	32%	15	41%
Society	2	8%	4	11%
Method		0%	12	32%
IT	8	32%	3	8%
Total	25		37	

HICSS the IS research one? Such an interpretation could perhaps be supported by the differences between the EGOV conference and workshop, with "Organization" being more common at the Conference and "IT" at the Workshop.

In 2003 we tried to differentiate between focus on practitioners and researchers respectively by counting the number of references. A low number would indicate a practitioner focus, a high would indicate more focus on research. As Tables 6a, b, and c show, the number of references has grown enormously at EGOV, while still not being as many as at HICSS.

While in 2003, 62% of the EGOV papers had less than 9 references, in 2005 93% at the conference and 90% at the workshop had nine or more (97% at HICSS). Forty three percent of the conference papers had more than 20 references (70% at HICSS). It should also be mentioned that the references at EGOV 2005 are much more academic than those of 2003. In 2003, there were many company and government Web sites, mainly promotional, in the reference list. These may still be there, but now there are also academic references to relevant literature discussing the issues under investigation. In this sense, academic quality has improved. For HICSS, there is not much difference between 2003 and 2006, simply because the number of references was already quite high in 2003. We did not count beyond nine in 2003. While the actual number of nine was somewhat situatedly chosen to match data, the underlying idea was that while academic quality usually requires some references to literature it is not meaningful to claim that 20 references are better than 10. Our counting reveals whether there is references at all to relevant literature, and the answer is that in 2003 this was often not the case at EGOV but in 2005 and 2006 it definitely is at all conferences.

Table 6a. Number of references 2003

References							
No of refs		EGOV 03		HICSS-03		ECEG-03	
	0-5	33	35 %	1	4 %	5	10 %
	6-8	25	27 %	2	8 %	5	10 %
	9+	36	38 %	22	88 %	41	80 %
Number of papers		94		25		51	

Table 6b. Number of references 2005

References						
	EGOV 05		EGOV workshop 05		Total	
<=5	1	3%	3	6%	4	5%
6 to 8	1	3%	5	10%	6	8%
>=9	28	93%	45	90%	73	91%
(>=20)	13	43%	10	20%	23	29%
(>=30)	2	7%	3	6%	5	6%
(>=40)	2	7%	1	2%	3	4%

Table 6c. Number of references, HICSS 2003 and 2006

	HICSS 03		HICSS 06	
<=5	1	4 %		
6 to 8	2	8 %	1	3%
>=9	22	88 %	36	97%
(>=20)			26	70%
(>=30)			15	41%
(>=40)			7	19%
Total	25		37	

Research Origin

The affiliation of the first author is still, and increasingly, overwhelmingly a university at all conferences. In 2003, the figure for all conferences were 83%, in 2005 the figure for EGOV conference is 97%, for the workshop 94%, and for HICSS 86%. In only five cases the first author came from a company, in four cases from government.

Collaboration

In 2003, around 1/5 of the papers were collaborative (involving more than one institution), and many of these involved no practitioners but researchers from more than one university or more than one discipline within the same university. Only 11 papers involved at least one practitioner and one researcher (six at EGOV, two at ECEG, and three at HICSS). In 2005, collaboration has increased at EGOV, both the conference and the workshop, to 39% in total, with a slightly higher figure for the workshop (Table 7). Still, collaboration with practice is low, indeed lower than in 2003, only seven papers (as one is double-counted).

Table 7. Collaborations

	EGOV 05		EGOV workshop 05		HICSS 06	
Non-collab	20	67%	29	58%	27	73%
uni-gov	1	3%	4*	8%	1	3%
uni-biz		0%	4*	8%	2	5%
uni-uni	9	30%	14	28%	7	19%
Total papers	30		50		37	

* One paper included gov-biz-uni and is here counted in both categories uni-biz and uni-gov.

At HICSS, in 2003 7 out of 25 papers were collaborative, in 2006 10, meaning there is no increase in percent.

Claim

A final factor indicating rigor is the credibility of the claims. To investigate this, we matched the categories "research type", "method", and "claim". A reasonable combination would be, for instance that a "descriptive" type implemented by an "argument" would result in modest claims. In 2003, we found no less that 49 dubious claims, equivalent to 29% of the papers. There were several combinations, the largest category being a descriptive case story resulting in normative claims (11 cases) and theoretical argument ending by normative claims. In 2005 we found a completely different picture. At EGOV, the number of dubious claims was now only five (6 %)—two at the conference and three at the workshop. At HICSS, we found two papers (5 %) This seems a huge improvement. Even though we were a bit disappointed in the increased amount of descriptive research and product descriptions, at least this time authors typically do not make unwarranted claims. We were wondering whether our 2004 paper at EGOV (Grönlund, 2004) scared people a bit and made them determined not to overstate their findings. One potential indication of that might be that perhaps instead this time papers were underclaiming. We found a very high number of "ongoing/no claim", no less thant 46 papers (58%). Many of these were theory testing (six), theory generating (12), or interpretative (13) making a total of 25 papers or 21% (some are double-counted as they fall under more than one of the categories) where—given the method used, not necessarily the actual content of the paper—claims could well have been stronger. In some cases the reason was that research was indeed ongoing, but in many cases the research was actually complete, however the author(s) made strong disclaimers of the kind "more research is needed before we can make claims".

Geographical Distribution

It appears e-government conferences reach an increasing audience in a geographical perspective. EGOV 2003 gathered researchers from 30 countries, for 2005 the figure is 35 (17 for the conference and 27 for the workshop). All continents were represented, and Eastern Europe and former Soviet states were included. HICSS 2006 gathered papers from 15 countries, an increase from nine in 2003 but was still U.S.-Western Europe focused. Only two papers came from other countries, and these were Korea and Taiwan, which are hardly representative for the developing world.

Conclusion

We set out to assess the maturity of the e-gov field as a research area, and we did so by comparing 2005/2006 papers to a study of 2003 papers. The results can be described as mixed. We find authors' efforts to comply with research publications standards have increased considerably. The number of references has increased greatly, indicating better involvement with previous research. The number of dubious claims has been reduced from 29% to 6%. "Arguments" and "philosophical research"—lacking empirical observations, theory or both—have been virtually eradicated. What remains is a more strict research where empirical data is described and interpreted using sometimes a theory but at least considerably more often than in 2003 some structured method, and where claims match the methods used.

On the disappointment side we find that descriptive research is increasing from 61% to 69%, and theory testing and creating is increasing only little. However, as also the descriptive papers are more integrated in the research literature, both as measured by number of references and by the agreement between method and claims, we conclude that the field has indeed matured as papers are now more rigorous. Further, one reason for there being more descriptive papers could be that the field has expanded lately to include for example the developing world, where e-gov is indeed yet a field for exploration.

It should be noted here, that while this method allows us to tell what *kind* of research is done, and whether conclusions are drawn that are *in principle* reasonable given the research method, it does not help us understand whether papers are *in fact* good or bad. Clearly, descriptive papers can be just as interesting, relevant and rigorous as theory testing and theory generating ones. And clearly theory generating and theory testing papers can be poorly conceived and poorly written. While investigating this would be a much more time-consuming endeavour, we believe the method chosen at least gives us support in saying that there has been a change in a positive direction over the two years that have passed between measurements.

Beyond the measurements made, our impressions from reading all the papers are that in fact, several "product descriptions" are well argued methods often based on realistic arguments; however, they are not theory based or empirically founded but rather based on arguments often heard in the e-gov debate.

There are some limitations to our study. We study only two out of a large number of conferences, and we do not at all consider journal publications. This suggests caution in generalization.

We still believe there is reason to discuss the findings in view of our maturity model, however. While we have seen a change towards less philosophical and argumentative research, we should also have seen a change towards more theory testing and theory building, which we did not really. As a final point for discussion we now propose a reason for that, open to confirmation or rejection by further research.

Our proposition is that the basis of research—the funding principles—has changed so dramatically that our model, which was based on our view of traditional academic discipline development, does not fit that well anymore simply because research is redefined in the view of funders. Today, research funding seems increasingly hard to find without joining up with business and some development project. Some would say it is impossible in a field such as ICT. Looking at the papers presented in the examined conferences, they are to a large extent reports from projects funded by the EU. We tried to count the number, but that turned out to be impossible. Only in some cases are the funding sources explicitly mentioned, and as project funding often come from many sources, including a university, it is often not clear exactly which euro or dollar went to a project report and to a research conference paper based on that report. In many cases we could recognize ingredients from projects we know of, but no direct references to that project were made.

The principle underlying the new funding mechanism is not to study and analyze the development to device better ways of doing things but to provide government support to industry in development projects decided by other mechanisms. Sometimes this is very explicit. For example, the (only) Swedish government agency funding e-gov research states in its 2005 call that "Researcher(s) in the project shall take part in developing the e-service, not just evaluate it" (Vinnova, 2005, p. 4; author's translation). Could it be that what we see here is an outcome of this funding principle, a huge amount of papers describing products—typically methods and IT artefacts, sometimes architectures and conceptual frameworks—with little of comparison and critical analysis? If so, e-gov is not a research field but one concerned with product development, and the maturity model does not really apply. Sometimes it is less explicitly stated, but in any case this tying of researchers to development projects means in practice is that researchers are tied up to contribute to developing methods, software, architectures etc., not to critically examine them and discuss alternatives. Given also the funding administration delay where funding is often finally decided months *after* a project period has started, project time is often cut short and hence the race to complete artefacts is on already from the outset, and so the time for analysis is reduced even if it originally was part of the plan. There might be other reasons. One might be the "publish or perish" demand on researchers which is increasingly a reality also in Europe (it has long been in the U.S.). Another could be the increasing volume and de-academization of higher education, parts of which includes research being increasingly project funded and competitive, and education being increasingly instrumentally job preparation-oriented and less academically intellectual. Clearly this study does not provide evidence to make conclusions on this issue, but we strongly believe it is worth further research as our findings match such a hypothesis. Independent science is historically a highly valued force in society, similar to the idea of an independent press, and if the current development is detrimental to this independence it should at least be discussed.

After all, there is a difference between research and development. Research is looking for the unknown—creating new knowledge. Research is looking with open eyes, that is, not being biased by having a stake in what is being researched. This way, knowledge stemming from research will be trusted to be as good—true, credible—as possible. A researcher will be happy to try out new methods for the purpose of being able to observe and measure the world from some new angle hence achieving more complete knowledge. We have measured the universe for long time without necessarily seeing direct economic outcome, such has occurred only much later. We want to know, that's it. It is a matter of degree, of course. In researching, in particular social phenomena, no one is completely objective. But it is not impossible to avoid many dangers. Independent financing, adherence to proper method, critical review are good measures to take. Competition for publication is another one, and the current abundance of publication outlets for e-gov research may in fact be detrimental in this respect. Certainly "knowledge dissemination" from research to practice is also important and has often been found lacking, but achieving this by directly linking researchers' incentives with those of practitioners may be risky.

Development is using known knowledge to create new things. In that process, new knowledge may be found, but development projects try to avoid the unknown and stick to tools and methods that are not new. An engineer may want to build a longer bridge than anyone before has built, or one innovatively designed, but s/he will hesitate to abandon old, proven calculation and measurement methods and try out new ones. Further, all developers have a stake. Either they are paid to develop something and have a schedule and or success criteria, or they will make a future gain from their developed artefact. Either way, they will not have time to look around for all alternative solutions. And, what's more, they have already sold a particular solution to some investor—private or public—and coming back six months later to say "well, maybe this wasn't such a good idea after all" is indeed just that, not a good idea. Of course we can learn also from practice. But research is supposed to help us avoid learning by trial and error only, to create general knowledge that can be applied as input to development projects.

In this respect, the findings presented here should trigger some discussion about e-gov as a research field. Our production has become more rigorous since last measure two years ago. But are we doing good research? As we have seen in this chapter, the e-gov field is today, as compared to 2003,

- increasingly descriptive,
- increasingly containing product descriptions, and
- increasingly focusing on traditional IS areas (IT, method, organization) rather than government and society.

Following our research maturity model, an e-gov research field should rather focus on the *role* of ICT in contexts of society, government organization, method and in-dividuals/citizens, and it should increasingly analyze rather than describe. We invite comments on this. As we seem to be living in a time of redefinition of research we believe we should discuss the new definition(s).

References

Andersen, K. V., Grönlund, Å., Traunmüller, R., & Wimmer, M. A. (2005). *Electronic government.* Workshop and Poster Proceedings of the Fourth International EGOV Conference. 2005, Denmark. Linz: Trauner.

Benbasat, I., Goldstein, D. K., & Mead, M. (1987). The case research strategy in studies of information systems. *MIS Quarterly, 11*(3), 369-385.

De', R. (2005, August). E-government systems in developing countries: Stakeholders and conflict. In M. A. Wimmer, R. Traunmüller, Å. Grönlund, & K. V. Andersen (Eds.), *Electronic Government. Proceedings of 4th International Conference, EGOV 2005,* Copenhagen, Denmark (pp. 26-37). Heidelberg: Springer, Lecture Notes in Computer Science, LNCS 3591.

Dubé, L. & Paré, G. (2003). Rigor in information systems positivist case research: Current practices, trends and recommendations. *MIS Quarterly, 27*(4), 597-635.

Eisenhart, K. M. (1989). Building theories from case study research. *Academy of Management Review, 4*(4), 532-550.

Grönlund, Å. (2004) State of the art in e-Gov research: A survey. In R. Traunmüller (Ed.), *Proceedings of Electronic Government Third International Conference EGOV 2004* (pp. 178-185). LNCS 3183. Berlin: Springer.

King, J. L., & Lyytinen, K. (2004). Reach and grasp. *MISQ, 28*(4).

Lee, A. (1989). A scientific methodology for MIS case studies. *MIS Quarterly*, *13*(1), 33-52.

Vinnova (2005). Cross-departmental public e-services for businesses (Gränsöver-skridande offentliga e-tjänster för företag). Call 2 within the programme E-services in public sector. Stockholm: Vinnova, 2005-02189.

Wimmer, M. A., Traunmüller, R., Grönlund, Å., & Andersen, K. V. (2005, August). Electronic government. *Proceedings of 4th International Conference, EGOV 2005,* Copenhagen, Denmark. Heidelberg: Springer, Lecture Notes in Computer Science, LNCS 3591.

Yin, R. (1994). *Case study research: Design and methods* (2nd ed.). Beverly Hills, CA: Sage.

Chapter XIII

E-Government Research:
Capabilities, Interaction, Orientation, and Values

Kim Viborg Andersen, Copenhagen Business School, Denmark

Helle Zinner Henriksen, Copenhagen Business School, Denmark

Abstract

A comprehensive analysis of 110 peer-reviewed journal papers suggests that the conceptual domains and application areas covered by e-government research focus predominately on capabilities and interactions, whereas value distributions and policy orientations are largely ignored. Onwards, e-government research is more concerned with conceptualizing government and e-services, than exploring the governmental role in technology diffusion and the role IT plays in democracy and participation. The orientation of the e-government research is an indicator that the legacy of IS-research themes dominates the e-government research body. Interdisciplinary research involving core public administration research along with IS-research is yet to emerge. It is proposed that the field could be more unified if considering both the "e" and "government" of e-government.

Introduction

The dot com meltdown and the subsequent debate on the role of IT in transforming the private sector (Carr, 2004; Porter, 2001) contrast a firm belief that IT can transform the public sector. This firm belief on IT in policy settings has been materialized within the areas of internal administration and services, legal control, and law enforcement. Consequently, on a global scale there is a set of labels, such as e-government, e-governance, one-stop government, digital government, and online government, that capture the governmental quest for online government services.

The policy commitment to transform government using IT has been echoed in the academic research advocating the necessity of strategic visions as part of the transformation (Armstrong, 2002; Burn & Robins, 2003; Deb, 1999; Luling, 2001; Stamoulis, Gouscos, Georgiadis, & Martakos, 2001; Watson & Mundy, 2001) and guidelines on managing the transformation to the more dynamic interaction brought about by the technology (Lenk, 2002; Tan & Pan, 2003). Within the research community, however, there has not been agreement on whether to applaud the intended IT-led transformation of the public sector or whether to view the developments as old wine in new bottles. It has been argued that "…this [belief] sounds all too familiar. Almost 20 years ago a similar debate arose...pitting proponents of new IT against those who suggested that existing organizational and political relationships would dramatically influence any use of new technology" (Bretschneider, 2003).

Although there have been published papers devoted to defining e-government (Marche & McNiven, 2003; Silcock, 2001), there is evidence of a persistent myth that "not much has been published on e-government" and that e-government still appears to be in its infancy. It is therefore in a state where no core common references or theoretical assumptions guide the research. A study of the research methods of the e-government literature at three international conferences (DEXA, HICSS, and ECEG 2003) found that, in general, there are few rigorous research methods applied and that theory building and testing are the exception rather than the rule (Grönlund, 2004). In general, studies often take a normative or consultative approach (Chadwick & May, 2003; Collins & Butler, 2002).

Possibly the most focused and longitudinal studies on IT in government during the 1980s and 1990s was done by the UC Irvine group. They found, for example, that IT seems to reinforce existing organizational structures rather than revolt them, and that "… the primary beneficiaries have been functions favored by the dominant political-administrative coalitions in public administrations, and not those of technical elites, middle managers, clerical staff, or ordinary citizens" (Kraemer & King, 2003). No sources known to the authors have assessed whether that is still the case in this second wave of IT in the public sector. The present study is seen as the first step towards uncovering this issue.

The objective of this chapter is to identify the methodological approaches to research within the domain of e-government and to access the ontology of e-government research. Our underlying assumption is that IT in the public sector as a research discipline has had a revival after the burst of the "dot com" bubble, now under the label "e-government." Furthermore, it is assumed that the field of e-government research is populated by a heterogeneous group of researchers, some coming from the e-commerce research domain while other researchers have previously studied IT in the public since the 1970s and 1980s while others are newcomers to studying IT.

Hence, it is assumed that the (many) disciplines involved in e-government research pose a dispersed research agenda rather than a unified research theme or "hard core" of research themes (Lakatos, 1970). Specifically, it appears to be a research domain suffering from methodological shortcomings, a lack of a common vocabulary and a paucity of commonly agreed issues/findings. This is, for example, reflected in the present use of the term e-government (and all variations of the term, e.g., e-governance, one-stop government, digital government, online government, etc.) which spans from broad definitions (digital information and online transaction services to citizens) to narrow definitions (e-procurement) with respect to creating new strategic opportunities and value as a rallying force (Deb, 1999).

In order to explore the e-government span with respect to the operating domains of government and application areas, we have conducted a comprehensive literature review of five years of research (1998-2003) publications on e-government. The database with the complete set of references identified keywords, classification along the eight variables used in this review, etc., which is available through AIS World resources at URL http://www.isworld.org/endnote/ and from URL http://www.pprgovernment.com. In this chapter we will not provide the complete list of the 110 papers but kindly ask the reader to access the coding and references at the URLs provided.

The remainder of the chapter is organized as follows. The next section presents our research method. The following section outlines the classification models in parallel with the presentation of the data from the review which is divided into the two dimensions of the classification model. The subsequent section analyzes and discusses the outcome of the classification of data. Additionally, a listing of characteristics of the "pre-e-government" domain is presented. The objective of this exercise is to outline what is, in our view a more sound direction for future e-government research, a direction where more traditional government characteristics are prevalent instead of the "e". Finally, the conclusion of the analysis of five years of scholarly work on e-government is presented.

We are indebted to comments provided during a presentation of an earlier and much less developed version of this chapter at the European Conference on Information Systems (ECIS) in Turku, Finland (Ahmed, Andersen, Arnthórsson, & Henriksen, 2004) and by the reviewers associated with IJEG.

Methodology

Our review of e-government literature has followed a methodology suggested by Swan, Scarbrough, and Preston (1999). Hence, the comprehensive online journal databases Social Sciences Citation Index (SSCI®) and ProQuest Direct (PQD) were consulted for research published during the period 1998-2003.

The parameter set in the SSCI retrieval of articles was the following keywords: e-government, e-governance, one-stop government and digital government including combinations of the listed keywords. In the PQD a more restricted search procedure was followed to filter those contributions not directly related to academic research. Apart from searching for articles containing the keywords listed above, a further filtering was made by adding the "Scholarly journals, including peer-reviewed" option as search criteria.

In the initial screen, articles with only peripheral reference to e-government were excluded for the further analysis. A public sector or political system focus was required in order to qualify the article to fall into the category of e-government research. Additionally, hits retrieved from the databases which were book-reviews, editorials to special issues on e-government, or contributions in conference proceedings were excluded in the further analysis. This search led to a total of 167 unique articles where at least one of the keywords occurred in the title, abstract, or keywords. From this identified base, a random selection was used to exclude another third of the articles, leaving us with 110 articles as the basis for this review chapter. All articles were read by at least one of the authors.

Among the potential concerns to the validity of our conclusions is the potential lack of capturing research on the impacts of IT on politics and public administration that is not categorized and indexed in the search engines used for our review. We recognize that there are numerous other valid sources of empirical research, including other journals, online media, books, book chapters, conference papers, and so forth. Thus, one should be careful viewing the articles collected as a miniature of the actual e-government initiatives and research.

A second limitation to validity is our exclusive reliance on English-language journals, which introduces certain biases regarding the scholars, countries studied, and perhaps even epistemologies and ontologies. Third, the research methods in the studies vary, generating challenges of comparability and generality when the findings are aggregated in the manner we utilize.

Fourth, we do not make quality assessments regarding methods or findings, and we do not weigh the findings on the basis of the power of evidence supporting the inferences. We assume that the journal's internal system of peer review provides a baseline of acceptability regarding the validity of the research and conclusions. Furthermore, our own conceptual framework for classifying findings or methods of establishing inter-analyst agreement could be found wanting.

Finally, there are methodological problems of doing citation studies, particularly in such a new field, and limiting the search to the past five years using only two search engines.

Despite these possible sources of error, we suggest that analyzing the articles in a sample of key academic journals is a constructive method for conducting a systematic survey of the research within the "universe" of sources on e-government, e-governance, one-stop government, and digital government. Also, our approach can help maturing the research field building on accumulated findings and pointing to areas in need for more research.

Classification Model and Results

Our classification model has two key dimensions: domains of impacts and contextual research domains. The domains of impacts capture classic themes in political science: capabilities, interactions, orientations and value distributions (Andersen & Danziger, 1994; Danziger & Andersen, 2002).

The contextual research domain investigates the ontology of e-government research, that is, what the researchers imply e-government to consist of Burrell and Morgan (1979). We have grouped the papers into four contextual settings: conceptualization of e-government, the governmental role in technology diffusion, a governmental administrative e-service focus, and democracy and involvement of citizens, including separation of power.

In Table 1 we have summarized the findings along the two dimensions capturing e e-government research domains of impact and contextual domains. The cross

Table 1. Cross tabulation of contextual research domains by domains of impacts

Contextual research domain	Domains of impacts				Total %
	Capabilities	Interactions	Orientations	Values	
Conceptualization of e-government	36%	27%	19%	19%	100%
Governmental role in technology diffusion	42%	36%	8%	14%	100%
Governmental administrative e-service focus	37%	36%	12%	15%	100%
E-democracy and involvement of citizens and separation of power	38%	31%	16%	15%	100%

tabulation of data indicates that regardless of the research domain, researchers focus on impacts related to capability and interactions.

In the following sections a more comprehensive description of the domains and the categorization of articles into the two domains is provided. The tables summarizing the findings on each domain are placed at the end of each section.

Domains of Impacts

Using the conceptual domains framework (capabilities, interactions, orientations, and values) to categorize the papers, we identified an uneven distribution of the papers, with capabilities being the most frequent research type of impact, closely followed by interactions. Combined, the two domains of impacts counted for about 70% of the studies included in our sample, whereas the remaining 30% were in the domains of orientations and value distribution. This indicates that researchers in the domain of e-government research pay particular attention to the capabilities of the IT-applications introduced in public sector institutions and to interaction with citizens, businesses, politicians, and other public employees through electronic means.

The capability category of impacts has the highest frequency of studies (38%), including studies on information quality (data access, data quality), efficiency (productivity gain, staff reduction/substitution, improved managerial control, time-saving measures), and effectiveness (improved decision processes, improved products and services, improved planning). This group encompasses digital delivery of documents within the courts and legal area (Doty & Erdelez, 2002), as well as the broader level of services (Potter, 2002).

The second highest occurrence of studies addresses interaction in areas such as coordination/cooperation, citizen-public sector interaction, private sector-public sector interaction, citizen-citizen interaction, and organizational control and power. The studies echo classic IS-discussions with respect to whether IS facilitate centralization or decentralization (Peled, 2001). This group of studies also addresses the boundaries of e-government in the study of aboriginals and the Canadian e-government plan (Alexander, 2001), as well as the Maori people's access to IT (Parker, 2003). Thus, there is a diverse, rather than unified, pattern of reality in the many e-government plans, for example in Asia (Holliday, 2002). This category of studies also addresses "…MPs who want great control of their own local campaigning and the party elite who want to ensure a consistent, coherent and controlled message" (Jackson, 2003).

Whereas most of the studies address citizen-public sector interaction, there is limited emphasis on interactions between private businesses and the public sector. Studies that focus on the business-to-government analysis are rarely studied although there have emerged a few such as e-procurement (Liao, Cheng, Liao, & Chen,

2003) and the building of a satisfactory infrastructure for businesses (Stamoulis et al., 2001). Noteworthy, it is within the domain of interaction that one finds the clearest examples of use and contribution to theory building, such as the work on structuralism (Devadoss, Pan, & Huang, 2002), institutionalism (Yang, 2003) and governance (Marche & McNiven, 2003).

The lowest frequency of studies are within the orientation (13%) and value (17%) categories. Orientations encompasses studies that address IT use in the structuring of problems and discretion of government. Only 13% of studies fall within this group. Dearstyne (2001) argues that a potential danger is that the digital stored and structured information is partly analyzed, whereas information streamed through physical meetings, log of chat-sessions, and so on, will not be analyzed nor would it serve as input to political decision making processes. An indicator of this danger is the findings in the Korean study where the public sector managers perceive e-government as much in terms of technology as they do in terms of effect (Hwang, Choi, & Myeong, 1999).

Studies on values include IS implementation and impact on protection and improvement of the private sphere, job satisfaction and enrichment, job enlargement, protection of legal rights, improved standard of health, safety, and well-being. In

Table 2. Conceptual domains and the occurrence in the e-government research body

Conceptual domain	Variable[a]	Occurrences in review
I. CAPABILITIES	Capabilities of a political unit address the manner in which the unit (individual or collective) deals with its environment, in an attempt to control the environmental effects on its behavior and to extract values from the environment.	38%
II. INTERACTIONS	Interactions between the political units assess how IT affects patterns of power and control, communication among units, the coordination of tasks or policies, and the cooperation among actors in performing a function within the public sector.	32%
III. ORIENTATIONS	Orientations capture the political unit's cognitive, affective and evaluative considerations.	13%
IV. VALUE DISTRIBUTIONS	Value distributions are measured by examining whether a political actor experiences a shift in values that is attributable to IT.	17%
Total		100%

Source: [a] Andersen and Danziger (1994) and Danziger and Andersen (2002)

Brazil, for example, the e-government strategy is linked to improvement of health standards in the country (Tigre, 2003). The group of articles in this category also explores the dangers of e-government in the context of collection and analysis of personal information (Jaeger, Bertot, & McClure, 2003) which in the age of terrorism has called for increased attention (Halchin, 2002).

Contextual Research Domains

Turning to the distribution of the studies along the contextual research domains of e-government, articles included in the *Conceptualization of E-Government* domain comprise conceptualization and a broad definition of e-government (Collins & Butler, 2002; Dale, 2001; Dearstyne, 2001; Waisanen, 2002). General technical issues, such as development of suitable architectures for digital government systems (Joshi, Ghafoor, Aref, & Spafford, 2001) and standards for interagency sharing of information (Bajaj & Ram, 2003), are included in this category. Also, several studies in this category outline general overviews of e-government initiatives at country level, for example, Australia (Clark, 2003), New Zealand (Deakins & Dillon, 2002), South Korea (Hwang et al., 1999), China (Zhang, 2002), and the UK (Bellamy, 2002). Onwards, general organizational challenges associated with e-government initiatives (Armstrong, 2002) and implications for e-government due to the threat of terrorism, which can decrease the newly gained transparency achieved by the application of ICT in public agencies (Jaeger et al., 2003) are elements in this category.

Articles focusing on *Governmental Role in Technology Diffusion* encompass 18% of the articles ranging from global and national level (Gibbs, Kraemer, & Dedrick, 2003; Tigre, 2003; Wong, 2003) to a local scope. The papers with a focus on "governmental role in technology diffusion" concentrate on specific bills of e-government (Stamoulis et al., 2001; Tillman, 2003). Some articles focus on particular aspects of e-government, especially studies from the U.S.; for example focusing on "The Government Paperwork Elimination Act" (Fletcher, 2002) or discussing Internet and terrorism and the need for regulation of access of information in order to prevent terrorism (Halchin, 2002). Further, Meer and Winden (2003) focus on how ICT policies can support local manifestations and dynamics of the information society. Special attention is paid to the role of the different stakeholders at the local level.

The most often occurring type of article in our review lies in the domain of *Governmental Administrative E-Service Focus* with a share of 34%. This might not come as a surprise, given that a very visible manifestation of e-government is to establish a portal thereby providing access to information and services for citizens and businesses. Provision of information through public portals is often outlined in articles regarding e-service. Some articles outline requirements for e-service provision (Atherton, 2002; Ho, 2002; Layne & Lee, 2001; Lu, Du, Zahng, Ma, & Le, 2002; Teicher, Hughes, & Dow, 2002). Some authors (Micheletti, 2000; Thomas &

Streib, 2003) go further and discuss the likelihood of citizens adopting eServices, what citizens want, and what the benefits of adoption are (Luling, 2001). Another perspective on eService provision is the architecture of eService portals with respect to technological architecture (Bannister & Walsh, 2002), development and implementation of city Websites (Jorgensen & Cable, 2002), and the design features (Barnes & Vidgen, 2003; Burn & Robins, 2003). Yet another approach to eServices is the requirement of the authorities offering eServices. Requirements to staff in general (Burn & Robins, 2003), quality of information provided (Laskowski, 2000), and considerations related to resources allocated to eServices (Kaylor, Deshazo, & Van Eck, 2001) have been analyzed. The question raised by Kaylor et al. is whether municipalities need to consider which eServices they can afford to offer and, more precisely, which services they can afford not to offer to their citizens.

Articles that report on issues related to *E-Democracy and Involvement of Citizens and Separation of Power* include Atherton (2002) who argues that portals for electronic community information are tools for democratization and that e-government brings democracy closer to citizens. This issue is also discussed by Chadwich (2003) and Yang (2003). A highly articulated attitude to involvement of citizens in democratic processes is presented by Vigoda (2002) who purports that e-government creates active roles for citizens. E-government is seen as a means for responsiveness and for collaboration of citizens and the public sector. By contrast, Shuler (2003) claims

Table 3. Contextual research domains and the occurrence in the e-government research body

Contextual research domain	Content of the contextual domain.	Occurrences in review
Conceptualization of e-government	Broad and conceptual aspects on or related to e-government. The domain differs from the three other domains in the sense that it is more overall in its approach to e-government.	24%
Governmental role in technology diffusion	Policy makers' efforts to promote e-government initiatives in countries, regions or other units.	18%
Governmental administrative eService focus	Initiatives where governmental services have been provided via electronic means to citizens and businesses.	34%
e-democracy and involvement of citizens and separation of power	Articles which specifically focus on ICT as a mean for involvement of citizens in political processes.	25%
Total		100%

that e-government regulation can lead to a redistribution of power due to a possible violation of the separation of power doctrine in the American Constitution.

One topic in the borderline between the two domains *Governmental Administrative E-Service Focus* and *E-Democracy and Involvement of Citizens and Separation of Power* is the sharing of information. A large number of articles discuss the Internet as a means for sharing of public information. Ambite et al. (2001) discuss the problem of providing statistical information through e-service portals since this actually reduces the users' capability of retrieving useful information due to problems with information overload (Ambite et al., 2001). A competing argument is that public access to information creates transparency to citizens and improves accountability (Barata & Cain, 2003; Barnum, 2002; Susman, 2001; Watson & Mundy, 2001).

Discussion of Findings

This review challenges the findings by Grönlund who argues that much research in e-government is at a scientifically immature stage of "anecdotal case stories" where the research is characterized by a case description without including any strict data collection procedure, and where theory building and testing are absent (Grönlund, 2004). Although almost one third of the studies are oriented towards conceptualization of e-government, two thirds of the reviewed research present data and cases founded on some methodological assumption.

Sixty percent of the articles either concentrate on e-service provision or mere conceptualization of e-government, rather than indicating outcomes and benefits of e-government adoption. Thus, there is a major gap to be filled studying not only uptake but also exploitation of the technologies and the impacts on government.

It is also striking that research is less focused on involvement of citizens, for example with respect to e-democracy (25%) compared to e-service applications (34%). The wave of e-participation and e-democracy as prompted by, for example, the European Commission appears to have little substance in what governments implement. However, it has to be stressed that we have in our search for a research domain excluded the work on virtual state, digital divide, and pure democracy oriented aspects (Fountain, 2001). Although the democracy issue clearly is part of e-government, we have focused our review of literature on the administrative and executive domain of government thus not including keywords directly related to e-democracy.

From the review it has become clear that there is not well defined e-government research paradigm. Though it was possible to classify the articles from the sample into the four domains of impact and the four contextual research domains, there are more issues that diversify e-government research, other than unifying aspects.

This turbulence in the e-government field makes it challenging to crystallize the domain of the e-government research paradigm. Our proposition is that the *domain of government* needs to be addressed explicitly to qualify for the e-government label. The domain of government encompasses in our view one or more of the following features: (1) labor intensive work processes, (2) a variety of activities within regulation and service provision that can only partly be understood from a singular perspective, (3) co-existence of political and administrative rationale along with more anarchical rationalities, (4) high exposure to demand on transparency, accountability and accessibility, (5) the existence of a demand paradox, and (6) strict rules and regulations for expenditures. Several of the six features are shared with settings such as insurances and airlines. Thus, we do not claim that the six features exist only in government. We do claim, however, that e-government researchers have largely ignored the six features and thereby put a limitation to the validity and the relevance of the studies. Below we argue how these proposed characteristics materialize in the field of information systems in government.

First, the public sector is overall a *labor intensive workplace* where case handling plays a central role in areas such as social welfare and application processing as in the DMV and building permission departments. Focusing on case work applications and with less orientation towards physical production optimization could impact the speed and nature of the uptake of IT applications. In contrast to this picture is the uptake of IT in areas as law enforcement, sensors in surveillance, tax departments' uptake of computing in processing tax forms, and e-learning in the educational sector.

Second, we take the position that government needs to *conduct a variety of activities and apply information technology in more of these activities, in a manner that, only marginally, can be understood from a single research domain as law.* Thus, rather than seeking a solely formal political view of government, in other words, who gets what, when, and how from government (Laswell, 1936), we find it much more appealing to define government as the structures, processes, actors and policies that determine or implement the allocation of public values in the collectivity (Easton, 1965). Easton's model brings awareness to the political environment, of which public administration is a part. The model provides insight into the complex way that public services have emerged, sustained and changed. Complementing Easton's model with modern *governance models* can aid our understanding of how governmental IT-initiatives and IT-practices unfold (Ham & Hill, 1993). One implication of this is that rather than voting and legacy systems as the cornerstones of e-government research, they will be one amongst other technologies that allow participation and governance in a more generic sense.

Third, we propose that there is a mixture of political, administrative-rationale and anarchical arguments for adoption and use of IT in government. Barry Bozemann takes the position that "all organizations are public" in so far as they are subject to public authority (Bozemann, 1989), whereas Allison and Klausen argue that the specific context, among other things, is constituted by the inherent political and regulated character of both goal-setting and performance (Allison, 1983; Klausen, 2000). Thus, there are a *number of political actors who are setting the goals (not only the leaders and managers of public institutions)*, with these goals subject to change whenever shifting political coalitions find it opportune, and typically being diverse, broad and ambiguous (Hoff, 1992). Therefore, we propose a pragmatic view suggesting that in some areas of government the political rationality dominates, such as in large scale, national IT-projects, whereas in others, administrative arguments in terms of internal use and budget savings, dominate the motives for IT. In yet others, anarchic arguments, such as muddling through and garbage can models (Lindblom, 1959; March & Olsen, 1985), appear to possess more explanatory power for IT adoption by government.

Fourth, e-government applications often have "*less direct market exposure* (and therefore more reliance on appropriations), resulting in less incentive for productivity and effectiveness, lower allocational efficiency, and lower availability of market information; more legal and formal constraints; and higher political influences, including impacts of interest groups and the need for support of constituencies" (Thong, Yap, & Seah, 2000). The irony is, however, that e-government applications are more *exposed to critique and demand on transparency, accountability and accessibility* than in the assumed market driven private sector. Finally, there are common expectations that public officials act fairly, responsively, accountably, and honestly. Although similar expectations can subsist in the private sector, there are legal means to seek these expectations being implemented.

Fifth, there is a fundamental *demand paradox* for implementation of information technology in the public sector, resulting in greater e-government services risk, representing a cost-driver. IT-expenditures are budget driven and frequently the focus is on the improvement of service provision. Contrasting the private sector, IT in government is less frequently applied to increase market shares or improve profit, although it can be argued that in some instances similar goals are identified. For example, local municipalities' internet-enabled campaigns to attract business investment or high-end tax payers can be interpreted as seeking an increased market share. Thus, IT in a government setting pays more attention to its cost-effectiveness and contribution to impacts on the short term and less attention to the strategic, long term impacts. Budgets in government are rarely a result of a long-term market enlargement strategy aiming to erode competing products or services. Instead, funding for IT is seen as a possible means of reducing current operating costs. Thus, this could impact the application of IT to a particular target for the operational and transactional tasks.

Sixth, there are often *strict rules and regulations* for planning and contracting IT-application and limited strategic maneuvering for replacing workers and routines with IT. A public institution can, for instance, neither change its line of production nor can it harvest and invest any profits it may gain from reducing the spending of resources or from performance pay (Klausen, 2000). At the managerial level, managers are left with "less decision-making autonomy, less authority over subordinates, greater reluctance to delegate, and a more political role. There is a more frequent turnover of top managers due to elections and political appointments; difficulties in devising incentives for individual performance; and lower work satisfaction and organizational commitment" (Thong et al., 2000).

Table 4. Proposed key dimensions of the e-government domain

Dimension	Government characteristics
1. Labor intensity in the work processes	Few physical products
	Lack of robot and product technologies
	Case work technologies
2. Regulation and service provision	Positive and negative regulation
	Service provision (general information services, specific services)
	Citizens, government and politicians and other governmental units the key users
3. Political, administrative-rational, and anarchic motives	Structures, processes, actors and policies that determine or implement the allocation of public values
	Many and often fragmented and conflicting political actors
	Back-tracking (logs) of activities to ensure that employees act fairly, responsively, accountably, and honestly
4. Limited market exposure	Limited market exposure and substitution options (products/ actors)
	Limited/ no competition on the services
	Indirect processes for budget allocation rather than direct from users
5. Demand paradox	IT a potential cost driver rather than a strategic tool
	Budget driven IT-applications
	Higher concern on direct cost-effectiveness than in the private sector
6. Strict rules and regulations	Main roles and tasks defined at policy level
	Investment and changes in IT-use requiring consultation on formal procedures/ law changes
	Less strategic decision-making autonomy

Conclusion

Our review has identified a large number of papers published within the domains of e-government, e-governance, online government, digital government, one-stop government, and electronic government. Thus, any speculations on "not much has been published" could not be verified. The research also challenges Grönlund's (2004) claim that e-government is anecdotal in nature. One of the most important findings of this review is the insight into the type of research populating e-government research.

The literature review of articles published during 1998-2003 clearly indicates that e-government research has partly taken up the legacy from IS research and that no particular strong emphasis is put on those key dimensions of the government domain outlined in a previous section. The findings suggest that parameters related to capabilities and interactions are in the hub of e-government research.

This trend is pronounced in the cross-tabulation of our findings (see Table 1). Regardless of the research theme, there is strong emphasis on impacts related to capability and interaction, rather than on the more qualitative impacts concerned with orientations and value distribution. This is understandable with respect to the Governmental role in technology diffusion, which is strategic in nature, and the Government administrative eService focus where customer-orientation, rather than the expected civil service, is in focus. However, in the realm of the Conceptualization of e-government, a more even distribution of impacts was expected. This is also the case with respect to the theme related to e-democracy and involvement of citizens and separation of power which by nature is more concerned with impacts and is more qualitative. About one third of the articles fall into this category, and 16% and 15%, fall into the categories of impact related to orientations and value distribution, respectively.

This article has identified numerous variations in domains of e-government, which seems to suggest that there are more issues that divide, rather than unite, the many scholars and practitioners using the e-government term. It is our claim that at present, e-government research is primarily founded on the legacy of IS research and fails to incorporate disciplines such as public administration and political science in an adequate manner. Changing this path could offer rewarding research and help move the research field to a unique position.

References

Ahmed, A. S., Andersen, K. V., Arnthórsson, H., & Henriksen, H. Z. (2004). *Stray dogs and wild cats tracking down information systems in government.* Paper presented at the European Conference on Information Systems, Turku, Finland.

Alexander, C. J. (2001). Wiring the nation! Including first nations? Aboriginal Canadians and federal e-government initiatives (Canada). *Journal of Canadian Studies-Revue D Etudes Canadiennes, 35*(4), 277-296.

Allison, G. T. (1983). Public and private management: Are they fundamentally alike in all unimportant respects? In J. L. Perry & K. L. Kraemer (Eds.), *Public management: Public and private perspectives* (p. 79-92). Palo Alto, CA: Mayfield Publishing.

Ambite, J. L., Arens, Y., Hovy, E., Philpot, A., Gravano, L., Hatzivassiloglou, V., et al. (2001). Simplifying data access: The energy data collection project. *Computer, 34*(2), 47-54.

Andersen, K. V., & Danziger, J. N. (1994). Information technology and the political world: The impacts of it on capabilities, interactions, orientations, and values. *International Journal of Public Administration, 18*(11), 1693-1724.

Armstrong, A. (2002). E-government work force planning: A pilot study. *The Journal of Government Financial Management, 51*(2), 32-35.

Atherton, L. (2002). Seamless UK-building bridges between information islands. *New Library World, 103*(11/12), 467-473.

Bajaj, A., & Ram, S. (2003). IAIS: A methodology to enable inter-agency information sharing in egovernment. *Journal of Database Management, 14*(4), 59-80.

Bannister, F., & Walsh, N. (2002). The virtual public servant: Ireland's public services broker. *Information Polity, 7*(2,3), 115-128.

Barata, K., & Cain, P. (2003). Records management toolkits from across the pond. *Information Management Journal, 37*(4), 40-46.

Barnes, S. J., & Vidgen, R. (2003). Measuring Web site quality improvements: A case study of the forum on strategic management knowledge exchange. *Industrial Management + Data Systems, 103*(5/6), 297-309.

Barnum, G. (2002). Availability, access, authenticity, and persistence: Creating the environment for permanent public access to electronic government information. *Government Information Quarterly, 19*(1), 37-43.

Bellamy, C. (2002). From automation to knowledge management: Modernising British government with ICTs. *International Review of Administrative Sciences, 68*, 213-230.

Bozemann, B. (1989). *All institutions are public: Bridging public and private organizational theories.* San Francisco: Jossey-Bass Publishers.

Bretschneider, S. (2003). Information technology, e-government, and institutional change. *Public Administration Review, 63*(6), 738-744.

Burn, J., & Robins, G. (2003). Moving towards e-government: A case study of organisational change processes. *Logistics Information Management, 16*(1), 25-35.

Burrell, G., & Morgan, F. (1979). *Sociological paradigms and organizational analysis*. London: Heinemann Educational Books.

Carr, N. G. (2004). *Does it matter? Information technology and the corrosion of competitive advantage*. Boston: Harvard Business School Press.

Chadwick, A. (2003). Bringing e-democracy back in: Why it matters for future research on e-governance. *Social Science Computer Review, 21*(4), 443-455.

Chadwick, A., & May, C. (2003). Interaction between states and citizens in the age of the internet: "E-government" in the United States, Britain, and the European Union. *Governance-an International Journal of Policy and Administration, 16*(2), 271-300.

Clark, E. (2003). Managing the transformation to e-government: An Australian perspective. *Thunderbird International Business Review, 45*(4), 377-397.

Collins, N., & Butler, P. (2002). The marketplace, e-government and e-democracy. *Irish Marketing Review, 15*(2), 86-93.

Dale, A. (2001). Letters from the corporanian war zone. *Journal of Information Science, 27*(5), 351-353.

Danziger, J. N., & Andersen, K. V. (2002). The impacts of information technology in public administration: An analysis of empirical research from the „golden age" of transformation. *International Journal of Public Administration, 25*(5), 591-627.

Deakins, E., & Dillon, S. M. (2002). E-government in New Zealand: The local authority perspective. *The international Journal of Public Sector Management, 15*(4/5), 375-398.

Dearstyne, B. W. (2001). E-business, e-government & information proficiency. *Information Management Journal, 35*(4), 16-24.

Deb, G. K. (1999). Electronic governance: A vehicle for the new world order. *Electronics Information & Planning, 27*(1), 29-33.

Devadoss, P. R., Pan, S. L., & Huang, J. D. (2002). Structural analysis of e-government initiatives: A case study of sco. *Decision Support Systems, 34*, 253-269.

Doty, P., & Erdelez, S. (2002). Information micro-practices in Texas rural courts: Methods and issues for e-government. *Government Information Quarterly, 19*(4), 369-387.

Easton, D. (1965). *A systems analysis of political life*. New York: John Wiley & Sons.

Fletcher, P. D. (2002). The government paperwork elimination act: Operating instructions for an electronic government. *International Journal of Public Administration, 25*(5), 723-736.

Fountain, J. E. (2001). *Building the virtual state: Information technology and institutional change.* Washington, DC: Brookings Institution.

Gibbs, J., Kraemer, K. L., & Dedrick, J. (2003). Environment and policy factors shaping global e-commerce diffusion: A cross-country comparison. *Information Society, 19*(1), 5-18.

Grönlund, Å. (2004). *State of the art in e-gov research – A survey.* Paper presented at the third eGov DEXA conference, Zaragoza Spain.

Halchin, L. E. (2002). Electronic government in the age of terrorism. *Government Information Quarterly, 19*(3), 243-254.

Ham, C., & Hill, M. (1993). *The policy process in the modern capitalist state* (2nd ed.). New York: Wheatsheaf Books.

Ho, A. T. K. (2002). Reinventing local governments and the e-government initiative. *Public Administration Review, 62*(4), 434-444.

Hoff, J. (1992). Evaluation of information technology in private and public sector contexts. *Informatization and the Public Sector, 2*(4), 307-328.

Holliday, I. (2002). Building e-government in east and southeast Asia: Regional rhetoric and national (in)action. *Public Administration & Development, 22*(4), 323-335.

Hwang, S. D., Choi, Y., & Myeong, S. H. (1999). Electronic government in South Korea: Conceptual problems. *Government Information Quarterly, 16*(3), 277-285.

Jackson, N. (2003). Mps and Web technologies: An untapped opportunity? *Journal of Public Affairs, 3*(2), 124-137.

Jaeger, P. T., Bertot, J. C., & McClure, C. R. (2003). The impact of the USA patriot act on collection and analysis of personal information under the foreign intelligence surveillance act. *Government Information Quarterly, 20*(3), 295-314.

Jorgensen, D. J., & Cable, S. (2002). Facing the challenges of e-goverment: A case study of the city of Corpus Christi, Texas. *S.A.M. Advanced Management Journal, 67*(3), 15-21.

Joshi, J., Ghafoor, A., Aref, W. G., & Spafford, E. H. (2001). Digital government security infrastructure design challenges. *Computer, 34*(2), 66-72.

Kaylor, C., Deshazo, R., & Van Eck, D. (2001). Gauging e-government: A report on implementing services among American cities. *Government Information Quarterly, 18*(4), 293-307.

Klausen, K. C. (2000). *Leadership and management: Roles and styles among local government CEOs.* Paper presented at the IPMN conference at the MGSM, Macquire University, Sydney, Australia.

Kraemer, K. L., & King, J. L. (2003). Information technology and administrative reform: Will the time after e-government be different? Retrieved November 1, 2004, from http://www.crito.uci.edu

Lakatos, I. (1970). Falsification and the methodology of scientific research programmes. In L. A. Musgrave (Ed.), *Criticism and the growth of knowledge* (pp. 91-196). Cambridge: Cambridge University Press.

Laskowski, M. S. (2000). The impact of electronic access to government information: What users and documents specialists think. *Journal of Government Information, 27*(2), 173-185.

Laswell, H. (1936). *Who gets what, when, how.* New York: Whittlesey House.

Layne, K., & Lee, J. W. (2001). Developing fully functional e-government: A four stage model. *Government Information Quarterly, 18*(2), 122-136.

Lenk, K. (2002). Electronic service delivery: A driver of public sector modernisation. *Information Polity, 7*, 87-96.

Liao, S. H., Cheng, C. H., Liao, W. B., & Chen, I. L. (2003). A Web-based architecture for implementing electronic procurement in military organisations. *Technovation, 23*(6), 521-532.

Lindblom, C. E. (1959). 'The science' of muddling through. *Public Administration Review, 19*(2), 79-88.

Lu, W., Du, J., Zahng, J., Ma, F., & Le, T. (2002). Internet development in China. *Journal of Information Science, 28*(3), 207-224.

Luling, D. (2001). Taking it online: Anyway, anyplace, anytime. Tennessee anytime. *The Journal of Government Financial Management, 50*(2), 42.

March, J. G., & Olsen, J. P. (1985). The new-institutionalism: Organizational factors in political life. *American Political Science Review, 78*(3), 734-749.

Marche, S., & McNiven, J. D. (2003). E-government and e-governance: The future isn't what it used to be. *Canadian Journal of Administrative Sciences, 20*(1), 74-86.

Markus, L. M., & Robey, D. (1988). Information technology and organizational change: Causal structure in theory and research. *Management Science, 34*(5), 583-598.

Meer, A. v. d., & Winden, W. v. (2003). E-governance in cities: A comparison of urban information and communication technology policies. *Regional Studies, 37*(4), 407-419.

Micheletti, M. (2000). End of big government: Is it happening in the Nordic countries? *Governance-an International Journal of Policy and Administration, 13*(2), 265-278.

Parker, B. (2003). Maori access to information technology. *Electronic Library, 21*(5), 456-460.

Peled, A. (2001). Centralization or diffusion? Two tales of online government. *Administration & Society, 32*(6), 686-709.

Porter, M. E. (2001). Strategy and the internet. *Harvard Business Review, 79*(2), 63-78.

Potter, A. (2002). Accessibility of Alabama government Web sites. *Journal of Government Information, 29*(5), 303-317.

Shuler, J. A. (2003). Citizen-centered government: Information policy possibilities for the 108th congress. *Journal of Academic Librarianship, 29*(2), 107-100.

Silcock, R. (2001). What is e-government? *Parliamentary Affairs, 54*(1), 88-101.

Stamoulis, D., Gouscos, D., Georgiadis, P., & Martakos, D. (2001). Revisiting public information management for effective e-government services. *Information Management & Computer Security, 9*(4), 146-153.

Susman, T. M. (2001). The good, the bad, and the ugly: E-government and the people's right to know. *Vital Speeches of the Day, 68*(2), 38-42.

Swan, J., Scarbrough, H., & Preston, J. (1999). *Knowledge management: The next fad to forget people?* Paper presented at the 7th European Conference on Information Systems (ECIS), Copenhagen.

Tan, C. W., & Pan, S. L. (2003). Managing e-transformation in the public sector: An e-government study of the inland revenue authority of Singapore (iras). *European Journal of Information Systems, 12*(4), 269-281.

Teicher, J., Hughes, O., & Dow, N. (2002). E-government: A new route to public sector quality. *Managing Service Quality, 12*(6), 384-393.

Thomas, J. C., & Streib, G. (2003). The new face of government: Citizen-initiated contacts in the era of e-government. *Journal of Public Administration Research and Theory, 13*(1), 83-102.

Thong, J. Y. L., Yap, C. S., & Seah, K. L. (2000). Business process reengineering in the public sector: The case of the housing development board in Singapore. *Journal of Management Information Systems, 17*(1), 245-270.

Tigre, P. B. (2003). Brazil in the age of electronic commerce. *Information Society, 19*(1), 33-43.

Tillman, B. (2003). More information could mean less privacy. *Information Management Journal, 37*(2), 20-23.

Vigoda, E. (2002). From responsiveness to collaboration: Governance, citizens, and the next generation of public administration. *Public Administration Review, 62*(5), 527-540.

Waisanen, B. (2002). The future of e-government: Technology-fueled management tools. *PM. Public Management, 84*(5), 6-9.

Watson, R. T., & Mundy, B. (2001). A strategic perspective of electronic democracy. *Communications of the ACM, 44*(1), 27-30.

Wong, P. K. (2003). Global and national factors affecting e-commerce diffusion in Singapore. *Information Society, 19*(1), 19-32.

Yang, K. F. (2003). Neoinstitutionalism and e-government: Beyond Jane Fountain. *Social Science Computer Review, 21*(4), 432-442.

Zhang, J. H. (2002). Will the government 'serve the people'? The development of Chinese e-government. *New Media & Society, 4*(2), 163-184.

Chapter XIV

E-Government Adoption in Canadian Municipal Governments:
A Survey of Ontario Chief Administrative Officers

Christopher G. Reddick, The University of Texas at San Antonio, USA

Abstract

This study examines Ontario, Canada's municipal e-government adoption. This chapter specifically focuses on how e-government has increased citizen-initiated contacts with these local governments. This study uses survey data of these local governments to determine the key factors that predict increased citizen contact with e-government. What these municipal governments most commonly are doing is informational e-government, such as providing downloadable forms for manual completion. Transactional e-government is done less often, with very few local governments offering online payment of taxes, for example. The regression results indicated that offering more online services or e-services and having a separate information technology (IT) department developing the e-government budget increased citizen contact with e-government. The traditional factors that are used to explain citizen-initiated contact, such as socioeconomic status of the community, were not found to have any impact on increasing citizen contact with e-government.

Introduction and Background

E-government has been defined as the use of the Internet to deliver services and information to citizens and businesses (Ho & Ni, 2004; Holden, Norris, & Fletcher, 2003; Reddick, 2004a). There are several studies that examine the adoption of e-government at the local level in the U.S. (Edmiston, 2002; Holden, Norris, & Fletcher, 2003; Ho, 2002; Reddick, 2004a; Moon, 2002; Reddick, 2004b). However, there are few studies that have empirically examined e-government at the local level outside the U.S. (Criado & Ramilo, 2003; Archer, 2005). Some recent research examines theoretically the impact of e-government on governance in Canada (Charih & Robert, 2004; Kernaghan, 2005). Therefore, most of the empirical evidence on local e-government adoption is provided from the analysis of a single country. In addition, most of the work on e-government literature focuses on the features of local governments that have adopted the Internet for information and e-service delivery (Edmiston, 2002; Ho, 2002; Moon, 2002; Reddick, 2004a). A smaller number of studies actually has tested the impact of key features that explain e-government adoption rates (Ho & Ni, 2004; Holden, Norris, & Fletcher, 2003; Reddick, 2004b; Moon & Norris, 2005).

Citizen-initiated contacts with government occur when individual citizens contact government personnel with requests for services or complaints (Thomas & Melkers, 1999). Increased citizen initiated contact with e-government is important, since it enhances political participation and validates government institutions (Thomas & Streib, 2003). E-government is a way to enhance efficiency, effectiveness, and equity of citizen and business access to local governments (Kernaghan, 2005).

Few studies have examined how e-government has changed citizens' interaction with their local governments (Thomas & Streib, 2003). The studies that have examined citizen-initiated contact with public administrators focus on the perceptions and characteristics of citizens and their contacts (Serra, 1995; Thomas, 1982; Thomas & Melkers, 2000). Few studies examine administrators' responses to citizen-initiated contacts (Green, 1982). Therefore, the existing literature presents only one side of the relationship between citizen-initiated contacts and government, because it has not extensively considered bureaucrats and their responses to contacts.

Increased citizen interaction with government is a tool for enhancing democracy, since it represents an avenue for increasing service delivery and confidence in government (Green, 1982). With such an emphasis on enhancing performance at all levels of government, e-government is an excellent mechanism with which to achieve this goal (Ho, 2002). Therefore, this study examines through survey research, municipal e-government adoption in Ontario, Canada, to see how developed these local governments are and to discern whether e-government has increased citizen-initiated contacts with government.

Ontario, Canada, was chosen for two reasons: (1) for four years in a row, this country was rated as the most e-government-enabled national government according to Accenture, an information systems consultancy firm (Accenture, 2004); and (2) it is the most populous province in Canada with the largest city in the country; namely, Toronto.

In order to examine the impact of e-government and its relationship on citizen-initiated contacts, this chapter first outlines the existing literature in both areas and demonstrates how this study fits into the literature. Second, the evidence of e-government adoption at the local level in Ontario is presented. Third, six key hypotheses are outlined, and a model of citizen-initiated contacts is tested empirically. The conclusion summarizes and suggests avenues for future research on e-government adoption at the local level.

Local E-Government Adoption Survey Literature

As previously mentioned, there are few studies that examine factors that precipitate e-government adoption at the local level, with most of this work being focused on the U.S. (Ho & Ni, 2004; Reddick, 2004b). The majority of the existing research examines the International City/County Management Association (ICMA) surveys of e-government adoption (Holden, Norris, & Fletcher, 2003; Moon, 2002; Reddick, 2004a).

The general consensus from their findings is that local e-government adoption is past stage one of the Layne and Lee (2001) model of cataloging information online (Holden, Norris, & Fletcher, 2003; Moon, 2002; Reddick, 2004a; Norris & Moon, 2005). Stage two of transaction-based e-government is not as common, partly because of issues of privacy and security of personally identifiable information (PII) (Edmiston, 2002; Holden, Norris, & Fletcher, 2003). Limited evidence exists for vertical and horizontal integration of e-government across organizational boundaries and functional areas of government (Ho, 2002). This study is different from the existing work on e-government adoption in that it focuses on whether e-government has increased citizen-initiated contact with government officials; most of the existing work has focused on explaining e-government features, as mentioned, and has concentrated mainly on the U.S.

Citizen-Initiated Contact Literature

The citizen-initiated contacts literature can be divided into two research areas, with the first examining perceived needs and awareness as the most important factors that increases contacts (Hirlinger, 1992; Jones, Greenberg, Kaufman, & Drew, 1977; Sharp, 1984; Thomas, 1982; Thomas & Melkers, 1999; Vedlitz, Dyer, & Durand, 1980) and the second examining the satisfaction with bureaucracy and its impact on citizen-initiated contacts. In the second research area, some scholars have argued that citizen-initiated contact will decrease, because the bureaucracy is overwhelmed with service requests (Serra, 1995; Vedlitz & Dyer, 1984). There are also studies that show the opposite effect of increased contact because of frustration with the bureaucracy (Moon, Serra, & West, 1993; Thomas & Melkers, 2000).

A significant question in public administration is how responsive municipal bureaucracies are to citizens' needs and demands and how these can be increased (Greene, 1982). Most studies (of contacting) have examined the contactors; few studies focus directly on administrators' attitudes toward contacts (Greene, 1982). The question of responsiveness is important not only for individuals who depend on municipal services but also for democracy and political participation, since administrators are supposed to be responsible directly to mayors and council members and ultimately to citizens (Greene, 1982).

As mentioned, one reason for citizen-initiated contact with municipal government is a perceived *need* for the services that a government offers, which is usually a specific government service or modification of service (Thomas & Melkers, 2000; Thomas & Streib, 2003). Contacting behavior is also related to the *awareness* of government as the appropriate provider of these services (Vedlitz, Dyer, Durand, & 1980). Finally, needs and awareness are related to the relative social well being of the individual, or socioeconomic status (Jones, Greenberg, Kaufman, & Drew, 1977). Empirical evidence indicates that contacting is related to a perceived need for information or services, and socioeconomic status is of secondary importance (Hirlinger, 1992; Sharp, 1984; Thomas, 1982; Thomas & Melkers, 1999).

Other factors that influence citizen-initiated contacts are related to bureaucratic response to citizen demands. Research shows that the greater the number of demands, the more difficult it is for local governments to respond (Vedlitz & Dyer, 1984). In addition, empirical evidence indicates that citizens who are unhappy with the bureaucracy are more likely to contact members of Congress (Moon, Serra, & West, 1993). Research also shows that citizen-initiated contact increases with greater satisfaction of the bureaucracy (Serra, 1995).

There are at least two important differences between these Web contacts and traditional citizen-initiated contacts (Thomas & Streib, 2003). First, contacting via the Web may be easier and quicker than contacting by phone or in person, meaning that many contacts that have been traditionally made by the phone or in person will be made over the Web (Horrigan, 2004). Second, the Web may not have a meaningful two-way communication, because the phone has greater personal contact than a Web contact. Despite these differences, the similarities between the two types of contacts are still enough to explore citizen-initiated contacts (Thomas & Streib, 2003). This study does so by focusing on survey evidence collected from municipal administrators in Ontario, Canada.

Data Collection Methods

The data collected for this local e-government study were from a survey conducted in the months of August and September 2004. There were 161 municipal governments surveyed in Ontario, Canada, that served populations of 10,000 or more. Chief administrative officers (CAO) of these local governments were surveyed to obtain their perceptions on e-government development. A total of 119 surveys were completed. The overall response rate was 74%. This response rate was very high, given the general hesitancy of professionals to answer surveys. This was accomplished first by sending a letter introducing the research project and then following up in a couple of weeks with the formal survey.

To maximize the response rate, there was a reminder letter sent two weeks before the survey due date. In addition, only 10 key questions were asked in order to maximize the return rate. The questions were taken from the 2004 International City/County Management Association (ICMA) e-government survey and adapted to the Canadian context (ICMA, 2004). The 10 questions were used to show the major aspects of e-government relationships, specifically government-to-citizen, government-to-business, and government-to-employees. The value of a survey is to provide information on Web site content and to identify opinions of key decision makers on e-government adoption. If this study only conducted a Web site content analysis, it would be limited, since the opinions of key e-government decision makers would not be accounted for (West, 2004).

Data on the unemployment rate, median personal income, and population of the communities were taken from the most recent Statistic Canada's 2001 Community Profiles database of local governments. These socioeconomic data were used in the test of the model of citizen-initiated contact with government discussed toward the end of this chapter. The responses to the survey questions are discussed in the following section in order to get a better understanding of the e-government climate that local governments face in Canada.

Ontario Local E-Government Survey Data

The most common services that local governments in Ontario offer to their citizens and businesses are presented in Table 1. The majority of the list of services in Table 1 was taken from ICMA e-government survey questions of e-services offered by local governments in the U.S. (ICMA, 2004). Most of the municipal governments offer informational services. For example, 103 of them post council meeting minutes

Table 1.

Please provide the following information about e-government on your local government Web site. (Check all applicable.)			
	Ontario Local Governments Total Responses	Ontario Local Governments Percent of Respondents	ICMA E-government Survey 2004 Percent of Responses
Council meeting minutes	103	91.2%	75.6%
Budget documents	83	73.5%	NA
Forms that can be downloaded for manual completion (e.g. voter registration, building permits, etc.)	77	68.1%	58.3%
Online communication with individual elected and appointed officials	63	55.8%	65.6%
Online complaints (e.g. reporting graffiti, missing trash pickup)	47	41.6%	NA
Online requests for local government records	36	31.9%	27.1%
Online requests for services (e.g. pothole repair)	33	29.2%	29.5%
Newsletters e-mailed to residents	26	23.0%	27.7%
Other (please specify)	25	22.1%	19.7%
Online registration for use of recreational facilities (e.g. reserving picnic areas, racquetball courts, and registering for classes).	23	20.4%	16.4%
Online delivery of local governments records to the requestor	20	17.7%	18.1%
Online payment of fines/fees	17	15.0%	7.3%
Online completion and submission of permit applications	17	15.0%	10.2%
Online payment of taxes	14	12.4%	8.6%
Online payment of utility bills	9	8.0%	9.2%
Police reports	5	4.4%	NA
Online completion and submission of business license applications/renewals	4	3.5%	6.3%
Online property registration (e.g. animal, bicycle registration)	3	2.7%	2.8%
Online voter registration	1	0.9%	2.4%
Note: NA= Not Available			

online. Other common information provided online was budget documents, with three-fourths of these local governments providing this type of financial information to its citizens.

E-government in Ontario has not progressed to higher stages of development (see Table 1). For example, only around 12% of the governments surveyed provided the option of online tax payment, and 20% offered online registration for recreational facilities. In fact, the third most common response, at 68%, was providing online forms that could be downloaded for manual completion. This demonstrates the limited development of providing electronic service delivery.

Table 1 also compares Ontario local e-government adoption to municipal governments in the U.S. with ICMA (2004) data. Comparing Ontario municipalities with local governments in the U.S. indicates some interesting observations. Providing council meeting minutes online is very common in Ontario municipalities with more than 90% of these governments doing this, compared to three-quarters in the U.S. Forms that can be downloaded for manual completion also are found more often in Ontario than the U.S. However, communication with individual elected and appointed officials is less common in Ontario than the U.S., possibly explained by more officials in the latter county running for elections. Ontario local governments also seem to be more advanced in online payment systems, with 15% doing this in Ontario and only 7.3% in the U.S. having online payments systems for fines or fees. Similarly, online payment of taxes is done by 12.4% in Ontario and 8.6% in the U.S. The overall results reveal that Ontario municipalities are not much further ahead than U.S. local governments. However, Ontario municiple governments conduct more online transactions than local governments in the U.S.

There is greater adoption of e-government when it comes to electronic purchasing compared to the services results in Table 1. Table 2 shows electronic purchasing with transactional-based e-government taking place when local governments purchase goods online from businesses. For example, local governments purchasing office supplies from businesses often is done, but equipment purchases are done less frequently, and government purchasing insurance online is not done at all. Therefore, the development of e-purchasing seems to be more developed than e-services provided to citizens and businesses (see Table 1). The nonexistence of local governments purchasing insurance online could be the result of the lack of acceptance and technology enabling digital signatures in municipal governments. Therefore, these transactions would have to be completed on paper.

Table 3 demonstrates how e-government is used internally by these municipal governments, if they use an intranet (a Web server accessible only to local government employees). Around half of these governments have an intranet. Some of the more common intranet uses involve providing news and information, documents, and job searches. The intranet is used less often for more advanced tasks, such as online training and procurement. When comparing what e-governments offer to its

Table 2.

Please indicate by checking the boxes below which procurement activities you complete online. (Check all applicable.)			
	Review product offerings online(Percent of Responses in brackets)	Make purchases online(Percent of Responses in brackets)	Respondents Total
Property and/or liability insurance	13(100%)	0(0%)	13
Equipment	66(93%)	25(35%)	71
Office supplies	62(81%)	53(69%)	77
		Total Respondents	80

Table 3.

Does your local government have an Intranet (a Web server accessible only to local governments employees)?		
	Total Responses	Percent of Responses
Yes	53	47.7%
No	58	52.3%
If "Yes" how do you use the Intranet? (Check all applicable.)		
Provide news and information	52	96%
Publish documents and manuals online to reduce printing costs	48	96%
Post job openings for internal recruitments	43	90%
Expand telecommuting staff access to information and data	29	71%
Provide employees benefit forms	28	67%
Enable project teams to collaborate	26	74%
Provide online report generation	25	60%
Provide online training	21	57%
Provide online procurement tools	18	51%

citizens, there seems to be little development in transactional based e-government (see Table 1). This is attributed to the general hesitancy of the public conducting online transactions because of privacy and security concerns. E-purchasing is more advanced (see Table 2), and the intranet seems to be the most promising venture (see Table 3).

Table 4 demonstrates the amount that these governments are planning to budget for e-government for fiscal year 2005. In the sample, around 55% of municipalities

Table 4.

How much (Canadian Dollars) do you plan to budget for e-government for the coming next fiscal year?	Total Responses	Percent of Responses
Under $5,000	30	30.6%
$5,000-$10,000	25	25.5%
$10,000-$25,000	6	6.1%
$25,000-$50,000	8	8.2%
$50,000-$100,000	8	8.2%
Over $100,000	21	21.4%

budgeted less than $10,000 Canadian for e-government, and 21% budgeted more than $100,000 Canadian a year. Since the sample is composed of many smaller-sized local governments, this is not surprising. It demonstrated that small amounts of money are allocated to e-government, most likely attributed to the meltdown of the dot-com industry in early 2001 (Roy, 2003). This has caused many municipal governments to be hesitant to spend expansively on e-government projects, unless a sound business model can be identified.

Table 5 asks CAOs if they have a separate budget for e-government and whether the IT department develops this budget. This will give this research a sense of whether organizational structure influences e-government adoption. Around two-thirds of the local governments surveyed did not have a separate budget for e-government. Around 30% did have a separate budget for e-government, and the IT department submitted it to the budget office. Having a separate department looking after the needs of e-government is important because of the intense competition for fiscal

Table 5.

Please check the box beside the option below that best describes the e-government budget process in your local government.	Total Responses	Percent of Responses
There is no separate budget item for e-government	75	67.6%
There is a separate budget item for e-government and the Information Technology (or equivalent) department develops and submits the e-government budget for the local government.	34	30.6%
There is a separate budget item for e-government and each department develops and submits its own e-government budget.	2	1.8%

Table 6.

How are your current e-government efforts funded? (Check all applicable.)		
	Total Responses	Percent of Responses
General tax revenue	75	79.8%
Federal or provincial grants	22	23.4%
Transaction fees from services provided	13	13.8%
Municipal bond financing	9	9.6%
Risk-sharing (a private sector firm provides the application and receives a percent of the revenue)	4	4.3%

resources. A separate department can fight for e-government more effectively, rather than being lumped together with other departments.

Table 6 demonstrates that most of the sources of funds for e-government initiatives are found in the general fund. There was not a lot of non-traditional funding being used, such as grants and transaction fees. In addition, entrepreneurial efforts, such as risk sharing with private sector entities, hardly ever was done by these local governments.

Table 1 provides the evidence that there is not much transaction-based e-government taking place. Table 7 gives some indication as to why this has happened. Some e-government barriers can partially explain the situation that local governments are facing. For instance, the top responses for the barriers to e-government initiatives

Table 7.

Which if any of the following barriers to e-government initiatives has your local government encountered? (Check all applicable.)		
	Total Responses	Percent of Responses
Lack of financial resources	84	75.7%
Lack of technology/Web staff	64	57.7%
Lack of technology/Web expertise	50	45.0%
Issues regarding security	41	36.9%
Issues regarding privacy	37	33.3%
Need to upgrade technology (PCs, networks, etc.)	34	30.6%
Issues relating to convenience fees for online transactions	26	23.4%
Staff resistance to change	21	18.9%
Lack of collaboration among departments	20	18.0%
Lack of support from elected officials	17	15.3%
Other (please specify)	17	15.3%
Lack of information about e-government applications	13	11.7%

were lack of resources (both financial and personnel) and issues regarding privacy and security that have not been adequately addressed. This is consistent with the lack of transaction-based e-government, as shown in Table 1. In order for citizens to feel comfortable about paying taxes online or having online voter registration, governments must address the critical issues of privacy and security. For instance, what is going to happen to citizens' PII, such as credit card information? As well, are there controls in place to prevent misuse of this PII? In addition, since transaction-based e-government is more expensive than simply providing online information, funding and staffing become critical issues that should be addressed.

Table 8 shows the most important response to what is being tested in this chapter. Has e-government increased citizen-initiated contact? This was the number-one change as a result of e-government. The results in this table demonstrate that almost half of those surveyed believed that e-government had increased citizen-initiated contact. Only two municipal governments believed that e-government had reduced the number of staff. This is somewhat surprising, since this has been one of the primary reasons for many fiscally stressed local governments initiating e-govern-ment projects. E-government actually has increased the demands on staff, which is the opposite of those who argue that it will reduce transaction costs. The results in Table 8 highlight that e-government is moving closer to achieving outcomes. There-fore, the argument presented in some of the e-government literature on reinventing government has some validity (Ho, 2002). The impact of increasing citizen contact with government officials and business processes being reengineered, the top two changes are consistent with the reinventing government movement. Reinventing municipal government through e-government was evident for almost half of the municipal governments surveyed.

Table 8.

How has e-government changed your local government? (Check all applicable.)	Total Responses	Percent of Responses
Increased citizen contact with elected and appointed officials	46	48.4%
Business processes are being re-engineered	45	47.4%
Increased demands on staff	43	45.3%
Business processes are more efficient	42	44.2%
Changed the role of staff	37	38.9%
Reduced time demands on staff	29	30.5%
Reduced administrative costs	19	20.0%
Other (please specify)	10	10.5%
Reduced the number of staff	2	2.1%
Increased non-tax-based revenues from fees advertising	1	1.1%

This data can now be compiled to test specific hypotheses that explain whether e-government has increased citizen-initiated contacts with elected and appointed officials.

Hypotheses

There are six hypotheses tested in this study that are relevant to the citizen-initiated contact and e-government literatures, namely:

1.   Increases in population and median personal income will increase citizen-initiated contact with e-government because of greater socioeconomic status of the community.

2.   Increases in the unemployment rate will decrease contact with e-government because of greater fiscal stress placed on local governments.

3.   The greater the number of barriers to e-government adoption, such as lack of financial resources, lack of technology, issues regarding security and privacy, and so forth, that a municipal government faces inhibits e-government adoption. Therefore, less citizen-initiated contact with government will occur.

4.   Having a greater Internet presence will be signaled by providing more e-services, having more e-purchasing, and having an intranet; these factors will increase citizen-initiated contact with government by providing greater opportunity for contacting.

5.   If a municipal government plans to use non-traditional financing sources and has a large budget for e-government, this will increase citizen contact because of having more resources and diversity of sources of revenue.

6.   If a municipal government has a separate e-government budget developed by the IT department, this will increase citizen-initiated contact with government because of increased budgetary clout.

Each of these six hypotheses will be briefly elaborated on. The first hypothesis addresses the socioeconomic status of the community. Greater socioeconomic status leads to more citizen-initiated contact with e-government because of greater resources and economies of scale in service provision (Jones et al., 1977; Thomas, 1982; Thomas & Streib, 2003). Larger and wealthier cities are able to supply more e-government services and, thus, enhance contact. Personal income is one measure of wealth of a community. Higher income would signify a greater ability to tax citizens, and therefore, more money could be devoted to e-government. Local governments that serve larger population centers would have the ability to reap economies of scale in service provision, which would mean greater e-government adoption (Holden, Norris, & Fletcher, 2003).

The second hypothesis argues that the higher levels of unemployment will decrease citizen contact because of greater fiscal stress (Ho & Ni, 2004). Communities that have a higher unemployment rate will not be able to afford as much e-government, thereby reducing citizen-initiated contact. When more workers are unemployed, less tax revenue is being collected, which creates fiscal stress. Some workers would leave the community, especially in northern Ontario, where there is less work. They would search for jobs in larger cities in the southern part of the province. This further shrinks the tax base and prospects for e-government adoption.

If a municipal government identifies many barriers to e-government adoption, this would signal less citizen-initiated contact with government (Reddick, 2004b). Issues such as lack of resources (financial and personnel), privacy, and security should inhibit contact. Cities that have fewer barriers to e-government should be able to secure higher levels of adoption. Leadership is important, since champions of e-government can push projects from start to finish, creating greater e-government adoption (Ho & Ni, 2004).

The more e-services, e-purchasing, and intranet signals that the government is well developed technologically when it comes to e-government and, therefore, increases the possibility of citizen contact. Offering more opportunities for contact reflects the citizen-initiated contact research that greater demands by citizens will increase contact. Therefore, providing more services and opportunities to engage in e-government increases contact (Thomas & Melkers, 2000; Thomas & Streib, 2003). For example, if citizens are able to file their taxes online or register for recreational facilities, this will enhance citizen contact with government. In addition, if the local government has the ability to purchase office equipment or supplies online, this will signal greater acceptance of e-government as a tool for contact. Having an intranet provides more services and resources to local employees. This will enable employees to become more proficient and comfortable working online and enhance e-government acceptance and development by staff.

Larger e-government budgets and use of non-traditional sources of finance should indicate higher levels of e-government adoption (Ho & Ni, 2004). For example, using transaction fees or convenience charges to fund an e-government project indicates a more entrepreneurial spirit in financing and an increased willingness to implement e-government. In addition, merely spending more on e-government should imply greater development, leading to increased citizen-initiated contact. A separate e-government budget developed by the IT department indicates the capability of the local governments to secure expenditures, since it has a representative that actively will pursue its interests (Reddick, 2004b). If e-government spending is lumped together with other departments, there may be no high-level official who has enough clout to find and secure appropriate funding (Wildavsky, 1974).

The following section presents the summary statistics of the dependent variable and independent variables used to test citizen-initiated contact with e-government.

Summary Statistics of Dependent and Predictor Variables

Table 9 demonstrates the descriptive statistics of data tested in this study. Since this study is interested in whether there has been increased citizen-initiated contact with elected and appointed officials, this is used as the dependent variable. The summary statistics demonstrated that, on average, 39% of CAOs believed that e-government had increased citizen contact with elected and appointed officials (This figure is less than that presented in Table 1, since there are 108 usable observations rather than 119).

In order to measure how many obstacles these governments faced in terms of implementing e-government, a barriers' index was composed (Table 9). The more barriers they faced, such as lack of financial resources and lack of technology (as reported in Table 2), the higher the index score these governments received. It is anticipated that more barriers to e-government adoption would decrease citizen-initiated contact with e-government. Out of nine possible barriers, these governments indicated that, on average, they experienced three of them.

On average, there was less than one e-purchase completed by these municipal governments (Table 9). In addition, out of the nine possible services that were available online, only two municipal governments offered eight of these e-services. (There was one city that offered nine services but wished to remain anonymous.) Two cities have the highest score for the e-services index—the City of Ottawa (http://www.ottawa.ca) with a population of three quarters of a million, and the City of Windsor (http://www.citywindsor.ca) with a population of just over 200,000. They both had an e-services index score of eight, meaning that they offered eight of the services listed in Table 1. The services considered were only those that are transaction-based, such as online payment of taxes and online payment of utility bills. There were five services that were not part of this index. They are forms that can be downloaded for manual completion, council meeting minutes, budget documents, police reports, and newsletters, since they do not involve a transaction. An intranet was found in less than half of these local governments. The average median personal income for residents was around $24,000 Canadian a year. In terms of nontraditional financing of e-government, this research found that less than one- third used this method. Most of the financing was taken from the general fund. Almost one-fifth planned to

Table 9.

Descriptive Statistics				
	N	Minimum	Maximum	Mean
Increased citizen contact with elected and appointed officials	119	0	1	0.39
Barriers index	119	0	9	3.42
E-purchases index	119	0	2	0.66
E-services index	119	0	9	2.41
Intranet	119	0	1	0.45
Log of median personal income (Canadian Dollars)	108	$17,382	$33,828	$24,591
Non traditional e-gov finance	119	0	1	0.31
Plan to budget > $50,000 (Canadian Dollars)	119	0	1	0.18
Log of population	108	10,059	988,948	89,635
Separate e-government budget developed IT department	119	0	1	0.29
Unemployment rate	108	1.4	11.9	5.44
Note: Dependent Variable Shaded				

budget more than $50,000 for fiscal year 2005. The average population that these governments served was almost 90,000, a typical medium-sized municipal government. Twenty-nine percent had a separate e-government budget developed by the IT department. On average, the unemployment rate was almost 6%, which was below the national average of 7%. The following section uses the data on e-government adoption and tests a model of citizen-initiated contact.

Results of Logistic Regression

In order to examine the impact that these predictor variables have on citizen-initiated contact with government, logistic regression was conducted. The dependent variable is increased citizen contact with elected and appointed officials. This is a binary variable, with a *1* if this statement is true and *0* if it is not true.

As shown in Table 10, of all of the social, economic, and organizational independent variables, the most important reasons for increased citizen-initiated contact were increased e-services and a separate e-government budget developed by an IT department. None of the socioeconomic status variables, such as median personal income and the unemployment rate, had an influence on increasing citizen contact with e-government. Therefore, size or wealth of a municipal government was not a

Table 10.

Logistic Regression Results				
	Dependent Variable: Increased citizen contact with elected and appointed officials			
Independent or Predictor Variables	Odds Ratio	Standard Error	Wald Statistic	Prob. Significant
Barriers index	1.16	0.11	(1.86)	0.17
E-purchases index	1.35	0.29	(1.07)	0.30
E-services index	1.45	0.12	(9.72)***	0.00
Intranet	0.59	0.54	(0.99)	0.32
Log of median personal income (Canadian Dollars)	1.04	0.45	(0.01)	0.93
Non traditional e-gov finance	1.52	0.53	(0.63)	0.43
Plan to budget > $50,000 (Canadian Dollars)	0.83	0.71	(0.07)	0.79
Log of population	0.64	0.45	(0.96)	0.33
Separate e-gov budget developed IT department	3.37	0.63	(3.73)**	0.05
Unemployment rate	0.91	0.13	(0.59)	0.44
Nagelkerke-R^2	0.30			
Log-Likelihood $\chi^2(10)$	(23.08)***			
N	108			
Note: *** Significant at the 0.01 level; ** Significant at the 0.05 level.				

good predictor of increased contact with citizens. Having more e-government barriers was not an impediment to increased citizen contact with e-government. Odds ratios can be used in logistic regression to find out the likelihood of observing a *1* in the dependent variable, or increased citizen-initiated contact with e-government. For the statistically significant e-services index, the odds ratio was 1.45, indicating that as a municipal government offers more online services, it was almost one and a half times more likely to have increased citizen-initiated contact. In addition, if there was a separate budget developed by the IT department for e-government, this indicated that local governments would be three times more likely to increase citizen-initiated contact with e-government (i.e., the odds ratio of 3.37).

The following section analyzes the key findings of this study and presents avenues for future research.

Discussion and Conclusion

What do these statistical results mean for public administrators and the study of e-government? First, having more e-government services is a good predictor of increased citizen-initiated contact with government. This confirms the key hypothesis in the citizen-initiated contact literature that increased *needs* drive contacts. By increasing online services, municipal governments must answer more e-service related questions with citizens. This is somewhat surprising, since one would think that more online services would indicate less contact, because the municipal governments would conduct transactional services online.

In addition, a separate e-government budget adopted by an IT department signals a stronger command of fiscal resources, because it can fight as an autonomous unit to secure more e-government funding. This is the classic validation of the budget game applied to e-government finance (Wildavsky, 1974). This should indicate that larger and more developed e-governments that have separate IT departments interact more with the public.

What was found not to be a significant predictor of citizen-initiated contact with e-government was equally interesting. Socioeconomic status of the community that the municipal government serves did not have an impact on contact. This is consistent with the citizen-initiated contact literature showing that socioeconomic status is not an important predictor of increased contact. Common factors cited in the literature, such as the unemployment rate, personal income, and population, did not have an influence on increasing citizen contact. Therefore, being a large city serving a wealthy population did not assure greater citizen-initiated contact with e-government. This is consistent and inconsistent with the e-government adoption literature. Some studies argue that larger population centers have a positive influence on e-government adoption (Holden, Norris, & Fletcher, 2003; Norris & Moon, 2005), while other studies claim that non-socioeconomic status variables have the most important influence, such as leadership (Ho & Ni, 2004).

One of the limitations of this study is that it relies on the self-reporting of CAOs, who may be prone to exaggeration (Ho & Ni, 2004). For example, an examination of ICMA surveys of e-government longitudinally has shown an overestimation of plans for e-government adoption by local governments in the U.S. (Norris & Moon, 2005). A future study should combine the survey analysis of Ontario municipal governments and content analysis of their Web sites in order to verify accuracy of responses. This combined methodological approach most recently has been done in the U.S. (West, 2004). In addition, future work should examine issues such as e-government demand by the public in Canada. For instance, many studies focus on what governments supply, but what the public demands is equally important, and it is a relatively unexplored area of e-government research.

References

Accenture. (2004). *eGovernment leadership: High performance, maximum value*. New York: Accenture.

Archer, N. P. (2005). An overview of the change management process in egovernment. *International Journal of Electronic Business, 3*(1), 68-87.

Charih, M., & Robert, J. (2004). Government on-line in the federal government of Canada: The organizational issues. *International Review of Administrative Sciences, 70*(2), 373-384.

Criado, J. I., & Ramilo, M. C. (2003). E-government in practice: An analysis of Website orientation to the citizens in Spanish municipalities. *International Journal of Public Sector Management, 16*(3), 191-218.

Edmiston, K. D. (2002). State and local e-government: Prospects and challenges. *American Review of Public Administration, 33*(1), 20-45.

Green, K. R. (1982). Municipal administrators' receptivity to citizens' and elected officials' contacts. *Public Administration Review, 42*(4), 346-353.

Hirlinger, M. W. (1992). Citizen-initiated contacting of local government officials: A multivariate explanation. *Journal of Politics, 54*(2), 553-564.

Ho, A. T. K. (2002). Reinventing local governments and the e-government initiative. *Public Administration Review, 62*(4), 434-444.

Ho, A. T. K., & Ni, A. Y. (2004). Explaining the adoption of e-government features: A case study of Iowa County treasurers' offices. *American Review of Public Administration, 34*(2), 164-180.

Holden, S. H., Norris, D. F., & Fletcher, P. D. (2003). Electronic government at the local level: Progress to date and future issues. *Public Performance & Management Review, 26*(4), 325-344.

Horrigan, J. B. (2004). *How Americans get in touch with government*. Washington, DC: Pew Internet & American Life Project.

ICMA. (2004). *Electronic government 2004*. Washington, DC: International City/County Management Association.

Jones, B. D., Greenberg, S. R., Kaufman, C., & Drew, J. (1977). Bureaucratic response to citizen-initiated contacts: Environmental enforcement in Detroit. *American Political Science Review, 71*(1), 148-   165.

Kernaghan, K. (2005). Moving towards the virtual state: Integrating services and service channels for citizen-centered delivery. *International Review of Administrative Sciences, 71*(1), 119-131.

Layne, K., & Lee, J. (2001). Developing fully function e-government: A four stage model. *Government Information Quarterly, 18*(1), 122-136.

Moon, D., Serra, G., & West, J. P. (1993). Citizens' contacts with bureaucratic and legislative officials. *Political Research Quarterly, 46*(4), 931-941.

Moon, M. J. (2002). The evolution of e-government among municipalities: Rhetoric or reality? *Public Administration Review, 62*(4), 424-433.

Moon, M. J., & Norris, D. F. (2005). Does managerial orientation matter? The adoption of reinventing government and e-government at the municipal level. *Information Systems Journal, 15*(1), 43-60.

Norris, D. F., & Moon, M. J. (2005). Advancing e-government at the grassroots: Tortoise or hare? *Public Administration Review, 65*(1), 64-76.

Reddick, C. G. (2004a). A two-stage model of e-government growth: Theories and empirical evidence for U.S. cities. *Government Information Quarterly, 21*(1), 51-64.

Reddick, C. G. (2004b). Empirical models of e-government growth in local governments. *e-Service Journal, 3*(2), 59-84.

Roy, J. (2003). The relational dynamics of e-governance: A case study of the city of Ottawa. *Public Performance & Management Review, 26*(4), 391-403.

Serra, G. (1995). Citizen-initiated contact and satisfaction with bureaucracy: A multivariate analysis. *Journal of Public Administration Research and Theory, 5*(2), 175-188.

Sharp, E.B. (1984). Citizen-demand making in the urban context. *American Journal of Political Science, 28*(4), 654-670.

Thomas, J. C. (1982). Citizen-initiated contacts with government agencies: A test of three theories. *American Journal of Political Science, 26*(3), 504-522.

Thomas, J. C., & Melkers, J. (1999). Explaining citizen-initiated contacts with municipal bureaucrats: Lessons from the Atlanta experience. *Urban Affairs Review, 34*(5), 667-690.

Thomas, J. C., & Melkers, J. (2000). Citizen contacting of municipal officials: Choosing between appointed administrators and elected leaders. *Journal of Public Administration Research and Theory, 11*(1), 51-71.

Thomas, J. C., & Streib, G. (2003). The new face of government: Citizen-initiated contacts in the era of e-government. *Journal of Public Administration Research and Theory, 13*(1), 83-102.

Vedlitz, A., & Dyer, J. A. (1984). Bureaucratic response to citizen contacts: Neighborhood demands and administrative reaction in Dallas. *The Journal of Politics, 46*(4), 1207-1216.

Vedlitz, A., Dyer, J. A., & Durand, R. (1980). Citizen contacts with local governments: A comparative view. *American Journal of Political Science, 24*(1), 50-67.

West, D. M. (2004). E-government and the transformation of service delivery and citizen attributes. *Public Administration Review, 61*(1), 15-27.

Wildavsky, A. B. (1974). *The politics of the budgetary process* (2nd ed.). Boston: Little Brown.

About the Authors

Donald F. Norris is the director of the Maryland Institute for Policy Analysis and Research and professor of public policy at the University of Maryland, Baltimore County (USA). He is a specialist in urban politics, public management, and the application, management and impacts of information technology, including e-government in public organizations. Dr. Norris' works have been published in a number of scholarly journals. He holds a BS in history from the University of Memphis and both an MA and a PhD in government from the University of Virginia. Dr. Norris is editor-in-chief of the *International Journal of Electronic Government Research*.

*　*　*　*　*

Kim Viborg Andersen is a professor at the Copenhagen Business School. KVA is co-founder of the AIS SIG on e-government and in various editorial boards for journals (i.e., *International Journal of Electronic Government Research* and *Information Communication & Society*) and international conference program committees. He was general chair of the DEXA 2005-conference. His publications include *EDI and Data Networking in the Public Sector* (Kluwer, 1998), *Information Systems in the Public Service* (IOS Press, 1995), *Interdisciplianry Approaches to E-business* (Kluwer, 2003), *The Past and Future of Information Systems* (Elsevier, 2004) and *Public Sector Process Rebuilding Using Information Systems* (Kluwer, 2004) and various journal contributions published in journals such as *International Journal on E-Government, International Journal of Public Administration, Information Society, European Journal of Information Systems, Social Science Computer Review,* and *Information Communication and Society, Government Information Quarterly,* and *European Journal of Information Systems*. KVA has been a visiting scholar at the University of California, Irvine, Tokyo University, Deakin University, Örebro University, Sweden, and Agder University, Norway, and Aalborg University.

Annika Andersson is a PhD student of informatics at Örebro University, Örebro (Sweden). Her research is focused on e-government and ICT4D (information and communication technologies for development) and she is currently participating in two projects in Bangladesh and Sri Lanka. Andersson has authored many publications at international conferences and has also been called in as ICT consultant for the Swedish government.

Yu-Che Chen is an assistant professor of e-government and public management at Iowa State University, USA. He is the lead faculty member of the Public Policy and Administration Program's e-government concentration. Dr. Chen's current research interests include: implementation and management of e-government projects; management of IT outsourcing and partnerships; e-civic engagement; and the role of management networks in the production and delivery of e-government services. He has published in *Public Performance and Management Review, International Journal of Electronic Government Research, Social Science Computer Review, Government Information Quarterly* and *Public Administration Quarterly*. In spring 2006, he published an IBM report on the use of information technology in preventing and responding to global health-related crises. Dr. Chen teaches e-government courses such as e-government and information policy and managing IT in the public sector. Moreover, he offers a course on legal and ethical issues in information assurance as a faculty member of the Information Assurance Program at Iowa State University. He has both national and international service appointments. He serves on the National Association of Schools of Public Affairs and Administration's Information Technology Committee. He is also on the editorial board for the *International Journal of Electronic Government Research*.

Kevin M. Esterling is an assistant professor of political science at the University of California, Riverside, USA.

Åke Grönlund is a professor of informatics at Örebro University, Örebro (Sweden). He is also affiliated with the Department of Informatics at Umeå University. Grönlund's research currently has a strong focus on e-government. In this field he has published international books including *Electronic Government – Design, Application and Management* and *Managing Electronic Services*. Grönlund's research covers the coordination of organizations and networks using ICT, including electronic service delivery, organizational redesign, electronic information infrastructures, and ICT-enabled coordination of work. Grönlund is chair of the two largest e-government researcher communities, one within the U.S.-based Association of Information Systems (sigegov.org) and one within IFIP (International Federation of Information Systems, IFIP WG 8.2 - http://falcon.ifs.uni-linz.ac.at/research/ifip85.html). Grönlund is also program chair of the International EGOV Conference. Grönlund has participated in several international e-gov projects. He is the founding faculty and member of the steering committee of the EU e-government "Network of Excellence" DemoNet and the Swedish research programme DemocrIT on ICT in democratic processes.

Helle Zinner Henriksen, PhD, is an assistant professor with the Department of Informatics, Copenhagen Business School. She has an MSc in law from the University of Copenhagen and a PhD from the Department of Informatics, Copenhagen Business School. Her PhD is in the field of MIS with particular interest on the implications of institutional intervention with respect to interorganizational adoption and diffusion. Her research interests include adoption and diffusion of IT in the private and the public sector in particular. Her most recent work focused on e-government and regulation of e-governmant. Henriksen is involved in the Center for Research on IT in Policy Setttings (CIPS), Copenhagen Business School.

Marc Holzer is chair and professor in the Graduate Department of Public Administration, Rutgers University, the State University of New Jersey, Newark, and executive director, National Center for Public Productivity. Dr. Holzer's primary work has been in public sector productivity, a field he helped develop. He is the founder and editor-in-chief of the *Public Performance and Management Review*. Currently, Dr. Holzer is developing the E-Governance Institute to evaluate such capacities at the local level in the state, as well as nationally and internationally with universities in Korea and China. The institute has been instrumental in developing worldwide e-government surveys.

Zlatko J. Kovačić is an associate professor in the School of Information and Social Sciences at The Open Polytechnic of New Zealand. Kovačić has a varied academic background and research interests, ranging from core interests relating to IT careers, learning and teaching, to e-commerce, e-learning, time series analysis, and multivariate analysis. His current research is focused on social and cultural aspects of e-government and on cognitive processes in distance education using computers and communications technologies.

Herbert Kubicek is a full professor of applied computer science in the Department of Computer Science and Mathematics of the University of Bremen, Germany, and director of the Institute for Information Management Bremen (ifib). His research interests include IT management, the usefulness and usability of IT applications, in particular in government and the educational sector as well as the digital divide resp. integration of underserved groups.

David M. J. Lazer is an associate professor of public policy and director of the Program on Networked Governance, at the John F. Kennedy School of Government at Harvard University, USA.

Harald Mahrer is chair of the Centre for Politial Studies at the METIS Institute in Vienna. He received an MBA (1998) and PhD (2000) from the Vienna University of Economics and Business Administration (Austria) where he was an assistant professor at the Department of Information Systems. He is also a managing partner of Pleon Publico, Austria's leading public relations and lobbying firm. Besides his activities as senior lecturer at the Vienna University of Economics and Business Administration, he has been a visiting professor at the Eisenstadt School of Information Management since 2002. He has been a member of the e-government board of the Austrian Federal Government and is currently working on strategies for the evolution of e-democracy. Over the years he has acted as active member of the IS community by chairing workshops, tracks, and mini-tracks at different conferences as well as organizing the 8th European Conference on Information Systems (ECIS) in Vienna in the year 2000. He is author of several scientific publications and consultant to leading global companies.

James Melitski is an assistant professor of public administration at Marist College, School of Management, USA. He previously served as a director of the E-Governance Institute at Rutgers University–Newark in the Graduate Department of Public Administration. Dr. Melitski's research examines the impact of information technology and the Internet on the ability of public organizations to communicate, enhance participation, and deliver services. In particular, his research interests include e-government, strategic planning for information technology, citizen participation, state science and technology policies, and performance measurement.

Michael A. Neblo is an assistant professor of political science at Ohio State University, USA.

Pippa Norris is the McGuire lecturer in comparative politics at Harvard University's John F. Kennedy School of Government. The author of almost three dozen books, she works on comparative public opinion and elections, political communications, and gender politics. For more information, visit pippanorris.com.

Alison Radl has worked in state government for 11 years and a state department of education agency for the last five years. During that period, she assumed the lead for the education department main school district data collection and is responsible for Common Core Data (CCD). Radl has a Master of Public Administration and a Master of Science in Information Assurance from Iowa State University.

Christopher G. Reddick is an assistant professor of public administration at the University of Texas at San Antonio. Dr. Reddick's research interests are in e-government, public budgeting, and employee health benefits. Some of his publications can be found in *Public Budgeting & Finance, Government Information Quarterly*, and the *e-Service Journal*.

Jeffrey Roy is an associate professor in the School of Public Administration at Dalhousie University in Halifax, Nova Scotia, Canada. He specializes in models of democratic and multi-stakeholder governance and electronic government reforms. In 2004-2005, Professor Roy was a visiting faculty member of the School of Public Administration at the University of Victoria. He served as managing director of the Centre on Governance at the University of Ottawa in 2001-2002. He is also: member of the Organization for Economic Cooperation and Development's E-Government Network; associate editor of the *International Journal of E-Government Research*; featured columnist in *CIO Government Review*, a Canadian publication devoted to the nexus between technology and government (www.itworldcanada. com <http://www.itworldcanada.com/>); and author of *E-Government in Canada: Transformation for the Digital Age* (University of Ottawa Press).

Hans J. (Jochen) Scholl is an assistant professor in the University of Washington's Information School, USA. He teaches and conducts research on information management, process change, and organizational transformation in government and other organizations. He employs both quantitative computer simulation techniques and qualitative research designs. His special interests include integration, interoperability, organizational transformation, and the strategic choices in mobile technology diffusion in digital government. He is the PI of the NSF-funded Fully Mobile City Government research project (2005 to 2008). Scholl is involved in the organization of the three major conferences on electronic government. He chairs the Electronic Government Track at the Hawaii International Conference on System Sciences (HICSS). He also serves as a member of the organizing committees of dgo2006 and the DEXA/EGOV conferences. In May of 2006 he was elected to the inaugural board of the Digital Government Society of North America.

Hilmar Westholm is a researcher and consultant in the Institute for Information Management Bremen GmbH (Germany). He is also an associate professor in the

Institute of Political Science at the University of Oldenburg (Germany). He worked as a journalist and in further education, as project manager of cross-disciplinary environmental courses at the University of Oldenburg (Germany), as lecturer and researcher at the University of Hamburg. From 1996 to 2000, he had a replacement of a chair at the University of Oldenburg in the course of social sciences (main emphasis on European and international environmental policies, political participation). In 1998, he was fellow of the German Marshall Fund of the United States, from 1996 to 2001 council member of the City of Oldenburg. Research fields have been (international) environmental politics and education, political participation, e-government, media-use and e-democracy.

Index